D0138261

# Cooking with Shakespeare

# Cooking with
# SHAKESPEARE

Mark Morton and Andrew Coppolino

FEASTING WITH FICTION

GP

**GREENWOOD PRESS**
Westport, Connecticut • London

**Library of Congress Cataloging-in-Publication Data**

Morton, Mark Steven, 1963–
    Cooking with Shakespeare / Mark Morton and Andrew Coppolino.
        p. cm. — (Feasting with fiction, ISSN 1552–8006)
    Includes bibliographical references and index.
    ISBN 978–0–313–33707–9 (alk. paper)
    1. Cookery, British—History—16th century. 2. Great Britain—History—Elizabeth,
1558–1603. 3. Shakespeare, William, 1564–1616. I. Coppolino, Andrew, 1961–
II. Title.
    TX717.M2875 2008
    641.5941—dc22        2007044407

British Library Cataloguing in Publication Data is available.

Library of Congress Catalog Card Number: 2007044407
ISBN: 978–0–313–33707–9
ISSN: 1552–8006

First published in 2008

Greenwood Press, 88 Post Road West, Westport, CT 06881
An imprint of Greenwood Publishing Group, Inc.
www.greenwood.com

Printed in the United States of America

The paper used in this book complies with the
Permanent Paper Standard issued by the National
Information Standards Organization (Z39.48–1984).

10   9   8   7   6   5   4   3   2   1

The publisher has done its best to make sure the instructions and/or recipes in this book are correct. However, users should apply judgment and experience when preparing recipes, especially parents and teachers working with young people. The publisher accepts no responsibility for the outcome of any recipe included in this volume.

**Copyright Acknowledgments**

Every reasonable effort has been made to trace the owners of copyright materials in this book, but in some instances this has proven impossible. The author and publisher will be glad to receive information leading to more complete acknowledgments in subsequent printings of the book and in the meantime extend their apologies for any omissions.

For Aubrey, Alyssa, and Joseph
and
Melanie, Brandon, and Laika
and for
Lois Morton, who made jonnycakes

Wee alter our Fashions and outward Habits daily; the whitest Ruffe being not long since thought the purest wearing; then the blew, and not the yellow: So, our Cookery, Pastry, Distillations, Conserves, and Preserves, are far otherwise now than not long since they were.... These are all of the newest straine: approved and beloved of those that try them.

—John Murrell, *A Daily Exercise for Ladies and Gentlewomen*, 1617

# CONTENTS

Contents

# PREFACE

Nothing but sit and sit, and eat and eat!

*—The Taming of the Shrew 5.2.12*

Getting to know how people cooked and what people ate in William Shakespeare's England is a bit like seeing yourself reflected in a silver teapot. Some of your features (such as your eyes) might seem familiar and recognizable, but others (maybe your nose or chin) will appear stranger than you could have imagined, so ridiculously bent or grotesquely stretched that you're not sure whether to find it funny or frightening.

That blend of the strange and familiar is something you're bound to find as you make your way through the chapters that follow. You'll encounter some sixteenth-century beliefs about nutrition that will sound very contemporary (like the digestive benefits of taking a walk after eating a meal), but there are others that will seem rather peculiar (like the dangers of drinking cold beverages between dinner and supper). You'll come across many culinary techniques that will seem quite ordinary (like frying batter to make pancakes), but others might initially give you pause (like boiling a whole chicken or roasting eggs). In terms of combining ingredients, you'll probably feel right at home making a dish of chicken, parsley, and asparagus, but you'll probably do a double-take when you find out what you're supposed to add to a cherry tart (hint: nowadays you usually put it on a hot dog). Sixteenth-century table manners, too, will sometimes have you nodding with approval (such as don't speak with your mouthful) but will occasionally make you wonder if Shakespeare's contemporaries came from another planet (for example, when you went for dinner, you were expected to bring your own knife and carve your own toothpick). All in all, then, you'll find much in this book that will feel comfortable and familiar, but many things, too, that might make you exclaim, like Horatio after he sees the ghost of Hamlet's father, "This is wondrous strange!" (*Ham.* 2.1.173). Equally apropos, however, is Hamlet's reply to his friend: "And therefore as a stranger give it welcome" (*Ham.* 2.1.174).

Because this book is about the food culture that thrived in England during Shakespeare's lifetime, we've aimed to limit our culinary sources to books that were published in England within the 52 years spanned by his birth in 1564 and his death in

1616. For example, 160 of the 189 recipes that we've included are from sources that fall within that stretch of time. The 29 recipes that exceed those limits don't do so by very much, usually by just a handful of years, including 19 that were published even before Shakespeare's friends and former colleagues published his collected plays in 1623, in an edition now known as the First Folio. Moreover, many of those slightly later recipes would have been in circulation, either orally or in manuscript form, well before they were gathered together by a printer, so in that sense they still fall within Shakespeare's lifetime. Likewise, we've justified the inclusion of seven recipes from *A Propre New Booke of Cokery*, which appeared in 1545, because they are recipes that Shakespeare's mother might have learned as a young girl and that she would no doubt have continued to prepare for her own children after she married John Shakespeare. (Unlike most women of the time, including his wife, Shakespeare's mother could read and write.) Other recent books that are devoted to food in Shakespeare's era have not been so scrupulous about their time frame. For example, Madge Lorwin's *Dining with William Shakespeare*, Francine Segan's *Shakespeare's Kitchen*, and Betty and Sonia Zyvatkauskas's *Eating Shakespeare* draw heavily on much later cookbooks such as *The Accomplisht Cook* from 1660, *The Whole Body of Cookery* from 1661, *The Closet of the Eminently Learned Sir Kenelme Digbie* from 1669, and *The Accomplisht Ladys Delight* from 1672. The problem with using such sources is that English cooking changed in significant ways in the half century after Shakespeare's death. For one thing, continued exploration and colonialism introduced foods and beverages that would have been virtually or entirely unknown to the Elizabethans, including potatoes, chocolate, coffee, and vanilla. Tastes changed, too. *The Accomplisht Cook* from 1660, for example, includes several recipes that involve lobster, but none of the 1,600 or so recipes that were published in various cookbooks within Shakespeare's lifetime even mention that crustacean. Accordingly, when Francis Segan presents a recipe for "Lobster with Pistachio Stuffing and Seville Orange Butter" in her sumptuous *Shakespeare's Kitchen*, its status as a "Shakespearean" dish needs to be taken with a grain of salt. With regard to non-recipe sources, which provide useful historical or cultural information, we've also tried to stick to works published in Shakespeare's lifetime, but on occasion we've strayed into sources a decade or so earlier or later.

Because Shakespeare is the raison d'etre of this book, our introduction begins with a section devoted to how he employs food and cooking in his poetry and plays. We then move from the literary to the cultural with sections that give an overview of how food fit into the ideological, medical, religious, and legal systems of Shakespeare's England. The next four sections proceed from the market, to the kitchen, to the table, and finally to the palate; in other words, these four sections focus on where Shakespeare's contemporaries acquired their food, how they prepared their food, how they conducted themselves when they sat down to eat, and what they tasted when they put spoon to mouth. The introduction then concludes with some remarks on the cookbooks from which we drew our recipes, including their authorship, their audience, and the manner in which they were compiled and printed. The remainder of the book comprises chapters that focus on recipes pertaining to particular kinds of food (such as beef or pork) or particular methods of preparing it (such as fritters or broths). There are 189 recipes in total, and each one is preceded by a relevant quotation from Shakespeare. In most cases, the quotation from Shakespeare is then followed by a brief paragraph that comments on either the quotation or the recipe. The original recipe is then presented, followed by our modern redaction. Each recipe is also assigned a 1 to 5 "makeability" rating; a rating of 1 means that an adolescent could successfully make the recipe, while a rating of 5 means that making the recipe would be a challenge even for an experienced cook, either because of its complexity or because some of its ingredients are difficult to procure. Makeability ratings of 2, 3, and 4 fall, obviously, somewhere between these two extremes. Four appendices, a glossary, and a bibliography appear at the end of the book. The first appendix provides some guidance on locating hard-to-find ingredients; the second appendix gives some indication of what food items cost in Shakespeare's England, relative to one another and to the wages of the day; the third appendix reproduces a complete dinner menu for "fish days," that is, days when eating meat was forbidden; and the fourth appendix is a transcription of a dinner table dialogue that appeared in a French/English language book that was published in 1605. The glossary provides brief definitions of all the potentially unfamiliar words that appear in the included recipes.

We're interested in hearing from our readers, especially with regard to our modern redactions of the original recipes. Although we've tested our redactions, they can always be improved: if you make a recipe, and find that it turns out better with a little more nutmeg or a little less verjuice, if it is baked at a slightly higher temperature, or if it is deep-fried rather than pan-fried, please let us know. We can be reached by e-mail at authors@cookingwithshakespeare.com.

# ACKNOWLEDGMENTS

We are grateful to friends, colleagues, family members, and students who contributed resources, advice, ovens, and taste buds: Richard Goodwin, Liwana Bringelson, Alan Marshall, Laura Briggs, Susan Huehnergard, Michael Hewson, David Williamson, Robyn Stalkie, Anna Wiebe, Hannah Miller, Laura Wismer, Susan Moyer, Sarah Higgins, Derick Haywood, and Zainab Ramahi. George Butler of Greenwood Press provided astute and timely editorial advice.

# WILLIAM SHAKESPEARE'S WORKS AND THEIR ABBREVIATIONS

The following abbreviations are employed in parenthetical citations.

| | |
|---|---|
| Ado | *Much Ado About Nothing* |
| Ant. | *Antony and Cleopatra* |
| AWW | *All's Well That Ends Well* |
| AYL | *As You Like It* |
| Cor. | *Coriolanus* |
| Cym. | *Cymbeline* |
| Err. | *The Comedy of Errors* |
| Ham. | *Hamlet, Prince of Denmark* |
| 1H4 | *The First Part of King Henry the Fourth* |
| 2H4 | *The Second Part of King Henry the Fourth* |
| H5 | *The Life of King Henry the Fifth* |
| 1H6 | *The First Part of King Henry the Sixth* |
| 2H6 | *The Second Part of King Henry the Sixth* |
| 3H6 | *The Third Part of King Henry the Sixth* |
| H8 | *The Famous History of the Life of King Henry the Eighth* |
| JC | *Julius Caesar* |
| Jn. | *King John* |
| LC | *A Lover's Complaint* |
| LLL | *Love's Labour's Lost* |
| Lr. | *King Lear* |
| Luc. | *The Rape of Lucrece* |
| Mac. | *Macbeth* |
| MM | *Measure for Measure* |
| MND | *A Midsummer Night's Dream* |
| MV | *The Merchant of Venice* |
| Oth. | *Othello, Moor of Venice* |
| Per. | *Pericles* |
| PhT | *The Phoenix and the Turtle* |
| PP | *The Passionate Pilgrim* |
| R2 | *The Tragedy of King Richard the Second* |
| R3 | *The Tragedy of King Richard the Third* |
| Rom. | *Romeo and Juliet* |

| Shr. | *The Taming of the Shrew* |
| Son. | *Sonnets* |
| TGV | *Two Gentlemen of Verona* |
| Tim. | *Timon of Athens* |
| Tit. | *Titus Andronicus* |
| Tmp. | *The Tempest* |
| TN | *Twelfth Night; Or, What You Will* |
| TNK | *The Two Noble Kinsmen* |
| Tro. | *Troilus and Cressida* |
| Ven. | *Venus and Adonis* |
| Wiv. | *The Merry Wives of Windsor* |
| WT | *The Winter's Tale* |

Additionally, when discussing Shakespeare's history plays, scholars usual shorten the titles. For example, *The Second Part of King Henry the Fourth* becomes *2 Henry IV*; *The Famous History of the Life of King Henry the Eighth* becomes *Henry VIII*; and so on.

# 1

# INTRODUCTION

## FOOD AND THE BARD

Hotspur: I had rather live
    With cheese and garlike in a windmill, far,
    Than feed on cates and have him talke to me
    In any summer house in Christendome. (*1 Henry IV* 3.1.157–160)

In the 38 plays, 154 sonnets, and handful of other poems that comprise the extant works attibuted to Shakespeare, there are well over a thousand references to foods, cooking, eating, and drinking (the word "wine" alone appears 79 times; "meat" occurs 70 times). Some of these references are incidental, like King Lear offering a piece of toasted cheese to an imaginary mouse (*Lr.* 4.6.88–90) or Pandarus calling Helen a "honey-sweet queen" (*Tro.* 3.1.141). Others take up entire scenes, like the strange banquet that Timon prepares for his erstwhile friends (*Tim.* 3.6.1–123). This large number of gastronomic allusions might seem to set Shakespeare apart from his contemporaries, but in fact many of his literary peers also made great use of details and imagery drawn from the market, kitchen, and dinner table. Thomas Heywood, for example, in his 1602 comedy *How a Man May Choose a Good Wife from a Bad*, includes a scene where Aminadab recites a food-laden prayer before the guests begin to eat:

Attend me now, whilst I say grace.
For bread and salt, for grapes and malt,
For flesh and fish, and every dish;
Mutton and beef, of all meats chief;
For cow-heels, chitterlings, tripes and souse,
And other meat that's in the house;
For racks, for breasts, for legs, for loins,
For pies with raisins and with proins,
For fritters, pancakes, and for fries,
For ven'son pasties and minc'd pies;
Sheeps'-head and garlic, brawn and mustard,
Wafers, spic'd cakes, tart, and custard;

For capons, rabbits, pigs, and geese,
For apples, caraways, and cheese;
For all these and many mo:
Benedicamus Domino!

Another of Shakespeare's rivals, Thomas Middleton, in his 1615 tragicomedy entitled *The Witch*, features a servant who uses food to entice a courtesan:

Please you withdraw yourself to yond private parlour:
I'll send you venison, custard, parsnip pie;
For banqueting stuff, as suckets, jellies, syrups,
I will bring in myself.

And dozens of other late sixteenth- and early seventeenth-century plays—such as *The Spanish Tragedy* and *Antonio's Revenge*—include full-blown banquet scenes, many of which are actually setups for elaborate acts of vengeance. In their poetry, too, Shakespeare's contemporaries often descanted on food and drink, as was the case with Shakespeare's great friend and rival, Ben Jonson. In his poem, "Inviting a Friend to Supper," Jonson seeks to charm a prospective guest with a vivid description of the meats, fruits, and strangely named fowls that he will order for dinner:

Yet shall you have, to rectifie your palate,
An olive, capers, or some better sallad
Ushring the mutton; with a short-leg'd hen,
If we can get her, full of eggs, and then,
Limons, and wine for sauce: to these, a coney
Is not to be despair'd of, for our money;
And, though fowle, now, be scarce, yet there are clerkes,
The skie not falling, thinke we may have larkes.
I'll tell you of more, and lye, so you will come:
Of partrich, pheasant, wood-cock, of which some
May yet be there; and godwit, if we can:
Knat, raile, and ruffe too.

If these were Jonson's usual dinner preparations, it's not surprising that he weighed almost 20 stone or 280 pounds (as he confesses in one of his poems). Elsewhere in his verse he laments that a would-be mistress "cannot embrace / My mountain belly," and that he visits friends only to "break chairs, or crack a coach." In contrast, Shakespeare, judging from the various portraits that purport to depict him, managed to retain a more trim figure. Both men, however, seem to have enjoyed their cups. In fact, according to a seventeenth-century tradition, it was while he was carousing with Jonson that Shakespeare "drank too hard," and subsequently caught a fever from which he died a few days later.

The pervasiveness of food and drink in the poetry of the late sixteenth and early seventeenth century had some of Shakespeare's contemporaries fuming, either because it seemed to condone the sin of gluttony (as we'll see later on in the Introduction) or because they considered puddings, salted beef, and ale to be topics beneath the dignity of poetry. That, at least, was the charge leveled by John Taylor, a professional waterman (he ferried people from one side of the Thames to the other), who frequently turned his hand to verse, as in this passage from his 1620 poem entitled "The Praise of Hemp-Seed":

> One doth heroicke it throughout our coast,
> The vertue of muld-sacke, and ale and toast.
> Another takes great paines with inke and pen,
> Approving fat men are true honest men.
> One makes the haughty vauty welkin ring
> In praise of Custards, and a bag-pudding....
> Anothers humour will nothing allow
> To bee more profitable than a Cow,
> Licking his lips, in thinking that his theame
> Is milke, cheese, butter, whay, whig, curds, and creame,
> Leather and Veale, and that which is most chiefe
> Tripes, chitterlings, or fresh powder'd beefe.

It should be evident, then, that Shakespeare was in good company—or in bad company, if you share John Taylor's perspective—in making food and drink an integral part of his poetic and dramatic endeavours. Moreover, Shakespeare tends to do so to achieve three different objectives: first, to conjure up the reality or immediacy of a place, occasion, or character through ordinary details pertaining to food or drink; second, to ascribe a quality or attribute to a person, thing, or event through a figurative reference to food or drink; and third, to represent through depictions of shared meals the harmonious social relations that characterize a well-ordered community or, alternatively, an ironic absence of those harmonious social relations.

The first of these objectives is nicely exemplified in a short passage from *2 Henry IV* where Justice Shallow, eager to extend Falstaff's visit, tells his servant Davy what the cook should prepare for supper (incidentally, "kickshaws"—which derives from the French "quelque chose," meaning "something"—refers to what we might now call dainties):

> Some Pigeons, Davy,
> a couple of short-legg'd Hennes: a joynt of Mutton, and
> any pretty little tiny Kickshawes, tell William Cooke. (5.1.24–26)

In just three lines, small details bring to life the household of Justice Shallow. An imaginative groundling standing in the Globe or Blackfriars Theatre might have envisioned the pigeons cooing in their wooden cotes, the chickens scratching for grubs in the yard behind the manor (oblivious to the fact that two of them are headed for the pot), the leg of mutton already hanging in the kitchen (the hoof having been removed and used to make jelly), and the day-long bustle of an aristocrat's kitchen where something was always being plucked, skinned, boiled, baked, fried, rolled, preserved, chopped, or scrubbed.

Elsewhere, Shakespeare uses such details to figure forth an occasion rather than a place. For example, in this passage from *The Winter's Tale*, the Clown—a sixteenth-century name for a country bumpkin—tallies up the ingredients he is to buy for an upcoming feast:

> Let mee see,
> what am I to buy for our Sheepe-shearing-Feast? Three
> pound of Sugar, five pound of Currence, Rice:
> What will this sister of mine do with Rice? But my father hath
> made her Mistris of the Feast, and she layes it on. Shee
> hath made me four and twenty Nose-gayes for the shearers
> (three-man song-men, all, and very good ones)
> but they are most of them Meanes and Basses; but one
> Puritan amongst them, and he sings Psalmes to horne-pipes.
> I must have Saffron to colour the Warden Pies,
> Mace: Dates, none: that's out of my note: Nutmegges,
> seven; a Race or two of Ginger, but that I may begge: Foure
> pound of Prewyns, and as many of Reysons o'th Sun. (4.3.36–48)

Characters, too, are given depth and reality through their food and drink, as with Edgar in *King Lear* who, in the guise of Poor Tom,

> Eats Cow-dung for Sallets;
> swallowes the old Rat, and the
> ditch-Dogge; drinkes the green Mantle of
> the standing Poole. (3.4.130–133)

More palatable, but no less effective, is the portrait of Falstaff that emerges from tavern receipts taken from his pockets after he falls into a drunken slumber (in the receipts, the "s" following a number represents "shillings," and the "d" represents "pence"):

Prince: Harke, how hard he fetches breath: search his Pockets.
       What hast thou found?

Peto:   Nothing but papers, my lord.

Prince: Let's see what they be: reade them.

Peto:   Item, A capon,............................................ 2s. 2d.
       Item, Sawce,................................................ 4d.
       Item, Sacke, two gallons,............................ 5s. 8d.
       Item, Anchoves and sacke after supper, ... 2s. 6d.
       Item, Bread,................................................ ob.

Prince: O monstrous! but one halfe-pennyworth of
       bread to this intollerable deale of sacke! (*1H4* 2.4.526–536)

Incidentally, when Peto reads the receipts and comes to "ob," he would have said "halfpenny," just as we now say "pound" when we read "lb." The abbreviation "ob" derived from the word "obulus," which once denoted a small Greek coin, just as "lb" derives from the Latin "libra," which denoted a certain weight.

The preceding passages are all examples of literal uses of food and drink: the capon that Falstaff purchased for 2 shillings and 2 pence was an actual castrated rooster, one that was probably roasted on a spit and then served with a sauce on a half-pennyworth of sliced bread, known back then as sops or sippets. In contrast are the hundreds of gastronomic metaphors in Shakespeare's works where a quality of a food or drink is figuratively ascribed to a person, thing, or event, such as when one of the servants in *1 Henry IV*, says that Falstaff is "as fat as butter" (2.4.519) or when Pistol in *Henry V* warns that "mens faiths are as Wafer-cakes" (2.3.50), that is, their promises are easily broken. Sometimes such figurative comparisons are humorous, as when Stephano says to Trinculo, after they wash up on shore in *The Tempest*, "Though thou canst swim like a ducke, thou art made like a goose" (2.2.131–132), or when Touchstone in *As You Like It* tells his wife-to-be that a woman should be honest or beautiful, but not both:

Audrey:      Would you not have me honest?

Touchstone:  No, truly, unless thou wert hard-favoured:
             for honestie coupled to beautie is to have
             honie a sawce to sugar. (3.3.26–29)

Somewhat more complex is the following extended comparison of rapid speech to pouring wine, an analogy propounded by Rosalind in *As You Like It* as she urges Celia to tell her about Orlando:

                         I pri'thee, tell me who is it
quickely, and speak apace. I would thou couldst stammer,
that thou mightst powre this conceal'd man out of
thy mouth, as Wine comes out of a narrow-mouth'd
bottle: either too much at once, or none at all. I pri'thee,
take the Corke out of thy mouth that I may drinke thy
tydings. (3.2.194–200)

And sometimes the figure of speech is a form of metonymy, where a part stands in for something greater. For example, in *Twelfth Night* Sir Toby uses "cakes and ale" to represent the entire world of good cheer and celebration that Malvolio in his prudery condemns:

Dost thou thinke, because thou art vertuous,
there shall be no more cakes and ale? (2.3.114–115)

On dozens of occasions, these metaphorical applications of food and drink take the form of insults, as when Hotspur in *1 Henry IV* calls a cowardly nobleman "a dish of skim'd milk" (2.3.32) or the Countess in *1 Henry VI* calls Talbot a "weake and writhled shrimpe" (2.3.23). Sometimes the historical context needs to be restored before the gravity of the insult is apparent to the modern reader. For example, the Prince takes offense when Falstaff calls him a "bread-chipper" (*2H4* 2.4.315), that is, a servant so low on the totem pole that his job is to chip the hard crust off loaves of bread. Likewise, Timon utters a grievous insult when he calls his guests "trencher-friends" (*Tim.* 3.6.96), implying that their loyalty is motivated by nothing more than the trenchers—or wooden plates—of food that Timon provides them. Later on, Timon further insults one of these trencher-friends when he tells him he looks like a medlar, that is, a kind of fruit (*Tim.* 4.3.313). The insult seems rather mild, until we realize that the other name for the medlar in the sixteenth century was "open arse" (so called because one end of the fruit is deeply indented).

Somewhat less common than insults involving food and drink are terms of endearment drawn from the realm of gastronomy. In *1 Henry IV*, the Prince says to Falstaff, after bailing him out of a sticky situation, "O, my sweet Beefe, I must still be good Angell to thee" (3.3.177). "Duck" also figures as a term of endearment in three plays, namely, *Henry V*, *Troilus and Cressida*, and *The Winter's Tale*. In *The Winter's Tale*, Camillo admiringly says of Perdita, "she is / The Queen of Curds and Creame" (4.4.161), and in *All's Well That Ends Well*, Helena is eulogized as "the sweete Margerom of the sallet, or rather the hearbe of grace" (4.5.17).

Shakespeare also employs certain foods as vehicles for sexual innuendo. Enobarbus, for example, predicts that Antony will return to Cleopatra by saying, "He will to his Egyptian dish againe" (*Ant.* 2.6.122). Even more bawdy is the "fleshy" metaphor that the aptly named Doll Tearsheet uses in *2 Henry IV* when she spurns the advances of Pistol in favor of his employer, Falstaff: "Away, you mouldie Rogue, away! I am meat for your master" (2.4.124). In *Pericles*, Thaisa likewise uses the word "meat" to imply her carnal desire for the play's title character:

By Juno, that is queen of marriage,
All viands that I eat do seem unsavoury,
Wishing him my meat. Sure, he's a gallant gentleman. (2.3.32–34)

*Measure for Measure* is especially laden with instances of foods being used to convey sexual intrigue, as in this passage where Lucio asks Pompey about Madame Overdone and her brothel:

Lucio:   How doth my deere morsell, thy mistris? Procures she
         still? Ha?

Pompey:  Troth, sir, shee hath eaten up all her beefe, and she is
         herself in the tub.

Lucio:   Why, 'tis good; it is the right of it: it must
         be so: ever your fresh Whore and your pouder'd
         Bawd: an unshun'd consequence, it must be so. (3.2.54–60)

In the preceding passage, "deere morsell" essentially means "tasty tidbit" or, in modern parlance, "a nice piece." The reference to Madame Overdone having "eaten up all her beefe" implies that she has used up all her prostitutes. Moreover, since she is out of young women, Madame Overdone herself has had to take on the customers, which has led to her getting into "the tub," hot baths being reputed as a treatment for venereal disease. Tubs, however, were also found in kitchens, where they were filled with powdered salt used to preserve meat. That association is what leads Lucio to contrast a "fresh whore" with a "pouder'd bawd," that is, an aging prostitute who has been artificially preserved.

Lucio again associates food with sex later in the same scene. He asserts that the Duke "would eate Mutton on Fridaies" (Friday being one of the days when eating meat was forbidden), implying that the Duke does not hesitate to enjoy illicit flesh, that is, prostitutes. Lucio then goes on to claim that the Duke is now too feeble to actually have sex, but that he would nonetheless "mouth with a beggar, though she smelt brown-breade and Garlicke" (3.2.176–177). Although the bawdy implications of many of these references to food are almost lost on a modern reader, they were apparently easily apprehended at the time. For example, when Pompey describes Claudio's crime as "groping for trowts in a peculiar river," Madame Overdone immediately knows what he is talking about: "What, is there a maid with child by him?" (1.2.83–84)

Shakespeare's third objective for making literary use of food and drink is to represent, through depictions of shared meals, the harmonious social relations that characterize a well-ordered community or, alternatively, an ironic absence of those harmonious social relations. In all eras and across all cultures, the act of eating together has been integral to the establishment and continuance of a community. This is apparent even in the word "companion," which derives from the Latin prefix "com," meaning "together," and "panis," meaning "bread"; companions are literally individuals who come together to share bread. An invitation to share a meal is therefore an invitation to set aside differences in order to participate in a harmonious community. George Page suggests as much in *The Merry Wives of Windsor* when he seeks to end the squabbling between Falstaff and Justice Shallow:

> Wife, bid these gentlemen welcome: Come,
> we have a hot Venison pasty to dinner; come, gentlemen,
> I hope we shall drinke down all unkindnesse. (1.1.179–181)

By the same token, refusing to share a meal is a profound rejection of community, as when Shylock, in *The Merchant of Venice*, refuses Bassanio's offer to dine together:

> I will buy with you, sell with you, talke with you,
> walke with you, and so following: but I will not eate
> with you, drinke with you, nor pray with you. (1.3.33–35)

Moreover, because most of Shakespeare's comedies conclude with the reestablishment of community, the final scenes of those plays often make direct reference to a promised banquet or feast, one that will both celebrate and formalize the renewed social relations. Consider, for example, the last four lines of *The Two Gentlemen of Verona*, where Valentine suggests that he and Proteus (and their respective sweethearts) should share a single wedding feast:

> Come, Proteus; 'tis your pennance but to heare
> The story of your loves discovered:
> That done, our day of marriage shall be yours:
> One feast, one house, one mutuall happinesse. (5.4.170–173)

Likewise, Theseus announces a feast at the close of *A Midsummer Night's Dream* to celebrate the restoration of community represented by the three impending marriages: "Away with us to Athens; three and three, / Wee'll hold a feast in great solemnitie" (4.1.183–184). The joyful reunion of husband and wife, parent and child, and brother and brother at the end of *The Comedy of Errors* also merits a feast where everyone can break bread, celebrate, and cheerfully "gossip":

> Aemilia: The Duke, my husband and my children both,
>               And you the Kalendars of their nativity,

> Go to a gossips feast, and go with mee;
> After so long greefe, such nativitie!

Duke:   With all my heart, I'le Gossip at this feast. (5.1.404–408)

With Shakespeare, feasts that are intended to celebrate the renewal of a community tend to occur off-stage, usually after the play has ended (a notable exception is *A Midsummer Night's Dream*, where the the marriage feast occurs off-stage between Act IV and Act V). The main reason for alluding to such feasts, rather than actually staging them, is that they can thereby remain inviolate: the pure "idea" of such feasts is more important than the actual blackbird pies, roast rabbits, and boiled turnips that would make up those feasts. In contrast are those feasts, banquets, or shared meals that function as ironic foils to an event or situation that is characterized by a lack of harmonious social relations. Such feasts tend to be shown on stage because it is dramatically effective to do so: a broken community seems all the more broken (and menacing) when it is depicted in a context that is usually associated with good cheer and companionship. The vengeful feast staged by Titus, in *Titus Andronicus*, is a good example. Tamora and the other enemies of Titus mistakenly believe—as does Marcus, his brother—that the banquet that has been prepared for them betokens an end to feuding and a renewal of order:

> Marcus:  These quarrels must be quietly debated.
> The feast is ready, which the carefull Titus
> Hath ordained to an Honourable end.
> For Peace, for Love, for League, and good to Rome:
> Please you, therefore, draw nie, and take your places. (5.3.20–24)

The audience, however, is aware that the baked pastries that Titus sets on the table before his enemies are made of the bones, blood, and severed heads of Tamora's sons. His secret intention, as he has previously revealed to his daughter, is "to make this banquet ... / More sterne and bloody than the Centaures Feast" (5.2.202–203). After Tamora has begun to eat, Titus gleefully reveals the whereabouts of her absent sons:

> Why there they are both, baked in that Pie;
> Whereof their Mother daintily hath fed,
> Eating the flesh that she herselfe hath bred. (5.3.60–62)

Titus then kills Tamora, and his revenge—all the more potent because it is set against the usual conviviality of a banquet—is complete.

In *Timon of Athens*, the titular protagonist also uses the communal supper table as a stage from which to rail against the treachery of former friends and allies. As his one-time friends lift the lids from the dishes that have been set in front of them, they discover them to contain nothing but steaming water. Timon then angrily explains this culinary symbolism:

> May you a better feast never behold,
> You knot of Mouth-Friends! Smoke and lukewarm water
> Is your perfection. This is Timons last;

Who, stucke and spangled with your Flatterie,
Washes it off, and sprinkles in your faces
Your reeking villany. (3.6.88–93)

Timon's device resembles the one used by Prospero, in *The Tempest*, when he seeks to afflict the men who rose against him twelve years earlier. As the stage directions indicate, the traitors are presented with a sumptuous banquet, carried in by wondrous spirits:

Enter severall strange shapes, bringing in a Banquet, and dance about
it with gentle actions of salutations, and inviting the King, etc., to eate,
they depart. (3.3.19 ff)

As the men step forward to eat, however, the table of food disappears:

Thunder and lightning. Enter Ariell, like a Harpey, claps his wings
upon the Table, and with a quaint device the Banquet vanishes. (3.3.52 ff)

Two final examples, both from *The Taming of the Shrew*, will suffice to demonstrate how the act of sharing a meal is used by Shakespeare either to figure forth a renewed and harmonious community or as an ironic backdrop to a broken and disordered community. In the first example, Katharina's shrewishness—that is, her refusal to act in harmony with her community—is externalized by Petruchio, who has ordered his servants to offer her delicious food only to withhold it:

Katharina: I prithee go and get me some repast;
          I care not what, so it be wholesome foode.
Grumio:   What say you to a neats foote?
Katharina: 'Tis passing good: I prithee let me have it.
Grumio:   I fear it is too chollericke a meate.
          How say you to a fat Tripe finely broyl'd?
Katharina: I like it well: good Grumio, fetch it me.
Grumio:   I cannot tell; I fear 'tis chollericke.
          What say you to a peece of Beefe and Mustard?
Katharina: A dish that I do love to feede upon.
Grumio:   Ay, but the Mustard is too hot a little.
Katharina: Why then, the Beefe, and let the Mustard rest.
Grumio:   Nay then, I will not: you shall have the Mustard,
          Or else you get no beefe of Grumio.
Katharina: Then both, or one, or any thing thou wilt.
Grumio:   Why then, the Mustard without the beefe.
Katharina: Go, get thee gone, thou false deluding slave,
          That feed'st me with the very name of meate.
          Sorrow on thee and all the packe of you,
          That triumph thus upon my misery.
          Go, get thee gone, I say. (4.3.15–35)

A bit later in the same scene, Petruchio enters with a dish of meat, ostensibly so that he can share it with his famished wife, but in reality so that his friend Hortensio can devour it all in front of her eyes. Only near the end of the comedy, after Katharina has come to accept her role in her community (that is, after she has been "tamed"), does a bona fide banquet occur, one where all the guests, including Katharina, are companions in the literal sense of the word:

> Lucentio: At last, though long, our jarring notes agree:
> And time it is, when raging warre is done,
> To smile at scapes and perils overblowne.
> My faire Bianca, bid my father welcome,
> While I with selfesame kindnesse welcome thine.
> Brother Petruchio, sister Katharina,
> And thou, Hortensio, with thy loving widow,
> Feast with the best, and welcome to my house:
> My Banquet is to close our stomakes up,
> After our great good cheere. Praie you, sit downe;
> For now we sit to chat as well as eate. (5.2.1–11)

This section of the Introduction has explored how Shakespeare makes literary use of food and drink to achieve three different objectives: to evoke the reality or immediacy of a place, occasion, or character through ordinary details pertaining to food or drink; to ascribe a quality or attribute to a person, thing, or event through a figurative reference to food or drink; or to represent through depictions of shared meals the harmonious social relations that characterize a well-ordered community or, alternatively, an ironic absence of those harmonious social relations. Described that way, the three objectives might seem very distinct from one another, but of course it is not uncommon to find all three at work in the same passage. Consider, for example, this passage from *The Comedy of Errors* where Dromio scolds his master for being late for dinner:

> Return'd so soon! rather approacht too late:
> The Capon burns, the Pig falls from the spit,
> The clock hath strucken twelve upon the bell;
> My Mistris made it one upon my cheeke:
> She is so hot because the meate is colde;
> The meate is colde because you come not home;
> You come not home because you have no stomach;
> You have no stomacke having broke your fast;
> But we that know what 'tis to fast and pray
> Are penitent for your default to-day. (1.2.43–52)

In this passage, the vivid details of the place and occasion speak to our imagination: we can hear the chiming dinner bell, see the flesh falling from the roast pig, and smell the capon as it turns from a delicious golden brown to an unpalatable charcoal black. All these details evoke the immediacy and reality of the meal. At the same time, figurative comparisons or analogies abound: the clock strikes its bell twelves times just as the frustrated mistress of the house strikes her servant's cheek once; the master's delay has made his wife hot with anger just as it has made the meat cold with waiting. And at a deeper level, the emphasis in this passage on time—or timing—is a theme that is at the very heart of *The Comedy of Errors*: split-second mis-timings are the source of the comical errors involving one twin being mistaken for another, and the play's happy ending results only because time has providentially reunited the long-separated family members. The result, as in so much of Shakespeare, is a passage where the literal, the figurative, and the thematic are effectively and inseparably bound up with one another.

## FOOD AND IDEOLOGY IN SHAKESPEARE'S ENGLAND

The Guineans diet is strange, as raw flesh, handfulls of graine, large draughts of Aquavita, Dogs, Cats, Buffles, Elephants.
　　　　　　　—James Hart, *Klinike, or The Diet of the Diseased*, 1633

Along with language and religion, food plays an important ideological role in how a culture defines itself (think of idioms such as "as American as apple pie") and also in how it defines other cultures (think of how we tend to associate Italy with pasta, Belgium with chocolate, Russia with vodka, and so on). The same held true in Shakespeare's England: writers often pointed to English beef, which they asserted to be the best in the world, as a symbol of the vitality and robustness of the English nation. Likewise, they often characterized foreign peoples, especially ones they considered to be exotic, in terms of the foods they ate. For example, Thomas Johnson, writing in his 1596 treatise *Cornucopiae*, summed up an entire continent in two neat sentences:

Africa, one of three parts of the world, lying toward the South: herein is Barbary and all Ethiope contained. The people of these countries lived in times past very uncivilly, feeding much upon serpents flesh.

Henry Cockeram, in his 1623 *English Dictionarie*, likewise defined various tribes or groups—some of which were real and some of which we now recognize as mythical—according to what they ate: "Arimpeans, people which live on mast and berries ... Asachae, people which live on the flesh of Elephants ... Chelonophagie, people which live by eating of tortoises, and they cover their caves with their shells ... Essenie, people which abstaine from flesh, wine, and women among the Jewes ... Zigantes, people that feed on apes flesh," and so on. Sometimes the gastronomic idiosyncrasies attributed to these foreign peoples were so fabulous that it is hard to imagine that anyone took them seriously. However, the authority and veracity of ancient philosophers was rarely doubted by their sixteenth-century admirers. For example, in this passage from a 1579 work called *A Thousand Notable Things*, Thomas Lupton dutifully affirms a chunk of "natural history" that he found in a work by a first-century philosopher, Pliny the Elder:

The people of Astomores (as Plinie reportes) have no mouth: and are clad with a wooly mosse growing in India, and live onely with the smelling of odours at their nose, of rootes and of flowres, and of apples that growe in the woods: which they carrie with them in their long journeys to susteyne and nourish them withall, lest they should want whereof to smell.

Incidentally, Lupton's apparent acceptance of such fantastic tales recalls that of Gonzalo, in *The Tempest*, who gives ready credence to the stories brought back by explorers who undertook dangerous voyages to remote lands (as Gonzalo implies, their reward for doing so was to receive five times their initial investment upon their safe return):

> When wee were boyes,
> Who would beleeve that there were Mountayneeres
> Dew-lapt, like bulls, whose throats had hanging at 'em
> Wallets of flesh? Or that there were such men
> Whose heads stood in their brests? which now we finde
> Each putter-out of five for one will bring us
> Good warrant of. (3.3.43–49)

Many of Shakespeare's contemporaries seem to have construed the uncouth diets of these real or mythical foreign peoples as evidence of their supposed inferiority. Some even abused the food customs of other cultures in order to cause intentional harm. William Harrison, for example, in his 1587 *Description of England*, described an incident involving the brawn of a pig:

> A friend of mine also dwelling sometime in Spaine, having certeine Jewes at his table, did set brawne before them, whereof they did eat verie earnestlie, supposing it to be a kind of fish not common in those partes: but when the goodman of the house brought in the head in pastime among them, to shew what they had eaten, they rose from the table, hied them home in haste, each of them procuring himselfe to vomit, some by oile, and some by other meanes, till (as they supposed) they had clensed their stomachs of that prohibited food.

Others, however, were more enlightened than Harrison's friend. James Hart, for example, was open-minded toward the unusual culinary habits of foreign peoples in his 1633 work, *Klinike*:

> In many place in Germany the country-people use commonly to eat hedge-hogges, as we doe other food, which are pleasant to the palate, strengthen the stomacke, and provoke urine.... Locusts, which wee commonly call caterpillers, are at this day much used for ordinary food among many nations, especially the Africans.

For Hart, the strange foods consumed in "outlandish" nations were not something to be disparaged but rather were evidence of "the great and extraordinarie bountie of our great and gracious god, in affording us [that is, all humans] such plentie and varietie of good and wholesome food."

## DIETARY THEORY

Now, our life consisteth in moisture and heat, neither is our life any thing else, but a joint-continuance of heat and moisture in our bodies. But since our heat doth daily consume & waste away this naturall and radicall moisture, it is againe by the like humidity repaired. Now, this is performed by means of food, both meat and drinke.
—James Hart, *Klinike, or The Diet of the Diseased*, 1633

In Shakespeare's England, ideological assumptions about food such as the ones described in the previous section were for the most part implicit: they were so embedded in the sixteenth- and early seventeenth-century worldview that they peek out only occasionally, and even then only with our advantage of four hundred years of hindsight. In contrast were the highly intentional efforts to develop explicit and elaborate theories about food as it pertained to human physiology and health. Books such as Andrew Boord's *Compendyous Regyment or a Dyetary of Helth* (first published in 1542, with four more editions following by 1576), William Bullein's *Governement of Healthe* (1558), Thomas Twyne's *The Schoolemaster, or Teacher of Table Philosophie* (1576), Michael Scot's *The Philosophers Banquet* (1614), William Vaughn's *Directions for Health* (1617), and Tobias Venner's *Via Recta ad Vitam Longam* (1620) all sought to synthesize, systematize, and propagate "best practices" about what to eat and why.

These best practices were, for the most part, ones that had been articulated more than a thousand years previously by Greek, Roman, and Arab philosophers. In Shakespeare's England, coming up with an original idea was more likely to provoke suspicion than admiration. Scholars strove not to be innovative but to acquire a comprehensive and detailed knowledge of what the ancients had said long ago. (In a somewhat different way, this is true even of Shakespeare: he borrowed rather than invented most of his plots, as in *The Comedy of Errors*, which he adapted from a third-century play called *Menaechmi*.) With regard to diet and health, the ancient authority that was most influential on Shakespeare's contemporaries was Galen, a second-century C.E. physician who had honed his craft tending the wounds of Roman gladiators. It was Galen who propounded the notion of the four humors, a medical theory readily embraced by sixteenth- and early seventeenth-century scholars. According to this theory, the human body produced four fluids or "humors": sanguine (or blood), choler (or yellow bile), melancholy (or black bile), and phlegm. Moreover, each of these humors possessed two qualities, just like the element with which it was associated: sanguine was hot and moist like air; choler was hot and dry like fire; melancholy was cold and dry like earth; and phlegm was cold and moist like water. The key to good health was to keep these humors in proportion, the ideal ratio being one quarter as much phlegm as blood, one sixteenth as much choler as blood, and one sixty-fourth as much melancholy as blood. Few people, however, achieved this ideal, which usually meant that they had an excess of one of the four humours. This excess resulted in a "complexion" or what we would now call a temperament, or predisposition to certain behaviors (as well as to certain physiological traits). These temperaments are briefly described in a didactic poem called *The Englishmans Doctor*, printed in 1608. First comes the sanguine individual, an essentially plump and cheerful bloke (note that in the first line, the phrase "nothing nice" means "not at all shy"):

The Sanguin gamesome is, and nothing nice,
Loves wine and women, and all recreation,
Likes pleasant tales, and newes, playes cardes and dice,
Fit for all company, and every fashion:
Though bold, not apt to take offence, nor irefull,
But bountifull and kind, and looking chearfull:
Inclining to be fat, and prone to lafter,
Loves myrth, and Musicke, cares not what comes after.

Next is the choleric individual, who tended to be scrawny, hairy, and argumentative:

> Sharpe Choller is an humour most pernitious,
> All violent, and fierce, and full of fire,
> Of quick conceit, and therewithall ambitious,
> Their thoughts to greater fortunes still aspyre,
> Proud, bountifull enough, yet oft malitious,
> A right bold speaker, and as bold a lyer.
> On little cause to anger great inclined,
> Much eating still, yet ever looking pined;
> In younger yeares they use to grow apace,
> In Elder hayry on their breast and face.

The phlegmatic individual was usually stout and unambitious, but was fortunate in being "fayre" or good-looking:

> The Flegmatique are most of no great growth,
> Inclining rather to be fat and square,
> Given much unto their ease, to rest and sloth,
> Content in knowledge to take little share,
> To put themselves in paine most loth,
> So dead their spirits, so dull their sences are:
> Still either sitting like to folke that dreame,
> Or else still spitting, to avoid the flegme,
> One quality doth yet these harmes repayre,
> That for the most part the Flegmatiques are fayre.

The melancholic individual was a studious, skeptical loner, much like *Hamlet*, the so-called "melancholy Dane":

> The Melancholie from the rest do varry,
> Both sport and ease, and company refusing,
> Exceeding studious, ever sollitary,
> Inclining pensive still to bee, and musing,
> A secret hate to other apt to carry:
> Most constant in his choise, tho long a choosing.
> Extreame in love sometime, yet seldome lustfull,
> Suspicious in his nature, and mistrustfull.
> A wary wit, a hand much given to sparing,
> A heavy looke, a spirit little daring.

The relevance of all this to gastronomy is that in Shakespeare's England it was commonly understood that your temperament determined what kind of foods you ought to eat. This was because foods, just like humans, had temperaments, or at least they had qualities that influenced the temperaments of the individuals who ate them. Horseradish, for example, was a choleric foodstuff in that its qualities were "hot and dry." Choleric individuals, therefore, needed to avoid horseradish because it would make them more angry and arrogant, whereas phlegmatic individuals, with their cold and moist temperament, would do well to add horseradish to their meal because it would counteract their sluggish and dreamy nature. Sometimes the "humoral" qualities ascribed to foods seem quite sensible. Mushrooms, for example, were cold and moist, and pepper was hot and dry. More often, however, it is hard to understand why certain foods were thought to have certain qualities. For instance, eggs were considered hot and moist, honey was hot and dry, pork was cold and moist, and beef was cold and dry. The thing to remember, though, is that these qualities pertained less to the texture or flavor of the foods, and more to their impact on the human body. A typical dietary injunction, therefore, read something like this passage from Andrew Boorde's *Compendyous Regyment* of 1547:

> Sanguine men be hote and moiste of complexion … wherefore they must abstaine to eate inordynately fruytes and herbes and rootes as garlyke, onyions, and leekes. They muste refrayne from eatyng of olde flesshe, and eschewe the usage of eatyng of the braines of beestes, and from eatynge the udders of keyne [i.e., of cattle].

What sanguine men should eat, according to William Bullein in his 1562 *Bulwarke of Defence*, was "sharpe Sauces, made wyth Vinegar, Onions, and Barberies" as well as "small Fishes that feede upon the stones" and "cucumbers and pure Frenche wyne." These foods "be good for the Sanguine Men," just as other kinds of food were said to be good for individuals with one of the other three temperaments.

Eating according to your temperament—that is, according to whether you were sanguine, phlegmatic, choleric, or melancholy—was further complicated by the belief that what a person did for a living also affected what he or she was able to safely digest. Common laborers were advised to eat coarse foods that were suitable for their hardy natures and strenuous lifestyles. The *Compendyous Regyment* affirmed that "beane butter"—a kind of paste made of ground beans or peas—"is good for plowmen to fill the paunche." Boorde added that "bacon is good for carters and plowmen, the whiche be ever laborynge in the earth or dung." Thomas Twyne in his *Schoolemaster, or Teacher of Table Philosophie* made the same point by telling an anecdote about a city girl who mistakenly tried to feed her new husband, a farmer, fancy meals that he literally could not stomach:

> A younge delicate Cocknie of the Citie was married unto a ritche Fermour of the Countery. And always against hee should come home to dinner or supper from his woorke, she prepared him some fine litle deintie dish in a potenger, wherewith he was mutch discontented. And once she dressed him a capon for his supper, whereat he was much more offended than before. This pretty parnel seeing that she could not please him, went and complayned to her mother of the matter, who asked of her what she gave him to eate, who answered, this, and that, and recited as before is written. Then sayd hir mother thou art much deceived, and henceforward set before him a great bowle full of Beanes and Peason, with browne Bread, for hee is a labourynge man, and must bee grosely fed. Now when the daughter had followed her mothers advise, he laughed and was mery, and sayd that he laughed at the Capon which shee dressed for him the day before, but truer it is, that he rejoysed bicause his belly was full.

On the other hand, the aristrocrats and gentry who were at the other end of the social scale required much more delicate foods, as Thomas Twyne makes clear: "As for sutch as take no great paine, but live a gentlemans lyfe, they cannot chuse a better kinde of meate than this [the flesh of young goats]." It is worth stressing that these were not just casual differences in preference, but actual differences in what their bodies were thought capable of handling: your social class had a direct impact on your digestive system.

A further complicating factor in determining one's ideal diet was the seasons. Just as every human and every food had a humor or temperament, so too did the seasons, with spring being hot and moist (sanguine), summer hot and dry (choleric), autumn cold and dry (melancholy), and winter cold and moist (phlegmatic). Thus, eating ginger (which was classified as hot and dry) in November could help to alleviate the cold and moist effects of the onset of winter. A lot of dietary advice therefore concerned not just what you should eat, but when. Gervase Markham, for example, in the 1623 edition of his *Countrey Contentments, or The English Huswife,* devised a month-by-month dietary calendar:

Januarie—eate sallets wel prepared with oyle and spices.

Februarie—eate confections, candied with honny, for that they purge the body ... but to eate often freshe Beef, or other meates that be moyst, or to eat anye potte-hearbs, except the Parcely or Smallach, is then thought hurtefull.

March—to bathe often in that Moneth is greatly commended.

Aprill—eate pleasaunt meates and the river fishe and salets often.

Maye—eate no head nor foot of any best in that moneth, because of the moysture of the herbes and grasse which the beasts do eat in that moneth.

June—beware of eating milke, unlesse the same be well sodden, & likewise take heede both of the eating of cheese and apples in that moneth.

July—it is not good to eat strong meats, for the hotnesse of the season, for that the dogge dayes be entred in that moneth.... And beware of eating eyther Beetes, or Lettuce in this moneth.

August—eate both pullets and veale, for that they then comfort the body. And use to eate often cinamon in your meates.

September—eate all maner of meats you list, for that in the same moneth all thinges be in theyr proper vertue.... And to eate Pomegranates, and Goates milke, is well commended in this moneth, for that they both encrease bloud, & cause good colour.

October—eat often apple-tartes prepared with comfortable spices and Sugar, in that they comforte greatly the stomack: but washe not the head in this moneth.

November—bathe not in this moneth, or but little if neede so requireth, for that it is thought to be the most perilous moneth of the yeare to bathe in.... And the Cinamon and Ginger drinke often in this moneth is greatly commended.

December—to eate then potage made of Coleworts, and Cabages, and to eate roasted Onions prepared in Sallets, & either roasted apples or peares after meales, be greatly commended.

One final consideration needed to be taken into account by those who wanted to eat properly in Shakespeare's England—namely, the method used to prepare or cook the food. At its best, cookery was seen as a way of "correcting" the humoral excess or deficiency of a given food. Frying, for example, was the best way to prepare gourds, at least according to James Hart in his 1633 *Klinike*: "Gourds ... never to be eaten raw; but boiled, or rather fried with butter or oile, and onions, or the like, which may correct this cold and moist quality." On the other hand, frying was the worst way to cook meat, as Andrew Boord asserted in his *Compendyous Regyment*: "Fryed meate is harder of dygestyon than bruled [broiled] meate is, and it doth ingendre cholor and melancoly." Other foods, such as most fruits, were "corrected" by boiling or roasting.

Similarly, eating overcooked or undercooked food could also exacerbate an individual's humoral imbalance, as Petruchio affirms in *The Taming of the Shrew*:

> Katharina: I pray you, husband, be not so disquiet:
> The meat was well, if you were so contented.
>
> Petruchio: I tell thee, Kate, 'twas burnt and dried away;
> And I expressly am forbid to touch it,
> For it engenders choller, planteth anger;
> And better 'twere that both of us did fast,
> Since, of ourselves, ourselves are chollericke,
> Than feede it with such over-rosted flesh. (4.1.156–163)

The judicious combining of foods of different temperaments could also result in a well-balanced dish or meal, with each food helping to correct the excess or deficiency of the others. Fruits, as Hart recommends in his *Klinike*, should usually be followed by a cup of wine. Most meats, on the other hand, needed to be corrected by being eaten with bread, at least according to Gervase Markham's 1616 translation of a French text called *Maison Rustique*:

> Againe other victualls, have they never so good a taste, can neither bee pleasant nor profitable for the health in eating, if bread bee not eaten with them, in as much as the bread by its owne good nature doth correct the faults that are in other meates, and maketh them stronger and of more power in their properties and qualities.

All in all, balancing your humours was a complicated business: you needed to consider your own temperament, the temperament of the season, the temperament of the foods at hand, how different cooking methods affected the temperaments of different foods, and even how your vocation made you more or less able to digest certain foods. Moreover, failing to appreciate these many factors could lead not only to humoral imbalance, but to a host of other pernicious ailments. For example, Thomas Twyne warned that "if a man that is of a Melancholick complexion, use to eate beefe: hee shal be greeved with the Spleene, fall into a quartaine fever, and come into a Dropsie. Also he shall waxe itchie, have the Morfew, Leprosie, Canker, ringewormes"—and that was only the start of it.

In addition to their preoccupation with humoral imbalances, dietary experts also turned their attention to other food-related matters. Some of their notions and concerns now seem, from the perspective of the twenty-first century, rather bizarre. There was a general consensus, for example, that many fruits, vegetables, and herbs had almost miraculous properties, ones that could be exploited by a cunning physician. Thomas Hill, for example, in his 1577 *The Gardeners Labyrinth*, reveals that an infant "sicke of the Ague" can be cured if he "bee layed on a Bedde made of the Cucumbers to sleepe" because the "feverous heate passeth into the Cucumbers." Garlic, on the other hand, as reported by Andrew Boorde in his *Compendyous Regyment*, "doth kyll all maner of wormes in a mans bely," including "small lytell longe wormes which wyll tyckle in the foundement." Raisins, according to Thomas Twyne, "increase motion unto venery, and woorke to the erection of the yeard"—that is, they enhance sexual desire and give men a Viagra-like boost. Certain foods were also reputed to help people fall asleep or stay awake. Christopher Langton, in his 1545 *Introduction into Phisicke wyth an Universal Diet*, tells his readers that "lettuce, popie, mandragon, mulberyes, and garlyke, provoke slepe. Tyme, rue, hysope and onyons styre up the senses, whereby they cause watche." A good night's sleep was also assured, according to Andrew Boorde, if "your nyght cap be of skarlet" and if you "lay your hande or your bed felowes hande over your stomacke."

In terms of digestive ailments, hiccuping strangely seems to have been a matter of grave concern. "It is peryllous, and mutch to bee feared," wrote William Bullein, and his cure was to "give the Pacient Goates milke or Womans mylke wyth Suger, and washe his heade wyth warme Wyne." Bullein and his fellow dieticians were also much preoccupied with what they called "putrefaction" and the "engendering of crudities." These two problems arose when the digestive process was hindered, which could be caused by eating foods in the wrong sequence, by too much exertion after eating, or by falling asleep too soon after eating. The proper sequence for eating—or for the "order of ingestion" as James Hart referred to it—was that "the lightest meat, and easiest of digestion ought first to be eaten," the reason being that "the lightest meates being first eaten, sooner descend into the guts after concoction, which if last eaten, are by the other hindered to descend, and so putrifie, and ingender crudities." In terms of exertion, it was generally held that moderate exercise after dining was healthy. William Bullein, for example, affirmed that "to walke an hundred Paces after meate, is wholsome," and added that "this is the cause why Faukeners, Shouters, Hunters, Runners, Tenis players, Plowmen, and Gardeners, and lyfters of wayghtes have so good digestion and strength of Body." By extension, falling asleep shortly after dining was deemed baleful, because the sleeper's prone position interfered with the action of the stomach:

> The Stomacke being full, desireth a more open action and vent; which sleepe ensuing hereupon sealeth up, thereby causing an inordinate heat in the stomacke, whereby the meats become crusted and baked, as bread in an Oven, over-heat without vent, whereupon ensue Rhumes, and other diseases in the head.

Implicit in all of the preceding passages pertaining to the avoidance of putrefaction and crudities is the assumption that the human stomach works much like a stew pot on a fire. In other words, the bottom of the belly is hottest and thus most fit for digesting "heavy" foods, the top is cooler and better suited to digesting "lighter" foods, and one must be careful not to slosh around the contents of the "belly pot" by lying down before food is digested, or by exercising excessively after eating. This way of imagining the stomach also led many sixteenth-century dietary authorities to conclude that drinking anything between supper and bedtime was unhealthy, because it would "cool" the digestive process. Worst of all, naturally, were cold drinks, which prompted an author known only as F.W. in 1641 to write *A Treatise of Warm Beer*, in which he argues over the course of 143 pages why warm beer is preferable to cold beer:

> The stomach is compared to a pot boyling over the fire with meat; now if you put cold water therein it ceaseth the boyling, till the fire can overcome the coldnesse of the water, and the more water you put in, the longer it will be before it boyl again, and so long time you hinder the meat from being boyled: So it is with the stomach. If you drink cold beer, you hinder the digestion of the meat in the stomach; and the more cold you drink, the more you hinder it.

The notion that the stomach was a kind of stew pot also informed conventional wisdom about how often people needed to eat. Generally, as Thomas Twyne advised, a person was not to begin a new meal until "the weight of the meate which we eate last before is sunck downwarde, and the bottome of the stomacke is become light." Effectively, Twyne added, this meant that eating just once a day was ideal, "or at the most twise in one day" or better yet only "thrice in two dayes." Moreover, with regard to the amount of food eaten, "it is alwaies good to use a moderation," as James Hart affirmed in his *Klinike*. For Hart, this meant an upper limit of about 40 ounces of food a day, and that was only for hardworking laborers living in cold climates; those who led more sedentary lives and who lived in warmer climates were to strive to limit themselves to about 13 ounces of food a day. (Nowadays the average North American consumes about 60 ounces of food a day.)

This meagre allowance of food was to be further reduced by occasional fasts, whose purpose was to purge the body of "superfluities," and which, according to William Bullein, would help to "correct the flesh, and make it obedient, and servaunt to the spirite." This mollifying effect is undoubtedly the one sought by Petruchio, in *The Taming of the Shrew*, when he tells his unruly wife, "For this night we'll fast" (4.1.165), adding that she "ate no meate today, nor none shall eate" (4.1.185). A similar effect is aimed at by the King of Navarre in *Love's Labor's Lost* when he invites his lords to join him in a three-year fast, during which time they will eat nothing at all for one day each week, and only one meal a day during the rest of the week. The king believes that avoiding sumptuous food will enhance their mental abilities, because "daynty bits / Make rich the ribbes, but bankrupt quite the wits" (1.1.26–27). Indeed, the King's contempt for "dainty bits" was shared by the dietary experts of the time, who had an abiding fear of anything that might tempt people from moderate consumption into over-indulgence or, as they then called it, gluttony. Moreover, gluttony did not merely denote excessive eating, as it now tends to, but rather any kind of excess with regard to food. For example, James Hart, in his 1633 *Klinike*, identifies three branches of gluttony:

> Now in Gluttony, there is a treble fault committed: First, in the substance of the meat, when it is too curious and delicate; Secondly, in the quantity, when it exceedeth in the same; and thirdly, in the quality, if it be too daintily seasoned, and too curiously cooked. And then is it not properly called nourishment, but junkets or wanton fare.

Gluttony, according to the dietary treatises of the time, was a pernicious and prevalent cause of ill health. A 1576 treatise entitled *The Mirror of Mans Lyfe* warned that "glutony is an enimie to health, a friend unto sicknesse, the mother of wanton lust, and the instrument of death." James Hart catalogued some of the diseases caused by "this belly-god sin of Gluttony," including "apoplexie, epilepsie, incubus (called night-mare), all manner of distillations or rheumes, oppression of the stomacke, crudities, vomits, lasks of several kindes, putrid Fevers of severall sorts, disquietnesse and watching." Even Edmund Spenser's *The Faerie Queene*, an allegorical poem written for Queen Elizabeth, includes a depiction of the figure of Gluttony that highlights his ill health:

> Full of diseases was his carcas blew,
> And a dry dropsie through his flesh did flow:
> Which by misdiet daily greater grew.

There was a collective sense, too, that gluttony was now a worse social ill than it used to be, and that England in particular was becoming a nation of "belly-gods." Phillip Stubbes, for example, affirmed that "I have heard my Father say, in his dayes, one dish or two of good wholsome meate was thought sufficient, for a man of great worship to dyne withall, and if they had three or four kinds, it was reputed a sumptuous feast." But now, Stubbes goes on to say, our nicenes and curiousnes in dyet, hath altered our nature, distempered our bodies, and made us more subject to millions of discrasies and diseases, than ever weare our forefathers subject unto, and consequently of shorter life than they.

James Hart concurred, lamenting that

> mans boldnesse hath yet extended it selfe to strange and prodigious dishes, so that now we are not contented to feed on Sheep and Cattell, Hens and Capons, and other such creatures useful for the maintaining of the life of man; and fit them for our tables: but prodigious gluttony hath now devised to feed upon the excrements of the earth, the slime and scum of the water, the superfluity of the woods, and putrefaction of the sea; to wit, to feed on frogs, snailes, mushroms, and oisters.

Hart acknowledged that eating such "superfluities" as mushrooms and "putrefactions" as oysters was not yet as common in England as in other European nations, but warned that unless the growing tide was reversed, "one of these daies these dishes may become as common as our new French fashions of apparell." Thomas Nashe, however, asserted that England had already outstripped other nations in its gluttonous gourmandizing. He writes in his 1592 *Pierce Penilesse* that "It is not for nothing, that other Countries whom we upbraide with Drunkennesse, call us bursten-bellied Gluttons: for wee make our greedie paunches powdring tubs of beefe, and eat more meate at one meale, than the Spaniard or Italian in a moneth." John Stephens concurred in a section of his 1615 *Essayes and Characters, Ironical and Instructive*, in which he charges that English "epicures" have "purchased the generall name to our Countrey of Sweet-mouth'd English-men."

Others tried to defend their nation from such accusations. William Harrison, for example, in his 1587 *Description of England*, explained that because England was a northerly and cold island, its inhabitants needed more food and that "it is no marvell therefore that our tables are oftentimes more plentifullie garnished than those of other nations." Fynes Moryson in his 1617 *Itinerary* took another tack, explaining that although the tables of some English families are laden with numerous dishes, diners are not expected to try all of the dishes but only those that are appropriate for his or her temperament, and that large quantities are intentionally made so that there will be leftovers to give to the poor:

> The old custome of the English make our tables plentifully furnished, whereupon other Nations esteeme us gluttons and devourers of flesh, yet the English tables are not furnished with many dishes, all for one mans diet, but severally for many mens appetite, and not onely prepared for the family, but for strangers and reliefe of the poore. I confesse, that in such plenty and variety of meates, everie man cannot use moderation, nor understandeth that these severall meates are not for one man, but for severall appetites, that each may take what hee likes.

Given that gluttony is one of the traditional seven deadly sins, it is not surprising that dietary authorities sometimes enlisted moral or theological arguments in their denunciation of it. For example, *The Mirror of Mans Lyfe*—a treatise that aimed to show "what miseries we are subject unto"—first asserts that gluttony "corrupteth the stomake," and then, in the next sentence, adds that "gluttony did shutte up the gates of Paradyse agaynst mankynde," the notion being that Eve's eating of the apple was an act of gluttony.

Set against these learned censures of gluttony, however, were popular texts that celebrated gluttons as if they were folk heroes:

> I tell you of a Champion bold,
> That fights not for the fame of gold,
> but for good belly cheare.

That passage is from a ballad called "A Wonder in Kent," which extols the astonishing (and certainly apocryphal) gastronomic feats of one Nicholas Wood. According to the ballad, Wood once ate, at a single sitting,

> A quarter of a good fat Lambe,
> And threescore Egges he overcame,
> and eighteen yards of blacke pudding,
> And a raw Ducke all but Bill and Wing,
> and after he had dined, as I doe find,
> he longed for Cherries that bravely shined
> then threescore pound they brought,
> which he consumed to nought,
> a thing unpossible me thought.

A *Wonder in Kent*, c1630. In the early seventeenth century, Nicholas Wood was celebrated as a folk hero, thanks to his prodigious (and apocryphal) gastronomic exploits. In an era where dearths were never far from anyone's mind, Wood's boundless consumption of food was a kind of wish fulfilment for the populace. In this woodcut, Wood is shown biting the head off a fully feathered bird, while a pig and lamb stand beside him, waiting to be devoured. Courtesy of the Pepys Library, Magdalene College, Cambridge.

A 1630 prose tract called *The Great Eater of Kent* also celebrated the "admirable teeth and stomack exploits" of Nicholas Wood, including a meal where he ingested an entire hog followed by nearly a bushel of plums. His ability to consume was depicted as a kind of super power:

His mouth is a Mill of perpetuall motion, for let the wind or the water rise or fall, yet his teeth will ever bee grinding; his guts are the rendez-vous or meeting place or burse for the Beasts of the fields, the Fowles of the Ayre, and Fishes of the Sea; and though they be never so wild or disagreeing in Nature, one to another, yet hee binds or grindes them to the peace, in such manner, that they never fall at odds againe.

The inordinate eating and drinking Falstaff, one of Shakespeare's most beloved characters, also attests to the fact that the popular attitude toward gluttony did not always align with that of the dietary and religious authorities. Indeed, according to an anecdote recorded in 1702, Queen Elizabeth found Falstaff to be such an engaging character that she commanded Shakespeare to write a play in which that "tun of man" (*1H4* 2.4.453) fell in love, which became *The Merry Wives of Windsor*.

Given this complex web of attitudes toward and theories about food, it is not surprising that cookery was seen sometimes as a friend and sometimes as a foe. On the one hand, cookery could help adjust the temperaments of food so that it would be more healthful, but on the other hand it could make food more delicious, which would result in more gluttony. A proponent of the former view was Andrew Boorde, who praised cooks as the near-equals of physicians:

For a good cooke is halfe a phisicion. For the chiefe phisicke ... dothe come from the kytchyn, wherfore the phisicion and the cooke for sicke men must consult togyther for the preparacion of meate for sicke men. For if the phisicion withoute the cooke prepare any meate ... he wyll make a werysshe [weak and tasteless] dysshe of meate, the whiche the sycke can nat take.

John Lyly, one of Shakespeare's rival playwrights, said much the same in his 1580 work *Euphues*:

Let the Cooke be thy Phisition, and the shambles [the butcher] thy Apothecaries shop: He that for every qualme wil take a Receipt [a prescription], and cannot make two meales, unlesse Galen be his Gods good: shall be sure to make the Phisition rich, & himselfe a begger, his body will never be without diseases, & his pursse ever with-out money.

In contrast, Francis Bacon contemned cookery as a "voluptarie art," one that "did marre wholsome Meates, and helpe unwholesome by varietie of sawces, to the pleasure of the taste." Even more critical was the author of *The Mirror of Mans Lyfe*, who saw a huge moral distinction between simple foods intended for nourishment and fancy dishes that catered to "greedy desire":

In the beginning of mans life, bread & water was his foode, & a simple garment with a poore cottage were thought sufficient to cover his deformities. But now the frutes of the trees, the sondry sorts of graynes, the rootes of herbes, the fishes of the sea, the beastes of the land, the foules of the ayre, do not satisfie the greedie appetite of glutons & ravening men. For nowe they seeke pleasant dishes with painted coloures: they procure delicate & hote spices, choyce cates, sugred morsels for their daintie mouthes. Those things do they feed upon, which be curiously wroght by the arte of Cookery, & cunningly prepared by the inventions of their officers. One by stamping & strayning changeth some things from their proper nature, laboring by art to make that an accidente whiche of it selfe is a substance. Another compoundeth things togither, to make that delicate, whiche of it selfe is unpleasant: and al this is to turne excesse to hunger, to bring an apetite unto the stomacke opprest with saturitie, and to fulfyll the gredy desire of gluttonie, rather than to susteyne the weakenesse of nature.

In short, cookery was sometimes construed as a science (though they didn't use that word four centuries ago) and sometimes as an art. As a science, it was the loyal sidekick of physicians, but as an art it was allied with dubious practices like writing plays, juggling, and casting spells (after all, both witches and cooks use recipes—the one in *Macbeth* calls for "eye of newt and toe of frog, / Wool of bat, and tongue of dog") (4.1.14–15).

# FOOD AND DRINK LAWS

Falstaff: Marry, there is another indictment upon thee,
　　　　for suffering flesh to be eaten in thy house, contrary to
　　　　the law; for the which I think thou wilt howl.
Hostess: All victuallers do so: what's a joint of mutton
　　　　or two in a whole Lent? (*2 Henry IV* 2.4.343–347)

Officially, religion had no influence on what people ate in Shakespeare's England. However, many of the laws that restricted consumption were in fact built upon a framework of interdictions that had existed up until 1534, when Henry VIII initiated the English Reformation by declaring himself, rather than the Pope, the head of the church in England. Under Roman Catholicism, certain forms of penance—such as fasting, which really meant eating fish rather than meat—had been mandated for soteriological reasons: that is, they were good for your soul. After the Reformation, however, the new Church of England, like other Protestant denominations, declared that "Popish" practices such as doing penance and buying indulgences were foolish superstitions; a person got into heaven not by doing things, but by simply accepting God's grace. The problem for England's Protestant monarchs, however, was that one of the abolished Roman Catholic practices—namely, the observance of "fish days"—also had economic and social benefits. Accordingly, in 1558, Queen Elizabeth affirmed that England would maintain the custom of observing fish days, but only because it was good for her people's welfare, not their souls. In fact, Elizabeth actually increased the number of fish days, until over one-third of the year was officially meat-free: all of Lent, all of Advent, every Wednesday, Friday, and Saturday, and certain other holy days (though she repealed the Wednesdays in 1585). Not surprisingly, many people found it difficult to forgo meat for so many days of the year. Elizabeth dealt with such resistance—which in one proclamation she blamed on the "develyshe and carnall appetite" of some of her subjects—through a combination of punishment and persuasion.

The punishment for anyone who ate meat on a fish day was three months of imprisonment or a fine of three pounds, which was about six months of wages for an ordinary laborer, though later in Elizabeth's reign this fine was reduced to one pound. Sometimes, alternative punishments were imposed: in his diary, William Machyn recorded that on March 9, 1557, a young man who ate meat during Lent was paraded through the streets of London in a horse-drawn cart, with his face toward the horse's tail and two large pieces of salted beef slung over him. Machyn also records that on April 7, 1563, the wife of a man who owned the Rose Tavern was put into a pillory for one day, as punishment for eating both raw and roasted flesh. Food vendors, too, such as "Innholders, Tablekeepers, Victuallers, Alehousekeepers, and Taverners," were subject to the fish day laws. They were required to provide authorities with a bond of one hundred pounds, an enormous sum that they would forfeit if they were caught selling meat dishes during Lent. Butchers were likewise required to cease their slaughtering on fish days, unless they were were fortunate enough to be granted a special license. In *2 Henry VI*, such a license is what Jack Cade promises Dick, "the butcher of Ashford," as recompense for fighting valiantly, or rather he makes the wild promise that Lent will now last for twice as long and that Dick will be granted a license every year for the next ninety-nine years:

> They fell before thee like Sheepe and Oxen, &
> thou behaved'st thy selfe, as if thou hadst beene in thine
> owne Slaughter-house: Therfore thus will I reward
> thee, the Lent shall bee as long againe as it is, and thou
> shalt have a License to kill for a hundred lacking one. (4.3.3–7)

A few such licenses notwithstanding, most butchers were idle for the forty days of Lent, a period that John Taylor, in a 1620 tract called *Jack a Lent*, fancifully construes as a kind of detente between humans and beasts:

> The Cut-throat Butchers, wanting throats to cut,
> At Lents approach their bloody Shambles shut:
> For forty dayes their tyrannie doth cease,
> And men and beasts take truce and live in peace:
> The Cow, the Sow, the Ewe may safely feed,
> And lough, grunt, bleate, and fructifie and breed,
> Cocks, Hens, and Capons, Turkey, Goose and Widgeon,
> Hares, Conies, Phesant, Partridge, Plover, Pidgeon:
> All these are from the break-neck Poulters pawes
> Secured by Lent, and guarded by the lawes,
> The goaring spits are hanged for fleshly sticking,
> And then Cookes fingers are not worth the licking.

Supplementing the punishments for those who flouted the fish days were various persuasive tactics, including reasoned arguments such as those found in a 1593 treatise entitled *A Briefe Note of the Benefits that Grow to this Realme, by the Observation of Fish-daies*. According to the anonymous author of that treatise, numerous fish days were necessary in order to keep fishermen employed, which was important not just

*Jack a Lent His Beginning and Entertainment*, John Taylor, 1620. The three figures in this wood-cut represent three phases of Lent. First comes Shrove Tuesday, fattened with overindulgence; then comes Jack a Lent, blithely riding a fish through the 40 meatless days of Lent; and finally comes Hunger, the inevitable consequence of fasting. © British Library Board. All Rights Reserved C.40d.31 pg 22.

for the maintenance of them and their families, but also because fishermen, in times of crisis, could be quickly pressed into the navy to defend England's shores. The author also points out that because many disobedient citizens had been flouting fish days, the price of beef and mutton had gone up, which had prompted many unscrupulous landowners to turn their arable fields into enclosed pastures so that they could graze more cows and sheep. This in turn meant that many rural inhabitants had lost their livelihood, and that "many Farme houses and Villages [are] now utterly decayed and put downe." Edward Jeninges, who in 1590 published a treatise devoted to the same issue, went so far as to estimate that a hundred thousand people had been put out of work by the nation's poor observance of fish days (though he doesn't indicate how he arrives at this figure). Worse yet, he adds, this unemployment had led to a "greater increase of idleness, rogues, and theeves." Jeninges also puts forth a further, rather peculiar, argument: namely, that because people were refusing to observe fish days, they had forgotten how to prepare some of the more unusual foods that the sea provides, including puffins, porpoises, and seals, all of which were considered fish. From these creatures, he writes, people once made "fine & delicate dishes," but they are now "utterly forgotten, how or in what sort it should be used, dressed, or served: and worst of all, how it should be eaten, and digested, for that the proportion and substance of them is by many forgotten, and the use and taste forgotten of all."

Not surprisingly, enforcing fish days was a difficult task. If a husband and wife nibbled a flitch of bacon in the privacy of their own home, it was unlikely that they would be caught. Nonetheless, judging from the diaries and household accounts of the time, it seems that most people actually did their best to avoid meat on fish days, and the cookbooks of the time include many meat-free recipes, some of which are specifically identified as "Lenten" dishes. For every person like the Hostess in *2 Henry IV*, who remarks "What's a joint of mutton or two in a whole Lent?", there was someone like Thomas Tusser who soberly advised, in his *Five Hundredth Points of Husbandry*, "Keepe fish daie and fasting daie," adding that if fish are scarce one can "supplie that want, with butter and cheese." Moreover, the law itself provided some flexibility. Pregnant women and the sick could request a temporary license from their priest or bishop that permitted them to eat meat on any day, and members of the gentry could purchase an annual license for a fee ranging from about 6 shillings to about 26 shillings, depending on their rank. On fish days, individuals with these licences were popular dinner guests, as their presence at the table meant that their host could serve meat dishes, to which the other guests would undoubtedly help themselves.

In addition to laws pertaining to fish days, other statutes in Shakespeare's England regulated the quality, price, and sale of certain foods and beverages. To some extent, these laws were necessary to protect customers from the dishonest practices of certain food vendors. A passage from an early seventeenth-century ballad implies that such outright deceptions were widespread (the "puffing" in the second line below refers to the ruse of inflating cuts of meat to make them appear bigger):

> The Butcher with his winde,
> doth love to puffe his meate:
> The Cooke doth in his kinde
> delight the world to cheate.
>
>          …
>
> Some Bakers pure doe show,
> although they use false weights.

In his diary, Henry Machyn recorded how such dishonest vendors were sometimes punished by being publicly shamed. For example, on July 1, 1552, he reported that a man and woman were set in the pillory for a day because they had sold pots of strawberries with fern leaves hidden under the fruit, so that their pots appeared more full than they actually were. On February 28, 1558, a man was set in the pillory with a garland of fish about his neck, because he had bought smelts for the Queen's household (as he was supposed to do), but had then sold them to "fishwives," pocketing the money for himself (as he was not supposed to do). And on January 31, 1560, a butcher was set in the pillory with rotten meat placed above his head, as a punishment for twice selling flesh that was unfit for consumption.

Other laws were intended not to curb the chicanery of food vendors, but rather to control the marketplace and to protect the interests of various professions. To this end, about seventy distinct guilds—or "worshipful companies" as they were then called—were granted the sole right to purvey certain goods. These included guilds that engaged in manufacturing, such as Goldsmiths, Masons, and Upholders (who made feather pillows); guilds that provided services, such as Musicians and Barbers (who also performed minor surgery, and advertised this fact by hanging bloody bandages from their storefronts); and guilds that supplied produce or made foodstuffs, such as Cooks, Grocers, Fishmongers, Poulterers, Fruiterers, Bakers, Butchers, Milkmen, Salters, Brewers, Vintners, and Distillers. Some of these guilds, such as the Grocers and Apothecaries, had close and amicable relationships, whereas others, such as the Fletchers (who made arrows) and Bowyers (who made bows), were often at odds. Moreover, the demarcations between guilds were sometimes, at least from our perspective, rather peculiar. There were, for example, two guilds for bakers: one for "white bakers" (who produced various kinds of wheat bread) and one for "brown bakers" (who produced coarse bread made from rye, barley, beans, and peas, with some of their loaves intended for human consumption and some for horses). Neither of these two guilds was allowed to make or sell the bread of the other guild. Moreover, thanks to a decree issued by Queen Elizabeth (and recorded in a 1592 treatise called *The Assize of Bread*), neither guild was allowed to bake "fancy" products such as "Spice Cakes, Bunnes, Biskets, or other spice breads … excepte it be at Burialls or upon the Friday before Easter, or at Christmas." Bakers who were caught using their ovens for such naughty purposes were required to forfeit their contraband spice cakes to the poor.

In London, the members of guilds that dealt in foodstuffs could sell their wares only in certain authorized neighborhoods. For example, a fishmonger could not set up a stall in the Eastcheap Market because Eastcheap was restricted to butchers; likewise, a butcher could not sell his meat in the Fish Street Market. Moreover, there were also further restrictions pertaining to residency: fishmongers who lived outside of London (they were called "foreigners," even though they might reside only a few miles away) were not allowed to vend their wares in the Fish Street Market. They could, however, do so in the Billingsgate market. Many of the neighborhood markets had several guilds within them. The Stocks Market, for example, had both fishmongers and butchers. The Gracechurch Market was intended for country vendors (that is, the "foreigners" mentioned previously), who were allowed to sell dairy products, fruit, and pork but not mutton; oddly, they were allowed to sell veal but not beef. In addition to the stalls or tables set up by these various guild members, certain food products could also be sold by licensed pedlars, who carried their wares in baskets or pulled them in small carts as they walked through the streets. Fishwives, for example, sold their goods this way, though the law required that they had to keep moving: they couldn't rest in one spot and hawk their wares. Bakers also employed women to sell pies in the street, and apple vendors—known then as costermongers—ambled about as well.

Partly to give local householders some respite from the hurly-burly of the markets, and partly to help ensure that market transactions did not occur under cover of darkness, civic authorities regulated when the food markets could be open: in London, they were open Monday to Saturday, from 6:00 A.M. to 11:00 A.M. and from 1:00 P.M. to 5:00 P.M. On Sundays they were closed, with the exception that milk, vegetables, and fruit could be sold first thing in the morning, from 6:00 A.M. to 7:00 A.M. in the summer and from 6:00 A.M. to 8:00 A.M. in the winter.

Other market laws were directed at three practices that were then considered unscrupulous: forestalling, engrossing, and regrating. Forestalling referred to the practice of intercepting goods as they were being carried to a designated market, buying them at the regular price, and then selling them at a higher price at the intended market, much as scalpers now do with concert tickets. Fishwives were often accused of forestalling. Engrossing was essentially a large-scale form of forestalling: rather than just buying a basket or two of herring for resale at a somewhat inflated price, the engrosser would purchase all available supplies of a given commodity; having thus "cornered the market," he would then resell the goods at an exorbitant price. Regrating meant buying a commodity in one market and then walking it over to another market to sell at a higher price. As the laws against forestalling, engrossing, and regrating suggest, the ideal market economy in Shakespeare's England was presumed to be one in which consumers could buy goods directly from the producer. Would-be middlemen, who sought to insert themselves between consumer and producer, were considered by authorities to be parasites who bred inflation. Hugh Alley, in a report submitted to London's Lord Mayor in 1598, called them "evill-disposed persons" who bought up "all the best and chief thinges," before "anie good citizens of this Citie can come by the same." Sometimes, much to the alarm of the authorities, the good citizens grew so frustrated with the "hucksters, hawkers, and haglers," as they were commonly known, that they took matters into their own hands. In 1595, a number of apprentices were sent by their various masters to buy mackerel at the Billingsgate Market. Upon arriving there, they discovered that the local fishwives had bought up all the mackerel and were about to start selling it in the streets at a higher price. The apprentices—about seventy in number—pursued the fishwives, confiscated the fish, and returned home with their mackerel in hand. Although the apprentices seem to have acted with some discretion (they even paid the fishwives the usual market price before confiscating the mackerel), several of them were later tried and punished.

## AT THE MARKET AND BEYOND

These buy with the penny, or looke not for any: capers, lemmans, olives, orengis, sampire.

—Thomas Tusser, *Five Hundredth Points of Good Husbandry*

The 189 recipes included in this book call for about 150 distinct ingredients, ranging from beef to sparrows, eels to onions, and lemons to cinnamon. Where did these items come from, and how did they get into the kitchens of the upper-class women (or their cooks) who were the target audience of the cookery books that were published in Shakespeare's England? One source was the aforementioned markets, where foodstuffs that had to be imported into England were typically made available for sale. These imported items included various spices, such as aniseed, caraway, cardamom, cinnamon, cloves, coriander, fenugreek, galingale, ginger, grains of paradise, licorice, mace, nutmeg, and pepper. The sources of such spices ranged from Indonesia (for cinnamon) to India (for nutmeg) to Egypt (for anniseed) to Africa (for grains of paradise). In most cases, however, exotic spices weren't imported directly from their place of origin to England, but rather came via an intermediary port such as Venice, Lisbon, or Amsterdam. In those cities, the spices would be resold to English merchants (sometimes after being adulterated with various "fillers") and then shipped to London or sometimes Bristol. Once in England, the spices were brought to market by members of the Worshipful Company of Grocers, who (as their name implies) acquired the spices "en gros," that is, in large quantities. Admittedly, some of these exotic spices—such as coriander—were also grown in England by curious horticulturalists, but not in significant quantities.

Many exotic fruits were also imported into England and sold at markets. Fresh oranges and lemons were shipped from Spain and France, though by the time they arrived they were sometimes in a rather sorry state. Other fruits were so perishable, or came from so far away, that they could only be imported in dried form. This included figs (from Spain and Italy), dates (from Africa and the Middle East), and raisins (from regions along the Mediterranean). Raisins were often called "raisins of the sun" (because the grapes were dried under the hot sun) or "raisins of coraunce," the latter word being a corruption of Corinth, a city in Greece through which the dried fruit was shipped. Currants, which are another kind of grape, also take their name from Corinth. Needless to say, shipping these items from remote regions made them both expensive and sometimes hard to come by. Falstaff alludes to the scarcity of raisins in *1 Henry IV* (his analogy involves a pun on "raisins" and "reasons"): "If reasons were as plentiful as blackberries, I would give no man a reason upon compulsion" (2.4.237–238).

Olives and olive oil were imported from France, Italy, and Spain. After being preserved in brine, the olives were called "colymbades." They were used in salads, while the oil that was pressed from them was used in cooking as a fancy alternative to cheaper nut oils (like walnut), vegetable oils (like rapeseed), and oils rendered from animal fat. Certain nuts, too, were imported and sold at markets, including pistachios (which were sometimes called "fisticke"), which came from Italy and from nations even further east. Pine nuts, which were used in tarts and pancakes, were also brought from Italy, as were almonds, which were used to make various whitemeats and marzipan. (Almonds were cultivated in England, but the native species was considered inferior to those that came from southern climes.) Rice, which was also used in whitemeats (such as "maunger blanche" or what we would now call "blancmange"), was imported from Spain. Imports also included some items that our cooks now happily do without, such as ambergris, which is a secretion vomited forth by sperm whales and then harvested from shores or from the surface of the sea. Several early seventeenth-century recipes for macaroons call for ambergris. Sanders and cochineal were both imported as food dyes. Sanders, which was derived from India's sandalwood tree, was used to give foods a reddish hue: a recipe for roast thrushes says, "therto put Saunders, that the sauce may bee red." Cochineal, which was made by grinding up the dried bodies of an insect found on cactus plants in Mexico, produced a scarlet food dye.

Perhaps the most important culinary import in Shakespeare's England was sugar, which is an ingredient in more than half of the nearly 2,100 recipes that were compiled in cookery books of this era. Sugar was acquired from sugarcane plantations held by Portuguese colonies in Brazil and by Spanish colonies in the Canary Islands, mostly through legitimate trade but sometimes through "privateering," a form of royally sanctioned piracy. Typically, an English ship would attack a Spanish ship, take its cargo, send its crew packing, and return to England to split the profits with Queen Elizabeth (her successor, King James, did not condone privateering). Sugar was also imported from English colonies in North Africa where Queen Elizabeth had granted the Barbary Company a trade monopoly in 1585. Various types of sugar were available, ranging from a white sugar (which had undergone two boilings in the refining process), to an off-white sugar, to a brown sugar, to a sugar syrup (known as molasses) that was produced during the refining of other sugars. Refined sugar tended to be sold in congealed "loaves" that weighed about four pounds each. Powdered sugar, produced by scraping or grinding a sugar loaf, was also a commodity, as was "sugar candy," made by adding almond oil during the refining process. A pound of refined sugar cost at least 20 pence, the amount that a common laborer earned in a week. Still, despite its high cost, sugar had become the sweetener of choice by the early seventeenth century: writing in 1633, James Hart, in his *Klinike*, complained that "our forefathers in former times found honie very wholesome; but now nothing but the hardest Sugar will downe with us in this our effeminate and gluttonous age."

Wine was also imported into England, where it was not only imbibed but used in numerous culinary recipes. Grapes can, in fact, be cultivated in some parts of England, and earlier in its history, wine had been vinted in its southern regions. William Harrison, in his 1587 *Description of England*, noted that native wines had been "verie plentifull in this Iland, not onlie in the time of the Romans, but also since the conquest," the conquest being that of the Normans in 1066. "Yet at this present," he goes on to say, "have we none at all or else verie little to speake of growing in this Iland: which I impute not unto the soile, but the negligence of my countrimen." Most of the imported wines—such as claret (from France), port (from Portugal), muscadine (from Italy and Greece), and sack and bastard (both from Spain)—originated in southern Europe, but some rhenish was also acquired from Germany. Wine differed from other imports in that it was not sold at markets, but rather was acquired directly from a wine merchant (in large vessels, like tuns and hogsheads, by the very wealthy) or from a local tavern (in small vessels of a gallon or so, by the less affluent). A gallon of wine cost 40 pence, two weeks' wages for a common laborer, meaning that most people in England had to be content with domestically produced ale and beer.

Other ingredients and foodstuffs didn't need to be imported because they were readily available in England or in its coastal waters. These included plants and animals that were indigenous (like strawberries and hares) as well as flora and fauna that the island's inhabitants had successfully introduced to the ecosystem at some time in the past. Damsons, for example, were a kind of plum that originated in Greece (their name comes from "Damascus"). The ancient Romans brought them to England, where they continued to flourish even after the Romans left in the fifth century. Gooseberries were a somewhat more recent introduction: Edward I brought gooseberry bushes from France and planted them in English soil in the thirteenth century. Apricot trees had been introduced as recently as the early sixteenth

*A Caveatt for the Citty of London*, Hugh Alley, 1598 (manuscript). Hugh Alley sketched the major London markets in a report pertaining to mercantile malfeasance, which he presented to the Lord Mayor, Sir Stephen Soame, in 1598. In this sketch, two men herd cattle through Eastcheap Market, assisted by a dog that is ambling onto the right side of the page. The two women, on the left side of the page, are engrossers who intend to "corner the market" for a given commodity in order to drive up its price. In the background one can see large joints of meat hanging in front of a row of butcher shops.

century: even by 1613, they were still sufficiently novel that Gervase Markham referred to them as a "curious outlandish stone-fruit." Attempts to introduce and cultivate foreign species continued throughout Shakespeare's lifetime: by 1587, William Harrison was able to write, "I have seene capers, orenges, and lemmons, and heard of wild olives growing here, beside other strange trees, brought from far, whose names I know not." Such exotic fruits, however, remained horticultural curiosities, rather than becoming cash crops.

Like the imported commodities, most of the foodstuffs that were grown or produced in England were available for purchase at designated markets in London and other centers. In London, we have a sense of what these markets looked like thanks to Hugh Alley, who included sketches of them in the report he presented to Lord Mayor in 1598. His drawing of the Eastcheap Market has the street running horizontally across the page, with a continuous row of two-story houses along each side of the street. In the middle of the street two men with staffs are herding a dozen calves and two full-grown oxen. Behind one of the men is a dog that is assisting them as they coax the animals forward, presumably to a nearby shambles where they will be slaughtered. In front of each house we see a post-and-beam frame, from which hang entire carcasses and joints of meat. These are clearly the butchers' shops, with the families of the butchers living on the second story. On the left side of the sketch, Hugh Alley has included a symbolic element, namely, a huge pillar with "Engrosers" written at the top and with two well-dressed individuals standing beside it, one of whom is holding a basket. They represent, no doubt, one kind of offender who flouted the laws of the market.

Alley's sketch of the New Fishstreet Market is similar in that it again features two rows of houses with a street running in between. Each house has a table set up in front on which are displayed a variety of whole and filleted fish—probably the cod, plaice, pike, carp, trout, and white fish that the Duke of Wirtemberg noted when he visited one of London's fish markets in 1592. The fish vendors can be seen standing within the shop part of their houses, their heads poking out the front windows as they keep an eye on their wares. In the middle of the street is a cluster of people: a man leading two horses, each with a pair of panniers on its back; a woman with a basket slung under her arm; and another woman with a basket on her head and one in her hand. To their left is another pillar, this one with "Regraters" written at the top, suggesting that the individuals in the street are more "hucksters, hawkers, and haglers" who have bought fish and are now heading off to sell it at a higher price in another street or market. A dog, which growls at one of the basket-toting women, seems to embody the animosity that was often directed at regraters.

Leadenhall, judging from Alley's sketch of that market, was set up somewhat differently. In the foreground, we see the open-air section of the market, with various vendors displaying their wares on small tables, side by side: one sells pies and pastries, another holds a live duck by the neck, another has a scale and appears to be weighing small items like spices, and yet another seems to be carving pieces of meat, including a cow's udder. Interspersed among these individuals are five pillars with place names written at the top: "London," "Middlesex," "Surrey," "Kent," and "Essex," implying that these are country vendors who have traveled to London from the outlying districts. In the background is the actual Leadenhall building, which was built in the fourteenth century as a private residence and then converted by the city into a granary and covered market in 1445. Attached to the front of the Leadenhall building are planks of wood (called "stall-boards") on which wares could be displayed and that folded up to cover the building's windows when the market closed.

One thing that Alley's sketches don't capture is the cacophony and hurly-burly that must have reigned in the markets of London and other large towns. In addition to the noises made by various kinds of livestock as they were herded through the streets, there were the cries of the vendors (and hawkers) as they advertised their wares. Some of those cries were recorded in an early seventeenth-century ballad called "Turners Dish of Lentten Stuffe":

The fish-wife first begins,
Any Musckles lilly white,
Hearings, Sprats, or Pleace,
or Cockles for delight?
Any Wallfleet Oysters? ...

Ripe Chery ripe,
the Coster-monger cries,
Pipins fine, or Peares ...

Hot Pippin pies,
to sell unto my friends:
Or pudding pies in pans,
well stuft with Candles ends.
Will you buy any Milke,
I hear a wench to cry.
With a pail of fresh Cheese and creame
another after hies.

These street cries would have added to the general commotion that throbbed in London during much of the day (with 200,000 residents, London was the second largest city in the world, surpassed only by Paris). Thomas Dekker described this street ruckus in 1606 in a pamphlet entitled *The Seven Deadly Sinnes of London*:

In every street, carts and Coaches make such a thundring as if the world ranne upon wheeles: at everie corner, men, women, and children meete in such shoales, that postes are sette up on purpose to strengthen the houses, least with justling one another they should shoulder them downe. Besides, hammers are beating in one place, Tube hooping in another, Pots clincking in a third, water-tankards running at tilt in a fourth: heere are Porters sweating under burdens, there Marchants-men bearing bags of money, Chapmen (as if they were at Leape-frog) skippe out of one shop into another: Tradesmen (as if they were dauncing Galliards) are lusty at Legges and never stand still.

The noise and commotion of the markets were probably surpassed only by the odor. The smell of scalded pigs, singed feathers, and rendered fat—or what Shakespeare calls "the uncleanly savours of a slaughter-house" (*Jn.* 4.3.112)—would have been prevalent. Moreover, there was no underground sewage system in London at this time, which meant the guts of butchered animals, human excrement, dead dogs, and rotting vegetables had to be removed from the city by carting it through the streets (or by allowing scavenger birds, which were protected by law, to peck and carry it away). Indeed, according to John Stow in his 1598 *Survey of London*, Pudding Lane acquired its name because it was the route butchers used when they transported animal guts—known then as "puddings"—down to the dung boats that awaited them along the shore of the Thames. Some butchers probably didn't even bother taking their refuse to the dung boats, but simply dumped it straight into the river, in spite of laws prohibiting this. Falstaff, in *The Merry Wives of Windsor*, exclaims, "Have I lived to be carried in a basket, like a barrow of butcher's offal, and to be thrown into the Thames?" (3.5.4–6). All this, combined with the fact that taking baths was considered unhealthy in some months, would have made buying foodstuffs in the city's markets a rather pungent experience.

The alternative, of course, was to grow, raise, or capture your own foodstuffs. This would have been somewhat difficult for most people living in London: the city was densely populated, and few people would have had access to more than a tiny patch of ground. In rural areas, however, even poor households had use of a more sizable amount of arable land. Typically, all of the land in the district belonged to the lord of the manor, but (thanks to a custom dating back to feudal times) the villagers were allowed to farm it in a communal fashion. About eighteen acres of land was allotted to each "husbandman," that is, to men who were heads of a household and who did not work as servants or laborers for another household. Of the husband-man's eighteen acres, one-third of it in a given year had to lie fallow so that the soil would not become depleted, leaving twelve acres for him to plant with various crops. Some meadowland was also held in common for grazing cattle and sheep. Occasionally, manorial lords tried to buck the system by asserting their legal claim to the land, so that they could either sell it or turn the fields into pastures for sheep and cattle, which were more profitable. Sometimes they succeeded, and sometimes they didn't.

The crops grown by villagers on these tracts of land included grains such as wheat and rye (for making bread) and barley (for making beer and ale). A plot, too, was devoted to a garden, where a surprisingly large number of vegetables, fruits, and herbs were grown. These included a good quantity of peas and beans, as well as root crops such as turnips, carrots, parsnips, skirrets, radishes, navels (similar to a turnip), and beets (bearing in mind, though, that beets were cultivated as much for their leaves, which were eaten like spinach, as for their root). Leafy vegetables included cabbage, lettuce, spinach, kale, and cauliflower. Squashes ranged from pumpkins and gourds to cucumbers and muskmelons. Plants and herbs that gave substance as well as flavor to pottage or salads included onions, artichokes, alexanders, avens, chervil, cress, French mallow, English Mercury, orach, pennyroyal, rampions, rocket, chives, leeks, asparagus, sorrel, scallions, clary, burnet, purslane, and lange de boeuf. Gardens also featured herbs, flowers, and seeds that were used primarily as flavoring agents, such as tansy, borage, savory, thyme, hyssop, sage, rosemary, marjoram, fennel, basil, tarragon, bay, lovage, cumin, dill, mint, pennyroyal, garlic, bugloss, parsley, hops, violets, and marigolds. Berries from creeping vines and bushes were also cultivated in gardens, including raspberries, strawberries, red currants, gooseberries, bilberries, and barberries. It should be noted that in appearance, and perhaps even in flavor, some of these plants differed significantly from their modern counterparts. Beets, for example, had roots resembling slender parsnips rather than the fat globes with which we are now familiar. Similarly, carrots were yellow: the orange variety was not introduced from Holland until the late seventeenth century. Perhaps even more surprising is the observation that John Gerard makes in his 1597 *Herball*, that the stalk of a carrot can reach four cubits—about six feet—in height.

By the end of the sixteenth century, produce such as that named above was grown and enjoyed not just by humble villagers but by the highest levels of society. This is notable because in previous generations the meat-loving gentry had tended to scorn vegetables as more fit for barnyard animals than dinner guests. William Forrest, for example, made this claim in 1548:

> Our English nature cannot live by roots [i.e., root vegetables]. By waters, herbs, or such beggary baggage. That may well serve for vile outlandish coats. Give English men meat after their usage, Beef, Mutton, Veal, to cheer their courage.

Just forty years later, however, William Harrison noted that the gentry had had a change of heart:

> Such herbes, fruits, and roots also as grow yeerlie out of the ground ... [were formerly] supposed as food more meet for hogs & savage beasts to feed upon than mankind.

> Whereas in my time their use is not onelie resumed among the poore commons, I
> meane of melons, pompions, gourds, cucumbers, radishes, skirets, parsneps, carrets, cab-
> bages, navewes, turneps, and all kinds of salad herbes, but also fed upon as deintie
> dishes at the tables of delicate merchants, gentlemen, and the nobilitie.

Indeed, many country gentlemen turned farming and gardening into a sophisticated hobby, experimenting with different varieties of crops, grafting one plant onto another, and even attempting to alter the very form of some fruits and vegetables. For example, in his 1577 *Gardeners Labyrinth*, Thomas Hill taught country gentlemen how to insert a young cucumber, while it was still on the vine, into a clay mould so that as the plant grew it would take on the shape of the mould. According to Hill, cucumbers take joy in doing this because they are "so wonderful desirous of a new forme." Some of Hill's other horticultural advice seems less plausible: he suggests, for example, that one can grow extra sweet pumpkins by first soaking the seeds in honey and milk; he also claims that if you mix the seeds of lettuce, basil, and endive in a ball of dung, a single plant will sprout forth that tastes like all three plants combined. Not everyone was in favour of such horticultural experimentation: William Harrison thought it was pre-sumptious to meddle with God's creation, "dallying as it were with nature and her course, as if her whole trade were perfectlie knowne unto them."

In the countryside, husbandmen and gentlemen alike harvested fruit from orchards. The husbandman's orchard—apart from a tree or two that might grow on the edge of his own garden—was the communally held grove of fruit trees that he tended with his neighbors. The country gentleman, in contrast, usually had a large and private orchard cared for by a professional "fruiterer." Such an orchard supplied fresh produce for the gentleman's household, but surplus fruit could also be sold to a local market for a bit of extra income. For the truly affluent, however, a huge or-chard was as much a status symbol as anything: in his 1617 *Itinerary*, Fynes Moryson writes that "the English are so naturally inclined to pleasure, as there is no Countrie, wherein the Gentlemen and Lords ... allot so much ground about their houses for pleasure of Gardens and Orchards." Andrew Boorde, in his *Compendyous Regyment*, also emphasized the pleasure rather than the utility of a gentleman's orchard: "It is a commodyous and a pleasaunt thynge to a mansion to have an orcherd of soundry fruytes."

The fruits most commonly harvested from orchards were those mentioned by Fynes Moryson: "England hath such aboundance of Apples, Peares, Cherries, and Plummes, such variety of them, and so good in all respects, as no countrie yeelds more or better." As well, peaches, nectarines, apricots, quinces, and medlars were not uncommon. Chestnuts, hazelnuts, and walnuts were also gathered. Moreover, there were numerous varieties of most fruits. An apple, for example, could be a pip-pin, pomeroy, pomewater, ruddock, scrab, sweeting, jenneting, red streak, deuzan, or long-laster, to name only a few. Different varieties were used for different purposes: pippins tended to be used in cooking, whereas red streaks were used to make cider.

One challenge for those tending the orchards was keeping the fruit safe from birds. Gervase Markham advised making noise, and lots of it:

> You must have some boy or young fellow that must every morning from the dawning of
> the day till the Sunne bee more than an houre high, and every evening from five of

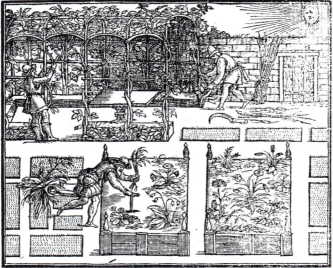

# The Gardeners Labyrinth.

Contayning the manifolde trauayles, great cares, and diligence,
to be yearly bestowed in euery earth, for the vse of a Garden:
with the later inuentions, and rare secretes therebnto added (as the like) not heretofore published.

The inuention of Garden plottes, by whom first deuised, and what
commoditie founde by them, in time past.      Chap. 1.

He worthie Plinie (in his xix. booke) reporteth, that a
Garden plotte in the Auncient time at Rome, was
none other, than a smal & simple inclosure of ground,
whiche through the labour and diligence of the hus-
bandmā, yeelded a commoditie and yearely reuenew
vnto him. But after yeares (that man more esteemed

*The Gardeners Labyrinth*, Thomas Hill, 1577. The ornate patterning of the arbor and garden depicted in this woodcut was typical of affluent households in Shakespeare's England, but probably not of ordinary folk. In the top half of the panel, two servants are entwining vines around a wood-framed trellis while an anthropomorphized sun gazes down at them. Within the arbor a bench and table are visible, and at the foot of the gardener on the right side is a sickle, used for cutting and hacking vegetation. In the bottom half of the woodcut a third gardener uses an awl to dig a hole for the plant he holds in his left hand. The plot he is working on seems to be devoted to flowers rather than vegetables. © Bodleian Library, University of Oxford Douce M 299 (detail pg 1).

the clocke till nine, runne up and downe your ground, whooping, showting, and making a great noise, or now and then shooting off some Harquebus, or other Peece.

Markham also cited thunder and lightning as a great threat to all kinds of flora, includ-
ing fruit trees. Yet another menace, according to Thomas Tusser in his *Five Hundredth Points of Good Husbandry*, was drabs—that is, promiscuous women—who would steal apples that had fallen to the ground: "For feare of drabs, go gather thy crabs."

Quince

in faire water, till they be foft, but not too violently for feare you
break them, when they are foft take them out, and boyle fome
*Quinces* pared, quarter'd, and coar'd, and the parings of the *Quin-*
*ces* with them in the fame liquor, to make it ftrong, and when
they have boyled a good time, enough to make the liquor of
fufficient ftrength, take out the quartered *Quinces* and parings,
and put the liquor into a pot big enough to receive all the *Quin-*
*ces*, both whole and quartered, and put them into it, when the
liquor is thorow cold, and fo keep them for your ufe clofe
covered.

To

*A Book of Fruits & Flowers*, Anonymous, 1653. In the cookery books of Shakespeare's England, the quince appeared in more recipes than any other fruit, though it has now fallen out
of favor and is virtually unknown in North America. The jottings that appear above the fruit
were inked onto the page after the book was published, presumably by whoever owned it; the
jottings at the top represent different stylized ways of writing the letter "Q" while the jottings
lower down represent the letter "Q" in different alphabets, including Arabic and Syriac. British Library Board. All Rights Reserved E.690(13) pg 4.

England's country dwellers also lived in close proximity to various four-footed
and two-footed dinner items. As mentioned previously, husbandmen were allowed
to graze sheep and cattle in communally held meadows; country gentleman would
have had larger herds and may have grazed them in a pasture enclosed by hedges.
Pigs and goats were easily kept, and chickens scratched for food in the yard of the
husbandman's house or in a pen behind the gentleman's house. Additionally, a gentleman might raise guinea-fowls, pea-fowls, American turkeys, and pigeons, and
would probably have a pond for ducks and geese.

In addition to the aforementioned domesticated animals there were many more
creatures that were captured or hunted in the wild. Small birds such as larks and
sparrows were often "limed": that is, a sticky substance was spread on the twigs of a
tree so that when the birds landed, they would not be able to escape and could be
gathered like fruit. Larks were also captured by distracting them with a piece of

scarlet cloth and a mirror until a net could be thrown over them. Larger birds—taken by nets or bow and arrow—were also served at the table, including snipes, rails, woodcocks, mallards, curlews, bustards, turtledoves, and blackbirds. Birds such as pheasants, partridges, and quails were much esteemed, but because they were harder to come by, they tended to be an upper-class dish. Young swans, known as cygnets, were prized for the table, but older swans were thought to acquire a fishy taste. Likewise, herons, cranes, bitterns, storks, and seagulls were considered to have a rather unpleasant savor and thus tended to be eaten only in poor households. Crows were consumed only as a last resort (at least according to Fynes Moryson), because they were thought to eat so many crop-damaging insects and worms.

Coneys, which we now call rabbits, were hunted with dogs by rich and poor alike and served in dishes such as "To boyle a Cony with a Pudding in his Belly." Writers of the time often commented on the large population of coneys in England, including Fynes Moryson who claimed there was an "infinite number." Hares, which are distinct from coneys, were also eaten, but were thought to be less tasty and to engender melancholy. Comparable animals, such as squirrels, hedgehogs, and badgers, are not mentioned in any of the 2,100 recipes dating from this period but were surely eaten in poorer households, especially in times of dearth.

There were three kinds of deer in Shakespeare's England—red, fallow, and roe—and they differed from other game animals in that they could not be legally hunted by commoners (Andrew Boorde cautioned that venison was a "meate for greate men"). Technically, all deer in England belonged to the crown, with the exception of those that were kept in parks on the private estates of wealthy gentlemen. Fynes Moryson, in his 1617 *Itinerary*, gives some indication of the size of these parks:

> The Kings Forrests have innumerable heards of Red Deare, and all parts have such plenty of Fallow Deare, as every Gentleman of five hundreth or a thousand pounds rent by the yeere hath a Parke for them inclosed with pales [i.e., stakes] of wood for two or three miles compasse.

Moryson adds that such game parks were so numerous, and so well stocked, that they were "thought to containe more fallow Deere, than all the Christian World besides." Hunting deer with dogs was considered an excellent sport—even Queen Elizabeth took part in a chase on occasion. The dogs themselves took center stage, as can be seen near the beginning of *The Taming of the Shrew* where the Lord and the Huntsman have a lengthy discussion about the relative merits of Merriman, Clowder, Echo, Silver, and Belman (Induction 1.15–18). Moreover, the dogs not only had to hunt well together, but their varying cries had to blend into what Theseus, in *A Midsummer Night's Dream*, calls "the musical confusion of hounds." Gervase Markham, in his 1615 *Country Contentments*, offers some advice on creating this music:

> If you would have your kennel for sweetness of cry, then you must compound it of some large dogs, that have deep solemn mouths, and are swift in spending, which must as it were bear the bass in the consort, then a double number of roaring, and loud ringing mouths, which must bear the counter-tenor, then some hollow plain sweet mouths, which must bear the mean or middle part; and so with these three parts of music you shall make your cry perfect.

A *Short Treatise of Hunting*, Thomas Cokayne, 1591. The deer depicted in this woodcut is a stag, which according to the text below the woodcut can be hunted after Whitsuntide, that is, the fiftieth day after Easter. Queen Elizabeth hunted deer, as do many characters in Shakespeare's plays, including the Lord in *The Taming of the Shrew*, Orsino in *Twelfth Night*, and the "aristocrats" in *Titus Andronicus*. When Jacques, in *As You Like It*, encounters a deer that has been wounded by a hunter, he uses the pitiful spectacle to "moralize" on the nature of humanity (2.1.44–63). © British Library Board. All Rights Reserved C.31.c.6 pg 11.

After the baying hounds had brought a deer to the ground (not too quickly, for it was thought that its flesh tasted best if it had been exhausted in the chase), it was killed and butchered on the spot. Its feet and guts were removed and fed to the dogs, while the rest was wrapped in a sheet and carried home. There, according to Thomas Cokayne in his 1591 *Short Treatise of Hunting*, it "will make delicate meate, if your Cooke season it, lard it, and bake it well." In earlier times, wild boars had also been hunted with dogs, but by the time Shakespeare was born, they were virtually extinct in England.

Fish, as noted previously, were a mandated component of everyone's diet in Shakespeare's England. Ocean fish—such as herring, cod, mackerel, flounder, and haddock—were of course only available at markets, but freshwater species could be caught by anyone with access to a nearby river or lake. (Officially, England's rivers belonged either to the crown or to the lords of manors, but in practice these rights were usually waived, so that commoners could fish from them.) Depending on the river or lake, netters or anglers might catch carp, eel, tench, bream, pike, salmon, perch, gudgeon, bullhead, barbel, roach, dace, ruff, luce, humber, shad, twait, mullet, and even something called a suant. Of these, salmon and carp were, in the estimation of James Hart, the fish that were most esteemed at the table. A country gentleman without easy access to a natural body of water might also construct a fish pond on his estate. John Norden, in his 1607 *Surveyors Dialogue*, explained how to do so, noting also that fishmongers in London and other towns would gladly buy the gentleman's surplus.

Gervase Markham's *Country Contentments* conveys an idealized view of what he calls "the art of angling," at least as it was supposed to be practiced by gentlemen. After describing the proper garb of the angler—"let then your apparell be plaine, and comely, of darke colour, as Russet, Tawny, or such like, close on your body, without any new-fashioned slashes, or hanging sleeves"—Markham goes on to detail the ideal angler's academic qualifications:

> A skilful Angler ought to be a general scholar, and seen in all the Liberal Sciences, as a Grammarian, to know how either to write or discourse of his Art in true and fitting terms, either without affectation or rudeness. He should have sweetness of speech, to persuade and entice others to delight in an exercise so much laudable. He should have strength of arguments to defend and maintain his profession, against envy or slander. He should have knowledge in the sun, moon, and stars, that by their aspects he may guess the seasonableness, or unseasonableness of the weather, the breeding of storms, and from what coasts the windes are ever delivered. He would not be unskillful in Music, that whensoever either melancholy, heaviness of his thought, or the perturbations of his own fancies stirreth up sadness in him, he may remove the same with some godly hymn or anthem.

The ideal angler should also be willing to try some of the alternative fishing techniques that Markham proposes: "Tie a hooke with a Frogge upon it with a string at the foot of a Goose, and put her into a Pond, where you shall see good tugging."

Some foodstuffs that we now consider quite ordinary were not procureable in Shakespeare's England, neither from the local market nor from one's own garden. These included chocolate, coffee, and tea; vegetables such as tomatoes, celery, and white potatoes; fruits such as bananas and pineapple; and flavoring agents such as vanilla. This is not to say that all these items were wholly unknown: Shakespeare's contemporaries knew, for example, that tomatoes were eaten in southern Europe (where they had been introduced from Central America), and no doubt a few English horticulturalists grew tomatoes as a curiosity. However, concern that the plant was poisonous (it was known to be related to deadly nightshade), prevented the tomato from being incorporated into English cooking until the eighteenth century. English explorers had also encountered bananas (which were originally called "muses"—the word "banana" did not enter the English language till 1697), but the first bunch of bananas to be brought to England did not arrive till 1633, and they did not become a common trade item until the nineteenth century.

One further foodstuff that was essentially unknown to Shakespeare's contemporaries was pasta, despite the best efforts of Hugh Plat. In a 1596 treatise entitled *Sundrie New and Artificiall Remedies Against Famine*, Plat advocated the adoption of a "certaine victuall" which, judging from his description, was surely pasta. He describes it as being "in the form of hollow pipes," and notes that it is light, durable, and "speedily dressed, for in one halfe houre, it is sufficiently sodden." He adds that it may be served "as delicate as you please, by the addition of oyle, butter, sugar, and such like." Plat claims that he furnished one of the ships of Francis Drake with this foodstuff, and that the mariners commended it upon their return from a voyage. Despite this early experiment, however, it wasn't until the eighteenth century that pasta began to appear on English tables.

# IN THE KITCHEN

Thrust it in againe as hard as you can cram it.
—*A New Booke of Cookerie*, John Murrell, 1615

Most people in Shakespeare's England didn't have a kitchen. The poorest of them had only a knee-high frame made of brick or iron in which they could tend a fire and over which they could hang a pot and bring it to a boil. The frame would probably be situated in the middle of their small hovel, beneath a hole in the roof through which the smoke would drift up and out. Those who were a bit better off might have an actual fireplace with a proper chimney, along with a few more pots and a frying pan, as well as a grate to set it on. They wouldn't have an oven, which meant that they had to make bread either by frying it (as was common in the north of England) or by using a baking pan (a lidded vessel onto which embers would be heaped). The estate of Robert Bendbowe, a scrivener who died in 1647, might be taken as typical. Upon his death, his possessions amounted to little more than four platters, three porringers (bowls for stew or porridge), one brass pot, two kettles, one posnet (a pot with a handle and three feet), one set of tongs, one fire shovel, and two candlesticks.

Needless to say, the members of such households were not the audience targeted by the cookery books that were published in Shakespeare's England. The authors of those books assumed that their readers were the privileged minority who had access to a well-equipped kitchen, which in affluent households—those of the gentry and wealthy merchants—was a separate room housing an oven and at least one large fireplace (the hall-place kitchen at Hampton Court had three fireplaces, each one eighteen feet wide, six feet deep, and seven feet high). The kitchen was adjoined by other rooms that supported the culinary work, such as a dairy house (where butter and cheese were made and kept), a larder (for storing preserved meats), a pantry (for storing bread and baking supplies), and a buttery (where "butts" or casks of wine were kept, along with other provisions). A brewing house, where beer and ale were made, was often a separate structure, some distance from the main house or manor, so that its smells would not afflict the residents. Households with a large number of servants often had two kitchens: a privy kitchen where the meals of the family were prepared and another kitchen where food for servants was made.

Most of the cooking in affluent households was done at the fireplace, using wood or coal as a fuel. Typically, a joint of meat was skewered on a spit (also known as a broach), which would then be set horizontally on a two-legged rack (also known as a cob-iron or gobert) that was positioned within the fireplace. The vertical legs of the rack could be free-standing and self-supporting, or they could lean against the back wall of the fireplace. Each leg of the rack had several hooks at different heights, so that the spit and its meat could be placed lower or higher, closer or further from the heat. Some racks, too, were designed so that the spit could be suspended in front of the fire, allowing the juices from the roasting meat to be caught in a dripping pan and used for sauces and gravies, rather than falling into the fire where they would create smoke. The spits were turned by a variety of means: by a young boy, known as a turn-broach; by a jack, a device made up of a heavy weight and gears; or by a dog wheel, a kind of treadmill on which a dog was trained to walk. In addition to being roasted, meat could also be broiled or grilled by affixing it to a gridiron, which would then be hung in front of the fire or over the coal embers, the meat being turned occasionally as it cooked.

The fireplace was also used to make stews or pottages: an iron or brass pot containing water, meat, and vegetables was suspended over the fire from a pair of hooks that were attached to the inner surface of the fireplace or from a horizontal bar known as a crane. The hooks were secured under two nubs—known as ears—on either side of the pot. Alternatively, the pot was placed over the fire by setting it on a trivet, a three-footed stand. In addition to pots, other kinds of vessels were also employed to boil food, such as pipkins, which were earthenware vessels with lids, and posnets, which had three short legs and a long handle that was used to lift the vessel on and off the coals. Kettles, which had a semi-circular handle that folded down when not in use, were also common. The fireplace was also used to heat wafer irons, the two sides of which were squeezed together after batter had been poured into it.

Apart from the fireplace, the only other device used for cooking was the chafing dish, a kind of iron basin into which hot coals were poured. Chafing dishes were sometimes used at the table, where they kept food warm, but they could also be used to cook food, especially dishes that required a gentle, simmering heat. The fuel for chafing dishes tended to be charcoal, because it produced much less smoke than either wood or coal.

Baking was done in ovens that, as mentioned previously, were found only in well-to-do households. These ovens were large domes of brick or masonry that had a cave-like recess at about waist height that extended two or three feet back from the front of the oven. The recess was twelve to eighteen inches in height, and about the same in width. Within this opening, a quantity of wood or coal would be set alight and allowed to burn for three or four hours, by which time the bricks or masonry of the oven would have heated up. The embers and ashes were then raked out of the recess and replaced by whatever needed baking, starting with foods that needed a high temperature (such as bread or meat pies) and followed, as the oven cooled, by

# THE
# LAMENTABLE
## COMPLAINTS

4

OF

Nɪᴄᴋ Fʀᴏᴛʜ the Tapſter, and
Rᴠʟᴇʀᴏsᴛ the Cooke.

*Concerning the reſtraint lately ſet forth,*
*againſt drinking, potting, and piping on the Sab-*
*bath day, and againſt ſelling meate.*

Printed in the yeare, 1 6 4 1.

*The Lamentable Complaints of Nick Froth the Tapster and Rulerost the Cooke,* Anonymous, 1641. This woodcut appeared in a book published 25 years after Shakespeare's death, but nonetheless the brick fireplace depicted in the top right corner of the panel is probably typical of what Shakespeare would have seen when he popped into a local inn for dinner. Visible within the fireplace are the two-legged racks (also known as cob-irons) upon which iron skewers or broaches were laid. On the left end of each skewer is a wheel, which would normally be connected to a "jack" that caused the skewers to rotate. On the skewers joints of meat are visible, as well as (on the top skewer, on the right) what appears to be a whole rabbit. Dripping pans, to catch the exuding fat and oil, seem to be placed beneath the skewers, and the little door in the brickwork at the bottom of the fireplace is for raking out ashes that fall through the grate. On the table in the lower left corner are visible several drinking vessels, including what appears to be a goblet, a mug, and a "black jack" made of leather and coated with tar. © British Library Board. All Rights Reserved E.156[4] pg 1.

items that needed a lower temperature (such as almond tarts). Each time a new item was added, the oven door would be lifted back in place (it was not hinged and was sometimes made of stone), and the edges sealed—or "luted"—with clay. Baked

¶Here beginneth the Booke, named
the Aſſiſe of Breade, what it ought to
weygh, after the price of a Quarter of wheate.
And alſo the aſſiſe of Ale, wyth all maner of
wood and Cole, Lath, Boord, and
Tymber, and the weyght of
Butter and Cheeſe.

*Here Beginneth the Booke Named the Assize of Bread*, Anonymous, 1580. The top two panels of this woodcut depict activities pertaining to the making of bread: in the top left corner, the two men appear to be weighing lumps of dough to ensure that they comply with the laws of the assize; in the top right corner, they are sliding the loaves into an oven. The assize also extended to other goods, including wood and coal, and butter and cheese. Hence, in the bottom left panel, the men are weighing bundles or "faggots" of firewood, while in the bottom right panel a dog guards what is probably a sack full of new cheese, which has been suspended over a barrel so that the excess whey can drip from it. © British Library Board. All Rights Reserved C.117.bb.5.

items were removed from the oven with a peel, a pole with a wide, flat blade on one end that slid under the foodstuff, just as pizzas are removed from commercial ovens today. Sheets of paper were sometimes placed under baked items before they went into the oven to prevent them from sticking.

When food wasn't being cooked or baked, it was probably being preserved. Large vessels, known as powdering tubs, were used to salt and pickle meat. Gallipots, which were smaller earthenware vessels, were used for storing items that had been preserved in syrup or vinegar. They were sealed using paper, leather, or an animal bladder rather than an earthenware lid. Other vessels used for storing preserved foods were known as galley glasses, gestelin glasses, jar-glasses, and butter pots, the latter being used for more than just butter.

Most of the utensils found in a well-equipped kitchen in Shakespeare's England were similar to those used nowadays. There were, for example, various cutting and piercing implements, including shredding knives, mincing knives, chopping knives, oyster knives, and trencher knives (which were used to slice or shape loaves of bread). Cleavers were used to hew large joints of meat. Rowel cutters, which were shaped rather like a cowboy's spur, were used to cut pastry shells in a fancy, zigzag fashion. Rasps were used to shave rinds from oranges and lemons, and graters were used to grate items such as bread or boiled liver. Piercers were used to bore holes into fruit such as apples, and larding pins were used to jab dry meats, such as venison, in order to insert fat into the flesh. A piercing utensil of another sort was required in a recipe included in Giovanni Rosselli's 1598 *Epulario*: "You must kill the Peacocke with a feather or quill pricked into her head."

Various utensils for stirring and dipping were also found in well-equipped kitchens. Long-handled wooden spoons would have been used for stirring hot liquids, but smaller pewter spoons were also used for measuring spices, drizzling sauces, mixing small quantities of ingredients, and so on. Occasionally, recipes specifically call for a silver spoon—for example, a recipe for candied sprigs of rosemary directs the cook to wet the sugar with "a little Rose-water in a silver spoone." Silver spoons likely tended to be smaller than pewter spoons, implying that a lesser quantity of an ingredient was being called for ("tablespoon" and "teaspoon" did not become standard measures until the eighteenth century). Ladles of wood, pewter, or brass were also used, as well as "spatters," which is an early form of the word "spatula." Flesh picks or flesh hooks were used to lift large pieces of meat from hot liquids. A utensil called a "slice" was used to turn items as they cooked in a frying pan.

Tools for separating or clarifying were of course on hand. Scummers, which were essentially a metal plate pierced with numerous small holes, were used to remove the "scum" that floated to the top of a boiling liquid. Metal colanders were used to wash herbs and leafy vegetables and to drain excess liquid from boiled foodstuffs. Strainers, made of a fabric such as canvas, were used to remove liquid from pulpy or viscous substances, sometimes by hanging them in the strainer for several hours. A specific kind of strainer was a linen hippocras bag, which was used like a coffee filter to remove spices that had been added to wine to give it additional flavor. Similar bags were used to strain excess fluid from jellies. Dry ingredients were sifted using sieves, boulters, and "searces," which were made from linen or the woven hair of a horse tail. Feathers and rabbit tails were used to brush on butter, icing sugar, and gold leaf.

Tools for crushing and rolling included the familiar rolling pin (also known as a "cane"), as well as mortars and pestles, which were made of a variety of materials. One recipe directs the cook to use a "stone morter with a pestell of wood," another calls for "an alabaster mortar with a wooden pestel," and yet another calls for "a morter of white marble." Molds and forms were used to give shape to jellies and sugar plate. John Murrell, in the preface to his *Delightfull Daily Exercise for Ladies and Gentlewomen*, even advised his readers on where they might procure them: "If any of you are desirous of any of the Moulds mentioned in the Booke, you may enquire at the shoppe of Thomas Dewe in St. Dunstans Church-yarde in Fleetstreete, where you may have them."

Measuring quantities, temperatures, and time was a rather inexact science in the kitchens of Shakespeare's England. In a world without thermometers, other benchmarks had to be used to estimate oven temperatures, the most common being the degree of heat ordinarily used to bake manchets, that is, small loaves of white bread. A recipe for macaroons, for example, directs the cook to "bake them in an Oven as hot as for Manchet." Similarly, another recipe instructs the cook to "heate the Oven no hotter than if it were after Pyes or cakes." A recipe for biscuits indicates that the oven should be "no whotter than you may abide your hand in the bottome," and even more subjective is a recipe for chicken pie that simply says, "heate your oven reasonablye." The instructions for an Italian pudding helpfully inform the cook that "if your Oven be too hot, it will burne." Gauging the doneness of roast meats was also an inexact science. Gervase Markham advised that large joints of meat were done "when the gravy which droppeth from it is clear without bloodiness." Whole pigs, he added, were sufficiently roasted "when the eyes are fallen out."

Liquid and dry measures did exist in Shakespeare's England, but they varied greatly according to region and according to what was being measured. Butter, beer, and herring, for example, were purchased by the barrel, but honey was bought by the bolle, and soft fruits by the frail. A bushel of oats at Andover was 40 gallons, while at Appleby it was 20 gallons, and at Dorchester it was 10 gallons. A chalder was 63 bushels in Hull, but only 36 bushels in London, and a mere 32 bushels in York. The number of liquid and dry measures, too, was dizzying. In addition to the bushels, pecks, gallons, quarts, pints, bolles, frails, and chalders, there were windles, tuns, firkins, barrels, hogheads, puncheons, sesterns, runlets, pipes, tertians, butts, pottles, topnets, and tierces. Other measuring units seem simply baffling. A "short hundred," for example, did not mean 100, but rather 112, at least when eggs were being counted; a "long hundred," on the other hand, meant 120 when certain kinds of fish were being counted, but 180 with regard to other kinds of fish. Measures for weight were somewhat more systematized, bearing in mind, though, that some things (like bread) were weighed using the Troy system, whereas other things (like cheese) were weighed using the Avoir Dupois system. Within the Avoir Dupois system, a stone weighed 14 pounds, a pound weighed 16 ounces, an ounce weighed 8 drams, a dram weighed 3 scruples, and a scruple weighed the equivalent of 20 grains of dried barley.

Things were not quite that confusing in the kitchen: the recipes from this period tend to stick with pounds and ounces, and with gallons, quarts, pints, and pottles (a pottle being half a gallon). Occasionally, more quaint measures were employed: a recipe for a bread called "Italian Crust" asks for "a thimble-full of the powder of an Oringe-peel," and a recipe for manchet for "as much salt as will into an eggshell." Another recipe for "the best fritters" calls for "a penny pot of sacke," that is, the amount of sack (a Spanish wine) that could be bought for a penny. Similarly, a recipe for "oister chewets" calls for "a pennyworth of suger." Figurative descriptions were also used to describe sizes and quantities, such as the following: "cut it overthwart in round peeces of the bignesse of your hand," "roule it in long roules as big as your little finger," "cutte it in peeces of the bigness of Ducks egges," "cut your bakon as thinne as a card," "take Sugar-candie beaten smal like sparks of diamonds," "make your balles as big as tennis balles," "take a litle peece of Butter as big as a walnut," and "the brawne of it must be pulled as small as a horse haire." Often the quantities were purely subjective, as with "take a good deale of spinnedge." Instructions such as "put in more according to your owne judgement" and "more or lesse by your discretion" were not uncommon.

Measuring time was also more of an art than a science. Mechanical clocks existed in Shakespeare's England (Shakespeare even puts one into *Julius Caesar*), but their cost was enormous. It is unlikely that anyone would buy a chiming "horologue" for 2,400 pounds (a sum larger than what a nobleman earned in a year) and then keep it anywhere near the smoke and steam of a kitchen. The alternative was a sand-filled hourglass: it was much less expensive, and tracked the passage of time sufficiently accurately for culinary purposes. Indeed, most of the recipes of the period advise cooking or baking times in terms of hours—the word "minutes" doesn't even appear in the recipes. When shorter durations needed to be measured in the kitchen, other methods were used. A recipe for a kind of almond biscuit, for example, instructs the cook to put them in the oven and then count to a hundred. Another recipe says that the ingredients should "not boile above the space of three Pater nosters," that is, no longer than it takes to recite the Lord's Prayer three times. The notion of a "wallop"— bringing something to a boil and then letting it subside—was also used to indicate how long to cook something: a recipe for quinces in syrup, for example, says that the pot should "stande upon the fire till it hath sodden a wallop or twaine."

In terms of ambience, kitchens in Shakespeare's England were probably not very pleasant places to work. For one thing, they were poorly lit by our standards. Kitchen windows tended to be small, so sunlight was minimal, especially in the winter. Artificial lighting was limited to oil lamps and wax or tallow candles, though the flames in the fireplace would have added a flickering illumination. In the winter, the temperature in most kitchens was probably very uneven: drafty and cold in most of the room, but feverishly hot near the fireplace and ovens. In his 1628 *Microcosmagraphie*, John Earle alludes to the heat that the cook daily endured: "The kitchen is his Hell and hee the Divell in it, Where his meate and he fry together." Hygiene may not have been a priority, as evidenced by the fact that dogs were sometimes used to turn spits. Keeping mice and rats at bay must have been difficult even with the assistance of ratsbane, which we now know as arsenic. Water had to be hauled into the kitchen from a well or, in London, from a public conduit in the street. Pots and pans, at least, were washed with soap and water and then scoured with fine sand. Brooms made of straw, rushes, or birch were used. Occasionally, the cookery books of the period encourage more hygenic practices: a recipe for preserving plums instructs the cook to "licke not the spoone in the making or stirring of it." Finally,

## A former part of the

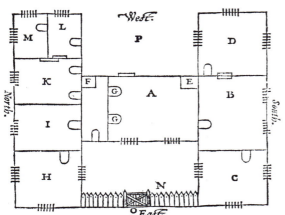

## Englifh Husbandman.

Architecture are able wonderfully to controle me; therefore that the Husbandman may know the vse of this facsimile, he shall vnderstand it by this which followeth.

A. Signifieth the great hall.
B. The dining Parlor for entertainment of strangers.
C. An inward closset within the Parlor for the Mistrisses vse, for necessaries.
D. A strangers lodging within the Parlor.
E. A staire-case into the romes ouer the Parlor.
F. A staire-case into the Good-mans romes ouer the kitchin and Buttery.
G. The Skreene in the hall.
H. An inward cellar within the buttery, which may serue for a Larder.
I. The Buttery.
K. The kitchin, in whose range may be placed a brewing lead, and conuenient Ouens, the bruing vessels adioyning.
L. The Dairy house for necessary businesse.
M. The Milke house.
N. A faire sawne pale before the formost court.
O. The great gate to ride in at to the hall dore.
P. A place where a Pumpe would be placed to serue the offices of the house.

This figure signifieth the dores of the house.

This figure signifieth the windowes of the house.

This figure signifieth the Chimnies of the house.

Now you shall further vnderstand that on the South side of your house, you shall plant your Garden and Orchard, as wel for the prospect thereof to al your best romes, as also because your house will be a defence against the Northerne coldnesse, whereby your fruits will much better prosper. You shall on the West side of your house, within your inward dairy and kitchin court, fence in a large base court, in the midst whereof would be a faire large

13

Here you behould the modell of a plaine country mans house, without plaster or imbossure, because it is as well to be intended that it is to be built of studde and plaster, as of lime and stone, or if timber be not plentifull it may be built of courser woode, and couered with lime and haire, yet if a man would bestow cost in this modell, the foure inward corners of the hall would be conuenient for foure turrets, and the foure gauell ends, being thrust out with bay windowes might be formed in any curious manner: and where I place a gate and a plaine pale, might be either a tarrisse, or a gatehouse: of any fashion whatsoeuer, besides all those windowes which I make plaine might be made bay windowes, either with battlements, or without, but the scope of my booke tendeth onely to the vse of the honest Husbandman, and not to instruct men of dignitie, who in Architecture

*The English Husbandman*, Gervase Markham, 1613. In this sketch, Gervase Markham depicts the first floor "of a plaine country mans house." Markham identifies the rooms as follows: "A" is the great hall; "B" is the dining parlor "for the entertainment of strangers"; "C" is a large storage room where the "mistriss" keeps her "necessaries"; "D" is an overnight room for guests; "E" is a staircase leading to the rooms above the parlor; "F" is a staircase leading to the rooms above the kitchen and buttery; "G" is a screen that provides ornamental separation between the great hall and the kitchen and buttery; "H" is the larder, for storing meat and other provisions; "I" is the buttery, for storing wine, ale, and other provisions; "K" is the kitchen, where the ovens are located; "L" is the dairy house; "M" is the milk house; "N" is a front courtyard or "pale"; "O" is the "great gate"; "P" is the backyard where a well or pump would be located. The "U"-shaped marks on the sketch represent doors, and the marks that look like this | | | | | | | represent windows. Courtesy Henry E. Huntington Library, Rare Books, 99553.

we shouldn't underestimate how strenuous kitchen work was in an age before microwaves and blenders: as a single example, a recipe for "bisket bread" instructs the cook to take the dough and "beate it the space of two hours." The work could be brutal, too: a recipe for broth instructs the cook to "take a red Cock that is not too olde, and beate him to death, and when he is dead, fley him and quarter him in small peeces." Worse yet is a recipe for blancmange in which the carving precedes the killing: "Take a capon and cut out the brawne of him alyve."

# AT THE TABLE

It is noted a folly to gyve meate to straunge dogges at the table: it is more folly to handle dogges at the table.

— Desiderius Erasmus, *A Lytell Booke of Good Maners for Chyldren*, 1532

How food was served to the table, and how it was eaten once it got there, varied from class to class. At one end of the social scale, a family of commoners would probably take their meal at a rough-hewn table near the firepit or fireplace where they cooked their food. Each family member would have a wooden bowl and a wooden or pewter spoon, and probably a mug made of stiffened leather, known as a "jack." A simple grace would be said, both before and after each meal.

For commoners, a typical breakfast might be bread and cheese or bread and pottage, washed down with ale. Breakfast lasted about half an hour and usually took place shortly after rising, which was just before sunrise—perhaps 4:00 A.M. in the summer and 5:00 A.M. in the winter. Thomas Tusser, in his *Five Hundredth Points of Good Husbandry*, advises husbandmen to have breakfast underway by the time Venus, also known as the "day star," appeared in the dawn sky:

Call servants to breakfast, by day star appear,
a snatch to wake fellows, but tarry not here.
Let huswife be carver, let pottage be eat,
a dishful each one with a morsel of meat.

The "snatch" to which Tusser refers is presumably a snatch of song, that is, a short burst of singing intended to rouse the husbandman's household.

Dinner was the largest meal of the day for most commoners, lasting an hour or so, and tended to be bread and pottage, cheese, and perhaps whatever fruit was in season. It was eaten at different times depending on one's occupation: in London and other centers, laborers and ordinary merchants dined around twelve o'clock, while in rural areas the husbandman's household dined at high noon (that is, whenever the sun reached its highest point, which varied according to the season). Supper time also varied by occupation: laborers and ordinary merchants around 6:00 P.M. and husbandmen at about 8:00 P.M. Thomas Tusser advised that, in the husbandman's household, supper was to be directly followed by slumber:

In winter at nine, and in sommer at ten,
to bed after Supper, both maydans and men.

Things were rather different for the gentry and for wealthy merchants who had the means to emulate the gentry. For one thing, family members rose later, and breakfast was taken alone in one's room, although many chose to forgo it entirely. Dinner was served around 11:00 A.M., and would sometimes last for hours. William Harrison remarked that "the nobilitie, gentlemen, and merchantmen, especiallie at great meetings doo sit commonlie till two or three of the clocke at afternoone, so that with manie it is an hard matter, to rise from the table to go to evening praier, and returne from thence to come time enough to supper." Supper, for the wealthy, was usually set for 5:00 P.M.

Among the gentry, formal meals featuring numerous guests were served in the great hall, which could be very great indeed: the one in Burghley House in Northhamptonshire measured thirty feet by sixty feet. When the family dined without guests, the meal might be served in a smaller and more informal parlor that was accessed off the great hall. Meals that were served in the great hall were elaborate and ostentatious. At one end of the hall was a dais, that is, a platform raised about six inches off the floor, where the family sat on ornate and cushioned chairs, along with select guests and high ranking servants such as the chaplain and the steward (in *Twelfth Night*, Malvolio, as the steward of Olivia, would expect to be placed on the dais). In the middle of the hall were several tables set end to end. These "ordinary" tables, unlike the fancy one on the dais, were essentially planks set upon trestles, so that they could be disassembled and set out of the way when more room was needed. This is what Capulet calls for in *Romeo and Juliet* when he orders his servants to create a space for dancing: "A hall, a hall! give roome! and foote it, girles. / More light, you knaves; and turne the tables up" (1.5.27–28). At the long stretch of trestle tables would be placed guests of lesser status and other household servants (such as footmen, stablemen, and huntsmen), who sat on benches that could be easily moved out of the way, or on joint stools that folded up—"Away with the joint-stooles," shouts one of the servants in *Romeo and Juliet*, as he helps clear the room (1.5.6). Even at these tables, seating arrangement reflected status: a salt cellar placed on the table marked the division between higher and lower. Those who sat above the saltcellar—that is, closer to the high table—were deemed to have greater rank than those who sat below it. Individuals of even lower rank—such as scullery maids—sat at separate tables scattered elsewhere in the hall. In some households, children were also placed at a separate table. For the most part, people knew (or could quickly figure out) their "seating status" in relation to others. Macbeth, for example, at his coronation banquet, tells his guests, "You know your owne degrees, sit downe" (3.4.1).

Tables were usually covered with linen, which is what Lorenzo tells Launcelot to do in *The Merchant of Venice*:

> Goe to thy fellowes, bid them cover the
> table, serve in the meate, and we will come in to
> dinner. (3.5.55–57)

Thomas Tusser, however, suggested that some servants, because of their carelessness, were better off eating without a tablecloth:

> Some cutteth thy linnen, some spilleth their broth,
> bare table to some, doth as well as a cloth.

A typical place setting in a wealthy household included a pewter or silver spoon and a trencher, the latter being a square piece of wood with a plate-sized hollow in its center, as well as a smaller cavity in its top right corner for salt. Plates of pewter, tin, and silver were becoming more common at table, but the traditional wooden trencher persisted: Launce, in *Love's Labour's Lost*, laments that his dog once snatched a capon's leg from Silvia's trencher. Knives were not supplied by the hosts, but were instead brought by their guests, who wore them sheathed on their person—men hung them from their belts, and women from their waistbands. These knives were sometimes inscribed by the cutlers who made them with mottos or bits of poetry. In *The Merchant of Venice*, Gratiano alludes to a verse that was "For all the world like Cutlers poetry / Upon a knife, 'Love me, and leave me not'" (5.1.149–150). In addition to being used to skewer and cut food, a guest might also lay his or her knife upon the table to claim that particular seat. This custom was known as "laying the knife aboard" and is alluded to in *Romeo and Juliet* (2.5.198).

Place settings also included napkins, which men draped over one shoulder and women kept on their laps. Napkins were sometimes called diapers, as in *The Taming of the Shrew*, where servants are ordered to treat Sly the tinker as if he is a lord:

Let one attend him with a silver bason
Full of Rose-water and bestrew'd with Flowers;
Another beare the Ewer, the third a Diaper,
And say, "Wilt please Your Lordship coole your hands?" (Induction 1.54–57)

Table forks were not in general use (except for small sucket forks, which were used to eat syrup-drenched sweetmeats). A travel writer named Thomas Coryate did, however, attempt to introduce the fork to England after returning from Italy in 1610. "I observed a custome," he wrote, "that is not used in any other nation that I saw in my travels." Coryate then went on to explain how the Italians used a fork to hold a piece of meat in place while they cut it with a knife. When Coryate imitated this practice in England, he was mocked: forks were seen as a mere affectation. Nicholas Breton, for one, said "we need no little Forkes to make hay with our mouths, to throw our meat into them." It wasn't until the 1630s that forks began to catch on in England, thanks in part to Charles I, who sanctioned their use.

Drinking vessels were kept on a nearby side table, partly because the tables at a formal dinner tended to be jammed with dishes of food, and partly (at least according to William Harrison) because it discouraged excessive tippling. If someone desired a drink, he or she beckoned a servant, who filled a goblet with wine or ale and brought it to the table. After drinking, the diner handed the goblet back to the servant, who rinsed it, and returned it to the side table. Goblets were traditionally made from silver or even gold, but ones made of expensive Venetian glass had also become fashionable.

The number of dishes served to the table in a wealthy household depended on the number of guests and the formality of the occasion. When a family dined alone, or with only one of two close friends, they probably contented themselves with a modest meal, as Thomas Tusser suggested in his 1577 *Five Hundredth Points of Good Husbandry*:

Three dishes well dressed, and welcome with all,
both pleaseth thy frend, and becommeth thine hall.

When the family dined more formally and with more guests, however, the quantity of dishes brought to the table could be staggering. On such occasions, food was usually brought to the table in two courses (also known as "messes"), with each course comprising a large number of dishes that were set on the table all at the same time. A sample dinner menu from a 1594 cookery book entitled *The Good Huswifes Handmaide for the Kitchin* proposes the following dishes as a first course:

> Brawne and Mustard; Capons stewed in white broth; A Pestell of Venison upon brewes; A chine of Beefe, and a brest of Mutton boyled; Chewets or Pies of fine mutton; Three greene geese in a dish, Sorrell sauce; For a stubble goose, mustard and Vinigar; After Alhallowen daye a Swanne, sauce Chaudron; A Pigge; A double ribbe of Beefe rosted, sauce Pepper and Vinigar; A loyne of Veale or breast, sauce Orenges; Half a Lambe or a Kid; Two Capons roasted, Sauce Wine & salt, Ale and Salt, except it be upon sops; Two Pasties of fallow Deere in a Dish; A Custard; A Dish of Leash.

The first course having been completed, the dishes would be "voided"—that is, cleared away—and the second course would be brought forth. The same menu from *The Good Huswifes Handmaide for the Kitchin* recommends the following dishes as a second course:

> Jellie; Peacockes, sauce Wine and Salte; Two Connies, or halfe a dozen Rabbets, sauce Mustard and Sugar; Halfe a dozen Pigions, Mallard, Toyle, sauce Mustard and Vergious; Gulles, Storke, Heronshew, Crab, sauce Galantine; Curlew, Bitture, Bustard, Feasant, sauce Water and Salt, with Onions sliced; Halfe a dozen Woodcockes, sauce Mustarde and Sugar; Halfe a dozen Teales, sauces as the Feasants; A Dozen of Quailes; A dish of Larkes; Two Pasties of red Deare in a dish; Tarte; Ginger bread; Fritters.

There was no expectation that dinner guests would try all of these thirty or more dishes; rather, they sampled only those dishes that pleased them best or that were most suited to their dietary "complexion." Some of what was leftover would be put aside for the family to eat the next day, but much of it would be given to the servants, and what they did not consume was often given to the poor who waited outside the gates of wealthy manors.

As the sample menus included in *The Good Huswifes Handmaide for the Kitchin* indicate, each course included among the many dishes two or three sweetmeats, such as custard, gingerbread, and leash (also known as "leach," usually made of almonds, milk, and sugar). In some circles, these sweetmeats evolved into an additional course made up entirely of what we would now call desserts. This third course was referred to as "the banquet," a somewhat confusing term as it was also used to refer to feasts in general. These "dessert banquets" emerged in the early sixteenth century and grew in popularity and elaborateness decade by decade (assisted in part by the increasing availablility of sugar). It became fashionable for such banquets to be enjoyed in a separate and special room in the house. The very wealthy even built designated "banquetting houses" to which guests would retire after the second course of the meal in order to snack on a medley of marzipan, wafers, candied fruit, and other "banquetting stuffe," as it came to be known. Christopher Hatton, the Lord Chancellor of England from 1587 to 1591, built a three-story banqueting house about a hundred yards from his usual mansion in order to entertain Queen Elizabeth. Unfortunately, she never visited.

As dessert banquets grew in popularity, cookery books began to offer advice on them so that wealthy commoners could emulate the gentry in preparing them. *The Good Huswifes Jewell* of 1596, for instance, provided an ingredients checklist of "all thinges necessary for a banquet," which included sugar, saffron, cinnamon, nutmeg, prunes, currants, raisins, dates, lemons, oranges, cherries, wafers, and more. Gervase Markham, in 1615, elaborated on the "ordering or setting forth of a banquet," suggesting that the first dish that comes to the banquet table should be "for shew only." Such ornamental centerpiece items, which were typically things like a bowl of artificial fruit made out of cast sugar, or a figurine of St. George made out of marzipan, were also known as "subtleties." Following the showpiece, other sweetmeats—which were sometimes called "junkets"—were brought in and arranged on the table so that they would "not only appear delicate to the eye, but invite the appetite with much varietie thereof." John Murrell, in his 1621 book entitled *A Delightful Daily Exercise for Ladies and Gentlewomen*, suggested several sample menus for banquets. Presumably, the way he arranged the names of the items on the page corresponded to how they were to be laid out on the table:

|                     | A Marchpaine       |                   |
| Shrewsbery cakes    |                    | Preserved Pippins |
|                     | Paste of Rasberies |                   |
| Preserved damsons   |                    | Dry peare-plums   |
|                     | Almond Jambales    |                   |
| Candied Citron      |                    | Sucket Lemons     |

The work of bringing the food to the dinner table was, in the wealthiest households, accomplished by a hierarchical chain of servants. Typically, the Clerk of the Kitchen would call up the dishes at the dresser, a kind of sideboard in the kitchen. He would then deliver it to an attendant known as the Sewer. The Sewer would then deliver it to the Yeoman Waiters, and the Yeoman Waiters would then carry it to the table. Sometimes, these roles would be conflated according to the number of available servants, and in a modest household (as Gervase Markham notes) all of these roles might be performed by the "huswife" herself. Children, too, were sometimes enlisted to prepare the table (or "board") and bear in the food, as is described in a 1619 handbook entitled *The Schoole of Vertue ... or, The Young Schollers Paradice*:

Be sure to be ready, the board to prepare
At times as accustom'd with diligent care:
The table-cloth first see fairely be spread,
Faire trenchers, cleane napkins, the salt & the bread,
Let glasses be scowred, in countrey guise,
With salt and faire water, and ever devise
The place most convenient, where they may stand,
The safest from breaking and neerest at hand.

...

Observe that nothing wanting be,
Which should be on the board.
Unlesse a question moved be,

Be carefull: not a word.
If thou doe give or fill the drinke,
With duty set it downe,
And take it backe with manlike cheere,
Not like a rusticke Lowne.

In terms of presentation, the ideal, at least according to Gervase Markham's 1623 edition of *Countrey Contentments, or The English Huswife*, was to crowd the table with food:

Setting the Sallets extravagantly about the table, mixe the Fricases about them; then the boild-meates amongst the Fricases, Rost-meates amongst the boyld, Bak't-meats amongst the Rost, and Carbonados amongst the bak't; so that before every trencher may stand a Sallet, a fricase, a Boyld-meate, a Rost-meate, a Bak't-meate, and a Carbonado, which will both give a most comely beautie to the Table, and very great contentment to the Gueste.

Any remaining space was to be filled with "made dishes and Quelquechoses," which were to be "thrust in into every place that is emptie, and so sprinckled over all the table." Not everyone, it has to be admitted, endorsed this sort of conspicuous consumption. The Puritan Phillip Stubbes, in his 1583 treatise *The Anatomie of Abuses*, complained that

now adaies if the table be not covered from the one end to the other as thick as one dish can stand by another, with delicat meats of sundry sorts, one cleane different from an other, and to every dish a severall sawce appropriate to his kinde, it is thought unworthye the name of a dinner. Yea so many dishes shal you have posteruing the table at once, as the devouringest glutton, or the greediest cormorant that is, can scarse eat of every one a litle.

Table manners in Shakespeare's England resembled ours in some respects but differed in others. Before sitting down to eat, guests would wash their hands in a nearby water basin—known as a ewer—with several people using the same water. There appears to have been some protocol about who washed with whom: in a dialogue published in a 1605 collection of English/French language lessons, the lady of the house says, "As for my cousin Du Petit-sens, I will give him leave to wash with the maydens, for he is not yet married." Once at the table, a grace would be said, such as this one from a 1619 treatise called *The Schoole of Vertue*:

Blessed is God in all his gifts,
And holy in all his deeds,
Our help is in the name of the Lord,
From whence all good proceeds,
Who gives repast to hungry hearts,
And comforts rich and poore,
His name be ever sanctified,
From henceforth evermore,
Blesse us (O Lord) and this our meat,
By thy grace to us sent,

God grant we use it moderately,
Our bodies to content. Amen.

During the meal, guests were expected to engage in amiable conversation, or as the humanist Erasmus put it in a 1532 translation of his handbook on etiquette, "At table nothynge ought to be blabbed forth that shulde dimynisshe myrthe." Thomas Twyne said much the same in his 1576 handbook entitled *The Schoolemaster, or Teacher of Table Philosophie*:

Talke ought to be merie at the table, more powdered with pleasure than sauced with severitie. And our communications at the boorde, as it ought to be faire with honestie: so must it be pleasant with delight.

To help hosts and guests achieve this pleasant goal, Twyne included in his handbook a chapter containing numerous "delectable and pleasaunt questions and pretie problemes to be propounded for myrth among companie at all times, but most conveniently at the table." These conversation starters included puzzlers such as "Which quencheth the thirst best of wine and water?" and "Do Fishes chewe their meat?" A further chapter included dozens of jokes and humorous anecdotes that were intended to be told to dinner guests, including the following:

There was a woman which could never make breade that would please her husbande. On a time strippying herselfe naked, and washing her selfe cleane all her body over, shee made dough and moulded it upon a stoole, and when she was wearie, she forgat herself and sat downe upon the stoole and the dough cleaved to her buttockes. Anon shee arose and sought for it, and her husband asked her what shee looked for, and she sayd, "For the loafe which I have made for thine own tooth." "Mary," quoth hee, "it sticketh to thy buttocks," and then the cleanly huswife remembred hir self.

While dining, eating with one's hands was considered good etiquette, so long as one's fingers were positioned appropriately. William Phiston, in his *Schoole of Good Manners*, explained the proper alignment of digits:

When thou receives anything at the Table with thy Hande, lay holde of it with no more but thy thumbe, and two forefingers, the hinder fingers being bowed in mannerly. In eating, thou must put thy morsels of Bread and Meate being cut, leysurely and modestly into thy Mouth with the Thumbe and forefinger of thy left hand, the other three fingers being bowed in, one beneath the other.

Plunging one's hand into a shared dish to retrieve a morsel was, however, more problematic. Erasmus tolerated that practice so long as it wasn't done too eagerly: "See that thou put not thy hande first in the dysshe," he advised, "bycause it sheweth thee to be greedy." However, an even better technique, he added, was for a guest to use his knife to remove the meat, because to "thrust his fingers in to his dysshe of potage is the maner of carters"—that is, of yokels who pull carts for a living.

There was no shortage of advice about how to behave at the dinner table. Walter Darrel, in his 1578 treatise *A Short Discourse of the Life of Servingmen*, shared etiquette tips such as the following:

It is a rude fashion for a man to clawe, or scratche him self, when he sitteth at the table. And a man should at such time have a very greate care that he spit not at all. But if neede inforce him, then let him doe it, after an honest sorte.

It is also an unmanerly parte, for a man to lay his nose uppon the cup where another must drinke: or uppon the meate that another muste eate, to the end to smell unto it.

Neither must you openly rynce your mouth with the wine, and then spit it fourthe.

When thou hast blowne thy nose, use not to open thy handkerchief, to glare uppon thy snot, as if thou hadst pearles and Rubies fallen from thy braynes.

Let not a man so sit that he turne his tayle to him that sitteth next to him: nor lye fottering with one legg so hygh above the other, that a man may see all bare that his cloathes would cover.

Neither is it gentleman like, to carry a sticke in your mouth from the table when you rise, like the birde that builds her a nest: or put it in your eare, for that is a Barbars tricke. And to weare a toothpicke, about your necke: of all fashions that is the worst.... I see no reason, why they should not as well carry a spoone, about their neckes, as a toothpicke.

William Phiston, in his 1609 handbook called *The Schoole of Good Manners*, added these words of counsel:

Leane not with thine Elbowes upon the table, for that is onely lawfull for old feeble persons: notwithstanding some Courtiers use it, judging all that they doe is to be tolerated. Take heede that thou trouble none of them that sit next thee with thine Elbowes, nor those on the other side the table with thy feete.

Some there be, that can scarse abide, till they be set at the Table, but they will fall to their meate like greedy Wolves, or Cormorants: but bee not thou too hastie, though it be among thy equals: for so thou mayest be noted of arrogancie and immodesty: and by putting a Morsell too hotte in thy Mouth, thou mayest be driven quickely to voyde out the same againe: than the which, nothing can bee more Slovenly, and make thee more laughted to scorne.

Some thrust so much into their mouthes at once, that their cheeks swel like bagpipes. Other open their Jawes so wide, that they smacke like Hogges: some blow at the nose. All which, are beastly fashions. To drinke or speake when thy mouth is full, is not only slovenly, but dangerous.

Richard West thought it best to put his tips into verse in his 1619 treatise, *The Schoole of Vertue*:

If thou of force doe chance to sneeze,
then backewards turne away
From presence of the company,
wherein thou art to stay.

If filthinesse, or ordure thou
upon the floore doe cast,
Tread out, and cleanse it with thy foot,
let that be done with haste.

If thou to vomit be constrain'd,
avoyd from company:
So shall it better be excus'd,
if not through gluttony.

Let not thy privy members be
layd open to be view'd,
It is most shamefull and abhord,
detestable and rude.

Retaine not urine nor the winde,
which doth thy body vex,
So it be done with secresie,
let that not thee perplex.

One wonders what dinners were like in households that could not afford these etiquette books.

# IN THE COOKERY BOOKS

It resteth now that I proceede unto Cookery it selfe, which is the dressing and ordering of meate, in good and wholsome manner; the which, when our hous-wife shall addresse her selfe, she shall well understand that these qualities must every accompany it: First, she must be cleanly both in body and garments, she must have a quicke eye, a curious nose, a perfect taste, and a ready care. She must not be butter fingered, sweet-toothed, nor faint hearted.
　　　　　—Gervase Markham, *Countrey Contentments, or The English Huswife*, 1615

The recipes that are included and redacted in this book are drawn from twenty-two books that were published in London between 1545 and 1627, as well as one manuscript collection of recipes, attributed to Elinor Fettiplace, which dates to around 1604 but which was not published until 1986 (and then only in part). A complete list of the recipe sources is provided in the Bibliography. Several of these sources were published anonymously (such as *The Good Hous-Wives Treasurie*) or by individuals who are only known by their initials (such as A.W. who authored *A Propre New Booke of Cokery*). Several others were written by the same author, such as *The Good Huswifes Jewell* and *The Second Part of the Good Hus-Wives Jewell*, both of which are by Thomas Dawson. Two other titles are essentially different editions of the same book, namely, the 1615 and 1623 editions of *Country Contentments*, which are very similar, with the exception of a few recipes that appear in one edition but not in the other, and vice versa. One of the books (*Epulario*) is a late sixteenth-century translation of an early sixteenth-century Italian text, and another (*The English Husbandman*) is not a book about cookery per se, but it does include some instructions for making cider that we've included in the chapter devoted to beverages.

The books that do explicitly concern cookery do so to varying degrees. Some, such as *A Book of Cookrye* and *A Good Huswifes Handmaide for the Kitchin*, comprise culinary recipes exclusively. More often, however, the books feature a medley of recipes—or "receipts," as they were then called—pertaining to cooking, preserving,

# The good Hus-wifes Handmaide for the Kitchin.

Containing

**Manie principall pointes of Cookerie,**
afwell how to dreffe meates, after fundrie
the beft fafhions vfed in England and o-
ther Countries, with their apt and proper
fawces, both for flefh and fifh, as alfo the
orderly feruing of the fame to the Table.

Hereunto are annexed, fundrie ne-
ceffarie Conceits for the prefer-
uation of health.

**Verie meete to be adioined to the good**
Hufwifes Clofet of prouifion
for her Houfhold.

**Imprinted** at London by Richard
**Iones.** 1594.

*The Good Huswifes Handmaide for the Kitchin*, Anonymous, 1594. This title page is typical of the cookery books published in Shakespeare's England. The subtitle reads "Containing manie principall pointes of Cookerie, aswell how to dresse meates, after sundrie the best fashions used in England and other Countries, with their apt and proper sawces, both for flesh and fish, as also the orderly serving of the same to the Table. Hereunto are annexed, sundrie necessarie Conceits for the preservation of health. Verie meete to be adjoined to the Good Huswifes Closet of provision for her Houshold." © Bodleian Library, University of Oxford Douce C 52, title page.

medicine, distilling (including perfumes), and sometimes even animal husbandry. The full titles of two of the books will give some indication of their wide ranging contents:

> *The Good Hous-Wives Treasurie Beeing a Verye Necessarie Booke Instructing to the Dressing of Meates. Hereunto is also Annexed Sundrie Holsome Medicines for Divers Diseases.*

> *The Widowes Treasure Plentifully Furnished with Sundry Precious and Approoved Secretes in Phisicke and Chirurgery for the Health and Pleasure of Mankinde: Hereunto are Adjoyned, Sundry Pretie Practises and Conclusions of Cookerie: With Many Profitable and Holesome Medicines for Sundrie Diseases in Cattell.*

The nonculinary recipes include ones such as "To make the haire of the bearde to growe," "To make one to pisse," "A medicine for the Plague," "Against the trembling of the heart," and "To make one slender." In some books, these nonculinary recipes are mixed in with culinary recipes in an apparently arbitrary manner, a fact that John Partridge acknowledges in the preface to *The Widowes Treasure* where he says, "perhaps they are not orderly set downe as manye of better skill might have doone." In other books, such as *Delightes For Ladies*, there are greater attempts at organization, such as a chapter devoted to distilling, a chapter devoted to cooking, a chapter devoted to medicinal concoctions, and so on. Overall, the books appear to have been carefully typeset and printed: spellings are variable (as is the case with any book published in this era), but actual typographical mistakes are infrequent. A recipe called "To make a tarte of damsons" has "yoyle" where the word "boyle" is clearly intended, and the recipe called "Fritters on the court fashion" has "togethrr" instead of "together," but considering that these books were set by hand with lead type (in dim light), from manuscripts that had been written with a quill pen, they are remarkably error-free. Many of these books were so popular that they went through several printings. *The Treasurie of Commodious Conceits*, for example, saw thirteen editions between 1573 and 1637. In some cases the author took the opportunity provided by a new printing to improve the organization of a recipe collection. John Partridge, for example, in the preface to *The Treasurie of Hidden Secrets*, brags that his new book has reproduced material from two of his earlier works, but in a more organized manner: "I have therefore placed each thing that was out of order in his due and convenient place."

Recipes were sometimes plagiarized from one author's book for reuse in another author's book. For example, "To make sirup of Violets" first appeared in 1591 in A.W.'s *A Book of Cookrye* and then reappeared, word for word, in 1597 in Thomas Dawson's *The Second Part of the Good Hus-Wives Jewell*. These borrowings occasionally resulted in revisions that improved the clarity, method, or flavor of a recipe. An example of this is "To boyle a Mallard with Cabage," which first appeared in 1594 in the anonymous *The Good Huswifes Handmaide for the Kitchin* and then resurfaced in 1596 in Thomas Dawson's *The Good Huswifes Jewell*:

> Take the Cabage and pick them cleane, and wash them, and parboile them in faire water: then put them in a colender, and let the water runne from them, then put them in a faire pot, and as much beefe broth as will cover them, and the Marie of three Mary bones whole. Then take a Mallard, and with your knife give him a launce along uppon each side of the breast. Then take him of, and put him unto your Cabage, and his dripping with him, for he must be roasted halfe ynough, and his dripping saved, and so let

them stew the space of one hower. Then put in some pepper and a little salt, & serve in your Mallard upon sops, and the Cabage about him, and of the uppermost of the broth.

> —*The Good Huswifes Handmaide for the Kitchin*, Anonymous, 1594

and

Take some cabbedge, and prick and wash them cleane, and perboyle them in faire water, then put them into a Collender, and let the water runne from them cleane, then put them into a faire Earthen Pot, and as much sweete Broth as will cover the cabbadge, and sweete Butter, then take your Mallard and roste it halfe enough, and save the dripping of him, then cut him in the side, and put the mallard into the cabbedge, and put into it all your dripping, then let it stew an houre, and season it with salte, and serve it upon soppes.

> —*The Good Huswifes Jewell*, Thomas Dawson, 1596

The later version of this recipe is more concise and clear and probably improves upon the earlier version in its change of beef broth to sweet broth and of marrow to butter. Sometimes revisions to later versions of a recipe reflect changes that were occurring in the English language itself. For example, recipes that appear in Thomas Dawson's 1596 *The Good Huswifes Jewell* reappear in his 1620 *A Booke of Cookerie*, but whereas the earlier recipes refer to "boiling" meat, the later versions refer to "stewing" meat. Other revisions gesture toward social changes. John Murrell's 1615 *A New Booke of Cookerie* includes a section called "London Cookerie"; in the 1639 reprint of that book, the section has become "English Cookerie," reflecting the fact that new culinary fashions had by then spread well beyond the city of London.

It must be admitted that some of the culinary recipes published in Shakespeare's England are so elliptical or convoluted that they are hard to follow. In some instances it seems evident that the author of a cookery book forgot, say, step two of a recipe and then remembered it only after already having written down steps three and four. Step two then makes an appearance as a kind of afterthought tacked on to the end of the recipe, leaving it up to the aspiring cook to untangle it all. Sometimes even short passages are rather riddling. For example, a recipe entitled "A Troute baked or minced" instructs the cook to take a pastry shell and "cut it in three corner waies in a small bignesse." Comparing one recipe with a similar one can often clarify a murky passage, but on occasion (as with "a small bignesse") one can only guess at what was intended. Fortunately, the authors of these cookery books seem to encourage their readers to interpret or alter the recipe as they see fit. Instructions such as "take so much water as you think convenient," "stirre it till you think it be enough," and "take what quantity of Mellons you think best" are common, as are (to a lesser extent) comments such as "season it according to the taste of the Master of the house" or "according to the fancy of the Cook." The authors also seem content to substitute one ingredient for another as necessity requires, as with "if you have no Orenges take Verjuice," "if you have no Almonds, thicken it with creame, or with yolks of eggs," "if you have not great store of Sugar, then take Rice," "cover it with Wafers or such like stuffe," and "put in a litle Orenge or Lemman peele if you have any."

The authors of these cookery books—at least the ones whose names are known—were all men: Gervase Markham, Thomas Dawson, John Partridge, John Murrell,

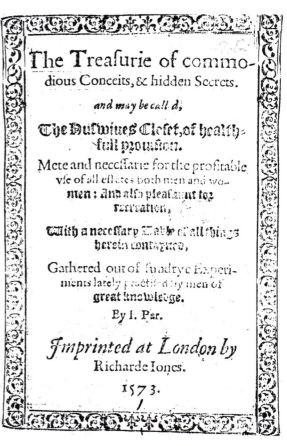

*The Treasurie of Commodious Conceits, & Hidden Secrets and may be Called, The Huswives Closet, of Healthfull Provision*, John Partridge, 1573. The figure seated at the desk presumably represents the author as he writes—or rather compiles—the recipes and lore contained within the book. The subtitle on the page reads, "Mete and necessarie for the profitable use of all estates both men and women: and also pleasaunt for recreation, with a necessary Table of all things herein contayned. Gathered out of sundrye experiments lately practised by men of great knowledge." Courtesy of Henry E. Huntington Library, Rare Books, 59164.

Hugh Plat, John Lacy, and Giovanni Rosselli. In all probability the cookery books published anonymously were also spearheaded by men. It is no accident that the one manuscript source attributed to a woman, Elinor Fettiplace, was not published until centuries after her death. In fact, if Fettiplace's recipes had been published in her lifetime, it is likely that they would have appeared in a book "authored" by a man. That, for instance, was the case with the culinary recipes found in Gervase Markham's *Countrey Contentments*, which he acknowledged acquiring from an unnamed "Honourable Countesse":

> I shall desire thee therefore to understand, that this is no collection of his whose name is prefixed to this worke, but an approved manuscript which he happily light on,

belonging sometime to an honorable Personage of this kingdome, who was singular amongst those of her ranke for many of the qualities here set forth. This onely he hath done, digested the things of this booke in a good method, placing every thing of the same kinde together, and so made it common for thy delight and profit.

Recipes in other cookery books also sometimes point to a woman as their originator. A recipe for thickened cream, for example, concludes with "this is called my Ladie Youngs clowted creame," while another for dried walnuts says, somewhat mysteriously, "This is of a kind Gentlewoman, whose skill I do highly commend, & whose case I doe greatly pitie; such are the hard fortunes of the best wits and natures in our daies." The titles of recipe, too, sometimes reveal their source, as with "To boyle a Capon with Oranges after Mistres Duffelds way" and "The making of manchets after my Ladie Graies use." In short, in many cases the male authors of these cookery books might be more accurately called compilers, with their recipes coming from the hands of anonymous noblewomen. (Curiously, although women in Shakespeare's England were discouraged from being authors, they were sometimes allowed to be publishers: *A Daily Exercise for Ladies and Gentlewomen*, for example, was printed by the Widow Helme in 1617.)

As for the backgrounds of the men who authored or compiled these cookery books, nothing is known about John Lacy, and very little (apart from their publications) about Thomas Dawson, John Murrell, John Partridge, or Giovanni Rosselli (or his anonymous English translator). The lives of Gervase Markham and Hugh Plat are, however, fairly well documented. Indeed, when Markham and Plat are set side by side, they exemplify the social mobility that was becoming a reality in Shakespeare's England. On the one hand, Markham was born into a well-connected aristocratic family that lived in the country, but his last years—despite having published many books about cookery, horsemanship, and military training, as well as poetry and drama—were spent in poverty in London. Plat, on the other hand, was born into a working class family—his father was a London brewer—but he became a wealthy landowner before he died. One of Markham's foibles, which may have contributed to his financial troubles, was his tendency to pirate his own books and reprint the material under a new title. He gained such notoriety for this practice that he was forced to sign an agreement with the Stationers' Company (which controlled book publishing in England) curtailing his output:

> Memorandum That I Gervase Markham of London gent Do promise hereafter never to write any more book or bookes to be printed, of the Diseases or cures of any Cattle, as Horse, Oxe, Cowe, sheepe, Swine and Goates &c. In witnes whereof I have hereunto sett my hand the 14th Day of Julie. 1617.

Plat, in contrast, was ever coming up with new material and inventions, such as a chafing dish that used a piece of hot iron rather than charcoal to keep food warm, a mechanism that allowed a cook to turn five spits with one hand, a "delicious" cake made with nothing more than flour and parsnips, and a crystal ring that allowed the wearer to spy on the cards of other players at a gaming table. Ironically, however, Markham may have had more of an impact on English literature than Plat, albeit indirectly: he is thought by some, including the respected scholar Robert Gittings, to have been the "rival poet" who is alluded to in Shakespeare's sonnets. And even if he isn't, it is fairly certain that Shakespeare drew upon one of Markham's books about animal husbandry in *The Taming of the Shrew*, where he has Biondello list a variety of peculiar horse diseases.

As for Elinor Fettiplace, she apparently began her collection of recipes (culinary and medicinal) around 1604 and continued to add to it until her death in 1647, when her manuscript was passed on to her niece. Lady Fettiplace belonged to an aristrocratic family that had connections with important figures such as Robert Cecil, Walter Raleigh, and Francis Bacon. Her household was occupied by a half dozen family members, as well as twenty or so servants and retainers, all of whom had to be fed. She would have also hosted occasional gatherings of a hundred or more guests, a task which was undoubtedly the raison d'etre of her recipe collection.

Presumably, Elinor Fettiplace supplemented her personal collection of recipes by purchasing some of the cookery books that were published in England in her life-time. Aristocratic women (and their kitchen staff) were, after all, part of the audience targeted by those books, albeit a small part: the English aristocracy comprised only about 160 families. More important, from a bookseller's point of view, were the "ladies" who headed the far more numerous households of the so-called "minor gentry," that is, descendents of the aristocracy who owned smaller tracts of lands, as well as the "huswives" who headed the middle-class households of successful merchants, tradesmen, and farmers (or "husbandmen," as they were then called). Many of the titles of the books in question confirm this target audience: *Delightes For Ladies*, *A Delightfull Daily Exercise for Ladies and Gentlewomen*, *A Good Huswifes Handmaide for the Kitchin*, and *The Good Huswifes Jewell*. The dedicatory letters that preface many of these books also affirm their intended audience. For example, John Partridge begins *The Treasurie of Hidden Secrets* with a letter to "Curteous Gentlewomen, honest Matrons, and vertuous virgins," while John Murrell begins *A Delightfull Daily Exercise for Ladies and Gentlewomen* with a letter addressing "Courteous Ladies and Gentlewomen, and all other well disposed whatsoever." Similarly, the 1591 edition of *The Treasurie of Commodious Conceits* includes a poem affirming that the book will benefit "Gentles state, the Farmers wife, / And Crafts-mans Huswife Cooke."

For such women, the implicit promise of these culinary and household books was twofold. First, the knowledge they gained from the books would ostensibly perfect them as women. Gervase Markham's *Countrey Contentments*, for example, advertised itself as "containing the inward and outward vertues which ought to be in a complete woman." Markham added that a woman who "is ignorant therein, is lame, and but the half part of a House-wife," because "a perfect skill and knowledge in cookery ... is a duty really belonging to the woman." Markham was not alone in equating culinary knowledge with perfect womanhood. Edmund Tilney, in his 1571 *Flower of Friendshippe*, maintained that it is "a great want in a woman, if she be unskilfull in dressing of meate." Second, these books offered wealthy middle-class huswives the opportunity to emulate the aristocracy. After all, what aspiring huswife wouldn't want to be able to make "Fritters in the court fashion" or, as another recipe claimed, the "Ginger bread used at the Court, and in all Gentlemens houses at festival times." Moreover, the task of keeping up with the Joneses (or, rather, the Cecils, Burghleys, and Fettiplaces) was made more difficult by the fact that new culinary fashions were coming into style. John Murrell affirmed this in A *Daily Exercise for Ladies and Gentlewomen* and promised that his recipes were the latest thing:

> Wee alter our Fashions and outward Habits daily; the whitest Ruffe being not long since thought the purest wearing; then the blew, and not the yellow: So, our Cookery, Pastry, Distillations, Conserves, and Preserves, are farre otherwise now, than not long since they were; Daily Practise and Observation finding out eyther what to adde or detract from olde Formes in eyther of these kindes; or to make new much more pleasing and profitable. These are all, (or, at least, the most) of the newest Straine: approved and beloved of those that try them.

One question that arises in relation to these cookery books is whether they accurately represent what most people living in Shakespeare's England ate on a regular basis. Putting aside, for a moment, the fact that the great majority of Shakespeare's contemporaries were not sufficiently literate to even read these cookbooks, it is instructive to tally up the cost of a typical dish. In the last decade of the sixteenth century, the price (in pence) of the key ingredients of "To boyle a Capon or chicken in Sacke and Pottage" would have been as follows:

| | |
|---|---|
| One capon: | 24 |
| Half a pound of rice: | 3 |
| One pint of sack: | 5 |
| Four eggs: | 1 |
| A pinch of saffron: | 1 |
| | |
| TOTAL: | 34 pence |

To purchase these ingredients for a single dish, a skilled craftsman would have had to work about three days and a common laborer about eight days. Not surprisingly, therefore, most people had to content themselves with more humble fare. Nicholas Breton, in his 1600 *Pasquils Mad-Cap*, suggested with perhaps only slight exaggeration that the typical peasant "only lives by Puddings, Beanes, and Pease." He added, years later in his 1626 *Fantasticks Serving for a Perpetuall Prognostication*, that "Butter, milke, and cheese, are the Labourers dyet." However, if there were many ingredients in the published recipes that ordinary laborers and peasants rarely or never enjoyed, there were also some common ingredients that rarely or never made their way into the published recipes. For example, in his 1584 *Haven of Health*, Thomas Cogan refers to the leek as an "hearbe which is so common in use," and yet it appears in only two of the 2,100 recipes published in this period. Likewise, Thomas Hill, in his 1577 *Gardener's Labyrinth*, noted that "garlike [is] much desired, and often eaten of the husbandman, with fat Beefe, and other sodden meates," and yet it is called for in none of the culinary recipes that originated in England (it does appear in recipes from *Epulario*, which was translated from Italian to English in 1598). Chestnuts, too, were apparently a common snack: one of the witches in Macbeth tells her sister-witch that "A Saylors Wife had Chestnuts in her Lappe, And mouncht, & mouncht, and mouncht." Yet nary a chestnut appears in the published recipes of the period.

# ON YOUR TASTEBUDS

If bangers and mash, fish and chips, and Yorkshire pudding are your idea of what English cooking has always tasted like, you're sure to be surprised by the recipes that follow. Indeed, the recipes that were published in Shakespeare's England probably have less in common with what is now thought of as "traditional" English food and more in common with, say, Moroccan cuisine. Consider, for example, that the most common flavoring agent (after sugar, which appears in about half of 2,100 recipes that were published in Shakespeare's England) was rosewater, which was called for in about 20% of the recipes. The most common spices were pepper (appearing in about 20% of the recipes), ginger (18%), mace (17%), cinnamon (15%), and cloves (15%). Almonds and raisins are each found in 10% of the recipes, and fruits—such as oranges, lemons, dates, and pears—abound, even in meat dishes. In short, roll up your sleeves and get ready to make some of the oldest and most exotic dishes that you've ever encountered.

# A NOTE ON OUR TRANSCRIPTIONS AND REDACTIONS

In our transcriptions of recipes and other texts from the sixteenth and seventeenth century, we have aimed to retain the original wording and spellings. After all, one of the pleasures of these centuries-old recipes is in savoring their archaic language and earthy descriptions. "Synamon," for example, seems like a more intriguing spice than "cinnamon," and an imperative such as "take your Pike and pull out all hys guttes" is far more vivid than "clean your fish." Nonetheless, our transcriptions have made a few minor orthographic changes for the sake of readability. For example, we have modernized the use of the letters "u" and "v." In texts printed in Shakespeare's England, those two letters were distinguished not by the sound they represented but by their placement in a word. The letter "v" was used at the beginning of a word, and "u" was used everywhere else. Thus a sentence such as "My uncle loves sour vinegar" would have been rendered as "My vncle loues sour vinegar." Additionally, the letter "i" was often used to represent "j"—as in "iuice" instead of "juice"—and we have modernized that usage as well. Another spelling convention of sixteenth- and seventeenth-century texts was to occasionally omit the letter "m" or "n" if it was preceded by a vowel, and to then imply the missing letter by putting a bar over the vowel. Thus the word "content" might appear as "cōtent. Similarly, a "y" with a mark over it was sometimes used to represent the word "that." Both of these forms we have modernized in our transcriptions. We have also changed double "v"s to "w"s—for example, "vvater" becomes "water"—and in a some places we have silently changed a letter or two in order to clarify the sense. For example, when an original source spells the adverb "then" as "than," we have altered the spelling to "then" to avoid confusion with the conjunction "than."

As for our redactions—that is, our modernized versions—of the sixteenth- and seventeenth-century recipes, we have aimed to be as faithful to the original recipes as possible. In a book devoted to food in Shakespeare's England, there would be little point in altering recipes to such an extent that they ceased to be dishes that Shakespeare or his contemporaries would recognize as familiar. Sometimes, however, we have had to modify a recipe to make it feasible for the modern cook. For

## A Booke.

Cream and seeth that with suger, and in the ende put in rosewater as into the other, and seeth it till it be thicke enough, and then vse it as the other, and when ye serue it ye may serue one dish and another of the other in roules, and cast on biskets.

### To make peascods in Lent.

Take Figs, Raisons, and a few Dates, and beate them very fine, and season it with Cloues, Mace, Cinamon and Ginger, and for your paste seeth faire water and oyle in a dish vppon coales, put therein saffron and salt and a little flower, fashion them then like peasecods, and when ye will serue them, frye them in Oyle in a frying panne, but let the Oyle bee verie hotte, and the fire soft for burning of them, and when yee make them for flesshe dayes, take a fillet of veale and mince it fine, and put the yolkes of two or three rawe egges to it, and season it with pepper, salt, cloues, mace, honie, suger, cinamon, ginger, small raisons, or great minced, and for your paste, butter, the yolke of an egge, and season them, and frye them in butter as yes did the other in oyle.

To

## of Cookerie. 30

### To bake Quinces, Peares and Wardens.

Take and pare and coare them, then make your paste with faire water and butter, and the yolke of an egge, then set your Oringes into the paste, and then bake it well, fill your paste almost full with Sinamon, Ginger and Suger. Also Apples must be taken after the same sorte, sauing that whereas the core should be cut out they must be filled with Butter euery one, the hardest Apples are best, and likewise are Peares and Wardens, and none of them all but the wardens may be perboyled, and the Ouen must be of a temperate heat, two houres to stand is enough,

### To make a Tarte of Spinadge.

Take Spinadge and seeth it stalke and all, and when it is tenderly sodden, take it off, and let it drayne in a Cullynder, and then swing it in a clowte, and stampe it and straine it with two or three yolkes of egges, and then set it on a chafindish of coales, and season it with butter and Suger, and when the paste is hardened in the Ouen, put in this Comode, strake it euen.

To

*The Good Huswifes Jewell*, Thomas Dawson, 1596. This page is typical of the cookery books published in Shakespeare's England. To the modern reader, the typeface used in the titles of the recipes is easier to read than the ornate "blackletter" typeface used in the recipes themselves. Some of the letter forms in that blackletter typeface are quite different from their modern counterparts: the letter "s," for example, sometimes looks like an "f" without its crossbar, as in the word "season" that appears at the end of the second line in the recipe called "To make peascods in Lent." Courtesy of Henry E. The Huntington Library, Rare Books, 59465.

example, with recipes that call for mutton, we have substituted lamb, simply because the former meat, at least in North America, is very difficult to acquire (unless you happen to live near a sheep farm, in which case you might be able to purchase mutton directly from the owner). For similar reasons, we've omitted the marrow that several recipes call for. In other cases, we've altered a recipe for reasons of safety: for example, the recipe for "lenthen haggess" calls for an herb known as pennyroyal, which is no longer considered safe for ingestion.

# 2

# HOUSE FOWL

Of the choyse and shape of the Cocke: he would be of a large and well sized bodie, long from the head to the rumpe, and thicke in the girth; his necke would be long, loose and curiously bending it, and his bodie together being straight, and high up erected.
—Gervase Markham, *Cheape and Good Husbandry*, 1614

In Shakespeare's England, the term "house fowl" denoted the various feathered bipeds that were commonly kept in pens, ponds, or yards in the vicinity of a household. These were chickens, turkeys, ducks, geese, and pigeons. As well, a gentleman with a special interest in animal husbandry might have on hand a few peacocks, and perhaps even some guinea fowl (the latter were valued because they uttered a harsh cry of alarm when a fox or other predator approached). The generic term "poultry" was also in use at the time, but it included not just house fowl but also birds that thrived in England's forests, meadows, and streams, such as partridges, pheasants, quails, godwits, larks, sparrows, and many more. Because we've dealt with those wild fowl in the chapter devoted to game, in this chapter we've limited ourselves to the so-called "house fowl."

From a culinary perspective, the most popular of the house fowls were chickens, which were further categorized as hens (or pullets), cocks (or roosters), and capons, the latter being castrated cocks. Of these three, the capon was most often served to the table: it appears in about a hundred recipes from this period, whereas hens appear in only about seventeen. Hens, of course, had special value in that they laid eggs, which was a good reason for keeping them out of the stew pot, whereas a capon's utility was more limited: Gervase Markham acknowledged that capons were better than hens at defending young chicks against hawks and buzzards, but their primary purpose in life was to grow fat and tasty. Cocks, on the other hand, were needed to fertilize a hen's eggs so that new chickens would hatch. They were also thought to be more tough and less tasty than either a hen or a capon. The few recipes that involve cock tend to be medicinal ones that call for its flesh because it reputedly possessed a unique power to restore strength. This restorative power arose from the belief that the cock, in the words of Gervase Markham, "is a Fowle of all other birds the most manliest." Extracting this manly virtue required some cruel techniques on the part of the cook. For example, the recipe entitled "To still a cock for a weake body that is consumed," instructs the cook to beat the cock to death.

Another one, called "A Jelly for one that is very weake," says that "the Cocke must be pulled alive"—that is, have its feathers removed while it is still squawking—and then "whipped to death." These agonies, it was presumed, would somehow activate the cock's manly virtues which would then be transferred to the person who ate its flesh. The whole process was surely inspired, at some level, by the passion of Jesus, who was beaten and whipped before being killed, and whose restorative virtues were transferred to believers through the consumption of his body as represented by the Eucharist. Indeed, the cock was associated with Jesus through the biblical story of Peter denying him three times before the cock crowed.

In comparison with capons—which appear, as previously mentioned, in about a hundred recipes—the other house fowls are relative rarities in the 2,100 recipes of this period. Pigeons (or house doves) are mentioned in thirteen recipes, turkeys in ten, geese in eight, ducks in eight, and peacocks in four. All of these birds, before they were slaughtered and cooked, would undergo a process known as "cramming." This meant that they were confined to a small pen and a doughy mixture of wheat meal and milk would be crammed down their throats several times a day. After a month or so of this force-feeding and idleness, they would—according to Gervase Markham—"bee as fat as is fit for any man to eate." With geese, this cramming process could begin at two points in their lives: either when they were just a month old (when they were known as "green geese," because of their youth rather than their color) or when they were six months old (when they were known as "stubble geese," because they had spent the fall eating the grain that was left in the stubble fields). Green geese and stubble geese were considered sufficiently different that distinct sauces were devised for each: a recipe entitled "Sauce for stubble Geese" was made from roasted apples, vinegar, barberries, breadcrumbs, sugar, and cinnamon, whereas one entitled "Sauce for green Geese" was made by mixing sorrel, sugar, and feaberries. As a final note, Gervase Markham suggested that all of these house fowl are "better for Idell folkes that labour not, than for them that use exercise." Hard-working laborers, he goes on to say, should confine themselves to "grose meates" such as beef and pork.

## NOTES FOR BOILING A CHICKEN

Several recipes in this chapter call for a boiled chicken. It is a relatively simple task but requires a bit of preparation time and may require planning ahead, depending on the recipe.

- Rinse the chicken with cold running water. Trim excess fat and skin if desired. Stuff the cavity or season if the recipe calls for it. It is a good idea to tie the legs with kitchen string to help keep the bird together and for ease of removing from the pot.
- Make sure you use a pot that is large enough to allow the chicken to be completely covered in water. Bring the water to a gentle boil and place the chicken in the pot. When the water returns to a boil, reduce the heat and let the chicken simmer for 45 to 50 minutes, or until a meat thermometer inserted in the thigh reads 180°F.
- As the pot returns to a boil, skim the water frequently to remove the effluent that rises to the surface.
- Have a large dish ready to receive the cooked chicken when it is removed from the pot.

## CUTTING POULTRY INTO EIGHT SECTIONS

A boiled chicken will be much easier to serve if you section it into eight pieces. Always use a sharp chef's knife.

- Allow the chicken to cool slightly.
- Set the chicken on its back with its legs toward you.
- Slice the skin where the breast meets the thigh and pop out the joint on both legs.
- Cut around the bone and remove the leg and thigh.
- Cut the drumstick where the leg meets the thigh on both legs.
- Cut the wings from the breast.
- Remove the breast meat by gently carving down along the breastbone on each side (a boneless breast), or flip the chicken onto its breast and cut out the backbone before cutting the breastbone in half, separating the two breasts.

# TO BOILE A CAPON OR A CHICKEN

*Elinor Fettiplace's Receipt Book, 1604*

> Biondello: I cannot tarry: I knew a wench maried in an afternoone
> as shee went to the Garden for Parseley to stuffe a Rabit,
> and so may you sir: and so adew sir. (*The Taming of the Shrew* 4.4.99–101)

Take a pinte of sack and annother of water, a little spinage, two or three sprigs of parseley, reasins of the Sunne, currans, large mace, put all into a pipkin, & boile it a good while, then put in dates, marrowe, prunes, and boile it againe, till the fruit bee soft, then take it up and put to a peece of sweet butter, sugar and a little ginger beaten, then take the yelk of an egg beaten with a spoonfull or two of verjuice, and put into it, and when your chickens bee boyled inough, put this broth to them.

---

 ## MODERN RECIPE                                      Makeability: 2

| | |
|---|---|
| 1 chicken | 2 TBS currants |
| 2 cups sack (substitute dry sherry) | 2 TBS dates |
| 2 cups water | 2 TBS prunes |
| 1 cup spinach | 1 TBS whole mace |
| 3 sprigs parsley | 1 tsp sugar |
| 1 TBS unsalted butter | 1 tsp minced ginger |
| 2 TBS verjuice (see Appendix 1) | 1 egg yolk beaten |
| 2 TBS raisins | |

Rinse out the chicken and tie the legs together. Using a large pot, place the chicken in enough gently boiling water to cover it. Add parsley, raisins, and currants and return to a gentle boil. Add dates and prunes. Simmer for 45 minutes, or until a thermometer inserted into the thigh reads 180°F. In the last 10 minutes of cooking, melt the butter in a small saucepan and add the sugar, ginger, egg, and verjuice and combine. Remove the chicken, drain, and carve into sections. Arrange the chicken pieces on a plate and garnish with the butter-verjuice sauce.

# TO BOILE A CAPON IN WHITE BROTH WITH ALMONDES

*The Good Huswifes Jewell, 1596*

Launce: When a mans Servant shall play the Curre with
him (looke you) it goes hard: one that I brought up of
a puppy: one that I sav'd from drowning, when three
or foure of his blinde brothers and sisters went to it: I
have taught him (even as one would say precisely,
thus I would teach a dog) I was sent to deliver him,
as a present to Mistris Silvia, from my Master; and I
came no sooner into the dyning-chamber, but he steps
me to her Trencher, and steales her Capons-leg: O, 'tis
a foule thing, when a Cur cannot keepe himselfe in all
companies. (*Two Gentlemen of Verona* 4.4.1–11)

*In Shakespeare's England, the soft tissue found inside bones—marrow—was often called "marie" or "marie bone." The substance was a common ingredient, appearing in more than 60 of the 2,100 published recipes of this period. Over the last few decades it has fallen out of culinary favor, at least in North America, and may be difficult to procure. If you are keen to use the real thing, you can probably get your local butcher to split a large beef bone for you, and then you can remove the marrow yourself. Alternatively, you can substitute suet or butter, which is what several of the recipes from this period instruct the cook to do when marrow is in short supply.*

Take your Capon with marie bones and set them on the fire, and when they be cleane skummed take the fattest of the broth, and put it in a little pot with a good deale of marie, prunes, raisons, dates, whole maces, & a pinte of white wine, then blanch your almondes and strain them, with them thicken your potte & let it seeth a good while and when it is enough serve it uppon soppes with your capon.

## MODERN RECIPE

Makeability: 3

| | |
|---|---|
| 1 chicken cut in pieces | 1/4 cup chopped dates |
| Marrow bones (substitute suet or butter) | 2 TBS raisins |
| 1/4 cup chopped prunes | 3 blades of mace |

*Continued on next page*

*Continued from previous page*

2 cups white wine

1 cup blanched almonds

60% lightly toasted whole wheat bread for sippets

In a large pot, cover the chicken and marrow bones with water and bring to a boil. Skim when necessary. Cook for about 30 minutes, or until chicken is cooked thoroughly. Into a saucepan, draw a cup of the broth, scoop the marrow from the bones, and add the prunes, raisins, dates, mace, wine, and almonds. Bring to a boil and simmer until the sauce thickens. Place the chicken pieces on the sops and spoon the almond mixture on top.

# TO BOYLE CHEKINS OR CAPON WITH PESCODS

*A Delightfull Daily Exercise for Ladies and Gentlewomen*, 1621

Touchstone: I remember when I was in
love, I broke my sword upon a stone, and bid him take
that for comming a night to Jane Smile, and I remember
the kissing of her batler, and the Cowes dugs that her
prettie chopt hands had milk'd; and I remember
the wooing of a peascod instead of her, from whom I
tooke two cods, and giving her them againe, said with
weeping teares, weare these for my sake. (*As You Like It* 2.4.44–51)

Take greene sugar Pease when the pods bee but young, and pull out the string of the backe of the podde, and picke the huske of the stalkes ende, and as many as you can take up in your hand at three severall times, put them into the pipkin, with halfe a pound of sweete Butter, a quarter of a pint of faire water, a little grose Pepper, Salt, and Oyle and Mace, and let them stue very softly till that they be very tender, then put in the yolkes of two or three rawe egges strained with six spoonefulls of Sacke, and as much Vinegar, put it into your Peascods and brewe them with a ladle, then dish up your Capon or Chickins upon sippets, then poure your Peascods and broath upon them, and strewe on salt and serve it to the table hott.

## MODERN RECIPE                                     Makeability: 2

1 chicken

3 cups shelled sugar-snap peas or sweet peas

$1/2$ lb butter

2 egg yolks

1 TBS whole mace

6 TBS vinegar

6 TBS sack (substitute dry sherry)

$1/2$ cup of water

1 TBS oil

Coarse salt

Cracked black pepper

6 slices of 60% whole wheat bread (toasted) for sippets

Rinse the chicken and tie the legs together. Using a large pot, place the chicken in enough gently boiling water to cover. Simmer for 45 minutes, or until a thermometer inserted in the thigh reads 180°F. In the last 15 minutes that the chicken is cooking, combine water, butter, oil, and mace in a saucepan over medium heat. Add peas and cook until tender. Add egg yolks, vinegar, and sherry. Combine. Remove and drain the chicken and cut into pieces. Arrange sippets on a large platter and place chicken pieces on sippets. Pour the pea mixture on the chicken and sprinkle with coarse salt.

# TO SMOORE A CHICKIN

*A New Booke of Cookerie, 1615*

Hotspur:  O, I could divide my selfe, and go to buffets,
            for moving such a dish of skim'd Milk with so
            honourable an Action. Hang him, let him tell the King we
            are prepared. I will set forwards to night. (*1 Henry IV* 2.3.31–34)

*Two recipes in this book call for "smooring," the other one being "For the fillets of a Veale, smoored in a Frying-panne." The verb denoted a method of stewing something in a closed vessel over a gentle fire. Although "smoor" is now obsolete in English, it persists in Dutch, where it means "to simmer." As for the clary that is called for in this recipe, we've substituted easier-to-find sage leaves (clary and sage are closely related). Clary was, however, formerly in common use: James Hart, in his 1633* Klinike, *observed that "the herbe Clary is in great use also, especially among women, which they esteeme soveraine good against their immoderate fluxes [i.e., excessive menstruation].... They use commonly here with us in the countrie to fry it with egges."*

Cut it in small pieces, and frye it with sweet Butter: take Sacke, or white Wine, Parsley, an Onyon chopt small, a piece of whole Mace, and a little grosse Pepper: put in a little Sugar, Vergis, and Butter. Then take a good handfull of Clary, and picke off the stalkes, then make fine batter with the yolkes of two or three new layd Egges, and fine flowre, two or three spoonfuls of sweet Creame, and a little Nutmeg, and so frye it in a Frying-panne, with sweet Butter: serve in your Chickins with the fryed Clary on them. Garnish your Dish with Barberryes.

---

 ## MODERN RECIPE                                    Makeability: 4

| | |
|---|---|
| 1 chicken cut in pieces | 1/4 cup chopped parsley |
| 3 TBS unsalted butter | 1 medium onion, finely diced |
| 1/4 cup dry sherry | 1 tsp whole mace |

*Continued on next page*

*Continued from previous page*

| | |
|---|---|
| $^1/_2$ tsp fresh-cracked black pepper | $^1/_4$ cup flour |
| 1 tsp sugar | 3 TBS 18% cream (as needed) |
| $^1/_4$ cup verjuice (see Appendix 1) | $^1/_2$ tsp nutmeg |
| 12 clary leaves (see Appendix 1) | Barberries for garnish (see Appendix 1) |
| 3 egg yolks | |

In a large frying pan, cook the onions in 2 TBS of butter until soft. Add the chicken and cook a few minutes. Add the sherry, verjuice, mace, sugar, pepper, and parsley. Simmer about 20 minutes. In the last 10 minutes while the chicken is cooking, prepare a medium-thick batter with the egg yolks, flour, cream, and nutmeg. Dip the clary leaves in the batter and fry in a pan with about 1 TBS of butter. Arrange the chicken on a platter and top with the fried sage. Garnish with barberries.

# TO BOYLE A CAPON OR CHICKEN WITH COLLE-FLOWERS

*A Delightfull Daily Exercise for Ladies and Gentlewomen, 1621*

Shepherd:  Fy, daughter, when my old wife liv'd: upon
This day, she was both Pantler, Butler, Cooke,
Both Dame and Servant: Welcom'd all: serv'd all,
Would sing her song, and dance her turne: now heere
At upper end o'th Table; now, i'th middle:
On his shoulder, and his: her face o' fire
With labour, and the thing she tooke to quench it
She would to each one sip. You are retyred,
As if you were a feasted one: and not
The Hostesse of the meeting: Pray you bid
These unknowne friends to's welcome, for it is
A way to make us better Friends, more knowne.
Come, quench your blushes, and present your selfe
That which you are, Mistris o'th' Feast. Come on,
And bid us welcome to your sheepe-shearing,
As your good flocke shall prosper. (*The Winter's Tale* 4.4.55–70)

*Andrew Boorde, in his 1547* Compendyous Regyment, *affirms that capons are "moste beste" in terms of digestibility. He does admit, however, that chickens can also be nutritious to eat in the summer, especially if they are "untrodden," that is, have not yet had sex. He does not comment on how the cook is to determine this.*

Out of the budds of your flowres, boile them in milke with a little Mace, till they be very tender: then take the yolkes of two eggs straine them with a quarter of a pint of Sacke then take asmuch thicke butter being drawne, with a little vineger and a sliced Lemmon, and brue them together, then take the flowers out of the Milke, and put them into the Butter and Sacke, then dish up your Capon, being tender boyld, upon sippets, strowing a little salt upon it, and so poure on the sawce upon it and serve it to the Table hotte.

**MODERN RECIPE** Makeability: 3

| | |
|---|---|
| 1 chicken | ½ cup dry sherry |
| 1 head cauliflower cut into medium-sized florets | ½ cup unsalted butter |
| 2 cups milk | 1 TBS cider vinegar |
| 1 TBS whole mace | Coarse salt |
| 1 lemon, sliced | 6 slices of 60% whole wheat bread (toasted) for sippets |
| 2 egg yolks | |

Rinse out the chicken and tie the legs together. Using a large pot, place the chicken in enough gently boiling water to cover it. Simmer for 45 minutes, or until a thermometer inserted into the thigh reads 180°F. When the chicken has 10 minutes left to cook, place the cauliflower in a saucepan of milk, lemon slices, and mace and cook just until tender. Remove the cauliflower from the milk, set it aside, and keep it warm. Whisk together the egg yolks, sherry, butter, and vinegar and heat in a sauté pan. Add the cauliflower to the egg and butter mixture and heat thoroughly. Remove the chicken, drain, and carve into sections. Place the sippets on a large platter and arrange the chicken pieces on top. Pour the cauliflower mixture on the chicken and sprinkle with salt.

# TO BOYLE CHICKENS WITH SPARAGUS

*A Delightfull Daily Exercise for Ladies and Gentlewomen, 1621*

Antony: I found you as a Morsell, cold upon
       Dead Caesars Trencher: Nay, you were a Fragment
       Of Gneius Pompeyes, besides what hotter houres
       Unregistred in vulgar Fame, you have
       Luxuriously pickt out. (*Antony and Cleopatra* 3.13.118–122)

*There were no "leftovers" in Shakespeare's England, because that term didn't develop until the late nineteenth century. Instead, they referred to food that was left on the table at the end of a meal as "remnants," "relics," "reliefs," "gobbets," "orts," or "fragments" (the latter appears in the quotation from* Antony and Cleopatra*). The phrase "broken meat" was likewise employed: in* King Lear*, Kent insults Oswald by calling him an "eater of broken meats." The insult gains power if we understand that food that had been broken open—such as a lidded pie—would grow mouldy much sooner than a dish that remained inviolate. Kent is essentially implying that Oswald scavenges rotten food.*

Boyle your Chickens in faire water, with a little whole mace, put into their bellies a little parsley, and a little sweete butter, dish them upon sippets and powre a little of the same broth upon it, and take a handfull of sparagus being boyld, and put them into a Ladle full of thicke butter, and stir it together in a dish, and powre it upon your Chickens or pullets, strew on salt, and serve it to the Table hot.

## MODERN RECIPE                                          Makeability: 3

1 chicken

2 TBS whole mace (or 1 tsp ground mace)

5 to 6 sprigs of parsley

5 TBS unsalted butter

1 bunch of asparagus

Coarse salt and fresh-cracked pepper to taste

6 slices of 60% whole wheat bread (toasted) for sippets

Rinse out the chicken. Put the mace, parsley sprigs, and 2 TBS of the butter into the cavity and tie the legs. Using a large pot, place the chicken in enough gently boiling water to cover. When the water returns to the boil, reduce the heat and let simmer for 45 minutes. In the last 15 minutes of cooking, add the asparagus. When it is cooked, remove the chicken (reserving 1 cup of broth), drain, and carve into sections. Melt the remaining butter in a sauté pan. Add reserved broth to the butter and combine for a thick consistency. Arrange the chicken pieces on the sippets and garnish with the asparagus. Spoon the butter and broth mixture on the dish and sprinkle with coarse salt and fresh-cracked black pepper.

# TO BOYLE A CAPON OR CHICKEN IN SACKE AND POTTAGE

*A Delightfull Daily Exercise for Ladies and Gentlewomen, 1621*

Falstaff:  Now Hal, what time of day is it Lad?

Prince.  Thou art so fat-witted with drinking of olde Sacke,
and unbuttoning thee after Supper, and sleeping upon
Benches in the afternoone, that thou hast forgotten to
demand that truely, which thou wouldest truly know. What
a divell hast thou to do with the time of the day? unlesse
houres were cups of Sacke, and minutes Capons, and
clockes the tongues of Bawdes, and dialls the signes of
Leaping-houses, and the blessed Sunne himselfe a faire hot
Wench in Flame-coloured Taffata; I see no reason, why
thou shouldest bee so superfluous, to demaund the time of the day. (*1 Henry IV*
1.2.1–12)

*This recipe calls for a quantity of saffron equal to the weight of three pennies. Throughout Shakespeare's lifetime, a penny weighed about 8 grains, which is about 0.018 ounces. Three English pennies from the late sixteenth or early seventeenth century therefore weighed about 0.054 ounces. A small paperclip weighs about 0.035 ounces, so the amount of saffron this recipe is calling for is equal to the weight of about one and a half paperclips.*

Boyle your Capons or Chickens in fayre water, with a little Oatmeale to make them looke white: then take ryse pottage when it is boyld and seasoned readie to eate, then put into it a pint of Sacke, strained with the yolkes of foure raw egs, and as much powder of Safron as the weight of threepence, a little salt, and as much Sugar as will season it, a pint of Sacke, and foure eges will season a pottle of your pottage: and then dish up your Capons or chickens upon sippets, and poure your Sacke & pottage upon them, and so serve it to the Table hotte.

## MODERN RECIPE                                    Makeability: 2

1 chicken, boiled according to the "Notes for boiling a chicken" on page 69 (add ¹/₄ cup rolled oatmeal for whiteness)

2 cups dry sherry

1 cup rice pottage; use "To make fine rice pottage" on page 202

4 egg yolks

¹/₄ cup sugar

2 pinches saffron

Coarse salt

6 slices of toasted 60% whole wheat bread for sippets

Cut the boiled chicken into pieces, set aside, and keep warm. In a saucepan, combine the rice pottage, sherry, sugar, egg yolks, saffron, and salt to taste. Bring to a gentle boil. Arrange the sippets on a large platter and then place the chicken on the sippets. Pour the sacke and pottage over the chicken and serve.

# TO BAKE CHICKINS WITH GRAPES

*A New Booke of Cookerie*, 1615

Cleopatra:  Give me my Robe, put on my Crowne, I have
            Immortall longings in me. Now no more
            The juyce of Egypts Grape shall moyst this lip. (*Antony and Cleopatra* 5.2.280–282)

Trusse and scald your Chickens season them well with Pepper, Salt, and Nutmeg: and put them into your Pye, with a good piece of Butter. Bake it, and cut it up, and put upon the breast of your Chickins, Grapes boyld in Vergis, Butter, Nutmegge, and Sugar, with the juyce of an Orenge.

## MODERN RECIPE                                    Makeability: 3

1 chicken, cut into pieces

Salt and pepper to taste

1 TBS nutmeg

4 TBS butter

1 cup grapes

¹/₂ cup verjuice (see Appendix 1)

2 TBS sugar

Juice of one orange

Pastry recipe "To make fine paste" on page 214, or buy premade pastry.

Prepare a pastry shell and top. Preheat oven to 350°F. Using a large pot, place the chicken in enough gently boiling water to cover it. Simmer for about 15 minutes. Arrange the chicken in the pastry shell and season with salt and pepper and place 2 TBS of the butter on the pieces. Cover with pastry and bake at 350°F for 35 to 40 minutes, or until the pastry is golden brown. In the

*Continued on next page*

*Continued from previous page*

meantime, in a saucepan, melt the remaining 2 TBS of butter and stir in the grapes, verjuice, sugar, and orange juice and simmer on low heat. Remove the chicken from the oven, cut the top pastry open, and pour in the grape mixture.

# TO BAKE CHICKENS IN A CAWDLE

*The Good Huswifes Jewell, 1596*

Apemantus:                              Will the cold brooke
                    Candied with Ice, Cawdle thy Morning taste
                    To cure thy o're-nights surfet? (*Timon of Athens* 4.3.227–229)

*Caudles were usally warm drinks made of gruel, ale or wine, spices, and sometimes eggs. In this recipe, the caudle is the mixture of egg yolks and wine. In the passage from* Timon of Athens, *"caudle" is being used as a verb meaning "to remedy": Apemantus is asking Timon whether the icy water from the brook will remedy the sour taste in his mouth caused by overindulging the night before.*

Season them with salt and pepper, and put in butter, and so let them bake, and when they be baked, boile a few barberries and pruines, and currants, and take a little white wine or vergice, and let it boile and put in a little suger, and set it on the fire a little, and straine in two or three yolkes of egges into the wine, and when you take the dish of the fire, put the pruines and currants and barberries into the dish, and then put them in altogether, into the pye of chickins.

## MODERN RECIPE                                                Makeability: 4

| | |
|---|---|
| 1 chicken cut in pieces | 1/4 currants |
| 1/2 tsp salt | 1 tsp sugar |
| 1/4 tsp pepper | 1 cup white wine |
| 4 TBS butter | 3 egg yolks |
| 1/2 cup barberries (see Appendix 1) | Pastry recipe "To make fine paste" on page 214, or buy premade pastry. |
| 1/4 chopped prunes | |

Prepare a pastry shell and top. Preheat oven to 350°F. Season the chicken with salt and pepper and sauté in the butter. Set aside and keep warm. Into a saucepan, add the barberries, prunes, currants, sugar, and wine. Bring to a boil and allow to reduce slightly. Take a few spoonfuls of the wine mixture from the saucepan and whisk into the egg yolks. Add the tempered yolks to the saucepan of wine and stir. Transfer the barberries, prunes, currants, and a few tablespoons of the wine to the pastry shell. Add the chicken pieces. Cover with the pastry and bake for 35 to 40 minutes, or until heated through and the pastry begins to brown.

# TO FRIE CHICKINS

*The Good Huswifes Jewell, 1596*

Foole:  How do you Gentlemen?
All:    Gramercies good Foole: How does your Mistris?
Foole:  She's even setting on water to scald such Chickens as you are.
        Would we could see you at Corinth. (*Timon of Athens 2.2.69–73*)

*Cookery books from this period allude to both "sweet broth" and "sharp broth." No actual recipe for either kind of broth exists, but a study of the other broth recipes reveals that they tend to fall into two kinds: those that call for wine or verjuice, and those that call for dried fruits such as raisins. Presumably, the former would be "sharp broths" (verjuice, especially, is quite acrid) and the latter would be "sweet broths." Accordingly, we've used the recipe called "To make ordinary stew'd broth"—which contains raisins, prunes, and dates—as our base for a sweet broth. As for the quotation from* Timon of Athens, *the Fool's harsh remarks refer literally to the technique of scalding chickens with boiling water to remove their feathers, and figuratively to the hot baths reputed to cure victims of venereal disease (who also, as a result of the disease, lost their hair).*

Take your chickins and let them boyle in verye good sweete broath a prittye while, and take the chickens out, and quarter them out in peeces, and then put them into a Frying pan with sweete butter, and let them stewe in the pan, but you must not let them be browne with frying, and then put out the butter out of the pan, and then take a little sweet broath, and as much Vergice, and the yolkes of two Egges, and beate them together, and put in a little Nutmegges, synamon and Ginger, and Pepper into the sauce, and then put them all into the pan to the chickens, and stirre them together in the pan, and put them into a dish, and serve them by.

---

 ## MODERN RECIPE                                           Makeability: 3

1 chicken

12 cups sweet broth (use "To make ordinary stew'd broth" on page 199, or substitute chicken broth)

3 TBS unsalted butter

1/2 cup verjuice (see Appendix 1)

2 egg yolks beaten

1 tsp grated nutmeg

1 tsp grated cinnamon

1/2 tsp minced ginger

1/4 tsp coarsely ground black pepper

1 tsp salt

Rinse out the chicken and tie the legs with kitchen string. Using a large pot, place the chicken in enough gently boiling sweet broth to cover. When the sweet broth returns to the boil, reduce the heat and let simmer for 45 minutes. Remove the chicken (reserving 1/2 cup of sweet broth), drain, and carve it into pieces. Melt the butter in a sauté pan and add the chicken pieces. Cook over medium heat. In a bowl, combine the verjuice, beaten egg yolks, nutmeg, cinnamon, ginger, broth, and salt and pepper. Add mixture to the chicken and heat thoroughly.

# TO MAKE BLEAW MANGER

*A Propre New Booke of Cokery, 1545*

| | |
|---|---|
| Benedick: | You are a villaine, I jest not, I will make it good how you dare, with what you dare, and when you dare: do me right, or I will protest your cowardise: you have kill'd a sweete Ladie, and her death shall fall heavie on you, let me heare from you. |
| Claudio: | Well, I will meete you, so I may have good cheare. |
| Don Pedro: | What, a feast, a feast? |
| Claudio: | In faith I thanke him, he hath bid me to a calves head and a Capon, the which if I doe not carve most curiously, say my knife's naught, shall I not finde a woodcocke too? |
| Benedick: | Sir, your wit ambles well, it goes easily. (*Much Ado About Nothing* 5.1.144–157) |

*The name of this dish—"bleaw manger"—is a corruption of "blanc manger," meaning "white food." Not surprisingly, its main ingredients are all white: milk, cream, sugar, rice flour, and chicken, presumably the white breast meat, which—as the recipe instructs—was carved from the bird while it still alive. This instruction, expressed so matter-of-factly in the recipe, is a reminder that brutality was a fact of life in Shakespeare's England. In London, Shakespeare would have walked by men without ears: they had been lopped off as punishment for some criminal infraction. He would have surely witnessed public beheadings of more serious criminals, and he would have walked along London Bridge where their heads were stuck on poles. He might even have seen a heretic being burned at the stake (though these were less frequent during Elizabeth's reign). And he would have seen cartloads of pustule-covered bodies trundling through the streets, as he hurried out of London during an outbreak of the plague and made his way back to the relative safety of Stratford. Bon appétit!*

Take a capon and cut out the braune of him alyve and parboyle the braune tyll the flesshe come from the bone and then drie him as drie as you can in a fayre cloth, then take a payre of cardes and carde him as small as is possyble and then take a pottell of mylke and a pottell of creame, and halfe a pownde of Ryc flower and your carded braune of the capon and put all into a panne, and stere it all togither and set it upon the fyer, & whan it begynueth to boyle put therto halfe a pounde of beaten suger and a saucer full of rosewater, and so let it boyle till it be very thicke, then put it into a charger till it be colde and then ye maie slice it as ye do leiche and so serve it in.

---

 ## MODERN RECIPE                                   Makeability: 3

| | |
|---|---|
| 1 chicken cut into pieces | 1/2 lb rice flour |
| 1/2 cup milk | 1/2 lb sugar |
| 1/2 cup cream | 2 TBS rosewater |

Boil the chicken in a pot of water until is thoroughly cooked, about 30 minutes. Remove the chicken, let cool, and dry with kitchen towels. Remove the meat by shredding it with its grain, using mostly the breast meat. In a large saucepan, combine the meat with the remaining ingredients and stir until very thick. Pour the mixture onto a large flat platter and allow to cool. Refrigerate for several hours (or overnight). Cut the bleaw manger into slices to serve.

# TO BOYLE A CAPON WITH ORENGES OR LEMMONS

*A Book of Cookrye*, 1591

Jacques:                                      And then, the Justice
              In faire round belly, with good Capon lin'd,
              With eyes severe, and beard of formall cut,
              Full of wise sawes, and moderne instances,
              And so he plays his part. (*As You Like It* 2.7.152–156)

*This recipe indicates that the broth should not be allowed to quail, that is, to thicken or curdle. The word has no connection to the identically named fowl, but rather derives from the Italian "quagliare," which in turn evolved from the Latin "coagulare," meaning "to coagulate."*

Take your Capon and boyle him tender and take a little of the broth when it is boyled and put it into a pipkin with Mace and Sugar a good deale, and pare three Orenges and pil them and put them in your pipkin, and boile them a little among your broth, and thicken it with wine and yolkes of egges, and Sugar a good deale, and salt but a little, and set your broth no more on the fire for quailing, and serve it without sippets.

 ## MODERN RECIPE                                      Makeability: 3

| | |
|---|---|
| 1 chicken | 3 egg yolks |
| 2 oranges sliced, peeled and white pith removed | 1 TBS whole mace |
| 1 lemon sliced, peeled and white pith removed | 1/4 cup white wine |
| 1/2 cup sugar | Coarse salt |

Rinse out the chicken and tie the legs. Using a large pot, place the chicken in enough gently boiling water to cover. When the water returns to the boil, reduce the heat and let simmer for 45 minutes, or until a thermometer inserted in the thigh reads 180°F. Remove chicken (reserve 4 cups of broth), drain, and keep warm. Place the reserved broth in a saucepan along with mace, sugar, and orange and lemon slices and cook for 10 minutes over medium heat. Whisk together wine and egg yolks and add

*Continued on next page*

*Continued from previous page*

to the orange and lemon mixture. Cook for another 5 minutes. Cut chicken into pieces and arrange on a platter. Spoon the orange and lemon sauce onto the chicken pieces and sprinkle with coarse salt.

# TO BOILE MUTTON AND CHICKENS

*The Good Huswifes Jewell, 1596*

Shallow: The Councell shall know this.
Falstaff: 'Twere better for you if it were known in
councell: you'll be laugh'd at.
Evans: Pauca verba, Sir John, good worts.
Falstaff: Good worts? good Cabidge. (*The Merry Wives of Windsor* 1.1.111–115)

*In this quotation from* The Merry Wives of Windsor, *Evans tells Falstaff to hold his tongue: "Pauca verba," he says, which is Latin for "few words." Evans then stresses that what he has just said in Latin are "good words"—but thanks to his Welsh accent, it sounds like he has said "good worts." Falstaff then mocks Evans' mispronunciation by saying "good cabbage," cabbage being a common wort or pot-herb.*

Take your mutton and Chyckens and sette upon the fire with faire water and when it is well skummed, take two handfull of Cabadge, Lettice, a handfull of currants a good peece of butter, the juyce of two or three Lemmons, a good deale of grosse Pepper and a good peece of Suger, and let them seeth all well together, then take three or foure yolkes of egges togeather harde rosted, and straine them with parte of your broth, let them seeth a quantitye of an houre. Serve your broth with meate uppon Sippets.

 ## MODERN RECIPE                                                  Makeability: 3

| | |
|---|---|
| 1 chicken | 1/4 cup sugar |
| 1 lb cubed stewing lamb | 4 hard-boiled egg yolks |
| 2 cups Savoy cabbage | Juice of 3 lemons |
| 2 cups Boston lettuce | 1 tsp cracked black pepper |
| 1/2 cup currants | 6 slices of toasted 60% whole wheat bread for sippets |
| 2 TBS unsalted butter | |

Rinse out the chicken and tie the legs. Using a large pot, place the chicken and lamb in enough gently boiling water to cover. When the water returns to the boil, reduce the heat and let simmer for 45 minutes, or until a thermometer inserted in the thigh reaches 180°F. Skim frequently. With 15 minutes left to cook the chicken and lamb, add the cabbage, lettuce, currants, butter, sugar, lemon juice, and pepper. Draw out 1/2 cup of the broth and pass the egg yolks through a fine-meshed sieve. Mix yolks and broth to a smooth consistency and return it to the pot. Remove the chicken, cut into pieces and serve with the lamb on sippets. Spoon the cabbage and lettuce onto the chicken and lamb along with some of the broth.

# TO BOYLE A TAME DUCKE, OR WIDGIN

*A New Booke of Cookerie, 1615*

Pyramus:  But stay: O spight!
             But marke, poore Knight,
             What dreadful dole is heere?
             Eyes do you see!
             How can it be!
             O dainty Ducke: O Deere! (*A* Midsummer Night's Dream *5.1.272–277*)

*In Shakespeare's England, people enjoyed boiling barnyard fowls, but they also liked to bestow the names of those fowls on their friends and sweethearts as terms of endearment. In the quotation from* A Midsummer Night's Dream, *for example, Pyramus (played by the bumbling Nick Bottom) calls Thisbe his "dainty duck," while in* Twelfth Night *Sir Toby Belch calls Malvolio his "bawcock," meaning "pretty rooster." Similarly, in* Henry V, *Pistol calls Fluellen "sweet chuck," the word "chuck" being a variant of "chick," and in* The Winter's Tale *Leontes asks his young son, "Art thou my calf?"*

Parboyle your Fowle well, take strong Mutton broth, a handfull of Parsley, choppe them fine with an Onyon, and Barberryes, pickt Endiffe washt: throw all into the Pipkin with a Turnup cut in pieces, and parboyld, untill the rankenesse bee gone: then put in a little white Wine, or Vergis, halfe a pound of Butter: boyle all together, and stirre it, and serve it with the Turnups, large Mace, Pepper, and a little Sugar.

---

 ## MODERN RECIPE                         Makeability: 3

1 duck

Mutton broth to cover duck (substitute chicken broth)

1 large turnip, cut into 1-inch pieces

1 diced onion

1 endive, leaves separated

1/4 cup of barberries (see Appendix 1)

1 TBS whole mace

2 TBS sugar

1/4 cup finely chopped parsley

1/2 lb unsalted butter

1/2 cup white wine

1/4 cup verjuice (see Appendix 1)

1 tsp cracked black pepper

Using a large pot, place the duck and onions in enough gently boiling mutton broth to cover. When the broth returns to a boil, reduce the heat and let simmer for 45 minutes, or until a thermometer inserted in the thigh reaches 180°F. Add the remaining ingredients and cook the duck for a further 30 minutes. Remove the duck, cut into pieces, and place on a platter. Spoon the turnip and endive mixture over the duck along with some of the broth.

# TO BOILE PIGEONS WITH RICE

*Delightes for Ladies*, 1609

Celia:     Heere comes Monsieur the Beau.
Rosalind: With his mouth full of newes.
Celia:     Which he will put on us, as Pigeons feed their young.
Rosalind: Then shal we be newes-cram'd. (*As You Like It* 1.2.87–90)

Boyle them in mutton broth, putting sweete hearbes in their bellies, then take a little Rice and boyle it in creame, with a little whole mace, season it with sugar, lay it thicke on their breasts, wringing also the juice of a Lemmon upon them and so serve them.

---

 ## MODERN RECIPE                                              Makeability: 3

4 pigeons (substitute quail or Cornish hens)

4 cups mutton broth (substitute beef broth)

1/2 cup minced parsley

1/2 cup minced basil

1 tsp marjoram

2 TBS finely chopped rosemary

1 1/2 cups cooked rice (boiled in 2 1/2 cups cream with 2 blades of mace and 1 TBS sugar)

Juice of 1 lemon

Combine the herbs and stuff the pigeons. In a deep skillet, arrange the pigeons and pour in enough broth to fill about half of the skillet. Bring the broth to a boil, reduce to a simmer, cover, and cook the pigeons about 1 hour. Baste the birds frequently and add more broth as needed. Arrange the pigeons on a platter and spread the rice thickly over top. Garnish with lemon juice and serve.

---

# TO DRESSE A PEACOCKE WITH ALL HIS FEATHERS

*Epulario*, 1598

Benedick: I would not marry her, though she were endowed with all
                that Adam had left him before he transgrest,
                she would have made Hercules have turnd spit, yea,
                and have cleft his club to make the fire too.
                (*Much Ado About Nothing* 2.1.239–242)

*We don't recommend that you actually make this dish, for several reasons. First, you would probably have to abduct the peacock from a local zoo. Second, the method of stuffing the cooked peacock back into its uncooked and still-feathered skin runs the risk of contaminating the flesh with salmonella. Third, the meat of a peacock, at least according to Gervase Markham, "is neither good, delicate nor wholesome." Fourth, the pyrotechnics that are supposed to spew from the bird's beak would probably set your tablecloth on fire.*

*Finally, you probably have better things to do with your gold leaf than glue it onto a roast peacock. Incidentally, the recipe's instruction to set the peacock's beak on fire is probably intended to recall the myth of the phoenix, which was said to live a thousand years before dying (and being reborn) in a kind of spontaneous combustion. Shakespeare's poem "The Phoenix and the Turtle" features that flaming fowl.*

To dresse a Peacocke with all his feathers, in such sort that when it is ynough it shall seeme to bee alive and cast fire out of the mouth. You must kill the Peacocke with a feather or quill pricked into her head, or els make her bleed under the throat like a Kid, then cleane the skin under the breast, that is from the neck unto the taile, and flea it off, and being fleaed turne the skin of the necke outward neere to his head, and cut the necke, so that his head be fast to the skin, and likewise let his legges hang to the skin, then stuffe it full of some dainty pudding, with spices, and take whole cloves, and stick them in his breast, and so spit him and rost him by a soft fire, and about his necke wrap a wet cloth, that the fire may not drie it over-much, still wetting the cloth: and when it is rosted, take it off the spit, and put it into the skinne, then you must have a certaine yron cunningly made fast to a trencher, which shall goe through the Peacockes feet and not bee seene, that so the Peacocke may stand upon his feet, with his head upright, as though hee were alive, and dress his taile in such a manner, that it may be round. If you will have the Peacocke cast fire at the mouth, take an ounce of Camphora wrapped about with Cotton, and put it in the Peacockes bill with a little Aquanity, or very strong wine, and when you will send it to the table, set fire to the cotton, and he will cast fire a good while after. And to make the greater shew, when the Peacocke is rosted, you may gild it with leafe gold, and put the skin upon the said gold, which may be spiced very sweet. The like may be done with a feisant, or any other birds.

---

 ## MODERN RECIPE           Makeability: 5

1 plump young peacock with lovely plumage

Dainty pudding (use "A Swanne or Goose Pudding," page 195)

1/2 cup whole cloves

Kitchen towels

Rebar and other iron rods and wires

1 oz camphor wrapped in cotton

Aqua vitae (substitute brandy)

3 TBS sugar

Gold leaf

Dispatch the peacock with a quick thrust of a quill to its head. Make a cut from just above the breastbone down to the base of its tail, trimming around the legs to leave them intact but hollow and connected to the skin. Remove the skin, turning it inside out, and pull it forward toward the head, which you must then lop off one-quarter of the way down the neck. The head is therefore attached to the skin something like a "cape." Insert cloves evenly into the peacock. Spit him and roast slowly over a low fire. Wrap a wet cloth around his neck so it does not dry out. Stuff the dainty pudding in the legs. When cooked, cover the roast with the peacock skin and use the rebar and wire

*Continued on next page*

*Continued from previous page*

devices, concealed from view, to show the peacock standing up, alive, with head erect and tail round—and breathing fire. Nail the peacock's feet to a heavy wooden trencher. For the pyrotechnics, soak the cotton-wrapped camphor in aqua vitae. As the bird is brought to the table, ignite the cotton, encouraging guests to marvel at this fiery centrepiece. To further adorn the peacock, decorate it with gold leaf.

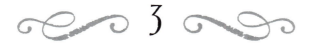

# 3

# BEEF AND VEAL

Leave off tittle tattle & looke to thy cattle.
—Thomas Tusser, *Five Hundredth Points of Good Husbandry*, 1577

Authors of dietary books in Shakespeare's England never tired of ranking various foodstuffs according to their digestibility. Usually, beef didn't fare very well, as it was thought to be more difficult to digest—or "concoct," as they then termed it—than most other meats. Moreover, even within the category of beef there were further nutritional hierarchies: beef from a cow (that is, a female bovine) was worse than beef from an ox (that is, a male bovine), and beef from an old animal was worse than beef from a young animal. The danger, as Andrew Boorde saw it, was that "olde beefe and cowe flesshe dothe ingendre melancoly and leprouse humours." Even harder on one's digestion was beef that had been "powdered"—that is, preserved in salt—and then hung to dry in a smoke house. Beef preserved in such a manner was often called martinmas beef, because it was usually salted on or around St. Martin's Day. According to Boorde, a slab of hard and dry martinmas beef made a better umbrella than a foodstuff. An alternative method for preserving beef was proposed by Hugh Plat: he suggested that sailors could tow barrels of flesh behind their ships, with the salty ocean acting as a circulating brine. Not surprisingly, Plat's idea didn't hold water.

Veal, which is the flesh of a young calf, was usually ranked much higher than beef in terms of its supposed nutritional value. Thomas Twyne, in his 1576 *Schoole-master, or Teacher of Table Philosophie*, asserted that veal "is good and holsome, as not having that sliminess and coldenesse which is in Beefe," and Andrew Boorde called it "the best flesshe and the moste nutrytyve meate that can be for mans sustenaunce." This privileging of veal was longstanding: even the knight in Chaucer's fourteenth-century "Merchant's Tale" says, "bet[ter] than olde boef is the tendre veel." The cookery books of the time also esteemed veal over beef. The 1596 *Good Huswifes Jewell*, for example, includes twenty recipes for veal and only three for beef (although beef broth and beef suet are also occasionally called for by other recipes).

Still, despite the caveats of dietary authorities and the predilections of cookbook authors, the reality was that more beef than veal was eaten in Shakespeare's

England. Slaughtering a 200-pound calf, rather than letting it grow into a 1,400-pound cow or ox, was a luxury that only the wealthy could afford. Like Sir Andrew in *Twelfth Night*, the typical citizen was "a great eater of beef" (1.3.84) rather than of veal. Similarly, the humble Christopher Sly, in *The Taming of the Shrew*, has no use for the delicacies that are offered him and instead insists "if you give me any conserves, give me conserves of beef" (H5.3.7.151). Indeed, by 1628, the French were calling the English "mangeurs de boeuf"—that is, "beef eaters"—and in one of Shakespeare's history plays, a French Duke smugly gloats that "these English are shrewdly out of beef" (Induction 2.6–7), meaning that they lack the one thing that makes them hardy Englishmen. One contemporary commentator, in a treatise called *A Briefe Note of the Benefits that Grow to this Realme, by the Observation of Fish-Daies*, estimated that London, with a population of around 200,000, consumed more than 67,000 head of cattle each year.

# TO BOYLE A RACK OF VEALE ON THE FRENCH FASHION

*A New Booke of Cookerie*, 1615

King Henry: You have Witch-craft in your Lippes, Kate:
there is more eloquence in a Sugar touch of them, than
in the Tongues of the French Councell; and they should
sooner perswade Harry of England, than a generall
Petition of Monarchs. (*Henry V* 5.2.278–282)

*Shakespeare's contemporaries were divided in their attitude toward French cuisine. For some, the culinary tradition of France was clearly superior to that of England, which explains why the cookery books of the era abound with recipes such as "To bake Calves feet after the French fashion," "To boile a Flounder or Pickrell of the French fashion," and "To bake a Hare on the French fashion." As well, the Earl of Leicester clearly enjoyed French cuisine: in 1588, he sent a letter to an acquaintance in France, asking him to look after a young man who had trained in his kitchen, and who was now going to "spend a year or two there with some good principal cook in Paris," before returning to England. Others, such as James Hart in his Klinike, vilified the French for eating "frogs, snailes, mushroms, and oisters," as well as other foods that were essentially considered excretions of the earth and ocean. As for the "steakes" referred to in this recipe, they aren't the thick slabs of meat that the word "steak" now denotes. Instead, the word formerly referred to much smaller pieces of flesh, perhaps cubes the size of dice, or strips as long and thick as a little finger.*

Cut it into Steakes, cut a Carrot, or Turnup in pieces, like Diamonds, and put them into a Pipkin with a pinte of white Wine, Parsley bound in a Fagot, a little Rosemary, and large Mace, and a sticke of Sinamon: pare a Lemmon, or Orenge, and take a little grose Pepper, halfe a pound of Butter: boyle all together untill they be enough: when you have done, put in a little Sugar, and Vergis. Garnish your Dish as you list.

**MODERN RECIPE**                                    Makeability: 2

2 lb veal cubes (or beef)

1 turnip, cut into diamond-shaped pieces
(or a few carrots)

2 cups white wine

1 bouquet garni of parsley, rosemary, and
cinnamon stick

1 blade of mace

1 peeled lemon (or 1 peeled orange)

1/2 tsp cracked black pepper

1/2 lb unsalted butter

1 tsp sugar

1/4 cup verjuice (see Appendix 1)

Place the veal, turnip, and bouquet garni into a large pot. Cover with the wine. Add the mace, lemon, pepper, and butter and bring to a boil. Simmer gently until the veal is tender. In the last few minutes of cooking, stir in the sugar and verjuice. Place the contents in a soup tureen and serve.

# HOW TO BAKE VAUNTS

*A Book of Cookrye*, 1591

Titus: For worse than Philomel you used my Daughter,
  And worse then Progne, I will be reveng'd,
  And now prepare your throats: Lavinia come.
  Receive the blood, and when that they are dead,
  Let me goe grind their Bones to powder small,
  And with this hatefull Liquor temper it,
  And in that Paste let their vil'd Heads be bakte,
  Come, come, be every one officious,
  To make this Banquet, which I wish might prove,
  More sterne and bloody than the Centaures Feast.
  So now bring them in, for I'le play the Cooke,
  And see them ready, gainst their Mother comes. (*Titus Andronicus* 5.2.194–205)

Take the kidney of Veale and perboile it till it be tender, then take & chop it small with the yolkes of three or foure Egs, then season it with Dates small cut, small raisins, Ginger, Sugar, Sinamon, Saffron and a little Salte, and for the paste to laye it in, Take a dozen of Egs both the white and the yolkes, and beate them well togither, then take Butter and put it into a frying pan, and fry them as thin as a pancake, then lay your stuffe therin, and so frye them togither in a pan, then cast sugar and Ginger upon it, and so serve it forth.

## MODERN RECIPE                                      Makeability: 2

2 veal (or beef) kidneys

4 hard-boiled egg yolks, chopped

1/4 cup finely chopped dates

1/4 cup raisins

1 tsp minced ginger

1/2 tsp sugar

1/4 tsp cinnamon

1 pinch saffron

1/4 tsp salt

For the paste:

12 eggs

1 TBS unsalted butter

Gently simmer the kidneys in a saucepan with just enough water to cover until tender and cooked. Cool. Chop the kidneys into small pieces and mix with the egg yolks, dates, raisins, ginger, sugar, cinnamon, saffron, and salt. Heat the mixture gently and reserve. Beat one dozen eggs thoroughly. Melt the butter in a large frying pan and make one large "pancake," allowing it to cook for a couple of minutes. Distribute the kidney mixture onto the pancake and fry together until it sets. Sprinkle with sugar and ginger.

# TO MAKE A FRYCASE OF COLDE MUTTON OR VEALE

*A Book of Cookrye*, 1591

Shylock:  O father Abram, what these Christians are,
Whose owne hard dealings teaches them suspect
The thoughts of others: Praie you tell me this,
If he should breake his daie, what should I gaine
By the exaction of the forfeiture?
A pound of mans flesh taken from a man,
Is not so estimable, profitable neither
As flesh of Muttons, Beefes, or Goates. (*The Merchant of Venice* 1.3.159–166)

Chop flesh small and fry it in sweet butter, and then put thereto a little white wine, Salt, and Ginger, and serve it forth in faire dishes.

## MODERN RECIPE                                      Makeability: 1

2 lb veal cutlets, cooked and chilled

2 TBS unsalted butter

1 TBS minced ginger

1/4 cup white wine

1/4 tsp salt

Chop the cutlets into small pieces. Melt butter in a frying pan and sauté the veal over medium heat for two minutes. Add the ginger and salt and continue to cook another minute. Add the wine and simmer two or three minutes more.

# TO BAKE A NEATES TONGUE TO BE EATEN HOT

*A New Booke of Cookerie*, 1615

Gratiano: Well, keepe me company but two yeares mo,
Thou shalt not know the sound of thine owne tongue.
Antonio: Fare you well, I'le grow a talker for this geare.
Gratiano: Thankes i'faith, for silence is onely commendable
In a neats tongue dri'd, and a maid not vendible. (*The Merchant of Venice*
1.1.108–112)

*"Neat" was the usual name for cattle, both male or female; "cow" was reserved for the
female of the species. Gratiano's jest about the "neats tongue" implies that women who
are unmarketable (presumably because of their homeliness or because they are already married) should be silent, like the severed tongue of a cow.*

Boyle it tender, and pill off the skinne, take the flesh out at the but-end: mince it
small with Oxe suit, and marrow. Season it with Pepper, Salt, Nutmeg, parboyld
Currens, and a minced Date cut in pieces. Take the yolkes of two new layd Egges,
and a spoonefull of sweet Creame, worke all together with a silver spoone, in a Dish,
with a little powder of a dryed Orenge pill: sprinckle a little Vergis over it, and cast
on some Sugar. Then thrust it in againe as hard as you can cram it. Bake it on a
Dish in the oven: baste it with sweet Butter, that it may not bake drye on the outside: when it is to be eaten sawce it with Vinegar and Butter, Nutmeg, Sugar, and
the juyce of an Orenge.

---

 ## MODERN RECIPE                                             Makeability: 3

1 beef tongue

$^1/_2$ cup suet

$^1/_4$ cup marrow (substitute suet or butter)

$^1/_4$ tsp pepper

$^1/_2$ tsp each salt and nutmeg

$^1/_4$ cup parboiled currants

$^1/_4$ cup parboiled dates, minced

2 egg yolks

1 TBS 18% cream

1 TBS finely minced orange peel (powder if available)

1 TBS verjuice (see Appendix 1)

1 TBS sugar

$^1/_4$ cup melted unsalted butter

For the sauce:

1 tsp white vinegar

2 TBS butter

$^1/_2$ tsp nutmeg

juice of an orange

Preheat oven to 350°F. Cover the tongue with several quarts of water in a pot and bring it to a boil.
Reduce to a simmer and cook for 2 hours. Peel the skin back, keeping it whole. Allow to cool, cut
out the meat, removing any gristle, and mince finely. In a large mixing bowl, combine the tongue

*Continued on next page*

*Continued from previous page*

and suet and season with salt, pepper, currants, and dates. In a separate bowl, whisk together the egg yolks and cream and add to the tongue along with the orange peel. Sprinkle with the verjuice and sugar, and stuff the mixture back into the skin and place in a baking dish. Bake 30 minutes, or until thoroughly cooked. Baste with butter frequently. In the meantime, prepare the sauce by blending the vinegar, butter, nutmeg, and orange juice in a small saucepan. Spoon the sauce over the tongue and serve.

# A DELICATE CHEWIT

*A New Booke of Cookerie*, 1615

Sir Andrew:    Mee thinkes sometimes I have no more wit than a Christian, or an ordinary man has: but I am a great eater of beefe, and I beleeve that does harme to my wit. (*Twelfth Night* 1.3.82–85)

Parboyle a piece of a Legge of Veal, and being cold, mince it with Beefe Suit, and Marrow, and an Apple or a couple of Wardens: when you have minst it fine, put to a few parboyld Currins, six Dates minst, a piece of a preserved Orenge-pill minst, Marrow cut in little square pieces. Season all this with Pepper, Salt, Nutmeg, and a little Sugar: then put it into your Coffins, and so bake it. Before you close your Pye, sprinckle on a little Rosewater, and when they are baked shave on a little Sugar, and so serve it to the Table.

 ## MODERN RECIPE                          Makeability: 3

2 lb ground veal

1/2 cup beef suet

1 apple, peeled and chopped fine

1/4 cup parboiled currants

6 minced dates

2 TBS minced orange peels (preserved peel if available)

1/4 tsp each pepper and salt

1/2 tsp nutmeg

1/2 tsp sugar

2 TBS rosewater (see Appendix 1)

Pastry recipe "To make fine paste" on page 214, or buy premade pastry.

Prepare pastry shell and top. Preheat oven to 350°F. Sauté veal and drain. Return veal to the pan and add the suet, apple, currants, dates, and orange peel. Season with the pepper, salt, nutmeg, and sugar and cook a few minutes more. Fill the pastry shells and sprinkle on a few drops of rosewater before closing the shell with pastry. Bake for 35 to 40 minutes, or until cooked through and pastry is golden brown. Remove from the oven, sprinkle with sugar, and serve.

# FOR THE FILLETS OF A VEALE, SMOORED IN A FRYING-PANNE

*A New Booke of Cookerie, 1615*

Troilus:  She strokes his cheek.
Ulysses:  Come, come.
Troilus:  Nay, stay; by Jove, I will not speak a word:
There is between my will and all offences
A guard of patience. Stay a little while.
Thersites: How the devil luxury, with his fat
rump and potato finger, tickles these together!
Fry, lechery, fry! (*Troilus and Cressida* 5.2.51–58)

*The "olives" referred to in the original of this recipe are not the small green ovoids that are plunked into martinis or sliced and scattered on pizza. Rather, "olives" here is a variant of "olaves," which indicates a way of cutting meat into strips. As for the word "smoored," it denotes a method of stewing something in a closed vessel over a gentle fire (in Dutch, the word "smoor" means "to simmer"). One other recipe in this book also calls for smooring, namely, "To smoore a Chickin."*

Cut them as for Olives: hacke them with the backe of a Knife: then cut Larde fine, and larde them, then put them in a Frying-pan with strong Beere or Ale, and frye them somewhat browne: then put them into a pinte of Claret Wine, and boyle them with a little Sinamon, Sugar and Ginger.

---

 ## MODERN RECIPE                                    Makeability: 2

| | |
|---|---|
| 4 veal cutlets | 1 cinnamon stick |
| 4 TBS suet | 1 tsp sugar |
| 1/2 cup ale | 1 TBS ginger |
| 2 cups red wine | |

Pound the fillets to 1/8-inch thinness. Spread suet on each of the fillets and roll them, securing with a toothpick if needed. Over medium heat, lightly brown the fillets before adding the ale. Cook for 5 minutes before transferring the fillets to a saucepan of the wine. Add the cinnamon, sugar, and ginger. Bring to a boil, and let simmer gently for 10 minutes.

---

# TO MAKE A RARE CONCEIT WITH VEALE BAKED

*The Good Huswifes Handmaide for the Kitchin, 1594*

Horatio:  My Lord, I came to see your Fathers Funerall.
Hamlet:  I pray thee doe not mock me, fellow Student,
I thinke it was to see my Mothers Wedding.

Horatio:  Indeed my Lord, it followed hard upon.
Hamlet:  Thrift thrift Horatio: the Funerall Bakt-meats
        Did coldly furnish forth the Marriage Tables. (Hamlet 1.2.175–181)

*Although beef was deemed a hearty food for common laborers, veal was the preferred meat of the gentry who purchased cookery books. Thomas Twyne, in his 1576 Schoolemaster, wrote that veal "is good and holsome, as not having that sliminess and coldenesse which is in Beefe, and is more sweete both to the mouth and nose, than any other fleash."*

Take Veale and smite it in litle peeces, and seeth it in faire water, then take Parsley, Sage, Hope and Savorie, and shred them small, and put them in the pot when it boyleth. Take powder of Pepper, Canel, Mace, saffron, and salt, and let all these boyle together till it be ynough. Then take up the flesh from the broth, and let the broth coole, when it is colde, take the yolkes of Egges with the whites, and straine them, and put them into the broth, so manie till the broth be stiffe ynough, then make faire coffins, and couch three peeces or foure in one coffin of the Veale: and take Dates minsed again, and let it bake a good while, when it is baken drawe it foorth, & cast Sugar & Rosewater upon it, and serve it in.

 ## MODERN RECIPE                                 Makeability: 4

| | |
|---|---|
| 1 lb cubed veal | Pinch of saffron |
| 1/2 cup parsley | 1 tsp salt |
| 1/4 cup sage | 3 eggs (or as needed), lightly beaten |
| 1/4 cup hops | 1/4 cup finely chopped dates |
| 1/4 cup savory | Sugar |
| 1/4 tsp ground pepper | Rosewater (see Appendix 1) |
| 1/4 tsp cinnamon | Pastry recipe "To make fine paste" on page 214, or buy premade pastry. |
| 1 blade of whole mace | |

Prepare four pasty shells (and tops), about the size of a muffin. Preheat oven to 350°F. Place veal in a large pot with just enough water to cover and bring it to a boil. Skim as necessary. Add the herbs, pepper, cinnamon, mace, saffron, and salt and simmer gently for 5 to 7 minutes. Remove the veal and reserve. When the broth has cooled to room temperature, strain the eggs through a fine-meshed sieve and add to the broth until it thickens. Into each pastry shell, place three pieces of veal (less or more as appropriate), and add broth and dates. Cover and bake in a 350°F oven for 25 to 30 minutes. Remove and sprinkle with sugar and rosewater.

# TO MAKE A HUTCHPOT ON THE DUTCH FASHION

*A Delightfull Daily Exercise for Ladies and Gentlewomen*, 1621

Sly: I am Christophero Sly, call not mee Honour nor
Lordship: I ne're drank sacke in my life: and if you
give me any Conserves, give me conserves of Beefe:
nere ask me what raiment Ile weare, for I have no
more doublets then backes: no more stockings than
legges: nor no more shooes than feet, nay sometime
more feete than shooes, or such shooes as my toes looke
through the over-leather. (*The Taming of the Shrew*, Induction 2.5–12)

*A "hutchpot" was a dish made by mixing a medley of ingredients. Its name was a compound formed from the French "hocher," meaning "to shake together," and "pot." The word "hodgepodge" derives from the same source.*

Take seven or eight pieces of the best Beefe, and every piece as broad as your hand, and set them on the fire in two gallons of water, and then when they boyle skumme them, letting it stew halfe away: then take a good handfull of Parsley, two handfulls of Spinage, halfe a handfull of Savory and Thime stript, wring them betweene your hands once or twise, and when that is done throwe it into your meate, then put in three or foure whole onions Pepper, three or foure blades of Mace, and a little Salt, three or foure quartered Carrets, if the Carrets bee small you may then put in the more according to your owne judgement, and then let it boyle againe close covered till halfe be boyled away, then dish it upon sippets and poure your Carrets and Hearbes upon the toppe thereof, and then throw Salt upon it and so serve it to the Table hotte.

---

 ## MODERN RECIPE                                   Makeability: 2

8 slices, quarter-inch thick, inside eye of sir–loin round steak

1 cup parsley

2 cups spinach

1/2 cup savory

1/4 cup thyme

1/2 tsp cracked black pepper

4 blades of mace

3 medium whole onions

4 carrots, peeled and quartered

1 tsp salt

6 slices of toasted 60% whole wheat bread for sippets

In a large pot, bring to a boil about 3 quarts of water. Add the slices of beef and simmer for 20 to 30 minutes, or until the stock is reduced by half. Skim the water regularly. Rub the parsley, spinach, savory, and thyme between your hands to release the oils and put them in the pot along with the mace and pepper. Add the onions and carrots and simmer until the carrots and onions are soft and the stock has further reduced. Arrange the sippets on a plate and add the stewed beef slices. Spoon out the carrots, onions, and herbs onto the beef, sprinkle with salt and serve.

# TO ROAST OLAVES OF VEAL

*The English Huswife, 1615*

| | |
|---|---|
| Katharine: | "Veale," quoth the Dutch-man: is not Veale a Calfe? |
| Longaville: | A Calfe, faire Ladie? |
| Katharine: | No, a faire Lord Calfe. |
| Longaville: | Let's part the word. |
| Katharine: | No, I'le not be your halfe: |
| | Take all and weane it, it may prove an Oxe. |
| Longaville: | Looke how you butt your selfe in these sharpe mockes. |
| | Will you give hornes, chast Ladie? Do not so. |
| Katharine: | Then die a Calfe before your horns do grow. (*Love's Labour's Lost* 5.2.248–254) |

*In the quotation from* Love's Labour's Lost, *Katharine and Longaville engage in pun-filled banter. Katharine begins by saying "veal," which is how a person with a Dutch accent would pronounce the word "well," a pun that may have been inspired by the resemblance of "veal" to the last syllable of Longaville's name. When Longaville says "A Calfe, faire ladie," Katharine replies by inverting his response so that she effectively calls him "a faire Lord Calfe." He then asks if they can come to some compromise—"Let's part the word"— but she refuses, and again mocks him by implying that he will mature from a calf to an ox, that is, from a little stupid animal to a big stupid animal. Longaville protests against Katharine's barbs—her "hornes"—but she warns him that his only hope of avoiding horns (which were a symbol of cuckoldry) is to die before he acquires them.*

You shall take a legge of Veal, and cut the flesh from the bones, and cut it out into thin long slices, then take sweete hearbes and the white part of Scallions, and chop them well together with the yolkes of eggs, then rowle it up within the slices of Veale, and so spit them and roast them; then boile verjuyce, butter, sugar, cinnamon, Currants, and sweet hearbes together, and being seasoned with a little salt, serve the Olives up upon the sawce with salt cast over them.

---

 ## MODERN RECIPE                                    Makeability: 2

| | |
|---|---|
| 4 veal cutlets | 1/4 cup olive oil |
| 1 tsp chopped basil | 1/4 cup verjuice (see Appendix 1) |
| 1 tsp chopped parsley | 1/2 cup butter |
| 1 tsp chopped marjoram | 1 TBS sugar |
| 1 tsp thyme | 1/2 tsp cinnamon |
| 1 TBS finely chopped scallions | 1/4 cup currants |
| 2 hard-boiled egg yolks, chopped | 1/2 tsp salt |

Pound the cutlets to 1/8-inch thickness. Mix together the herbs, scallions, and egg yolks into a stuffing. Place stuffing onto each cutlet and roll the cutlets securing with a skewer or toothpick. Place the cutlets in a baking dish and brush lightly with olive oil. Bake at 350°F for 15 to 20 minutes, turning occasionally. In the meantime, for the sauce, heat the verjuice and butter in a saucepan and add the sugar, cinnamon, currants, and salt. Simmer gently. To present the dish, pour the sauce onto a plate and arrange the cutlets on top. Sprinkle with salt to taste before serving.

# HOW TO MAKE CHUETS

*A Book of Cookrye*, 1591

King Henry: You have not sought it: how comes it then?
Falstaff: Rebellion lay in his way, and he found it.
Prince: Peace, Chewet, peace. (*1 Henry IV* 5.1.27–29)

*A chuet, or chewet, was a pie that was small in diameter but tall in height—that is, it was rather cylindrical in shape. In this passage from* 1 Henry IV, *the Prince uses the word to address Falstaff much as one might call a sweetheart a "sugarpie." In calling Falstaff a "chewet," the Prince might also be alluding to the gluttonous nature of his friend, but in fact "chewet" is not connected to the word "chew."*

Take Veale and perboyle it and chop it very fine, take beefe Suet and mince it fine, then take Prunes, Dates and Corance, wash them very clean and put them into your meat, then take Cloves, Mace, and pepper to season your meat withal and a little quantity of salt, vergious and Sugar, two ounces of biskets, and as many of Carowaies, this is the seasoning of your meat, then take fine flowre, yolkes of Egs, and butter, a little quantitye of rosewater and sugar, then make little coffins for your Chewets and let them bake a quarter of an houre, then wet them over with butter, then strewe on Sugar and wet the Sugar with a little Rosewater, and set them into the Oven again, then take and serve five in a dish.

 **MODERN RECIPE**            Makeability: 3

2 lb ground veal

1/2 cup suet

1/4 cup chopped prunes

1/4 cup chopped dates

1/4 cup currants

1/2 tsp ground cloves

1/2 tsp ground mace

1/4 tsp cracked black pepper

1/4 tsp salt

1/4 cup verjuice (see Appendix 1)

1 tsp sugar

2 oz biskets (see recipe for "To make English Bisket" on page 237, or substitute two dry ginger snap cookies)

2 oz caraway seeds

1/4 cup melted butter

Sugar

Rosewater

Pastry recipe "To make fine paste" on page 214, or buy premade pastry.

*Continued on next page*

*Continued from previous page*

Prepare a pastry shell and top. Preheat oven to 350°F. Mix together all the ingredients except for the butter, sugar, and rosewater. Fill the pastry shells with the veal mixture and cover with pastry. Place in a 350°F oven and bake for 20 minutes. Remove and brush with melted butter and return to oven. Remove after a further 10 minutes, sprinkle with sugar and rosewater, and return to the oven for 5 minutes to finish.

# A FLORENTINE OF VEALE

*A New Booke of Cookerie*, 1615

Macbeth: Me thought I heard a voyce cry, "Sleep no more:
Macbeth does murther Sleepe," the innocent Sleepe,
Sleepe that knits up the ravel'd Sleeve of Care,
The death of each dayes Life, sore Labors Bath,
Balme of hurt Mindes, great Natures second Course,
Chiefe nourisher in Life's Feast. (*Macbeth* 2.2.39–44)

*In the preceding quotation, Macbeth suggests that the second course of a feast is the more substantial one, the "chief nourisher" of the meal. The feast menus of the day, however, seem to indicate that the first and second courses were similar with regard to their number and kinds of dishes. Macbeth may, in fact, be thinking of the salads—which often preceded the meal proper—as the first course, which would indeed seem meagre compared to the myriad of meat dishes that appeared with the subsequent courses.*

Mince colde Veale fine, take grated Bread, Currins, Dates, Sugar, Nutmeg, Pepper, two or three Egges, and Rosewater: mingle all well together, and put it on a Chafing-dish of coles, stirre them till they be warme, and then put some betweene two sheetes of puft-paste, and bake it, put the rest upon slices of a white loafe and frye it in a Frying-pan, washt before with the yolke of an Egge: serve it with Sinamon and Ginger, at the second course.

---

 ## MODERN RECIPE                                    Makeability: 2

| | |
|---|---|
| 2 lb ground veal, cooked and cooled | 2 TBS rosewater |
| 1/2 cup bread crumbs | 4 to 6 slices of 60% whole wheat bread |
| 1/4 cup currants | 3 egg yolks for egg wash |
| 1/4 cup roughly chopped dates | 2 TBS cup cinnamon |
| 1 tsp sugar | 1/4 cup grated ginger |
| 1 tsp nutmeg | Puff pastry recipe "To make puffe paste" on |
| 1/4 tsp cracked black pepper | page 213, or buy premade puff pastry. |
| 3 eggs | |

Preheat the oven to 425°F. Prepare a puff pastry. In a mixing bowl, combine veal, bread crumbs, currants, dates, sugar, nutmeg, pepper, eggs, and rosewater. Cook the mixture gently in a frying pan until just warm and integrated. In a loaf pan, spoon most of the veal mixture onto the puff pastry and place in the oven. Turn the heat down to 350°F and bake about 30 minutes (or according to the packaged pastry instructions). Dip the slices of bread into the egg yolk and place in a frying pan. Add the remaining veal mixture to the bread and fry, topping with the cinnamon and ginger.

# TO MAKE BALLES OF ITALIE

*The Good Huswifes Handmaide for the Kitchin, 1594*

Clown:                          Let mee see,
        what am I to buy for our Sheepe-shearing-Feast? Three
        pound of Sugar, five pound of Currence, Rice: What
        will this sister of mine do with Rice? But my father hath
        made her Mistris of the Feast, and she layes it on. Shee
        hath made-me four and twenty Nose-gayes for the shearers
        (three-man song-men, all, and very good ones)
        but they are most of them Meanes and Bases; but one
        Puritan amongst them, and he sings Psalmes to horne-pipes.
        I must have Saffron to colour the Warden Pies,
        Mace: Dates, none: that's out of my note: Nutmegges,
        seven; a Race or two of Ginger, but that I may begge:
        Foure pound of Prewyns, and as many of Reysons o'th Sun. (*The Winter's Tale*
        4.3.36–50)

*In this passage from* The Winter's Tale, *the Clown—the kind of character that we would now call a country bumpkin—expresses surprise that his sister has asked him to buy rice. His consternation reflects the fact that rice was a relatively uncommon ingredient: only twenty of the 2,100 recipes that were published in this period call for that grain, which was usually imported from Spain.*

Take a peece of a legge of Veale, parboyle it, then pare away all the skin and sinewes and chop the Veale verie small, a litle salt and pepper, two yolks of Egges hard rosted, and seven yolkes rawe, temper all these with your Veale, then make balles thereof as big as walnuts, and boyle them in beefe broth, or mutton broth, as ye did the other before rehearsed, and put into your broth ten beaten cloves, a race of Ginger, a litle Vergious, foure or five lumpes of marrowe whole, let them stew the space of an howre. Then serve them upon sops, eight or nine in a dish, and betwixt the balles you must lay the lumps of marrow.

## MODERN RECIPE                                        Makeability: 2

2 lb ground beef (or veal)                2 TBS salt
3 quarts beef broth                       1/2 tsp pepper

*Continued on next page*

*Continued from previous page*

| | |
|---|---|
| 2 hard-boiled egg yolks | $^1/_2$ cup verjuice (see Appendix 1) |
| 7 egg yolks | Marrow (substitute suet or butter) |
| 10 whole cloves, lightly cracked | 60% lightly toasted whole wheat bread for sippets |
| 2 TBS minced ginger | |

Bring the beef broth to a gentle boil. In a large mixing bowl, gently combine the beef, salt, pepper, and eggs. Mix the meat gently and form meatballs about the size of a walnut. Place the meatballs in the broth and add the cloves, verjuice, and marrow. Simmer for about an hour. On platters, place 8 or 9 meatballs on sippets with pieces of marrow between.

# TO STEW FILLETS OF BEEFE

*A Delightfull Daily Exercise for Ladies and Gentlewomen, 1621*

Hamlet:                               Nay, but to live
In the ranke sweat of an enseamed bed,
Stew'd in Corruption; honying and making love
Over the nasty Stye. (*Hamlet* 3.4.93–96)

*In Shakespeare's time, a cook could make "stew" but not "soup." The latter word didn't appear in English until the middle of the seventeenth century. In Shakespeare's plays, most of his references to "stews" are to brothels, so called because they often housed hot tubs where individuals afflicted with venereal disease could try (vainly) to sweat out their infection.*

Take a rawe fillet of beefe and cut it in thin slices halfe as broad as your hand and fry them till they bee halfe fried in a frying-panne with sweete butter upon each side with a soaft fire, then powre them into a dish or pipkin putting in a pint of claret-wine, a faggot of sweete hearbes, and two or three blades of whole mace, and a little salt, the meate of a Lemon cut in slices, then stewe these all together very softly for the space of two or three houres till it be halfe boyled away, then dish it upon sippets and throwe salt upon it, and serve it to the table hot.

 ## MODERN RECIPE                                     Makeability: 2

| | |
|---|---|
| 2 lb rib eye roast | 1 TBS salt |
| 2 TBS unsalted butter | 1 lemon, peeled, pith removed, and sliced |
| 2 cups red wine | Beef broth or water |
| Bouquet garni of rosemary, thyme, and sage | 60% lightly toasted whole wheat bread for sippets |
| 3 blades of mace | |

Cut the roast into slices ¼ inch thick and about 2 inches wide. Heat the butter in a large frying pan, searing all sides of the beef fillets but not cooking them through. Place the beef into a large enough pot (or a large heavy skillet) with the red wine, bouquet garni, mace, salt, and lemon. Bring to a boil and let simmer for 2½ hours. Add beef broth or water as the liquid reduces. Arrange the sippets on a large platter and cover with the fillets. Sprinkle with salt and serve.

# TO BOILE A BREAST OF VEALE

*Elinor Fettiplace's Receipt Book*, 1604

Therefore are feasts so solemn and so rare,
Since seldom coming in that long year set,
Like stones of worth they thinly placed are,
Or captain jewels in the carcanet. (Sonnet 52, 5–8)

*The printers who made the cookery books from which we've drawn our recipes tended to use the word "and" and the ampersand (the "&" symbol) interchangeably. That is, there doesn't seem to be any rhyme or reason as to when they used one and when they used the other. For the most part, however, they favored the word "and": two-thirds of the 2,100 recipes from the period don't use the ampersand at all, and those that do tend to use it less frequently than "and." This recipe is rather unique in reversing that pattern: it contains thirteen ampersands and just one "and," which might lead us to wonder why. Was the typesetter trying to save space? Was he running out of "a"s or "n"s or "d"s? Was he trying to save time by grabbing the one-piece ampersand rather than the three pieces of type needed to compose the word "and"? We'll never know.*

First boile the veale, in water with a bundle of good herbs, untill it bee very tender, then take some of that broth, & some tyme & parselie, & marjerome & spinage, & a little winter saverie, & the yelks of three hard eggs, chop the herbs and the eggs together, & put it into the broth with some whole mace, let the broth bee very thick with herbs, let it boile all together, till it bee boyled inough, then when you dish up the veale, you must take some vineger & butter & sugar & put it in the dishe wherin you serve it, & warme it, & so with the herbs upon the veale serve it, you must lay some capers in warme water, & lay them on the veale.

 ## MODERN RECIPE                                    Makeability: 2

| | |
|---|---|
| 1 veal breast roast (or blade roast) | ½ cup chopped parsley |
| 1 bouquet garni of parsley, rosemary, and bay leaf | 2 TBS marjoram |
| 1 TBS thyme | ½ cup spinach |

*Continued on next page*

*Continued from previous page*

| | |
|---|---|
| 2 TBS savory | 5 TBS unsalted butter |
| 3 hard-boiled egg yolks, chopped | 1 tsp sugar |
| 3 blades of mace | $1/2$ cup capers |
| 2 TBS red wine vinegar | |

In a large pot, place the veal along with the bouquet garni and bring to a boil. Reduce the heat and simmer until tender, about an hour. When the veal is done, put 2 cups of the veal broth in a saucepan and add the thyme, parsley, marjoram, spinach, savory, egg yolks, and mace. Cook until thick. Using a small saucepan, heat the vinegar, butter, and sugar. Heat the capers in warm water. Cover a platter with the vinegar-butter, on which to place the veal. Spoon the herb and egg sauce on the veal and top with capers.

# TO MAKE MINST PYES

*The Good Houswives Treasure, 1588*

Pandarus: Well, well! Why, have you any discretion?
Have you any eyes? Do you know what a man is? Is
not birth, beauty, good shape, discourse, manhood,
learning, gentleness, virtue, youth, liberality, and such like,
the spice and salt that season a man?
Cressida: Ay, a minc'd man; and then to be bak'd
with no date in the pie, for then the man's date is out. (*Troilus and Cressida* 1.2.253–259)

*As Cressida knows, recipes for minced pies (including the one below) usually called for dates. Accordingly, when she responds to Pandarus by saying that his description of the ideal man is like a mince pie made without dates, she is suggesting that such a man lacks something essential. Additionally, she is making a pun on "date," suggesting that such a man would be "out of date," that is, a kind of fossil.*

Take your Veale and perboyle it a little, or mutton, then set it a cooling: and when it is colde, take three pound of suit to a legge of mutton, or fower pound to a fillet of Veale, and then mince them small by themselves, or together whether you will, then take to season them halfe an unce of Sinamon, a little Pepper, as much Salt as you think will season them, either to the mutton or to the Veale, take eight yolkes of Egges when they be hard, half a pinte of rosewater full measure, halfe a pound of Suger, then straine the Yolkes with the Rosewater and the Suger and mingle it with your meate. If ye have any Orrenges or Lemmans you must take two of them, and take the pilles very thin and mince them very smalle, and put them in a pound of currans, six dates, half a pound of prunes laye Currans and Dates upon the top of your meate. You must take two or three Pomewaters or Wardens and mince with your meate, you maye make them woorsse if you will, if you will make good crust put in three or foure yolkes of egges, a little Rosewater, and a good deale of Suger.

## MODERN RECIPE                                        Makeability: 3

| | |
|---|---|
| 2 lb ground veal | $1/2$ cup sugar |
| 1 cup suet | 1 peel of orange, minced |
| 2 finely chopped apples | 1 peel of lemon, minced |
| 1 TBS cinnamon | $1/2$ cup currants |
| $1/2$ tsp cracked black pepper | 6 chopped dates |
| 1 tsp salt | $1/2$ cup chopped prunes |
| 8 hard-boiled egg yolks | Pastry recipe "To make fine paste" on page |
| 1 cup rosewater (see Appendix 1) | 214, or buy premade pastry. |

Prepare a 9-inch pastry shell and top. Preheat oven to 350°F. Sauté veal until cooked and drain. In a large mixing bowl, combine the suet, apples, cinnamon, salt, and pepper. Sauté the mixture over medium-high heat for a few minutes. Into a separate bowl, force the egg yolks through a fine-meshed strainer and add the rosewater and sugar. Whisk vigorously and stir into the veal. Cook a few minutes more. Place the veal mixture into the pastry shell. Combine the minced orange and lemon peel with the currants, dates, and prunes and spread this on top of the veal mixture. Cover the pie with pastry and bake at 350°F for 35 to 40 minutes, or until pastry is golden brown.

# 4

# MUTTON AND LAMB

Touchstone: That is another simple sinne in you, to bring the Ewes
and the Rammes together, and to offer to get your
living, by the copulation of Cattle, to be bawd to a
Belwether, and to betray a shee-Lambe of a
Twelvemonth to a crooked-pated olde Cuckoldly Ramme,
out of all reasonable match. If thou bee'st not
damn'd for this, the divell himselfe will have no
shepherds, I cannot see else how thou shouldst scape. (*As You Like It*
3.2.76–83)

Mutton and lamb differ with regard to the age of the sheep from which they are derived: meat from a sheep that is less than a year old is lamb, whereas meat from a sheep that is more than a year old is mutton. In England and Australia there would be no need to mention the difference between mutton and lamb. But in North America, "sheepmeat" is little known, having gradually fallen out of favor since the 1940s. In the United States, the annual consumption of sheepmeat is now less than one pound per person, whereas annual pork consumption is just under 50 pounds. In the United Kingdom, the ratio is not quite as lopsided: about 14 pounds of sheepmeat per person annually, versus about 50 pounds of pork per person. However, in Shakespeare's England, that ratio was reversed, at least for those who could afford to eat whatever meat they wanted. For example, in 1591 the royal household of Queen Elizabeth—which accommodated between 1,000 and 1,500 people—consumed 8,200 sheep but only 1,870 pigs (in addition to 2,330 deer, 1,240 oxen, and 760 calves). That ratio is echoed in the cookery books: about 170 of the 2,100 recipes that were published in this period mention sheepmeat, whereas fewer than 80 call for pork (including ham, bacon, pig's feet, and so on). Moreover, of the 170 recipes from Shakespeare's England that involve sheepmeat, the vast majority (155) call for mutton, which has a strong flavor, rather than lamb (15), which has a mild flavor. This is in stark contrast to the United States where, of the meager amount of sheepmeat that is consumed, most of it is lamb rather than mutton. In fact, unless you live in one of a handful of small regions (such as western Kentucky, where mutton remains popular), you'll be hard pressed to find a grocery store or butcher who sells mutton. For that reason, we've substituted lamb in all of the mutton recipes we've included, but you can certainly revert to mutton if you can find a local source.

With regard to sheepmeat, Shakespeare's contemporaries considered mutton from a female sheep (a ewe) or from a castrated male sheep (a wether) to be preferable to that of an uncastrated male sheep (a ram). Edward Topsell, however, in his 1607 *Historie of Foure-Footed Beastes*, describes a ruse by which the less desirable ram's flesh was sold (illegally) as expensive venison. The live ram was shorn of its wool, then beaten and whipped until its flesh grew red. This abuse would cause the flesh of the creature, after it was finally slaughtered, to resemble that of a deer. Topsell expresses revulsion at such "cruel meates" and compares the abuse of the ram to what "Pilate did with Christ, who was first of all whipped and crowned with thornes, and yet afterward did crucifie him."

Sheep were prized not just for their flesh, but also for their wool. By the late sixteenth century, wool made up two-thirds of England's exports (much of it went to Holland, where it was finished into various textiles). Because the wool trade was profitable, the crown attempted to control who was allowed to buy and sell that product, which led to Shakespeare's father being charged in 1572 when he illegally bought about three tons of wool with the intention of selling it at a higher price. The skin of sheep was also used to make parchment (as Hamlet notes at 5.1.112), but it began to be superceded by paper in the sixteenth century.

In contrast with sheep, which outnumbered people three to one in Shakespeare's England, goats were relatively uncommon. Gervase Markham, for one, noted in 1614 that "goates are not of any generall use in our Kingdome, but onely nourished in some wilde and barraine places ... as in the mountainous parts of Wales." Not surprisingly, therefore, only a handful of the 2,100 recipes that were published in England in this period mention goat flesh—specifically, kid, which is a goat less than six months old—and most of those are in *Epulario*, whose recipes originated in Italy.

This had not always been the case, for goat meat had been popular up until the end of the Middle Ages. Perhaps it was the goat's sinister associations that led to its demise. For one thing, it was associated with lechery, as when Iago implies that Desdemona and Cassio are "as prime as goats, as hot as monkeys." The randy mythological creature known as the satyr was likewise half goat. Moreover, Ben Jonson, in a footnote he supplied for *The Masque of Queens*, suggested that "the goat is the devill himselfe," an identification that King James had also made in his 1597 treatise on witches called *Daemonology*.

# TO MAKE SPECIAL GOOD PIES EITHER OF MUTTON OR VEALE

*The Good Huswifes Handmaide for the Kitchin*, 1594

Buckingham: The divell speed him: No mans Pye is freed
From his Ambitious finger. (*Henry VIII* 1.1.52–53)

*In the quotation from* Henry VIII, *the reference to a pie being violated by an overly ambitious finger recalls the nursery rhyme about Little Jack Horner sticking his thumb into a Christmas pie in order to pull out a plum. Both the quotation and the nursery rhyme may* be alluding to Thomas Horner who, according to legend, plucked a land title out of a Christmas pie, where it had been hidden by the Abbot of Glastonbury in an attempt to keep Henry VIII from finding and claiming it.

Let your meat bee perboyled, and mince it verie fine, and then your suet by it selfe: and after put to the meat, and mince them well together, then put thereto five or six yolkes of Egs, being hard sodden and minced, smal Corrans, Dates fine minced: season it with Synamon, ginger, Cloves, and Mace, a handful of Carowayes, Sugar and Vergious, and some salt and a litle Pepper, and so put it into your paste, whether they be Chewets or Trunk pies.

---

 ## MODERN RECIPE                                    Makeability: 3

| | |
|---|---|
| 2 lb ground lamb | 1/4 tsp ground mace |
| 1 cup ground suet | 2 TBS caraway seeds |
| 6 hard-boiled egg yolks | 1 tsp sugar |
| 1/2 cup currants | 1/4 cup verjuice (see Appendix 1) |
| 1/2 cup finely chopped dates | 1/2 tsp salt |
| 1/2 tsp cinnamon | 1/4 tsp cracked black pepper |
| 1/2 tsp ginger | Pastry recipe "To make fine paste" on page 214, or buy premade pastry. |
| 1/4 tsp ground cloves | |

Prepare a pastry shell and top. Preheat oven to 350°F. In a mixing bowl, combine the lamb, suet, and egg yolks and cook in a large pan for about 10 minutes. Pour into the pastry shell, cover with pastry, and bake for 35 to 40 minutes, or until pastry is golden brown.

---

# TO DRESS A SHOWLDER OF MUTTON

*Elinor Fettiplace's Receipt Book, 1604*

Iago: Zounds, Sir, y'are rob'd, for shame put on your Gowne,
    Your heart is burst, you have lost halfe your soule.
    Even now, now, very now, an old blacke Ram
    Is tupping your white Ewe. (*Othello* 1.1.88–91)

Take a showlder of mutton and beinge halfe Roasted, Cut it in great slices and save the gravie then take Clarret wine and sinamond & suger with a little Cloves and mace beaten and the pill of an oringe Cut thin and minced very smale. Put the mutton the gravie and these thinges together and boyle yt Betweene two dishes, wringe the Juice of an oringe into yt as yt boyleth, when yt is boyled enough lay the bone of the mutton beinge first Broyled in the dish with it. Then Cut slices of limonds and lay on the mutton and so serve yt in.

## MODERN RECIPE

Makeability: 3

1 shoulder roast (or boneless shoulder roast)

1 bottle red Bordeaux wine

1 tsp cinnamon

1 TBS sugar

1/2 tsp ground cloves

1/2 tsp ground mace

Peel of one orange, minced

Juice of one orange

1 lemon cut into slices

Preheat oven to 450°F. Place the lamb in the preheated oven and immediately turn the heat down to 325°F. Calculating 30 minutes to the pound, roast the lamb until it is half done. Cut the roast into half-inch slices, retaining all the liquid in a large pot. Add the slices of lamb and cover with the wine. Add the cinnamon, sugar, cloves, mace, and orange peel and bring to a boil, covering it with a lid. Add the orange juice. Cook just until tender. Arrange the slices on a platter, spoon on the gravy, and garnish with lemon slices.

# TO MAKE A STEW AFTER THE GUISE OF BEYONDE THE SEA

*A Propre New Booke of Cokery, 1545*

Capulet:  So many guests invite as here are writ,
            Sirrah, go hire me twenty cunning Cookes.
Servant:  You shall have none ill sir, for I'le trie if
            they can licke their fingers.
Capulet:  How canst thou trie them so?
Servant:  Marrie sir, 'tis an ill Cooke that cannot licke
            his owne fingers: therefore he that cannot licke his
            fingers goes not with me. (*Romeo and Juliet* 4.2.1–8)

Take a pottell of fayre water, and as muche wyne & a brest of mutton chopt in peces, than set it on the fyre & scome it clene, than put thereto a disshe ful of sliced onions and a quantite of synamon, gynger, Cloves and Mace, with salte and stew them all togither, and than serve them with soppes.

## MODERN RECIPE

Makeability: 2

2 lb lamb stew cubes

2 cups red or white wine

1 large onion, sliced in rings

1 tsp cinnamon

1 tsp ginger

6 cloves

3 blades of mace, minced

1 tsp salt

6 slices of lightly toasted 60% whole wheat bread for sippets

*Continued on next page*

*Continued from previous page*

In a large saucepan, pour the wine over the lamb and add water to just cover the meat. Bring to a boil and skim when necessary. Add the remaining ingredients and simmer gently for 2 to 2$^1$/$_2$ hours until tender. Add more wine as the liquid reduces if needed. Arrange the sippets on a platter and top with the stew.

# OF THE TOASTING OF MUTTON

*The English Huswife*, 1615

First Servingman:                                   He was too hard for him directly,
                            to say the Troth on't before Corioles; he scotcht him,
                            and notcht him like a Carbinado.
Second Servingman:   And hee had bin Cannibally given,
                            hee might have boyld and eaten him too. (*Coriolanus* 4.5.194–198)

*The 1615 version of this recipe says that the meat should be "scorcht"; the same recipe, however, in a 1685 edition of the same book, has "scotcht," which is probably what the recipe actually intends. Scotching refers to the technique of slicing or slashing a joint of meat, either to allow the heat to penetrate more deeply into the flesh or to allow the juices of the meat to exude more easily. That such a technique was associated with carbonados— that is, with grilled or broiled meat—is affirmed by the quotation from Coriolanus, where the General is said to have been "scotched" like a carbonado.*

Touching the toasting of Mutton, Venison, or anie joint of meate which is the most excellentest of all Carbonadoes; you shall take the fattest and the largest that can possibly be got: for leane meat is losse of labour, and little meate not worth your time, and having scorcht it and cast salt upon it, you shall set it on a strong forke with a dripping panne underneath it, before the face of a quick fire; yet so farre off that it may be no meanes scorch but toast at leasure, then with that which falls from it and with no other basting see that you baste it continually, turning it ever and anon many times, and so oft that it may soake and browne at great leasure, and as oft as you baste it so oft sprinkle Salt upon it, and as you see it toast so scorch it deeper and deeper; especially in the thickest and most fleshy parts where the blood most resteth; and when you see that no more blood droppeth from it but the gravy is cleere and white, then you shall serve it up either with Venison sauce, or with Vinegar, Pepper and Sugar, Cinnamon, and the juice of an Orenge mixt together, and warmed with some of the gravie.

---

 ## MODERN RECIPE                                   Makeability: 3

1 leg of lamb                              1 tsp sugar

$^1$/$_4$ cup salt                           $^1$/$_2$ tsp cinnamon

$^1$/$_4$ cup vinegar                        Juice of 1 orange

$^1$/$_2$ tsp fresh-cracked black pepper

Sprinkle the leg with salt and arrange on the barbecue rotisserie with a pan to catch drippings. Roast the lamb, basting it regularly with the drippings and sprinkling frequently with salt. Cook until the internal temperature of the lamb reaches 145°F. Let the meat rest covered. Scrape the pan drippings into a saucepan on the stove and heat. Add the vinegar, salt, pepper, cinnamon, and orange juice and simmer. Arrange the lamb on a platter and pour on the gravy. If not barbecuing, roast the leg of lamb in a heavy pan in an oven preheated to 450°F. Put the leg in, reduce heat to 325°F, and roast until done. Prepare the gravy as before.

# TO MAKE PEARES TO BE BOILED IN MEATE

*The Second Part of the Good Hus-wives Jewell, 1597*

Falstaff:                     I warrant
    they would whip me with their fine wits, till I were as
    crest-falne as a dride-peare: I never prosper'd, since I
    forswore my selfe at Primero: well, if my winde were but
    long enough; I would repent. (*The Merry Wives of Windsor* 4.5.93–97)

Take a peece of a legge of Mutton or Veale raw, being mixed with a little Sheepe sewet, and halfe a manchet grated fine, taking foure raw egges yolkes and al. Then take a little time, & parsely chopped smal, then take a few gooseberies or barberies, or greene grapes being whole. Put all these together, being seasoned with Salte, saffron and cloves, beaten and wrought altogether, then make Rowles or Balles like to a peare, and when you have so done, take the stalke of the sage, and put it into the ends of your peares or balles, then take the freshe broth of beefe, Mutton or veale, being put into an earthen pot, putting the peares or balles in the same broth with salt, cloves, mace and Saffron, and when you be ready to serve him, put two or three yolkes of egs into the broth. Let them boile no more after that but serve it forth upon soppes. You may make balles after the same sorte.

 MODERN RECIPE          Makeability: 4

2 lb ground lamb

1 cup mutton suet (substitute beef suet)

1 cup bread crumbs

4 eggs

2 TBS thyme

2 TBS parsley

1/2 cup chopped barberries (see Appendix 1)

1 tsp salt

1 pinch saffron

1/4 tsp ground cloves

Sage stalks as needed

For the broth:

8 cups mutton broth (substitute beef broth)

1 TBS salt

3 whole cloves

*Continued on next page*

*Continued from previous page*

3 blades of whole mace

1 pinch of saffron

3 egg yolks

Slices of lightly toasted 60% whole wheat bread for sippets

In a large mixing bowl, combine the lamb, suet, bread crumbs, eggs, barberries, and spices. Work the meat into a paste and form pear-shaped balls. Insert a bit of sage stalk into the top of the pear. In a large pot, bring to a boil the broth seasoned with the salt, cloves, mace, and saffron. Slip in the lamb "pears." Simmer gently for 30 to 35 minutes or until tender and cooked through. Turn off the heat and add the eggs. Arrange the sippets on a platter, add the lamb pears, and pour on a few ladles of broth.

# TO HASH A SHOULDER OF MUTTON, OR A LEGGE OF LAMBE

*A New Booke of Cookerie*, 1615

| | |
|---|---|
| Petruchio: | Come Kate sit downe, I know you have a stomacke. Will you give thankes, sweete Kate, or else shall I? What's this, Mutton? |
| First Servant: | Aye. |
| Petruchio: | Who brought it? |
| Peter: | I. |
| Petruchio: | 'Tis burnt, and so is all the meate: What dogges are these? Where is the rascall Cooke? How durst you villaines bring it from the dresser And serve it thus to me that love it not? There, take it to you, trenchers, cups, and all: You heedlesse jolt-heads, and unmanner'd slaves. (*The Taming of the Shrew* 4.1.146–154) |

*A number of the mutton and poultry recipes included in this book call for barberries, a tart red berry that grows on an evergreen shrub (Berberis vulgaris), varieties of which are indigenous to every continent except Australia and Antarctica. Although barberry shrubs are often grown as ornamental plants, finding a store that sells the berries may be difficult. They are often used in Iranian cooking, so you may be able to find them in a Persian food market. In appearance and flavor, barberries resemble red currants, which can be used as a substitute. Incidentally, in the recipe, the phrase "if you want Oysters" means "if you lack Oysters."*

Take your meat off the Spit, and hash it into a Pewter Dish: put in some Rennish Wine, Razins of the Sunne, sliced Lemmon, raw Oysters: put them altogether into a Pipkin, and stirre them. If you want Oysters, and Razins, then take two Onyons whole, put them into the meat. If you want Wine, take strong broth, Vergis, and Sugar. Throw a few Barberryes into the Dish, and serve it on toasts or sippets.

## MODERN RECIPE                                    Makeability: 2

1 cooked boneless shoulder of lamb or leg of lamb

1 cup red wine

1/2 cup raisins

1 lemon sliced

12 raw oysters

1/2 cup barberries (see Appendix 1)

6 slices of lightly toasted 60% whole wheat bread for sippets

Chop the meat into a fine hash and put into a saucepan. Add the wine, raisins, lemon, and oysters and heat to a gentle simmer. Add the barberries and serve the hash on sippets. Broth, verjuice, and sugar may be substituted for wine. Onions may be substituted for raisins and oysters.

# TO BOYLE A LAMBES HEAD AND PURTENANCE

*The Good Huswifes Jewell, 1596*

Elizabeth:  No doubt the murd'rous Knife was dull and blunt,
          Till it was whetted on thy stone-hard heart,
          To revell in the Intrailes of my Lambes. (*Richard III* 4.4.227–229)

*The "purtenance" of an animal is its edible innards, such as the heart, liver, and lungs. In a curious analogy, John Foxe, in his 1583* Actes and Monuments, *compares a Christian's belief in Christ to eating a lamb's head and purtenance: "We doe eate the lambes head, when wee take holde of Christes divinitie in our beliefe…. What bee the lambes purtenaunce but Christes secrete precepts, and these we eate when we receive … the word of life."*

Straine your broth into a pipkin, and set it on the fire, and put in butter, and skumme it as cleane as you can, and put in your meate, and put in endive, and cut it a little, and straine a little yeast and put into it, and currans and prunes, and put in all maner of spices, and so serve it upon soppes.

## MODERN RECIPE                                    Makeability: 5

1 lamb's head and variety meats

4 quarts mutton or beef broth

1/2 lb unsalted butter

1 roughly chopped endive

2 packets active dry yeast

1 cup currants

1 cup roughly chopped prunes

3 blades of mace

*Continued on next page*

*Continued from previous page*

6 cloves

1 tsp nutmeg

1 tsp cinnamon

Salt and pepper to taste

Slices of lightly toasted 60% whole wheat bread for sippets

In a large pot, bring the broth to a boil and add the lamb's head. Skim as necessary. Add the butter, endive, yeast, currants, prunes, and spices. Cook several hours (topping up the broth as needed). Serve on sippets. Sprinkle with salt and pepper to taste.

# ROASTING MUTTON WITH OYSTERS

*The English Huswife, 1615*

Proteus: But do'st thou heare: gav'st thou my Letter to
Julia?

Speed: Aye Sir: I (a lost-Mutton) gave your Letter to her
(a lac'd-Mutton) and she (a lac'd-Mutton) gave mee (a lost-Mutton)
nothing for my labour.

Proteus: Here's too small a Pasture for such store of Muttons. (*The Two Gentlemen of Verona* 1.1.95–101)

*In the quotation from* The Two Gentlemen of Verona, *Speed calls himself a "lost mutton" because Proteus, a few lines earlier, had described him as a lost sheep seeking a shepherd. Speed then makes a bawdy pun by referring to Julia as a "laced mutton," which was sixteenth-century slang for a prostitute. The slang term probably arose because both prostitutes and mutton were "laced": with prostitutes, the word referred to the tightly-laced bodices they wore, whereas with mutton it referred to the slashes (called "laces") that were cut into joints of meat in order to help the juices run out (as is done, for example, in the recipe called "To boile a legge of mutton").*

If you will roast mutton with oisters, take a shoulder, a loine, or a legge, and after it is washt parboile it a little, then take the greatest oisters and having opened them into a dish, draine the gravy cleane from them twice or thrice, then parboile them a little, Also then take spinage endive, succory, strawbery leaves, violet leaves and a little parsly, with some scallions; chop these very small together: Then take your oisters very drie draind and mixe them with an halfe part of these hearbes: Then take your meate and with these oisters and hearbes farce or stop it, leaving no place empty, then spit it & roast it, and whilst it is in roasting take good store of verjuice and butter, and a little salt, and set in a dish on a chafing-dish and coales; and when it begins to boile, put in the remainder of your herbes without oisters, and a good quantity of currants with cinamon, and the yelke of a couple of egges: And after they are well boiled and stir'd together, season it up according to tast with sugar, then put in a fewe lemmon slices, and the meat being enough, drawe it and lay it upon this sawce remooved into a cleane dish, the egges thereof being trimmed about with Sugar, and so serve it foorth.

MODERN RECIPE                                       Makeability: 4

| | |
|---|---|
| 1 rolled boneless leg roast | $^{1}/_{2}$ cup verjuice (see Appendix 1) |
| 12 large oysters | 2 TBS unsalted butter |
| 1 cup finely chopped spinach | $^{1}/_{2}$ tsp salt |
| 1 cup finely chopped succory (also known as chicory, radicchio, and endive) | $^{1}/_{2}$ cup currants |
| | 1 tsp cinnamon |
| $^{1}/_{4}$ cup finely chopped violet leaves (if available) | 2 egg yolks |
| | Sugar to taste |
| $^{1}/_{2}$ cup finely chopped parsley | 1 lemon sliced |
| $^{1}/_{2}$ cup finely chopped scallions | |

Preheat oven to 450°F. Bring a pot of water to the boil and put in the roast. Let simmer for 5 minutes. Shuck the oysters, drain, and rinse. Remove a cup or two of the boiling water to a saucepan and parboil oysters for one minute. Drain and dry well. Chop the herbs and scallions finely and mix half with the oysters. Unroll the roast and stuff with the mixture. Tie and secure the roast. Place in a 450°F oven and immediately turn the heat down to 325°F. In a saucepan, combine the verjuice, butter, and salt and simmer gently. Add the remaining herb mixture along with the currants, cinnamon, and egg yolks. Continue to simmer and add sugar according to taste. Add the lemon slices (reserving 5 or so). Hold the sauce on a low simmer while the meat rests. Pour the sauce onto a platter and set the roast on it. Sprinkle lightly with sugar and garnish with the reserved lemon slices.

# TO MAKE STEWED STEAKES

*The Good Huswifes Jewell, 1596*

Jack Cade:                                    Is not this a lamentable thing,
            that of the skin of an innocent Lambe should be
            made Parchment; that Parchment being scribbled
            o're, should undoe a man? (*2 Henry VI* 4.2.76–79)

*In this recipe, the word "faggot" means "bundle." The word was also used, as early as the sixteenth century, as a pejorative name for old women, probably because they often eked out a living by gathering and selling faggots of firewood. It was not until the early twentieth century that this pejorative use of the term was transferred to male homosexuals.*

Take a peece of Mutton, and cutte it in peeces, and washe it very cleane, and put it into a faire potte with Ale, or with halfe Wine, then make it boyle, and skumme it cleyne, and put into your pot a faggot of Rosemary and Time, then take some Parsely picked fine, and some onyons cut round, and let them all boyle together, then take prunes, & raisons, dates, and currans, and let it boyle altogether, and season it with Sinamon and Ginger, Nutmeggs, two or three Cloves, and Salt, and so serve it on soppes and garnish it with fruite.

**MODERN RECIPE**                                        Makeability: 3

| | |
|---|---|
| 2 lb lamb stew cubes | $1/4$ cup currants |
| 2 cups ale or enough to cover the lamb | $1/4$ tsp cinnamon |
| 1 bouquet garni of 2 sprigs rosemary and 2 sprigs thyme | $1/2$ tsp ginger |
| $1/2$ cup roughly chopped parsley | $1/4$ tsp nutmeg |
| 1 medium yellow onion cut into rings | 3 cloves |
| $1/4$ cup roughly chopped prunes | $1/4$ tsp salt |
| $1/4$ cup raisins | Slices of lemon and orange |
| $1/4$ cup roughly chopped dates | 6 to 8 slices of lightly toasted 60% whole wheat bread for sippets |

Cover the lamb cubes in the ale and bring to a gentle boil. Skim the fluid when necessary and add the bouquet garni. Add the parsley and onions and let them simmer for 10 minutes before adding the fruit and spices. Simmer for 2 to $2^1/2$ hours until the lamb is tender. On a platter, spoon the lamb onto the sippets and top with the fruit. Pour a bit of the broth over the lamb and garnish with lemon and orange slices.

# 5

# PORK

Richmond: The wretched, bloody, and usurping Boare,
(That spoyl'd your Summer Fields, and fruitfull Vines)
Swilles your warm blood like wash, & makes his trough
In your embowel'd bosomes: This foule Swine
Is now even in the Centre of this Isle. (*Richard III* 5.2.7–11)

Shakespeare's contemporaries had a love–hate relationship with pigs. On the one hand, they denounced them as vile creatures. Andrew Boorde, for example, in his 1547 *Compendyous Regyment*, wrote that "a swyne is an unclene beast and they do lye upon fylthy & stynkynge soyles." To bolster his claim, Boorde noted that the Bible contemns pigs and that Jews and Muslims—whom he praises as having expert knowledge in medicine—spurn the flesh of pigs. Similarly, William Bullein, in his 1562 *Bulwarke of Defence*, declared that swine "in their lives be most vile, noysome, and never good untill they die," a sentiment echoed two decades later by William Harrison, who said that they "doo never anie good till they come to the table." On the other hand, 45 of the 2,100 recipes of this period call for various parts of the pig, which suggests that it was a popular foodstuff. Moreover, a dish made of the foreparts of the pig—the head, neck, and shoulders—was traditionally given pride of place at the feasts that occurred throughout the twelve days of Christmas. Known as soused brawn, it was served by the gentry at the beginning of each dinner, usually accompanied by a wine such as malvesey, bastard, or muscadel. As William Harrison described it, preparations for the dish began well in advance, when a pig was selected, penned up, and then served a diet of oats and peas for the next year or two. At the end of that long confinement, the pig was slaughtered, and its foreparts were boiled in a cauldron until it was so tender that, in the words of Harrison, "a man may thrust a brused rush or soft straw cleane through the fat." The brawn was then put into lidded vessels and a brine known as sousing drink—made from ale, verjuice, and salt—was poured in before the vessels were sealed. The soused brawn was then set aside for weeks or months, until it was needed for the Christmas season. Harrison added that soused brawn was a uniquely English dish and that when a barrel of it was sent to a gentleman in France who had never before encountered it, he mistook it for fish and ate it during Lent.

Harrison also noted another culinary practice involving pigs, one that he by no means approved of. The testicles of the pig, known as stones, were traditionally thrown away when the creature was slaughtered. "Some delicate dames," however, "have now found the meanes to dresse them also with great cost for a deintie dish." This innovation, Harrison complained, was not motivated by the women's gastronomic curiosity, but by "their desire to the provocation of fleshlie lust." The pig's cooked testicles, in other words, were being served as aphrodisiacs.

# HOW TO BOYLE PIGGES PETITOES

*A Book of Cookrye, 1591*

Autolycus: My Clowne (who wants but something
to be a reasonable man) grew so in love with
the Wenches Song, that hee would not stirre his
Petty-toes, till he had both Tune and Words, which
so drew the rest of the Herd to me, that all their
other Sences stucke in Eares. (*The Winter's Tale* 4.4.607–612)

*Pettitoes are the feet of a pig, but in* The Winter's Tale *Shakespeare applies the word to the rustic Clown in order to equate him with a swine. That identification then sets up a further comparison between "the rest of the herd"—that is, the Clown's fellow rustics— and the herd of demon-possessed swine that hurl themselves off a cliff in the New Testament (Matthew 8:28–33). The "lights" that the recipe calls for are lungs, so called because those organs, filled with tiny air sacs, are light in weight. Although Shakespeare refers to "lungs" on sixteen different occasions in his plays, he never uses the word "lights" in that regard, preferring to reserve it to denote sources of illumination, as when Mercutio says, "We waste our lights in vaine, like lamps by day" (Rom. 1.4.45).*

Take your Pigs feet, and the Liver and Lightes, and cut them in small peeces, then take a little mutton broth and apples sliced, Corance, sweet butter, vergious and grated bread, put them altogither in a little pipkin with salt and Pepper, perboyle your petitoes or ever you put them in your Pipkin, then when they be ready, serve them upon sippets.

 ## MODERN RECIPE
Makeability: 5

4 pig trotters, boiled and cut into small pieces

1 pork liver, boiled and cut into small pieces

4 cups chicken broth

2 apples sliced

2 TBS currants

2 TBS unsalted butter

$1/2$ cup verjuice (see Appendix 1)

$1/2$ cup dry bread crumbs

Salt and pepper

Thin slices of toasted 60% whole wheat bread for sippets

In a large saucepan or Dutch oven, combine all the ingredients and simmer gently for 1 hour. Arrange the sippets on a large serving dish and spoon the pig's feet and liver over the sippets.

# TO ROST A PIG

*Epulario*, 1598

Jessica: Nay, you need not feare us Lorenzo, Launcelet
and I are out, he tells me flatly there is no mercy for mee
in Heaven, because I am a Jewes daughter: and hee saies
you are no good member of the common wealth, for in
converting Jewes to Christians, you raise the price of
Porke. (*The Merchant of Venice* 3.5.29–34)

*As with several of the recipes from* Epulario, *this one calls for garlic. That root, according to Joannes de Mediolano, has a "secret power" that protects anyone who eats it from poisoned drinks and infected air. That protective benefit, he adds, makes garlic worth eating, despite its undesirable side-effects: "Since Garlicke then hath power to save from death, / Beare with it though it make unsavoury breath: / And scorne not Garlicke like to some, that think / It onely makes men winke, and drinke, and stink."*

First let him be scalded white and cleane, then cut him in the belly and take out the guts and entrailes, and wash it cleane, then shred Garlike very smal with larde, grated Cheese, Egges, Pepper, and a little Saffron, mixe them togither and put them into the Pig, then sow it up and spit it, but let him rost sokingly, & let him be well rosted both outwardly and inwardly, then make a little liquor with vineger, Saffron, and two branches of Rosemary or Sage, and bast the Pig therewith. The like may be done with Geese, Duckes, Crane, Capon, Pullet, and other Birds.

---

 ## MODERN RECIPE                                        Makeability: 4

For the pork:

1 pork tenderloin

1 cup grated hard cheese (Lancashire or Cheshire, for example)

3 hard-boiled eggs, roughly chopped

2 garlic cloves, minced

1/2 tsp cracked black pepper

For the basting juice:

1/4 cup red wine vinegar

1/4 tsp ground saffron

1 TBS chopped rosemary

Preheat oven to 350°F. Combine in a mixing bowl the cheese, eggs, garlic, and pepper. Cut open the tenderloin along its length, maintaining a quarter-inch thickness to prepare it for stuffing. Spread the stuffing onto the tenderloin, roll it, and tie it together with kitchen string. Place the tenderloin in a heavy iron pan and roast it in the oven for 30 to 35 minutes per pound. Mix together the red wine vinegar, saffron, and rosemary and baste the tenderloin at regular intervals. Any remaining juices can be seasoned and made into a sauce while the pork is resting. Remove the tenderloin from the oven, cover, and let it stand a few minutes.

# TO SOWCE A PIGGE

*The Good Huswifes Jewell, 1596*

Shylock:   May I speake with Anthonio?
Bassanio:  If it please you to dine with us.
Shylock:   Yes, to smell porke, to eate of the habitation
           which your Prophet the Nazarite conjured the divell
           into: I will buy with you, sell with you, talke with you,
           walke with you, and so following: but I will not eate
           with you, drinke with you, nor pray with you. (*The Merchant of Venice*
           1.3.29–35)

*The "sowce" that appears in the title of this recipes means "to pickle," though the method employed in this recipe is perhaps more similar to what we would now call a marinade. "Sowce"—usually spelt "souse"—was also used in relation to drunkenness: a 1613 play by Francis Beaumont and John Fletcher refers to a "soused soldier."*

Take White Wine and a little sweete broth, and halfe a score Nutmegs cut in quarters, then take Rosemarye, Bayes, Time, and sweet Margerum, and let them boyle altogether, skimme them very clean, and when they be boyled, put them into an earthen pan and the sirrope also, and when you serve them, a quarter in a dish, and the Bayes, and nutmegs on the top.

---

 ## MODERN RECIPE                                    Makeability: 2

1 large pork tenderloin

2 1/2 cups sweet broth (use "To make ordinary stew'd broth" on page 199, or substitute chicken broth)

2 cups white wine

3 bay leaves

2 nutmegs, quartered or crushed

1/2 tsp thyme

1/2 tsp rosemary

1/2 tsp marjoram

1 1/2 tsp salt

Combine the ingredients in a covered saucepan, bring to a boil, and then simmer for 20 to 30 minutes or until the internal temperature is 170°F, skimming frequently. Allow to cool, then transfer the contents of the saucepan to an earthenware vessel. Refrigerate for a week, turning the meat every day or so. When serving, cut the meat into four pieces and garnish with some of the bay leaves and pieces of nutmeg from the marinade.

---

# TO FRY BAKEN TO SERVE WITH THESE EGGES

*A Delightfull Daily Exercise for Ladies and Gentlewomen, 1621*

Launcelot:                        This making of Christians will
                 raise the price of Hogs, if wee grow all to be porke-eaters,

wee shall not shortlie have a rasher on the coales for money. (*The Merchant of Venice* 3.5.21–23)

*In the quotation from Shakespeare, Launcelot's joke alludes to the fact that Shylock's daughter has converted from Judaism to Christianity, which means that she can now eat nonkosher foods such as pork. If such conversions continue, says Launcelot, pork will be in such demand that one won't be able to buy even a single rasher—or slice—of bacon. Incidentally, Andrew Boorde, in his 1547* Compendyous Regyment, *asserted that "bakon is good for carters and plowmen, whiche be ever laborynge in the earth or dung."*

Cut your bakon as thinne as a card and parboyle it, then fry it in a panne without any liquor upon a very coole fire, then fry them good and browne on the other side, then take them up and put them in a warme dish and set them by the fire and it will be very crispe and never rise in the stomake, then dish up your egs in a warme dish and lay the baken all over them with a dish, and serve them to the table hot.

---

 ## MODERN RECIPE                                          Makeability: 2

1 lb whole bacon                          12 eggs

Cut the bacon into very thin slices and parboil 2 to 3 minutes. Remove and fry the bacon in a cast iron pan until brown on both sides. Keep bacon in a warm dish while cooking the eggs. Place the cooked eggs in a warm dish and arrange bacon on top.

---

# TO BAKE A PIGGE

*A Book of Cookrye*, 1591

Titus: Why there they are both, baked in that Pie,
       Whereof their Mother daintily hath fed,
       Eating the flesh that she herselfe hath bred.
       'Tis true, 'tis true, witnesse my knives sharpe point. (*Titus Andronicus* 5.3.60–63)

*Nowadays we tend to refer to "salt and pepper" rather than "pepper and salt," but in Shakespeare's England the preferred sequence appears to have been reversed: in the 2,100 recipes that were published in this period, the phrase "salt and pepper" appears only nine times, while "pepper and salt" appears 57 times.*

Take your Pig and flea it, and draw out all that clean which is in his bellye, and wash him clean, and perboyle him, season it with Cloves, mace, nutmegs, pepper & salt, and so lay him in the paste with good store of Butter, then set it in the Oven till it be baked inough.

## MODERN RECIPE                    Makeability: 4

1 loin or shoulder roast

1 tsp ground cloves

1 tsp ground mace

1 TBS ground nutmeg

1 tsp fresh-cracked pepper

$^1/_2$ tsp salt

3 TBS unsalted butter

Pastry recipe "To make fine paste" on page 214, or buy premade pastry.

Prepare a pastry shell and top. Preheat oven to 350°F. In a mixing bowl, combine cloves, mace, nutmeg, pepper, and salt. Place the pork roast in enough gently boiling water to cover it and simmer for 10 minutes. Remove and let the roast cool slightly. Rub the roast with the spice mixture. Place the roast in a pan lined with pastry. Put bits of butter on and around the roast. Cover with a pastry top, pinch the edges closed, and bake in the oven for about 80 minutes (25 to 35 minutes per pound).

# TO ROAST A PIGGE

*The English Huswife, 1615*

First Gaoler:  Come Sir, are you ready for death?
Posthumus:    Over-roasted rather: ready long ago.
First Gaoler:  Hanging is the word, Sir, if you bee readie
              for that, you are well Cook'd.
Posthumus:    So if I prove a good repast to the
              Spectators, the dish payes the shot. (*Cymbeline* 5.4.151–156)

To roast a Pigge curiously you shall not scald it, but draw it with the haire on, then having washt it, spit it and lay it to the fire so as it may not scorch: then being a quarter roasted and the skinne blistered from the flesh, with your hand pull away the haire and skinne, and leave all the fat and flesh perfectly bare: then with your knife scorch all the flesh downe to the bones, then bast it exceedingly with sweet butter and creame, being no more but warme; then dredge it with fine bread crummes, currants, sugar and salt mixt together, and thus apply dredging upon basting, and basting upon dredging till you have covered all the flesh a full inch deepe: then the meat being fully roasted, draw it and serve it up whole.

## MODERN RECIPE                    Makeability: 3

2 to 2$^1/_2$ lb pork roast

2 TBS unsalted butter

$^1/_2$ cup 18% cream

3 cups dry bread crumbs

$^1/_4$ cup roughly chopped currants

1 TBS sugar

1 tsp salt

Preheat oven to 350°F. Warm the butter and cream slightly in a saucepan. Mix the bread crumbs, currants, sugar, and salt and put them in a large flat dish. Pour the butter and cream mixture over the pork and dredge the roast. Drizzle with more of the butter and cream and dredge. Repeat until the roast has a thick coating. Roast the pork until the internal temperature reaches 160°F, about 25 to 30 minutes per pound.

# TO BAKE A GAMMON OF BACON

*A Book of Cookrye*, 1591

| William Page: | Articles are borrowed of the Pronoune; and be thus declined. *Singulariter nominativo hic, haec, hoc.* |
| Evans: | *Nominativo hig, hag, hog*: pray you marke: *genitivo huius*: Well: what is your Accusative case? |
| William Page: | *Accusativo hinc.* |
| Evans: | I pray you have your remembrance, childe. *Accusativo hung, hang, hog.* |
| Quickly: | Hang-hog, is Lattin for Bacon, I warrant you. |
| Evans: | Leave your prables woman. What is the Focative case, William? |
| William Page: | *O, Vocativo, O.* |
| Evans: | Remember William, Focative, is caret. |
| Quickly: | And that's a good roote. (*The Merry Wives of Windsor* 4.1.37–50) |

*The humor in this quotation from* The Merry Wives of Windsor *arises from Mistress Quickly's attempts to make sense of Latin, a language she has surely never studied. Evans initiates the confusion when he attempts to say "hunc, hanc, hoc" (that is, the accusative singular forms of the demonstrative pronoun), but mangles it to "hung, hang, hog." This prompts Mistress Quickly to speculate that "hang-hog" is Latin for "bacon." A few lines later, Evans refers to a caret, that is, a diacritic that is written over the exclamation "O" when it is used in the vocative case. Mistress quickly assumes that they are talking about a carrot, rather than a caret, which prompts her to affirm, "that's a good roote."*

Take your Bacon and boyle it, and stuffe it with Parcely and Sage, and yolks of hard Egges, and when it is boyled, stuffe it and let it boyle againe, season it with Pepper, cloves and mace, whole cloves stick fast in, so then lay it in your paste with salt butter.

---

 ## MODERN RECIPE                                      Makeability: 3

1 lb bacon

1/2 cup chopped parsley

1/2 cup chopped sage

2 hard-boiled egg yolks

1/2 tsp cracked black pepper

1/4 tsp ground cloves

1/2 tsp ground mace

6 whole cloves

Pastry recipe "To make fine paste" on page 214, or buy premade pastry.

3 tsp salted butter

*Continued on next page*

*Continued from previous page*

Prepare a pastry shell and top. Preheat oven to 350°F. Boil the bacon in a pot for 10 minutes. Remove and allow to cool. Mix the parsley, sage, and egg yolks. Slit the top of bacon and stuff it with the parsley mixture. Season with pepper, cloves, and mace and insert whole cloves around the bacon. Line a loaf pan with pastry, put in the bacon and pieces of butter, and cover with pastry crust. Bake for 35 to 40 minutes.

# THE ORDER TO BOYLE A BRAWNE

*The Good Huswifes Jewell*, 1596

And with that word she spied the hunted boar;
Whose frothy mouth bepainted all with red,
Like milk and blood being mingled both together,
A second fear through all her sinews spread,
Which madly hurries her she knows not whither. (*Venus and Adonis* 900–904)

*In this recipe, the willow branches that are placed beneath the meat are presumably intended to prevent the meat from sticking to the metal surface of the pot.*

Take your Brawne, and when ye have cut him out, lay him in faire water foure and twenty houres, and shifte it foure or five times, and scrape and binde up those that you shall thinke good, with Hempe, binde one handfull of greene Willowes together, and laye them in the bottome of the panne, and then put in your Brawne, and skimme it very cleane, and let it boyle but softlye, and it must be so tender, that you may put a straw through it, and when it is boyled enough, let it stand and rowle in the panne, and when you take it up, let it lye in Trayes an houre or two, and then make sowsing drinke with Ale and water, and salte, and you must make it verye strong, and so let it lye a week before you spende it.

 ## MODERN RECIPE                                    Makeability: 5

1 pork shoulder

Hemp and green willows (if available)

4 cups ale

2 cups water (enough to cover the pork)

1 cup pickling salt

Soak the pork in water in the refrigerator for 24 hours, turning it four or five times. Place the willows bound with hemp in the bottom of a large pot. Put in the pork shoulder and bring to a boil, skimming as necessary. Reduce to a simmer and cook until very tender, about 3 hours. Remove the shoulder to another pot and allow to cool two hours. Pour in the ale, water, and salt, and let the pork pickle one week.

# 6

# GAME

Orsino: O, when mine eyes did see Olivia first,
Methought she purg'd the ayre of pestilence!
That instant was I turn'd into a hart;
And my desires, like fell and cruell hounds,
E'er since pursue me. (*Twelfth Night* 1.1.18–22)

This chapter employs the word "game" rather loosely to denote any undomesticated animal, large or small, that was served to the table in Shakespeare's England. Sparrows, for example, which were stewed or baked, are not the kind of beast that we usually associate with "the hunt," but they did have to be caught in the wild. Other wild varmints that commonly appear in the recipe books of this period include hares, rabbits, and several kinds of deer, along with a host of water fowl (like mallards, widgeons, teals, curlews, bustards, and herons) and other birds (such as larks, quails, pheasants, blackbirds, and woodcocks).

Attitudes toward the palatability of game animals varied greatly. Thomas Twyne asserted that the "flesh of wilde beasts is drie, and hard of digestion" and "no good nutriment." On the other hand, Andrew Boorde claimed that "the brawne of a wylde bore, is muche more better than the brawne of a tame bore" and that venison "is good for an Englysheman, for it dothe anymate him to be as he is: whiche is stronge and hardy." Others, such as James Hart, admitted that venison was hard to digest, but added that it could be made more tender if the deer were hunted to exhaustion before it was killed. Still others insisted that venison was "never good untill it be mouldy," and therefore they hung the meat in the open air until it began to decompose. The flesh of hares was thought by many to induce melancholy, but its cousin the coney—which we now call a rabbit—was prized by many, especially if it was slaughtered at a young age. Andrew Boorde, for example, considered the meat of suckling rabbits to be "the best of all wylde beestes," and James Hart affirmed that they made "a good & wholsom dish, in sickness and in health." This was fortunate, because England had an enormous population of rabbits—an "infinite number," according to Fynes Moryson.

The three kinds of deer found in Shakespeare's England were fallow, roe, and red, which roamed about in large private parks belonging to wealthy gentlemen or in the huge forests belonging to the crown. Either way, they were off-limits for commoners (though surely poaching was not uncommon). For the gentry, deer hunting was a noble sport, more popular in England, according to Andrew Boorde, than in any other European nation. Gervase Markham noted that the art of venery, as it was sometimes called, was undertaken more "for the exercise of the body and recreation of the spirits" than for the meat that it brought to the table. Hunting developed an elaborate language of its own—a "recheat," for instance, was a note blown on a horn to gather the hounds together, and a "hart" was a male red deer that was more than five years old. Elaborate protocols also had to be learned and observed during the hunt. For example, the huntsman, according to Thomas Cocayne, "must remember to blowe at the death of every stagge six long notes," and after the last note everyone else in the hunting party must "blowe altogether their double recheates."

# TO BAKE A FESANT

*The Good Huswifes Handmaide for the Kitchin, 1594*

Shepherd:  My Businesse, Sir, is to the King.
Autolycus:  What Advocate ha'st thou to him?
Shepherd:  I know not (and't like you.)
Clown:  Advocate's the Court-word for a Pheazant:
          say you have none.
Shepherd:  None, Sir: I have no Pheazant Cock, nor Hen. (*The Winter's Tale* 4.4.742–747)

*In the quotation from* The Winter's Tale, *the rustic Clown assumes that an "advocate"— a word he has probably never heard before—is some sort of bribe that Autolycus is demanding in exchange for arranging an audience with the king. Accordingly, he whispers to the Shepherd, "Advocate's the court-word for a pheasant," and advises him to pretend that they have no pheasants to give.*

Trusse him like a hen, and perboyle him, then set him with cloves, then take a litle Vergious and Saffron, and colour it with a feather, then take Salt, Mace, and Ginger to season it, and so put it in the paste, and bake it till it bee halfe enough. Then put in a litle Vergious, and the yolk of an Egge beaten together: then bake it till it be ynough.

---

 ## MODERN RECIPE                                                    Makeability: 4

| | |
|---|---|
| 1 young pheasant | ½ tsp finely chopped mace |
| 6 whole cloves | 1 tsp minced ginger |
| 3 TBS verjuice (see Appendix 1) | 1 egg yolk, lightly beaten |
| 2 pinches saffron | Pastry recipe "To make fine paste" on page |
| 1 tsp salt | 214, or buy premade pastry. |

Prepare a pastry shell and top. Preheat oven to 350°F. Truss the pheasant and parboil in a large pot. Remove and pat dry. Although the original recipe calls for baking the pheasant whole, it is probably most practical to section the bird. Insert the cloves evenly around the pheasant. Sprinkle with 1 TBS of verjuice and season with the saffron, salt, mace, and ginger. Place in the pastry shell and bake for 30 minutes. Mix together the remaining 2 TBS of verjuice with egg yolk, and remove the bird from the oven. Open up the pastry topping carefully and pour in the verjuice-butter mixture and gently tilt the dish to distribute. Return to the oven and bake another 30 minutes.

# TO ROAST VENISON

*The English Huswife, 1615*

Duke Senior:  Come, shall we goe and kill us venison?
And yet it irkes me the poore dapled fooles
Being native Burgers of this desert City,
Should in their owne confines with forked heads
Have their round hanches goard. (*As You Like It* 2.1.21–25)

*The "soking fire" that is alluded to in this recipe might sound like an oxymoron, but in fact it simply means a slow or gentle fire, the kind where the heat gradually "soaks in" to the meat. Another recipe from* Epulario, *for example, instructs the cook to "make a soft fire that it may rost sokingly."*

If you will Roast any Venison after you have washt it, and clensed all the blood from it, you shall sticke it with Cloves all over on the out side; & if it be leane you shall larde it either with Mutton lard, or pork larde: but Mutton is the best: then spit it and roast it by a soking fire, then take vinegar, bread crummes, and some of the gravy which comes from the Venison, and boile them well in a dish: then season it with sugar, cinamon, ginger and salt. And so serve the venison foorth upon the sauce when it is roasted enough.

 ## MODERN RECIPE — Makeability: 4

| | |
|---|---|
| 1 saddle of venison | Pan drippings from the roast |
| 1/4 cup whole cloves | 2 TBS sugar |
| Pork fat for larding (substitute bacon) | 1 tsp cinnamon |
| | 1 tsp ginger |
| For the sauce: | 1 tsp salt |
| 1 3/4 cup red wine vinegar | |
| 1 cup bread crumbs | |

*Continued on next page*

*Continued from previous page*

Insert cloves evenly throughout the venison. If it is particularly lean, stab the meat with a slender knife in a dozen or more places, and insert pork fat into the punctures as deeply as possible. Alternatively, wrap the meat with bacon, affixing it with toothpicks. If using a rotisserie, spit the roast and cook it until the thermometer reads 145°F. Catch the drippings in a pan. Remove from the spit and allow it to rest. Meanwhile, bring to a boil the gravy ingredients and allow them to reduce. Pour the gravy onto a platter and plate the venison on top. If roasting in an oven, preheat the oven to 450°F, place the venison on a rack in a roasting pan, and reduce the heat to 350°F. Roast for 20 minutes per pound. Prepare the gravy as before.

# TO BAKE A WILDE BOARE

*The Good Huswifes Handmaide for the Kitchin, 1594*

Maecenas:   We have cause to be glad, that matters are so
well digested: you staid well by't in Egypt.
Enobarbus:  Aye, Sir, we did sleepe day out of countenaunce:
and made the night light with drinking.
Maecenas:   Eight Wilde-Boares rosted whole at a breakfast:
and but twelve persons there. Is this true?
Enobarbus:  This was but as a Flye by an Eagle: we had
much more monstrous matter of Feast, which worthily
deserved noting. (*Antony and Cleopatra* 2.2.185–193)

*In a dialogue that appeared in a 1605 language book called* The French Garden for English Ladyes, *a dinner guest expresses surprise at one of the dishes: "From whence had you this wilde pig, Madame? For there is no wilde Bores in England." Wild boar were indeed extinct in England by the time Shakespeare was born (or not long after), but as the hostess in the dialogue explains, they continued to run wild on the Continent, where they were sometimes caught and shipped live to England. The meat was much prized, as it was considered both more flavorful and more nutritious than that of domestic swine.*

Take three parts of water, and the fourth part of white wine, and put therto salt, as much as shall season it, and let it boyle so til it be almost ynough: then take it out of the brothe, and let it lie till it be through cold: Then Larde it, and laye it in course paste, in pastries, and then season it with Pepper, salt, and Ginger, & put in twise so much Ginger as pepper. And when it is halfe baken, fill your pastries with white wine, and all to shake the Pastrie, & so put it into the Oven againe, til it be enough, Then let it stand five or six dayes, or ever that you eate of them, and that tyme it will be verie good meat.

 ## MODERN RECIPE                    Makeability: 4

| | |
|---|---|
| 1 pork shoulder | 1 cup of wine |
| 3 cups of water | 1 TBS salt |

Pork fat for larding

$^1/_4$ tsp pepper

$^1/_4$ tsp salt

$^1/_2$ tsp ginger

$^1/_2$ cup white wine

Pastry recipe "To make fine paste" on page 214, or buy premade pastry.

Prepare a pastry shell and top. Preheat oven to 350°F. Combine the water, wine, and 1 TBS of salt and bring to a boil. Put in the shoulder and simmer for 15 minutes, turning frequently. Remove it from the liquid and allow it to cool thoroughly. Slice pieces of the shoulder, season with pepper, salt, and ginger and arrange in the pastry shell. Place a small amount of pork fat on each piece of shoulder, cover with pastry crust, and bake for 25 minutes. Remove and cut a hole in the pastry crust. Pour in the wine and return to the oven for another 20 minutes, or until pastry crust is golden brown.

# TO DRESSE A HARE

*The Good Huswifes Jewell, 1596*

Falstaff: Depose me? If thou do'st it halfe so gravely, so
majestically, both in word and matter, hang me up by
the heeles for a Rabbet-sucker, or a Poulters Hare. (*1 Henry IV* 2.4.430–432)

*Fynes Moryson, in his 1617* Itinerary, *noted that the English preferred eating rabbits to hares. That preference may have been partly inspired by the belief that hare meat caused melancholy. This recipe calls for hare, but in our redaction we have substituted rabbit, not because we are afraid of provoking melancholy, but because it is easier to find a butcher who sells rabbit than hare. As for the use of the feminine pronoun in this recipe—"larde her and roste her"—it is a bit unnerving. Other recipes of this period also use "her" to refer to hens, ducks, peacocks, coneys (rabbits), and tenches (a kind of fish). It is unlikely, though, that the recipe is specifically calling for a female animal, but rather that it is an idiosyncrasy of the recipe's author. Another recipe, for example, uses "him" to refer to the stomach of a calf, and yet another one uses "him" to refer to a spoonful of butter.*

Wash her in faire water, perboyle her, then lay her in colde water, then larde her and roste her, and for sauce take red wine, salt vineger, ginger, pepper, cloves and mace, put these together, then mince onions and apples and frye them in a panne, then put your sauce to them with a little suger, and let them boyle together and then serve it.

## MODERN RECIPE
Makeability: 4

1 large rabbit

Pork fat for larding (substitute bacon strips)

For the sauce:

1 cup red wine

*Continued on next page*

*Continued from previous page*

| | |
|---|---|
| 1 tsp salt | 2 blades of mace |
| 1/2 tsp minced ginger | 1 medium yellow onion, finely diced |
| 1/4 tsp fresh-cracked black pepper | 1 firm apple, peeled, cored, and finely diced |
| 2 whole cloves | 2 tsp sugar or to taste |

Preheat oven to 450°F. Wash the hare, parboil it a few minutes, and then plunge it into cold water. Pat dry, stab the meat with a slender knife in a dozen or more places, and insert pork fat into the punctures as deeply as possible. Alternatively, wrap the meat with bacon, affixing it with toothpicks. Place the hare in a baking dish and put in the oven. Reduce the heat to 350°F. Bake until tender, about 80 to 90 minutes. Turn the hare when half-way through the cooking time. Remove and cover warm while making the sauce. Drain off most of the fat in the baking dish (retaining 1 TBS), and deglaze with the red wine, adding the spices. Stir and reduce. In another pan, sauté the apple in the reserved tablespoon of fat until soft. Pour in the wine and spice mixture, add the sugar, and bring to a boil. Reduce and serve on the hare.

**The order how to breede your Hounds for the Hare, and other chafes.**

Herein muſt you bee moſt carefull in breeding your Hounds both for ſhape and making, and foreſee you harken them forth of ſuch a kinde as bee durable, well mouthed,

B 3

*A Short Treatise of Hunting*, Thomas Cokayne, 1591. In Shakespeare's England, the flesh of hares was thought to induce melancholy and it was generally thought to be less tasty than the flesh of rabbits—or coneys as they were then called—but they were nonetheless hunted with hounds and served to the table. © British Library Board. All Rights Reserved C.31.c.6 pg 7.

# FOR TO MAKE NUMBLEIS STUED

*Wyl Bucke His Testament, 1560*

Falstaff:  Go, fetch me a quart of Sacke, put a tost in't.
Have I liv'd to be carried in a Basket
like a barrow of butchers Offall? and to be throwne
in the Thames? Wel, if I be serv'd such another tricke,
Ile have my braines 'tane out and butter'd, and give them
to a dogge for a New-yeares gift. (*The Merry Wives of Windsor* 3.5.3–8)

*Numbles are the edible entrails or viscera of an animal, especially deer. Numbles—which were also known as "umbles"—were sometimes baked in a pastry shell as "umble pie," which some etymologists claim was the origin of the phase "to eat humble pie." The word "lire," which appears near the end of the recipe, means "to thicken," while "egre dowce" is a French term that literally means "sharp sweet," or what we would now call sweet and sour.*

Take the Numbleis and loke that they be clene wasshed and dight, and then cut them to the length of the brede of halfe a thombe and sum what more, and then put them on a broche and roste them til they be halfe Inough and put them in a faire pot and caste therto strong broth and wine together, and a good quantite of Canell and powther of Peper, & Resons of Corans, and lete them boyle together and then lire him up with crustes of brede drawne with with wine or els with brede tosted, other els the yolkes of Egges when they be sodin herde, and breke them small and cast there amonge powther of ginger, & powther of Clowes and of Mace, and melt all these together & when thou shalt serve hit forth cast therin vergis & a litell vineger, and if thou lire him up with breade caste therin vineger and vergius, and ginger, & powther of clowes & mace, & give him a colour of saffron and loke that he be sum what egre dowce and serve it forthe in disshes.

---

 ## MODERN RECIPE                                     Makeability: 4

Assorted variety meats: liver, kidneys, heart, thymus gland, tripe

2 cups broth (Use to make ordinary stew'd broth on page 199)

1 cup red wine

1 TBS chopped cinnamon stick

1 tsp pepper

1/4 cup raisins

1/4 cup currants

Crusts of 4 slices of bread soaked in wine (or 3 hard-boiled egg yolks)

1 tsp minced ginger

1/2 tsp ground cloves

1/2 tsp ground mace

2 TBS red wine vinegar

2 TBS verjuice (see Appendix 1)

2 pinches saffron

Sugar to taste

*Continued on next page*

*Continued from previous page*

Wash and trim the variety meats and cut them into one-inch cubes. Thread the meats onto a skewer and grill on a barbecue over medium heat (or on a roasting rack in a 350°F oven), until they are half-cooked. Put the pieces into a pot of strong broth and wine, adding cinnamon, pepper, and raisins. Bring to a boil and reduce to a simmer. To thicken the broth, add bread crusts that have been soaked in wine (or, hard-boiled egg yolks that have been pressed through a strainer). Add powdered ginger, cloves, mace, and saffron and stir. Put in the vinegar and verjuice before serving. Add sugar as desired.

# TO BOYLE A MALLARD WITH CARETS AND ONYONS

*A Delightfull Daily Exercise for Ladies and Gentlewomen, 1621*

Scarus:  The Noble ruine of her Magicke, Anthony,
Claps on his Sea-wing, and (like a doting Mallard)
Leaving the Fight in heighth, flyes after her. (*Antony and Cleopatra* 3.10.19–21)

*Joannes de Mediolano, who published a book called* The Englishmans Docter *in 1607, would not have approved of this recipe for stewed duck: "Good sport it is to see a Mallard killed, / But with their flesh your flesh should not be filled." His concern was that the meat of ducks (and swans) was not healthy because they spent too much time in the mud. As for the onions that are called for in this recipe, those too had their detractors. Thomas Hill, in* The Gardeners Labyrinth, *wrote that they "hinder reason, and procure terrible dreames," though he does admit in another book (*The Profitable Arte of Gardening*) that a crushed onion, mixed with salt and honey, can be used as a poultice to get rid of warts. Carrots were also used for nonculinary purposes. John Parkinson, in his* Theatrum Botanicum, *notes that gentlewomen would often "gather the leaves, and sticke them in their hats or heads, or pin them on their armes in stead of feathers."*

Take a Mallard being halfe roasted, and cut her up as you doe eate them, put her into a pipkin with the brest downeward, put to her two or three sliced Onyons, and Carrets, sliced square the bignesse of a Butchers prick, an inch long, a little grose pepper, a little salt, a little whole mace, a piece of sweete butter, a little parsley, a little savory and time, a pint of strong broth, a quarter of a pint of white-wine: let these boyle halfe a way very softly, then dish up your Ducke upon sippets, and powre your broath on the toppe, and serve it hot to the Table.

 ## MODERN RECIPE                                    Makeability: 4

| 1 whole duck | 2 large carrots cut in one-inch sections |
| 3 medium yellow onions, sliced | 1 tsp whole peppercorns |

2 tsp salt

2 blades of whole mace

2 TBS unsalted butter

1/2 cup chopped parsley

1/2 cup chopped savory

2 cups strong beer

1/2 cup white wine

Slices of lightly toasted 60% whole wheat bread for sippets

Preheat oven to 450°F. Place the duck in a roasting pan in the oven, reduce heat to 325°F, and roast for 30 minutes. Remove the duck, allow it to cool, and cut into pieces. Transfer the duck into a large casserole dish and add the remaining ingredients. Bring the mixture to a gentle simmer and braise until the broth has reduced by half and the duck has cooked for 55 to 60 minutes, depending on size. Arrange the sippets on a large platter, top with the duck pieces, and pour the broth over.

# TO STUE SPARROWES

*A Book of Cookrye, 1591*

Thersites:  Lo, lo, lo, lo, what modicums of wit he utters!
His evasions have ears thus long. I have bobb'd
his brain more than he has beat my bones. I will buy
nine sparrows for a penny, and his pia mater is not
worth the ninth part of a sparrow. (*Troilus and Cressida* 2.1.69–73)

*Never one to avoid an anachronism, Shakespeare often infuses his plays, even ones that are set in remote places and ancient eras, with details drawn from his own life and times. The sparrows that Thersites offers to buy are a good example: they were sold nine for a penny in Shakespeare's London, but not in ancient Troy. Needless to say, you'll be hard-pressed nowadays to find a market that sells sparrows (or larks, the favorite small bird that was formerly served to the table). You could, of course, do what Shakespeare's contemporaries did, and trap them by coating a tree branch with sticky birdlime—but you'll probably enjoy them more if you just let them chirp outside your window. Incidentally, eating the testicles of a sparrow, according to James Hart in his 1633* Klinike, *will help a man to engender sperm. Considering the size of those organs, however, you may want to fill up on bread first.*

Take good Ale a pottel, or after the quantities more or lesse by your discretion, and set it over the fier to boyle, and put in your Sparowes and scum the broth, then put therin Onions, Percely, Time, Rosemary chopped small, pepper and Saffron, with Cloves and Mace, a fewe. And make sippets as you doo for Fish, and laye the Sparrowes upon with the said broth, and in the seething put in a peece of sweet Butter, and vergious if need be.

MODERN RECIPE                                                    Makeability: 4

| | |
|---|---|
| 8 sparrows (or smallest game bird available) | 2 pinches saffron |
| 6 cups ale | 6 whole cloves |
| 3 yellow onions, diced | 3 blades of whole mace |
| 1 cup parsley | 2 TBS unsalted butter |
| 1/4 cup rosemary | 2 TBS verjuice (see Appendix 1) |
| 1/4 cup thyme | Slices of lightly toasted 60% whole wheat |
| 1 tsp fresh-cracked pepper | bread for sippets |

Bring to a boil a large skillet of ale and set in the sparrows. Skim as necessary. Add the remaining ingredients, cover, and let the sparrows stew for 30 to 40 minutes. On a serving platter, arrange the sippets and add some of the broth. Place the sparrows on top and garnish with a bit more broth.

# 7

# FISH AND SEAFOOD

Falstaff: She's neither fish nor flesh; a man knowes not
        where to have her.
Host:      Thou art an unjust man in saying so; thou, or anie
        man knowes where to have me, thou knave thou. (*1 Henry IV*, 3.3.128–131)

As a nation surrounded by water, dotted with lakes, and criss-crossed by rivers and streams, it's not surprising that fish and other seafood were an important part of the average person's diet in Shakespeare's England. Species that were eaten included herring, cod, mackerel, flounder, haddock, carp, eel, tench, bream, pike, salmon, perch, gudgeon, bullhead, barbel, roach, dace, ruff, luce, humber, shad, twait, and mullet. Fish that had to be sent a long ways to market were sometimes first preserved by drying them into stockfish or salting them into saltfish, but the demand for fresh fish also prompted some fishermen to dump their catch into barrels of water and then transport them by cart to wherever they were needed. Crustaceans were also eaten: shrimp, for example, appear in two recipes published in this period, and crabs in one, and it's known that lobsters were sold in London markets, even though they don't appear in any of the published recipes. Oysters were enjoyed both cooked and raw and were even sold in the street as a snack. Mussels and periwinkles were also eaten.

Curious lore pertaining to fish and other sea creatures also circulated in Shakespeare's England. One belief, which actually has its origin with St. Augustine, was that every creature on land had a counterpart in the ocean. Thus there are horses and sea horses, lions and sea lions, elephants and whales, and so on. The land and sea parallels even extended to humans, as confirmed by the reports of mariners who occasionally spotted mermaids and mermen. The explorer Henry Hudson, for example, recorded such a sighting in a journal entry dated June 15, 1608, which was later published by Samuel Purchas:

This morning, one of our companie looking over boord saw a Mermaid … from the Navill upward, her backe and breasts were like a womans, her body as big as one of us; her skin very white; and long haire hanging downe behind, of colour blacke: in her going downe they saw her tayle, which was like the tayle of a Porpose, and speckled like a Macrell.

*A Briefe Note of the Benefits that Grow to This Realme, by the Observation of Fish-Daies*, Anonymous, 1627. These two woodcuts appeared side by side at the top of a one-page broadsheet that explained why eating fish was good for England. In the left panel one man pulls in a net of fish while the other appears to hold the boat steady with an oar or pole. In the right panel, an unrealistically large fish approaches two ships in full sail. Woodcuts such as these were probably not created for this particular publication, but instead had likely been created for an earlier book and were re-used because they happened to be at hand. © Bodleian Library, University of Oxford Fol Theta 659 (2) (detail).

Even descriptions of real sea creatures sometimes mixed fact with fancy. A 1621 dictionary entitled *An English Expositor* defined "dolphin" as follows:

> A fish friendly to man, and especially to children; the Females of this fish, have breasts like to women, which are well stored with milke … They sometime break foorth of the Sea, but presently die as soone as they touch land.

Tales of strange fish also made their way into popular ballads, including the one that the unscrupulous Autolycus tries to sell to the naive shepherds in *The Winter's Tale*:

> Here's another ballad of a fish, that appeared upon the coast on Wednesday the fourscore of April, forty thousand fathom above water, and sung this ballad against the hard hearts of maids: it was thought she was a woman and was turned into a cold fish for she would not exchange flesh with one that loved her: the ballad is very pitiful and as true. (*Winter's Tale* 4.4.274–280)

The "four-score of April" is April 80th, which is when the fish in the ballad was seen hovering in the sky at a height of forty thousand fathoms, which equals 240,000 feet. That figure, divided by 5,280, equals 45.454545454545 miles. Shakespeare's sonnets were, of course, published when he was 45, and Queen Elizabeth reigned for 45 years. It all sounds rather fishy.

# TO STEW FLOUNDERS

*A Delightfull Daily Exercise for Ladies and Gentlewomen, 1621*

Falstaff: There's never any of these demure Boyes
come to any proofe: for thinne Drinke doth so over-coole
their blood, and making many Fish-Meales, that they
fall into a kinde of Male Greene-sicknesse: and then, when they marry, they
get Wenches. They are generally Fooles,
and Cowards; which some of us should be too, but for
inflamation. (*2 Henry IV* 4.3.89–95)

Take two faire Flounders, cut off the heads and the finnes, crosse them overthwart
with a sharpe knife two or three cuts, then put them in a pewter dish the white side
downeward, put in halfe a pint of sweete butter, halfe a pint of vinegar, a handfull
of shred parsley, three or foure blades of Mace, a faggot of sweete herbes, three or
foure whole Onions, strow on a little salt, and let them stewe halfe an houre, then
turne them and let them stew halfe an houre more, then dish it upon sippets and
strew salt upon it, and then serve it to the table hott.

## MODERN RECIPE                    Makeability: 2

2 lb flounder (substitute sole)

1/2 lb melted unsalted butter

1 cup white vinegar (or less depending
on taste)

1/2 cup parsley, roughly chopped

4 blades of mace

1 bouquet garni of thyme, basil, marjoram,
rosemary, bay leaf

3 medium-sized yellow onions

1 tsp salt

6 slices 60% lightly toasted whole wheat bread
for sippets

Score the fillets gently and place them in a deep pan. Add the butter, vinegar, parsley, mace, onions,
salt, and the bouquet garni. Bring to a boil and reduce to a simmer for 7 to 10 minutes or until the
flesh is flakey and opaque (the internal temperature should read 145°F). Place the sippets on a dish
and arrange the flounder on top, pouring on a little of the broth and using the onions for garnish.

# TO BROYLE MACKRELL ON THE DUTCH FASHION

*A Delightfull Daily Exercise for Ladies and Gentlewomen, 1621*

Falstaff: Worcester is stolne away by Night: thy Fathers Beard is
turn'd white with the Newes; you may buy Land now
as cheape as stinking Mackrell. (*1 Henry IV* 2.4.355–357)

Lay your Mackrells in Hysope and Mints, bind them close with a thred that they come
not off, then parboyle them in water and salt, and a little vinegar, then broyle them while

they are very browne and crispe, then dish them up and take off the threds, then put vinegar and butter upon them and serve them to the table hot, throwing salt upon them.

---

 MODERN RECIPE                                    Makeability: 3

| | |
|---|---|
| 4 pieces of mackerel fillets | 1 TBS salt |
| 4 sprigs hyssop (see Appendix 1) | ¼ cup white vinegar plus 2 more TBS |
| 4 sprigs mint | ¼ cup melted butter |

Preheat the oven broiler. Tie sprigs of hyssop and mint onto each mackerel fillet. Bring a pot of water to the boil, add the salt and ¼ cup of vinegar. Gently place the mackerel fillets in the water and parboil for a few minutes. Place the mackerel on a cooking sheet under the broiler and cook slowly until they are brown and crisp, about 20 minutes. Baste frequently with a bit of butter. Remove the string holding the herbs and arrange the mackerel on a plate. Drizzle with the 2 TBS of vinegar and the melted butter. Sprinkle with salt to taste.

---

# TO FRY WHITINGS

*A Book of Cookrye, 1591*

> What have
> Trinculo: we here, a man, or a fish? dead or alive? a fish, hee
> smels like a fish: a very ancient and fish-like smell: a
> kinde of, not of the newest poore-John: a strange fish:
> were I in England now (as once I was) and had but
> this fish painted; not a holiday-foole there but would
> give a peece of silver. (*The Tempest* 2.2.24–30)

*Many different kinds of fish have been called whitings, but the one denoted in this recipe is probably the species known scientifically as* Merlangius merlangus, *commonly known in North America as the English whiting. The fish that Trinculo refers to in the quotation from* The Tempest—*the Poor-John, also known as the hake—is not identical to the whiting, but they both belong to the same* Gadidae *family.*

First flay them and wash them clean and scale them, that doon, lap them in floure and fry them in Butter and oyle. Then to serve them, mince apples or onions and fry them, then put them into a vessel with white wine, vergious, salt, pepper, cloves & mace, and boile them togither on the Coles, and serve it upon the Whitings.

---

 MODERN RECIPE                                    Makeability: 3

| | |
|---|---|
| 1 lb whiting (silver hake) fillets | 1 finely diced onion |
| 1 cup flour | 1 finely diced apple (leaving peels on) |

<table>
<tr><td>½ cup white wine</td><td>¼ tsp ground cloves</td></tr>
<tr><td>2 TBS verjuice (see Appendix 1)</td><td>½ tsp ground mace</td></tr>
<tr><td>½ tsp salt</td><td>unsalted butter</td></tr>
<tr><td>¼ tsp fresh-cracked black pepper</td><td>canola (rapeseed) oil</td></tr>
</table>

In a sauté pan, cook the onion in a bit of butter and oil until just soft. Add the apple and continue to cook for a few minutes, or until the apple begins to soften. Add the remaining ingredients and simmer until cooked and reduced slightly. Meanwhile, mix some salt and pepper into the flour and dredge the fillets. Over a medium-low heat, fry the fillets in butter and oil until golden brown, about 5 to 6 minutes per side. Add more butter and oil as needed. Arrange the fish in rows on a platter and spoon on the apple-onion sauce.

# A HERRING PYE

*The English Huswife, 1623*

Feste: No indeed sir, the Lady Olivia has no folly,
     shee will keepe no foole sir, till she be married, and fooles
     are as like husbands, as Pilchers are to Herrings—the
     Husbands the bigger. (*Twelfth Night* 3.1.32–35)

*Of all the fish that were caught off the coasts of England, herring were probably the most important. Vast numbers of them were taken, salted on board the ships, barrelled, and then sold throughout England, as well as exported to Germany, France, Italy, and even Turkey. The city of Yarmouth was the hub of the herring fishery: according to Thomas Nashe, who wrote a treatise in praise of herring entitled* Nashes Lenten Stuffe, *Yarmouth alone sent out eighty ships to catch herring, an industry that also gave work to thousands of "carpenters, shipwrights, makers of lines, roapes and cables, dressers of hempe, spinners of thred, and net-weavers," who would have otherwise "starvd with their wives and brattes." Nashe adds that herring is not only cheap but delicious: "The poorer sort make it three parts of there sustenance; with it, for his dinnier [i.e., denier, a coin], the patchedest leather-pilched laboratho may dine like a Spanish duke when the niggardliest mouse of beef will cost him sixpence." Some herring, after being soaked in brine, were also smoked, which turned them a red color. These so-called red herrings were renowned in Shakespeare's England for their strong smell, but the notion of a "red herring" as a false clue did not arise till the nineteenth century. As for the pilchards or "pilchers" to which Feste refers in the quotation from* Twelfth Night, *they are better known as sardines.*

Take white pickled Herrings of one nights watering, and boil them a little, then pill off the skin, and take only the backs of them, and picke the fish cleane from the bones, then take good store of raysins of the Sunne, and stone them and put them to the fish: then take a warden or two, and pare it, and slice it in small slices from the chore, and put it likewise to the fish: then with a very sharp shredding knife shred all as small and as fine as may be; then put in a good store of currants, sugar, cinammon, slic't dates, and so put it in the coffin with good store of very sweete butter, and so cover it, and leave only a round vent-hole on the top of the lid, and so bake it like pies of that nature: When it is sufficiently baked, draw it out and take Claret-wine and a little verjuyce, sugar, cinammon, and sweet butter, and boyle them together; then put it in at the vent hole, and shake the pie a little, put it again into the Oven for a little space, and so serve it up, the lid being candied over with sugar, and the sides of the dish being trimmed with sugar.

 ## MODERN RECIPE                                       Makeability: 4

For the pie filling:

1 lb pickled herring, cleaned of bones and skin

1/4 cup raisins

2 large Bartlett pears, peeled and cored

2 TBS currants

1 tsp sugar

1/4 tsp cinnamon

1 TBS sliced dates

4 TBS unsalted butter

For the basting liquid:

1/2 cup red wine

1 TBS verjuice (see Appendix 1)

1/2 tsp sugar

1/4 tsp cinnamon

2 TBS unsalted butter

Pastry recipe "To make fine paste" on page 214, or buy premade pastry.

Preheat oven to 350°F. Prepare a pastry shell and top, and precook the pastry shell for 10 minutes or just until it starts to brown. After rinsing the herring, parboil it for 1 minute and drain and dry with kitchen towels. Mince the herring finely and do the same with the apples. In a mixing bowl, combine the herring and apple along with the raisins, currants, sugar, cinnamon, and dates. Drain any fluid, and then use a slotted spoon to transfer the mixture into the pastry shell along with dollops of the butter. Cover the shell and cut out a small vent-hole in the center. Place in the oven and bake for 45 to 50 minutes. Meanwhile, in a small saucepan heat the wine, verjuice, sugar, cinnamon, and butter to a simmer. Remove the pie from the oven after 30 to 35 minutes and pour the wine mixture into the vent-hole. Gently rock the pie back and forth to distribute the fluid. Mix a little water and sugar, and brush the top and edges of the pie shell so that it is "candied over with sugar." Return to the oven for the final 15 minutes of baking.

# TO BOILE A BREAME

*The Good Huswifes Jewell, 1596*

Cleopatra:  Give me mine Angle, weele to' th' River. There
My Musicke playing farre off, I will betray
Tawny fine fishes. My bended hooke shall pierce
Their slimy jawes: and as I draw them up,
I'le thinke them every one an Anthony,
And say, "Ah ha; y'are caught."

Charmian:                                    'Twas merry when
          you wager'd on your Angling, when your diver
          did hang a salt fish on his hooke which he
          with fervencie drew up. (*Antony and Cleopatra* 2.5.10–18)

*The bream is a general name for a variety of fresh-water fish that are allied to the carp. In the sixteenth century, bream were also called "copper nose," "old wife," "plosher, "ruffle," and "pargo" (the latter term became the still-current "porgy"). As for the quote from Antony and* Cleopatra, *the incident that Charmian refers to—when Cleopatra had a diver surreptitiously attach a "salt fish" to Antony's hook—gains humor when we realize that "salt fish" referred not to a salt-water fish, but to a fish that had been dried out and preserved with salt. The equivalent jest nowadays would be to tie a can of sardines to someone's hook.*

Take White wine and put it into a pot, and let it seeth, then take your breame and cut hym in the midst, and put him in, then take an Onion and chop it small, then take nutmegs beaten, cinamon and ginger, whole mace, and a pound of butter, and let it boile altogether, and so season it with salt, serve it uppon soppes, and garnish it with fruite.

---

 MODERN RECIPE                                    Makeability: 2

| | |
|---|---|
| 1 lb bream or porgy (or whitefish such as turbot or sole) | 2 blades of mace |
| 2 cups white wine | 1 lb unsalted butter (or to taste) |
| 1 medium yellow onion, finely chopped | 1/2 tsp salt |
| 1 tsp ground nutmeg | 6 slices lightly toasted 60% whole wheat bread for sippets |
| 1 tsp cinnamon | Lemon, orange, barberries, gooseberries, |
| 1 TBS minced ginger | strawberries as available for garnish |

Cut the fish into four pieces. In a large pot, bring the wine to a simmer and gently put in the fish. Add the onion, spices, and butter and simmer for about 10 minutes, or until the fish is opaque and the temperature reads 145°F. Put the sippets on a plate and arrange the fish on them, adding some of the onions. Garnish the dish with fruit as available.

---

# A TROUTE BAKED OR MINCED

*The Second Part of the Good Hus-wives Jewell, 1597*

Maria:                                    Lye thou there:
          for heere comes the Trowt, that must be
          caught with tickling. (*Twelfth Night* 2.5.20–21)

*Among the first five hundred or so books ever printed in England was an anonymous one published in 1508 called* Here Begynneth the Boke of Kervynge. *The book, which* explained how to carve and serve food to the table, was sufficiently popular that further editions followed in 1513, 1560, and 1613. Its opening section lists the terms that are to be used to describe the carving or dressing of various kinds of meat and fish. For example, one does not simply carve a chicken but rather "frushes" it. Likewise, a duck is "unbraced," a heron is "dismembered," and a peacock is "disfigured." The verbs used in relation to fish are especially peculiar and include the following: "chine that salmon, string that lampry, splat that pike, sauce that tench, splay that breme, side the haddock, tusk that barbel, culpon that troute, finne the chevine, transen that eele, traunch that sturgion, undertranch that porpas, tame that crab, barbe that lobster."

Take a Troute and seeth him, then take out all the bones, then mince it verie fine with three or foure dates minced with it, seasoning it with Ginger, and Sinamon, and a quantitie of Sugar and Butter, put all these together, working them fast, then take your fine paste, and cut it in three corner waies in a small bignesse, of foure or five coffins in a dish, then lay your stuffe in them, close them, and so bake them and in the serving of them baste the covers with a little butter, and then cast a little blaunch pouder on them, and so sarve it foorth.

---

 ## MODERN RECIPE                                           Makeability: 3

2 rainbow trout, gutted and cleaned

4 dates, finely minced

1 tsp minced ginger

1/4 tsp cinnamon

1 tsp unsalted butter plus 1/4 cup

1/2 tsp sugar

Blanch powder (see the recipe on page 260)

Pastry recipe "To make fine paste" on page 214, or buy premade pastry.

Prepare four 4-inch pastry shells and tops. Preheat oven to 350°F. In a frying pan with enough water to cover the trout, gently simmer the fish for about five minutes. Remove and allow to cool. Mince the trout finely, adding the dates, ginger, cinnamon, sugar, and butter. Stir the ingredients together. Fill the pastry shells with the trout mixture, cover with pastry, and bake for 30 minutes. Just before serving, brush the tops of the pastries with butter and sprinkle with a little blanch powder.

---

# TO MAKE OISTER CHEWETS

*The Good Huswifes Jewell, 1596*

Benedick:                                                    May I be
so converted, & see with these eyes? I cannot tell, I think not:
I will not bee sworne, but love may transforme me to an oyster,
but I'le take my oath on it, till he have made an oyster of me, he
shall never make me such a foole. (*Much Ado About Nothing* 2.3.21–25)

*According to the* Oxford English Dictionary, *it was Shakespeare who coined the saying, "the world is my oyster."*

Take a pecke of Oisters & wash them cleane, then sheal them and wash them faire in a Cullendar, and when they be sodden, straine the water from them, and chop them as small as pye meate, then season them with pepper, halfe a penniworth of cloves and Mace, halfe a penniworth of sinamon and ginger, and a pennyworth of suger, a little saffron & salt, then take a handfull of small raisons, six dates minced smal and mingle them altogether, then make your paste with one pennyworth of fine flower, tenne yolkes of Egges, a halfe penniworth of Butter with a little saffron and boyling water, then raise up your chewets and put in the bottom of every one of them a little Butter, and so fill them with your stuffe, then cast Prunes, Dates, and small Raisons upon them, and being closed, bake them, let not your Oven be too hotte for they will have but little baking then draw them, and put into every one of them two spoonefull of vergice and butter, and so serve them in.

---

 ## MODERN RECIPE                                          Makeability: 4

2 cups oysters fresh or smoked

1/2 tsp fresh-cracked black pepper

1/4 tsp ground cloves

2 blades of mace

1/2 cup raisins, plus a few for topping

6 minced dates, plus some for topping

1/4 tsp cinnamon

1/4 tsp ground ginger

1 tsp sugar

1 dash saffron

1/2 tsp salt

6 prunes, finely chopped

Pastry recipe "To make fine paste" on page 214, or buy premade pastry.

1/2 cup verjuice (see Appendix 1)

Unsalted butter for the bottom of the pastry shells

Prepare four 4-inch pastry shells and tops. Preheat oven to 350°F. Finely chop the oysters and add the remaining ingredients except the prunes. Put a teaspoon of butter in the bottom of each chewet and fill with the oyster mixture. Add a few raisins, dates, and prunes before topping with pastry. Bake in the oven for 15 minutes. Remove, lift the pastry tops gently, and add a dollop of the remaining butter and 2 tsp of verjuice. Continue baking another 15 minutes.

---

# TO MAKE ALLOES OF FRESH SALMON TO BOILE OR TO BAKE

*The Second Part of the Good Hus-wives Jewell, 1597*

Iago:       She that in wisedome never was so fraile,
To change the Cods-head for the Salmons taile:
She that could thinke, and nev'r disclose her mind,

> See Suitors following, and not looke behind:
> She was a wight, (if ever such wightes were).

Desdemona:    To do what?

Iago:    To suckle Fooles, and chronicle small Beere. (*Othello* 2.1.154–160)

*In the passage from* Othello, *Iago lists the qualities of a virtuous woman, including her refusal to exchange the head of a codfish (which represents the intellect) for the tail of a salmon (which represents sexuality). Iago's conclusion, however, is that such a woman, despite her virtue (or perhaps because of it), is fit for nothing more than nursing foolish babies and tallying up how much her household has spent on weak beer. As for the recipe, its use of "a woman's hand" to indicate the length of the salmon slices probably needs to be adjusted, to account for the fact that men and women nowadays are larger than they were in Shakespeare's England because of improved nutrition. Thomas Johnson, for example, in a 1596 treatise called* Cornucopiae, *claims that the length of a typical man—not his height, but his length when his arms are stretched upward—is six feet. Such a man would only be about five feet in height.*

Take your Salmon and cut him small in peeces of three fingers breadth, and when you have cut so many slices as you will have, let them be of the length of a womans hand, then take more of the salmon, as much as you thinke good, & mince it rawe with six yolkes of hard Egges very fine, and then two or three dishes of Butter with small raisons, and so worke them together with cloves, Mace, Pepper, and Salt, then lay your minced meat in your sliced Aloes, every one being rolled and pricked with a feather, fall closed, then put your aloes, into an Earthen pot, and put to it a pinte of water, and another pint of Claret wine, and so let them boile til they be enough, & afterwarde take the yolkes of three rawe egges with a litle vergious, being strained together, and so put into the pot, then let your aloes seeth no more afterwarde, but serve them upon Soppes of bread.

---

 ## MODERN RECIPE                                        Makeability: 4

| | |
|---|---|
| 1 side of salmon | 1/2 tsp salt |
| 6 hard-boiled egg yolks | 2 cups water |
| 3 TBS unsalted butter | 2 cups red wine |
| 1/4 cup raisins | 3 egg yolks |
| 1/4 tsp ground cloves | 2 TBS verjuice (see Appendix 1) |
| 1/4 tsp ground mace | 6 to 8 slices lightly toasted 60% whole wheat |
| 1/4 tsp fresh-cracked black pepper | bread for sippets |

Slice four pieces of salmon 3 inches wide and 6 inches long. Score the salmon lightly. Mince the remaining salmon and mix with the hard-boiled eggs, butter, raisins, and spices. Place 2 tsp of the mixture on each piece of salmon and roll neatly into a cylinder. If necessary, secure with a toothpick. Place the salmon rolls into a baking dish and pour in the water and red wine. Bring to a boil and hold at a gentle simmer for about 10 minutes, or until the salmon is opaque and the stuffing is thoroughly cooked. Beat the verjuice lightly into the raw eggs and add to the salmon rolls. Simmer for another 5 minutes. Place the sippets on a platter and arrange the salmon rolls on top.

# TO DRESSE A CRAB

*A Propre New Booke of Cokery*, 1545

Puck:  And sometime lurke I in a Gossips bowle,
        In very likenesse of a roasted crab. (*A Midsummer Night's Dream* 2.2.47–48)

*The quotation from* A Midsummer Night's Dream *is a red herring: the crab to which Puck is referring isn't a multi-legged crustacean but rather a crab apple. That signification is more apparent in a passage from Henry Peacham's 1638 treatise entitled* The Truth of our Times, *where he alludes to impoverished children whose "drinke is many times but a roasted Crab, crush'd into a dish of faire water." Other passages, from other sixteenth-century sources, are even clearer: for example, some of them refer to crabs that are roasted and then peeled and cored. Shakespeare's original audience would, of course, have immediately known which crabs were being referred to because they would have been familiar with a long-standing trope that depicted old women as sitting at a fire while roasting crab apples. The modern reader, however, lacks that frame of reference and therefore Puck's roasted apple becomes susceptible to misinterpretation. A similar ambiguity arises in* 1 Henry IV *where Falstaff complains that his sack has lime in it. The sack, of course, is wine (not a woolen bag) and the lime is calcium oxide (not the green citrus fruit), which was used to make a flat beverage sparkle.*

First take awaie all the legges and heddes, and then take all the fisshe out of the shelle & make the shelle as clene as ye can and putte the meate in to a disshe and butter it upon a chafyng dishe of coles and putte there to sinamon and suger and a little vineger, and when ye have chafed it and seasoned it, then put the meate in the shelles again and bruse the heddes and set them upon the disshe side and serve it.

---

 ## MODERN RECIPE                                      Makeability: 4

| | |
|---|---|
| 1 large snow or blue crab | 1/2 tsp cinnamon |
| 1 tsp baking soda | 1/2 tsp sugar |
| 1/4 cup unsalted butter | 1/4 tsp white vinegar |

Remove the legs and head. Cut open the top of the shell and remove the meat to a mixing bowl. Scrub and wash the empty shell and then place it in boiling water to which the baking soda has been added. Boil the shell for 20 minutes. Combine the cinnamon, sugar, vinegar, and crab meat. Add the butter to a sauté pan and simmer the crab meat, seasoning it with a little salt and pepper. Cook over medium-low heat for 10 minutes. Stuff the meat mixture into the shell. Crack open the head slightly. Set the shell on a large plate and arrange the legs and head in their proper position.

# HOW TO SEETH SHRIMPS

*A Book of Cookrye, 1591*

Holofernes: Great Hercules is presented by this Impe,
Whose Club kil'd Cerberus that three-headed Canus,
And when he was a babe, a childe, a shrimpe,
Thus did he strangle Serpents in his Manus.
(*Love's Labour's Lost* 5.2.584–587)

*Considering that England is an island nation, it is surprising that shrimp appear in only two of the 2,100 recipes that were published in this period and that lobsters appear not at all. This apparent culinary aversion to these two shellfish may reflect the sixteenth-century belief that shrimp and lobster were aphrodisiacs and therefore were to be avoided by "good huswives." Michael Drayton, for example, in a sequel to his vast poem Poly-Olbion, describes lobster as "fit for wanton Venus" and "voluptuaries." Shrimp, he adds, are likewise "for wanton womens tastes." Edward Topsell, in his Historie of Foure-Footed Beastes, does find a use for shrimp, albeit not a culinary one: he recommends rubbing crushed shrimp on a mare's genitals in order to "increase her lust." In contrast with shrimp and lobster, other shellfish— such as oysters and mussels—do appear in many of the recipes published in this period.*

Take halfe water and halfe beere or Ale, and some salt good and savery, and set it on the fire and faire scum it, and when it seetheth a full wallop, put in your Shrimpes faire washed, and seethe them with a quick fire, scum them very clean, and let them have but two walmes, then take them up with a scummer, and lay them upon a fair white cloth, and sprinkle a little white salt upon them.

---

 ## MODERN RECIPE                                    Makeability: 2

1 cup water                           1 ½ lb shrimp, shelled and deveined
1 cup beer                            Salt to taste
1 TBS salt

Salt the water and beer and bring to a boil, skimming if necessary. Add the shrimp, and simmer gently no more than 3 to 5 minutes, or until just pink. Remove to a "fair white cloth" for presentation and sprinkle with salt.

---

# TO BOILE A PIKE WITH ORENGES A BANQUET DISH

*The Second Part of the Good Hus-wives Jewell, 1597*

Beatrice: The Count is neither sad, nor sicke, nor merry,
nor well: but civill Count, civill as an Orange, and something of
a jealous complexion. (*Much Ado About Nothing* 2.1.279–281)

"Pike" and "pickerel" are often used interchangeably, but their connection is a bit more complicated than that. Originally, the word "pickerel" denoted a young pike fish, and it is often still used with that sense today. However, "pickerel" has also come to be used to denote the adults of certain subspecies of pike. Moreover, "pickerel" is sometimes used for the walleye, even though that fish is unrelated to the pike. Ichthyologists avoid the confusion by referring to the pike as Esox, but if your local fishmonger is taken aback by that term, just say that you want a pike or a pickerel but not a walleye. Incidentally, in the recipe, the phrase "rosemary, slipped" means that the needles of the rosemary have been stripped from the stem. As for the quotation from Much Ado About Nothing, the pun that Beatrice makes turns on the word "civil": the civil count is like a Seville orange (that is, an orange from the Spanish city of Seville), because he, like the color orange, stands for jealousy. Oranges were a popular ingredient: their flesh, juice, or peels are called for in over a hundred of the 2,100 recipes that were published in this period.

Take your pike, split him, and seeth him alone with water, butter, & salt, then take an earthen pot and put into it a pint of water, and another of Wine, with two Orenges or two Lemmons if you have them: if not, then take foure or five Oringes, the rines being cut away, and slyced, and so put to the licour, with six Dates cut long wayes, and season your broth with ginger, pepper and salte, and two dishes of sweete butter, boyling these together, and when you will serve him, lay your pike upon soppes, casting your broth upon it, you must remember that you cut of your pikes head hard by the body & then his body be spletted, cutting every side in two or three partes, and when he is enough, setting the body of the fish in order: then take his heade & set it at the foremost part of the dish, standing upright with an Orrenge in his mouth, and so serve him.

---

 ## MODERN RECIPE Makeability: 4

| | |
|---|---|
| 1 pike, pickerel, or other similar fish (gutted but head intact) | 2 lemons, peeled and sliced |
| ½ cup unsalted butter | 6 dates cut in quarters along their length |
| 1 TBS salt | 1 TBS minced ginger |
| 2 cups water | ¼ tsp fresh-cracked black pepper |
| 2 cups white wine | ½ tsp salt |
| 2 oranges, peeled and sliced | 6 to 8 slices lightly toasted 60% whole wheat bread for sippets |

Prepare the sauce first. In a saucepan, combine the water and wine along with the oranges and lemons, the dates, ginger, pepper, salt, and butter. Bring to a boil and reduce to a gentle simmer. Meanwhile, place the fish in a large enough pot and just cover with water. Add the butter and salt and bring to a boil, reducing the heat to a gentle simmer immediately. Depending on thickness of the fish, cook for 7 to 10 minutes. Arrange the sippets on a platter and plate the fish, pouring on the sauce. Place the head at the front of the plate with a small orange in its mouth.

# TO FRYE MUSSELS, PERYWINCKELS, OR OYSTERS, TO SERVE WITH A DUCKE, OR SINGLE BY THEMSELVES

*A New Booke of Cookerie*, 1615

Prospero: Speake not you for him: hee's a Traitor: come,
Ile manacle thy necke and feete together:
Sea water shalt thou drinke: thy food shall be
The fresh-brooke Mussels, wither'd roots, and huskes
Wherein the Acorne cradled. (*The Tempest* 1.2.464–468)

*Periwinkles, also known as sea snails, are a spiral-shelled mollusk, somewhat similar to, but smaller than, a whelk. Unlike mussels and oysters, they are not commonly sold, but you might find them in an Asian food market.*

Boyle these shell fishes: then flowre and frye them: then put them into a Pipkin, with a pinte of Claret Wine, Sinamon, Sugar, and Pepper. Take your Ducke boyled or roasted, and put them into two severall Pipkins, if one be boyled, and the other roasted and a little Sugar, large Mace, and fryed toasts, stuck around about it with Butter.

---

 ## MODERN RECIPE                                       Makeability: 4

| | |
|---|---|
| 1/2 lb mussels | 2 cups red Bordeaux |
| 1/2 lb periwinkles (substitute clams) | 1 tsp sugar |
| 12 oysters | 1/2 tsp ground mace |
| 2 cups flour | 1/4 tsp fresh-cracked black pepper |
| 3 TBS unsalted butter | |

Boil the mussels, periwinkles, and oysters in salted water until cooked and then remove them from their shells. Discard any shells that do not open. Allow to cool, dredge in flour, and fry in butter. Remove the shellfish to a large saucepan with the wine and spices and simmer gently. Arrange the shellfish on a boiled or roasted duck (for example, use "To boil a tame ducke or widgin" on page 83), add fried toasts, and garnish with sugar, mace, and pieces of butter.

---

# TO CONGAR EELES, IN COLLARS, LIKE BRAWNE

*A New Booke of Cookerie*, 1615

Lear:  Oh me my heart! My rising heart! But downe.
Foole:  Cry to it Nunckle, as the Cockney did to the Eeles,
when she put 'em i' th' Paste alive, she knapt 'em

o' th' coxcombs with a sticke, and cryed downe wantons,
downe; 'twas her Brother, that in pure kindnesse
to his Horse buttered his Hay. (*King Lear* 2.4.119–124)

*Although the word "congar" in this recipe's title looks like a verb, it is actually a noun denoting a particular kind of eel. "Conger and fennel," for example, is a dish that the Prince and Poins are said to eat in 1 Henry IV. The recipe's title was likely intended to be something like "To boil congar Eeles, in collars, like Brawn," but the word "boil" was inadvertently omitted by the seventeenth-century printer.*

Cut them open with the skinne on, and take the bone cleane out, large Mace, grosse Pepper, some fine sweet Hearbs, chopt under your Knife. Then straw the Hearbes and the Spices, all along the inside of your Eele, and rowle it like a collar of Brawne: so may you doe with Tenches, boyled in fayre water, white Wine, and a quantitie of Salt, so put in some sliced Ginger, Nutmeg, and Pepper in graine. When it is well boyled put it into an earthen Pan, covered with the owne liquour, and a little white Wine-vinegar.

---

 **MODERN RECIPE**  Makeability: 4

| | |
|---|---|
| 3 lb eel | 1 cup white wine |
| 1 tsp ground mace | 1 TBS salt |
| 1 TBS fresh-cracked black pepper | 2 TBS sliced ginger |
| 1/4 cup parsley roughly chopped | 1 TBS nutmeg |
| 1/4 cup roughly chopped basil | 5 peppercorns |
| 2 TBS chopped chives | 1/2 cup white wine vinegar |
| 1 TBS thyme | |

Slice the eel open along its length, de-bone, and season the inside with mace and pepper. Roll the lengths like a "collar" and boil in water for 20 minutes, adding white wine, salt, ginger, nutmeg, and pepper. Remove the eel to an earthenware dish and cover with the stewing liquid, adding the vinegar.

---

# TO SEETH A DORY OR MULLET

*A Book of Cookrye, 1591*

Hamlet: A man may fish with the worme that hath eate
of a King, & eate of the fish that hath fedde of that
worme.
King: What doost thou meane by this?
Hamlet: Nothing but to shew you how a king may goe
a progresse though the guts of a begger. (*Hamlet* 4.3.27–32)

*The deep-sea fish known as the dory probably takes its name from its color: the body of the fish has a golden tint, and the French "dorée" means "gilded." The dory has also been known as the "John Dory" since the early seventeenth century. The addition of "John" may simply have been a humorous nod to the familiarity of this commonly eaten fish. It is also tempting, though, to see "John" as a corruption of the French "jaune," meaning "yellow." As for the mullet, it is name may derive from a Greek source meaning "black." There are many varieties of mullet, but none of them keep well after being caught, so it is imperative to buy it fresh.*

Make your broth light with yest, somewhat savery with salt, and put therin a little Rosemary, and when it seethes put in your fish and let it seeth very softly, take faire water and vergious a like much, and put therto a little new Yest, corance, whole pepper and a little Mace, and Dates shred very fine, and boyle them wel togither, and when they be well boyled, take the best of your broth that your fish is sodden in, and put to it strawberyes, gooseberyes, or barberyes, sweet Butter, some Sugar, and so season up your broth, and poure upon your Dorry or Mullet.

 ## MODERN RECIPE

Makeability: 3

4 cups broth (use "To make ordinary stew'd broth" on page 199)

1 TBS active dry yeast

1 TBS salt

1 TBS finely chopped rosemary

1 lb silver mullet fillets

1/2 cup water

1/2 cup verjuice (see Appendix 1)

1/2 cup currants

6 whole peppercorns

1 blade of mace

1/4 cups finely chopped dates

1 cup strawberries

1 cup gooseberries (if available)

1 cup barberries (see Appendix 1)

1 TBS unsalted butter

1 tsp sugar

Combine the broth, salt, and rosemary and bring to a boil. Add the fish, water, verjuice, yeast, currants, peppercorns, mace, and dates. Return to a boil and let simmer gently. Depending on thickness of fish, cook for 7 to 10 minutes, or until the fish is opaque. Draw off most of the fish broth and add to it the strawberries, gooseberries, barberries, butter, and sugar. Heat thoroughly. Plate the mullet on a platter and pour the strawberry sauce over it.

# TO BAKE PORPOSE OR SEALE

*The Second Part of the Good Hus-wives Jewell, 1597*

First Fisherman:   Alas, poor souls, it grieved my heart
to hear what pitiful cries they made to us to help them,
when, well-a-day, we could scarce help ourselves.

Third Fisherman: Nay, master, said not I as much
                when I saw the porpus how he bounced and tumbled?
                they say they're half fish, half flesh: a plague
                on them, they ne'er come but I look to be washed.
                Master, I marvel how the fishes live in the sea. (*Pericles 2.1.20–27*)

*Although we now know that porpoises and seals are mammals, in Shakespeare's time they were considered fish. William Bullein, for example, warned that "greate Fishes, which bee devourers in the Sea, as Seale, Porpose, and sutch like, bee unholsome." Still more strangely, Shakespeare's contemporaries considered the diving bird known as a the puffin to be a fish, as well as the tail (but not the rest) of the beaver—this classification meant that those animals (or parts of animals) could be eaten on the mandated fish days. In the Middle Ages, porpoise and seal were both considered aristocratic delicacies, but by the time Shakespeare was born, they had fallen out of favor, prompted in part by dietary warnings such as the one just quoted. Indeed, of the 2,100 recipes that were printed in this period, only three of them involve porpoise or seal, including a recipe for "white pease pottage," which names both creatures as optional ingredients.*

Take your porpose or Seale, and perboile it, seasoning it with Pepper and Salt, and so bake it, you must take off the Skinne when you doe bake it and then serve it forth with Gallentine in sawcers.

---

 ## MODERN RECIPE           Makeability: 5

2 lb cubed seal meat (or 4 seal flippers)

2 tsp each salt and pepper

Pastry recipe "To make fine paste" on page 214, or buy premade pastry.

Galantine sauce (see "To make Gallantine for flesh or fish" on page 263)

Prepare a pastry shell and top. Preheat oven to 350°F. In a large pot of boiling water, parboil the seal meat for 10 minutes, skimming when necessary. Drain and remove to a mixing bowl and season with salt and pepper. Arrange the meat in the pastry shell, cover with pastry top, and bake for 50 to 60 minutes, or until the meat is tender. Serve the baked seal in small dishes with the galantine sauce.

# 8

# VEGETABLES

Eating of lettuce is both dangerous to such women as bee apt to conceave with childe, and such as be with childe … those which be with childe shall after bee delivered of children farre unlike their fathers in that they shall be both raging in minde and foolish in wit.
—Thomas Hill, *The Profitable Arte of Gardening*, 1593

When Shakespeare's grandparents were born, vegetables were considered to be second-rate fare, more fit for animals than humans, or at least that was the attitude of those in England who had the means to be choosey when it came to their meals. William Harrison, in his 1587 *Description of Britain*, claimed that this aristocratic disdain for vegetables dated back to the thirteenth century, specifically to the reign of Edward I, though he doesn't reveal how he ascertained this fact. By the latter part of the sixteenth century, however, vegetables (and fruits, for that matter) had made a comeback and were again being served, according to Harrison, "at the tables of delicate merchants, gentlemen, and the nobilitie." The vegetables cited by Harrison and others as being commonly cultivated for consumption include carrots, parsnips, cabbages, turnips, radishes, cucumbers, beans, peas, spinach, beets, asparagus, artichokes, onions, cauliflower, skirrets (a kind of water parsnip), and navets (a kind of turnip). Pumpkins were also eaten, but other gourds and squashes appear to have been grown primarily for ornamental purposes or were dried and fashioned into containers.

In one sense, it is actually a misnomer to use the word "vegetable" in the context of Shakespeare's England. That word didn't come to denote a plant eaten for food until the eighteenth century. Instead, the kinds of things that we now consider vegetables were called, by Shakespeare's contemporaries, "pot herbs" and "salad herbs." It is this broad sense of "herb" that Andrew Boorde had in mind when, in his *Compendyous Regyment*, he asserted that "there is no herbe, nor weede, but god have gyven vertue to them, to helpe man." In other words, all plants were thought to have special "virtues" or attributes, many of which didn't even pertain to nutrition. Thomas Hill, for example, in *The Gardeners Labyrinth*, asserts this about the parsnip: "It is thought that no venemous beast may hurte the creature which weareth or carrieth the roote about him." Similarly, lettuce was thought to prevent drunkenness, skirrets were believed to be an aphrodisiac, and onions, according to Hill, "take away the stinke of the mouth" (which makes one wonder what the breath of

Shakespeare's contemporaries normally smelt like). Hill adds that onions can also be used to facilitate covert communications: "letters drawen and written with the juice of the onion, are invisible, whych then shewe and appeare evidentlye, when the paper shall be heated at the fire." On the other hand, many "pot herbs" and "salad herbs" also had the power to do harm: for example, onions "maketh a man dimme sighted" and spinach "dothe ingender Melancholie."

Curious lore was also propounded about the best way to grow vegetables. For example, the seeds of artichokes, according to Thomas Hill, should be steeped in "pleasant wine" before being planted, in order to produce an especially sweet plant. Hill also claims that you can safeguard whatever seeds you plant by dragging a speckled toad around your garden and then putting it into an earthen pot and burying it. Gervase Markham advises that gardens should have laurel trees planted against their walls to protect the pot herbs and salad herbs from thunder and lightning.

# A FRIDAYES PYE, WITHOUT EYTHER FLESH OR FISH

*A New Booke of Cookerie, 1615*

Lucio:                    The Duke (I say to thee againe)
would eate Mutton on Fridaies. He's now past it,
yet (and I say to thee) hee would mouth with a beggar,
though she smelt browne-bread and Garlicke: say that I
said so: Farewell. (*Measure for Measure* 3.2.174–178)

*This dish is called a "Fridayes pye" because it is meat-free, making it suitable for eating on Fish Days, which included not just Fridays but also Wednesdays, Saturdays, and all of Lent and Advent. Lucio alludes to this practice in the quotation when he says that the Duke would "eat mutton on Fridays," by which he means to imply that the Duke has an appetite for the illicit flesh of prostitutes. As for the recipe itself, its reference to picking out the "middle string" (that is, the reddish vein that runs from one end of a beet leaf to the other) makes it clear that this pie is made from the leaves of the beet rather than its root. The word "relisht," which is applied to the apples, means "nicely flavored."*

Wash greene Beetes cleane, picke out the middle string, and chop them small with two or three well relisht ripe Apples. Season it with Pepper, Salt, and Ginger: then take a good handfull of Razins of the Sunne, and put all in a Coffin of fine Paste, with a piece of sweet Butter, and so bake it: but before you serve it in, cut it up, and wring in the juyce of an Orenge, and Sugar.

 ## MODERN RECIPE                              Makeability: 3

4 cups of chopped beet leaves        1/4 tsp pepper
3 ripe apples, peeled and diced      1/4 tsp salt

*Continued on next page*

*Continued from previous page*

2 tsp minced ginger

$^1/_2$ cup raisins

Juice of one orange

2 TBS sugar

3 TBS unsalted butter

Use pastry recipe "To make a fine paste" on page 214, or buy premade pastry

Prepare a pastry shell and top. Preheat oven to 350°F. Clean the beet leaves and remove the thick central stalk. Chop the leaves into 2-inch squares. In a mixing bowl, combine the beet leaves, apples, spices, raisins, orange juice, and sugar. Pour into the pastry shell, place dollops of butter on the mixture, and cover. Brush the top with a bit of butter and bake for 35 to 40 minutes, or until golden brown.

# TO FARSE A CABBADGE FOR A BANQUET DISH

*The Second Part of the Good Hus-wives Jewell, 1597*

Benedick: He was wont to speake plaine, & to the
purpose (like an honest man & a souldier) and now is
he turn'd orthography, his words are a very fantasticall
banquet, just so many strange dishes. (*Much Ado About Nothing* 2.3.18–21)

Take litle rounde cabbage cutting off the stalkes, and by the cabbadge then make a round hole in your cabbadge, as much as will receive your farsing meat, take heede you breake not the brimmes, thereof with your knife, for the hole must be round and deep, then take the kidney of a mutton or more, and chop it not smal. Then boile six egges hard, taking the yolkes of them being smal chopped & also take rawe egges and a manchet grated fine, then take a handfull of proynes, so many great raysons, seasoning al these with salte, pepper, cloves and Mace, working all these together, and so stuffe your Cabbedge. But if you have Sawsedge you may put it among your meate at the putting in of your stuffe, but you must leave out both the ends of your sawsage at the mouth of the cabbadge when you shall serve it out. In the boyling it must be within the cabbadge, and the cabbadge must be stopped close with his cover in the time of his boyling, and bound fast round about for breaking: the cabbadge must bee sodde in a deepe pot with fresh beefe broth or mutton broth, and no more then will lye unto the top of the cabbadge, and when it is enough take away the thrid, and so set it on a platter, opening the heade & laying out the Sawsadge endes, and so serve it forth.

 ## MODERN RECIPE

Makeability: 5

1 large Savoy cabbage

1 lamb kidney, roughly chopped

6 hard-boiled egg yolks, finely chopped

$^1/_2$ cup bread crumbs

$^1/_2$ cup prunes

$^1/_2$ cup raisins

$^1/_4$ tsp each salt and pepper

$^1/_4$ tsp ground mace

1 large cooked sausage

6 quarts beef stock

Quantity of kitchen string for trussing the cabbage

Remove the two or three outer leaves of the cabbage. Slice off the top 2 inches of the cabbage and reserve for a lid. Bore a wide and deep hole down into the centre of the cabbage, but leave a 1-inch "wall" around the hole. In a mixing bowl, combine the mutton, egg yolks, bread crumbs, prunes, raisins, and seasonings. Sauté the stuffing gently until just cooked through. Stuff the cabbage with the mixture and tuck in the sausage. Bind the cabbage with the kitchen string and seal it with the lid (use large toothpicks or skewers to secure the lid). Place the cabbage in a large, deep stock pot and fill with the beef stock to just below to lid. Bring to a boil and reduce to a simmer for one hour or until cooked through. Carefully remove the cabbage from the stock, remove the kitchen string, and arrange the sausage so that both ends are peeking out of the top of the cabbage. Set the cabbage on a platter and serve.

# HOW TO BUTTER A COLLE-FLOWRE

*A Delightfull Daily Exercise for Ladies and Gentlewomen, 1621*

Hotspur: O, I could divide my selfe, and go to buffets,
for moving such a dish of skim'd Milk with so honourable
an Action. Hang him, let him tell the King we are
prepared. I will set forwards to night. (*1 Henry IV* 2.3.31–34)

Take a ripe Colle-floure and cut off the buddes, boyle them in milke with a little Mace while they be very tender, then poure them into a Cullender, and let the Milke runne cleane from them, then take a ladle full of Creame, being boyled with a little whole Mace, putting to it a Ladle-full of thicke butter, mingle them together with a little Sugar, dish up your flowers upon sippets, poure your butter and creame hot upon it strowing on a little slicst Nutmeg and salt, and serve it to the Table hot.

 ## MODERN RECIPE                                   Makeability: 2

1 head cauliflower, sectioned into florets

2 cups whole milk (or enough to cover)

6 blades of whole mace

1 cup whipping cream

1/2 lb unsalted butter

1 TBS sugar

1 TBS nutmeg

1/2 tsp salt

6 slices lightly toasted 60% whole wheat bread for sippets

Place the cauliflower in a large pot with the milk and four blades of mace. Bring to a boil and reduce heat, simmering gently for about 6 to 8 minutes, or until tender. Drain the cauliflower in a colander and keep it warm. In a saucepan, bring the cream and remaining two blades of mace to a simmer, add the butter and sugar, and stir. Arrange the cauliflower on the sippets on a platter. Pour on the cream and butter mixture and sprinkle with the nutmeg and salt.

# TO FRYE BEANES

*A Propre New Booke of Cokery, 1545*

Lear:  Why, this would make a man, a man of Salt
    To use his eyes for Garden water-pots. (*King Lear* 4.6.195–196)

*In the quotation from* King Lear, *the outcast Lear means that his plight is so woeful that it would cause even a man made of salt to weep like a watering can. Salt, incidentally, was considered a symbol of eternity because, according to Michael Scot in his 1633* Philosophers Banquet, *it is "not onely able to preserve it selfe from rottennesse and corruption, but all other things." This may help account for the special status bestowed on salt at the dinner table: those who sat above the salt cellar—that is, closer to the high table—were deemed to have greater rank than those who sat below it.*

Take your Beanes and boyle them and put them into a fryenge pan with a disshe of butter & one or two onyons and so let them fry tyll they be browne all together, than cast a lytell salt upon them, & then serve them forth.

## MODERN RECIPE                                   Makeability: 1

2 cups canned navy beans, rinsed and drained    1 medium yellow onion, diced
2 TBS unsalted butter                           ¼ tsp salt

In a sauté pan melt the butter and sauté the onions until soft. Add the beans and stir frequently. Add the salt and cook the beans until they brown slightly.

# TO MAKE A DISHE OF ARTECHOKES

*The Good Huswifes Jewell, 1596*

Enobarbus:  He will to his Egyptian dish againe. (*Antony and Cleopatra* 2.6.128)

*The artichoke was introduced to England from Italy during the reign of Henry VIII, and gradually became a popular foodstuff, its acceptance perhaps slightly slowed by the fact that it was sometimes called "garden thistle" and even "cow thistle." A hundred years after it was introduced, James Hart, in his 1633* Klinike, *commented that the artichoke "is in no small request, and used by most people. It is most commonly eaten boiled with butter, vinegar, pepper, and salt." The artichoke was usually prepared as a dish in its own right (as with this recipe) but sometimes as a secondary ingredient in other dishes (a recipe for "marrow-bone pie," for example, calls for the bottoms of artichokes). Shakespeare's contemporaries also consumed the unrelated Jerusalem artichoke, which acquired that name only because its flavor somewhat resembles that of the artichoke (the "Jerusalem" part of its name is a corruption of the Italian "girasole," meaning "sunflower"). John Gerard, in his 1597 Herball, admitted that Jerusalem artichokes were popular—"some boile them in water, and after stew them with sacke and butter, adding a little Ginger: others bake them in pies, putting Marrow, Dates, Ginger, Raisons of the Sun, Sack"—but added that he personally thought they were "a meat more fit for swine than men," because they cause "a filthie loathsome stinking winde within the bodie, thereby causing the belly to bee pained and tormented."*

Take your Artechokes and pare away all the top even to the meate and boyle them in sweete broth till they be somewhat tender, and then take them out, and put them into a dishe, and seethe them with Pepper, synamon and ginger, and then put in your dishe that you meane to bake them in, and put in Marrowe to them good store, and so let them bake, and when they be baked, put in a little Vinegar and butter, and sticke three or foure leaves of the Artechoks in the dishe when you serve them up, and scrape Suger on the dish.

---

 ## MODERN RECIPE                                     Makeability: 2

12 artichokes, fresh or canned               1/4 cup marrow (see Appendix 1)

4 cups chicken stock                          1 tsp vinegar

1/2 tsp fresh-cracked pepper                  2 TBS unsalted butter

1/4 tsp cinnamon                              2 TBS sugar

1 tsp minced ginger

Preheat oven to 350°F. If using fresh artichokes, clean them and boil them in the chicken stock. Reserve a few of the outer leaves for garnish. In a saucepan, combine the artichokes, pepper, cinnamon, and ginger and heat the mixture thoroughly. Pour the artichoke mixture into a baking dish, add the marrow or suet, and bake for 45 minutes. Remove the dish with 15 minutes left and add the vinegar and butter. Continue cooking. Garnish with a few artichoke leaves and sprinkle with sugar to taste.

---

# TO MAKE A CLOSE TARTE OF GREEN PEASE

*The Good Huswifes Jewell, 1596*

Berowne:  This fellow pickes up wit as Pigeons pease,
          And utters it againe, when Jove doth please.
          He is Wits Pedler, and retailes his Wares,
          At Wakes, and Wassels, Meetings, Markets, Faires.
          And we that sell by grosse, the Lord doth know,
          Have not the grace to grace it with such show. (*Love's Labour's Lost* 5.2.316–321)

Take half a peck of green Pease, sheale them and seeth them, and cast them into a cullender, and let the water go from them then put them into the Tart whole, & season them with Pepper, saffron and salte, and a dishe of sweet butter, close and bake him almost one houre, then drawe him, and put to him a little Vergice, and take them and set them into the Oven againe, and so serve it.

 MODERN RECIPE                                        Makeability: 3

| | |
|---|---|
| 4 cups sweet peas or shelled sugar-snap peas | 1/4 lb unsalted butter |
| 1/4 tsp pepper | 2 TBS verjuice (see Appendix 1) |
| 1 pinch saffron | Pastry recipe "To make fine paste" on page 214, or buy premade pastry. |
| 1/2 tsp salt | |

Prepare a pastry shell and top. Preheat oven to 350°F. Bring to a boil a large saucepan of water. Pour in peas and return water to a boil. Simmer gently for four minutes and drain. Pour the cooked peas into the pastry shell and season with pepper, saffron, and salt. Place small dollops of butter throughout the peas. Cover with pastry and bake for 30 minutes. Remove the tart, slit a few small openings, and pour in the verjuice. Return to the oven and bake a further 10 minutes.

# TO MAKE A TARTE OF BEANES

*A Propre New Booke of Cokery*, 1545

Troilus: But still sweet love is food for fortunes tooth. (*Troilus and Cressida* 4.5.294)

Take beanes and boile them tendre in faire water, then take theim out and breake theim in a morter and strayne them with the yolkes of iiii egges, curd made of milke, then ceason it up with suger and halfe a disshe of butter and a litle synamon and bake it.

 MODERN RECIPE                                        Makeability: 3

| | |
|---|---|
| 2 cups white kidney beans | 1 TBS unsalted butter |
| 4 egg yolks | 1/4 tsp cinnamon |
| 1/2 cup cottage cheese (drained of fluid) | Pastry recipe "To make fine paste" on page 214, or buy premade pastry. |
| 1/2 tsp sugar | |

Preheat oven to 350°F. Prepare a pastry shell and precook it for 10 minutes, or just until it begins to brown. Drain beans and crush them (in a mortar and pestle if available). Mix thoroughly with the egg yolks and drained cottage cheese, adding the sugar, butter, and cinnamon. Pour into the pastry shell and bake for 35 to 40 minutes, or until the pastry is golden brown and the filling has set.

# TO DRESSE GOURDS WITH ALMOND MILKE OR WITH OTHER MILKE

*Epulario*, 1598

Menenius:                                        There is no
              more mercy in him, than there is milke in a male-Tyger;
              that shall our poore City finde. (*Coriolanus* 5.4.27–29)

Seeth the Gourdes in water, then presse the water out of them and straine them, then seeth them with almond milke or other milke, with sugar, and a little verjuice as you thinke good.

## MODERN RECIPE                                        Makeability: 2

2 cups pumpkin, cut into 1-inch cubes          1 TBS sugar

2 cups almond milk (see recipe on page 276,    1 tsp verjuice (see Appendix 1)
or substitute whole milk)

In a large saucepan, cover the cubes of pumpkin with water and bring to a boil. Simmer gently for 15 to 20 minutes, or until just tender. Drain the pumpkin cubes in a colander, pressing them gently. Return the pumpkin to the saucepan, add the almond milk, sugar, and verjuice and bring to a gentle boil.

# TO MAKE TATTES OR BALDE MEATES FOR FISH DAIES

*The Second Part of the Good Hus-wives Jewell*, 1597

Suffolk:  How often hast thou waited at my cup,
              Fed from my Trencher, kneel'd downe at the boord,
              When I have feasted with Queene Margaret?
              Remember it, and let it make thee Crest-falne,
              Aye, and alay this thy abortive Pride. (*2 Henry VI* 4.1.56–60)

Take your dish and annoint the bottom well with butter, then make a fine past to the bredth of the dish, and lay it on the same dish upon the butter, then take

Beetes, Spinage, and Cabbadges, or white Lettice, cutting them fine in long peeces, then take the yolkes of viii rawe eggs, and six yolkes of hard Egges, with small Raisons and a little Cheese fine scraped, and grated bread, and three or four dishes of Butter melted and clarified and when you have wrought it together, season it with Sugar, Sinamon, Ginger and salt, then lay it upon your fine past spreading it abroad, then the cover of fine paste being cut with prettie work, then set it in your oven, bake it with your dish under it and when it is enough, then at the serving of it you must newe paste the cover with butter, and so scrape suger upon it, and then serve it foorth.

---

 MODERN RECIPE                                    Makeability: 3

2 cups beet leaves

3 cups of spinach, washed and dried

2 cups Savoy cabbage

8 egg yolks

6 hard-boiled egg yolks

1/2 cup raisins

1/2 cup grated hard white cheese

1/2 cup bread crumbs

3 TBS unsalted clarified butter plus 3 TBS for brushing on the pastry

1 tsp sugar

1/4 tsp cinnamon

1 tsp ginger

1/4 tsp salt

Pastry recipe "To make fine paste" on page 214, or buy premade pastry.

Preheat oven to 350°F. Prepare a pastry shell and top, and precook the shell for 10 minutes, or just until it begins to brown. Cut the beet leaves and cabbage in 1-inch strips. Combine with the spinach, eggs, raisins, cheese, bread crumbs, and butter and integrate well. Add the sugar, cinnamon, ginger, and salt, and pour the mixture into the pastry shell. Cover with the pastry top, scallop the edges, and decorate with bits of pastry cuttings. Bake in the oven for 25 to 30 minutes. Remove the dish and brush with melted butter and sprinkle with sugar. Return to the oven and bake for another 10 minutes, or until golden brown.

# TO MAKE A MADE DISH OF TURNEPS

*A Delightfull Daily Exercise for Ladies and Gentlewomen, 1621*

Touchstone: Truly, and to cast away honestie upon a foule slut, were to put good meate into an uncleane dish. (*As You Like It* 3.3.33–34)

*Shakespeare's England had plenty of turnips (which were sometimes called rapes and navets), but no rutabagas (which were also known as swedes). The latter vegetable was developed in the seventeenth century, presumably in Sweden, by crossing the turnip with the cabbage, but was not introduced to England until much later. As late as 1799, for example, J.B. Bordley referred to "the new turnip, called roota baga," suggesting that the rutabaga had only recent crossed the North Sea. The "butcher's prick" to which the recipe alludes was a wooden skewer, probably used to pierce a dry joint of meat so that lard or fat could be inserted. A proverb current in Shakespeare's England was "to whittle an oak to a butcher's prick."*

Pare your Turnepes as you would pare a Pippin then cut them in square pieces, an ynch and a halfe long and as thicke as a Butchers pricke or skewet, put them into a pipkin with a pound of butter, and three or foure spoonefuls of strong broath, and a quarter of a pint of Vineger seasoned with a little Pepper, Ginger, Salt and Sugar, and let them stue very easily upon a soft fire, for the space of two houres or more, now and then turning them with a spoone, as occasion shall serve, but by all meanes take heede you breake them not, then dish them up upon Sippets, and serve them to the Table hot.

---

 ## MODERN RECIPE                                    Makeability: 2

2 cups white turnips cut into cubes 1$^1$/$_2$-inch long and $^1$/$_4$-inch thick

$^1$/$_2$ lb unsalted butter

4 TBS strong chicken broth

$^1$/$_2$ cup white vinegar

$^1$/$_4$ tsp pepper

1 tsp ginger

$^1$/$_4$ tsp salt

1 TBS sugar

6 slices lightly toasted 60% whole wheat bread for sippets

Place the turnips into a large saucepan with the remaining ingredients and bring to a boil. Reduce heat to a simmer and cook until tender. Turn the turnips gently on occasion. Arrange the sippets on a platter, spoon the turnips over the top, and serve.

---

# TO MAKE A FRIED MEAT OF TURNEPS

*Epulario*, 1598

Anne:            Good mother, do not marry me to yond foole.
Mistress Page: I meane it not, I seeke you a better husband.
Quickly:         That's my master, Master Doctor
Anne:            Alas I had rather be set quick i' th' earth,
                 And bowl'd to death with Turnips. (*The Merry Wives of Windsor* 3.4.83–87)

*Lawn bowling was a popular sport in Shakespeare's England and in fact had been enjoyed since at least the early fifteenth century. The turnips to which Anne refers in the quotation from* The Merry Wives of Windsor *would not, of course, have rolled in a straight line, but neither did the wooden bowling balls that were actually used: they were weighted or "biased" on one side with lead, so that they could be made to curve as they trundled along.*

*Petruchio alludes to this in* The Taming of the Shrew *when he comments on how his wife has "straightened up": "Forward, forward, thus the bowle should run, / And not unluckily against the Bias" (4.5.24–25).*

Rost the Turnops in the embers, or else seethe them whole, then cut or slice them in peeces as thicke as halfe the hast of a knife, which done, take cheese and cut them in the same form and quantity, but some what thinner, then take Sugar, Pepper, and other spices mingled together, and put them in a pan under the peeces of cheese, as if you would make a crust under the cheese, and on top of them likewise, and over it you shall lay the peeces of Turneps, covering them over with the spices aforesaid, and plenty of good butter, and so you shall doe with the faire cheese and Turneps till the pan bee full, letting them fry the space of a quarter of an houre, or more, like a Tart, and this would be one of your last dishes.

---

 ## MODERN RECIPE — Makeability: 3

| | |
|---|---|
| 6 white turnips | 1/4 tsp cinnamon |
| 6 oz hard white cheese | 1/4 tsp ground cloves |
| 1/4 cup sugar | 1/4 tsp ground mace |
| 1/4 tsp fresh-cracked black pepper | 4 TBS unsalted butter |

Preheat oven to 350°F. Boil the whole turnips for 30 minutes, cool, and peel. Cut the turnips in slices a quarter-inch thick and the cheese slightly less than a quarter inch. Mix together the sugar and spices. Put a half-inch layer of the sugar and spice mixture in the bottom of a deep skillet. Follow with a layer of cheese and then a layer of turnip. Add more spice mixture and dollops of butter. Repeat the sequence of layers. Bake for 25 to 30 minutes.

---

# TO MAKE A TART OF SPINNAGE

*The Good Huswifes Handmaide for the Kitchin, 1594*

Falstaff: I am the veriest Varlet that ever chewed with a Tooth. (*1 Henry IV 2.2.23*)

*Falstaff's reference to teeth, in the quotation from 1 Henry IV, raises a grim subject: namely, dental health in Shakespeare's England. Generally speaking, it was bad. Dentistry, such as it was, was practiced by barbers, who advertised their skill by hanging bloody bandages outside of their shops (an emblem that eventually evolved into the red-and-white-striped barber's pole). Sulpha drugs and antibiotics for treating "abscesses" were of course nonexistent. Anesthetics were limited to whatever quantity of distilled spirits one could drink. Things were probably worst for the wealthy, whose diets included far more sugar than the lower classes. Even teeth cleansers often included sweeteners: Hugh Plat, for example, proposed a mouthwash made of honey, wine, and vinegar. In the last decade or two of her life, Queen Elizabeth's teeth reached an advanced state of decay. Paul Hentzner, a German traveller who wrote an account of his travels through England in 1598, gave an unflattering description of the Queen with "her nose a little hooked, her lips thin, and her teeth black," adding that the latter feature was "a defect the English seem subject to, from their too great use of sugar." A few years earlier, the Queen had required the extraction of a decayed tooth, which she refused until one of her councillors, John Aylmer, volunteered to have one of his healthy teeth pulled so that she could see that the process was less painful than she feared.*

Take some cast creame, and seeth some Spinnage in faire water till it be verie soft, then put it into a Collender, that the water may soake from it: then straine the Spinnage, and cast the creame together, let there be good plentie of Spinnage: set it upon a chafingdish of coales, and put to it Sugar and some Butter, and let it boyle a while. Then put it in the paste, and bake it, and caste blanche powder on it, and so serve it in.

---

 ## MODERN RECIPE                                      Makeability: 3

6 cups spinach

$1/2$ cup cast cream (see the recipe "To make cast Creame another way" on page 170, or substitute sour cream)

Blanch powder (see the recipe on page 260)

1 TBS sugar

2 TBS unsalted butter

Pastry recipe "To make fine paste" on page 214, or buy premade pastry.

Prepare a pastry shell and top. Preheat oven to 350°F and precook the pastry shell for about ten minutes or just until it begins to brown. In a pot of boiling water, blanch the spinach for one minute. Drain the spinach in a colander and remove as much water as possible. In a sauté pan, gently heat the cast cream and spinach for a few minutes. Add the sugar and butter and combine, simmering gently for a few more minutes. Pour the spinach into the pastry shell and cover. Brush the top with a bit of butter and bake for 30 to 40 minutes until golden brown. Sprinkle on some blanch powder.

---

# TO DRESSE MUSHROMES

*Epulario, 1598*

Prospero:  Ye Elves of hils, brooks, standing lakes & groves,
And ye, that on the sands with printlesse foote
Doe chase the ebbing Neptune, and doe flie him
When he comes backe: you demi-Puppets, that
By Moone-shine doe the greene sowre Ringlets make,
Whereof the Ewe not bites: and you, whose pastime
Is to make midnight-Mushrumps, that rejoyce
To heare the solemne Curfewe. (*The Tempest* 5.1.33–40)

*In Shakespeare's England, conventional wisdom held that mushrooms were fit to be eaten only by fools, rodents, and Italians. James Hart, for example, wrote that "it is a food (if so it deserveth to be called) in small request here amongst us" but acknowledged that in "Italy, and adjacent countries, it is in no small esteem." Stephen Bradwell, in his 1633 treatise called* Helps for Suddain Accidents, *called them "an excrescence of the earths superfluitie" but admitted that some of his English countrymen "out of wantonnesse, and apish imitation of Strangers" have taken up eating them. Bradwell added that he once saved a man who ate a poison mushroom by making him a beverage of dried hen's dung, white wine, and vinegar. Not surprisingly, in Shakespeare's England the only recipes that call for mushrooms are those that originated, like this one, in Italy.*

Make the Mushromes very cleane, and seeth them with two or three heads of Garlike, and crummes of bread, this is done because naturally they are venomous, then take them up, and let the water runne out of them until they be dry, then fry them in oyle, and when they are fried, cast pepper and other spices on them, in flesh time fry them as aforesaied. You may dresse them another way, make them very cleane, then set them on the fire, putting to them larde and Garlike beaten together, with pepper, you may likewise dresse them with oyle, you may fry them also in a frying pan like a pancake.

---

 ## MODERN RECIPE                                     Makeability: 2

| | |
|---|---|
| 12 oz button mushrooms | 1/4 tsp fresh-cracked pepper |
| 2 cloves minced garlic | 1/4 tsp salt |
| 2 TBS vegetable oil | 1/4 tsp nutmeg |
| 6 slices of cooked bacon, roughly chopped | 1/4 tsp cloves |
| 1/4 cup bread crumbs | 1/4 cup lard (optional) |

Brush any dirt off the mushrooms, wipe them with a damp kitchen towel, and slice. Heat the oil and add the garlic, cooking it gently. Do not allow the garlic to brown or it will be bitter. Sauté the mushrooms and add the bacon, bread crumbs, and spices. Alternatively, you can add lard to the sautéed garlic and then sauté the mushrooms.

---

# TO FRY BEANS IN A PAN

*Epulario, 1598*

Pistol:     Dye, and be dam'd, and Figo for thy friendship.
Fluellen:  It is well.
Pistol:     The Figge of Spaine.
Fluellen:  Very good. (*Henry V* 3.6.57–60)

*As far as Shakespeare's contemporaries were concerned, Italy and Spain were breeding grounds of iniquity, lust, and political scheming. Accordingly, English playwrights tended to set their revenge tragedies in one of those two nations (Hamlet, set in Denmark, bucks the trend). One of the tools of revenge associated with Italians and Spaniards was the poisoned fig: references to people being knocked off with "the Italian fig" or "the Spanish fig" abound from the late sixteenth century to the late eighteenth century. Thus, when Pistol says "The Figge of Spaine" to Fluellen, he is essentially threatening him (in modern parlance) with concrete shoes.*

Take Beanes, Sage, Onions and Figges as aforesaid, with other good hearbes, and mingle them together, then frie them in a frying pan with oyle, and make it like a pancake, and when it is baked take it out, and cast spice upon it.

---

 ## MODERN RECIPE                                        Makeability: 3

| | |
|---|---|
| 1 cup cooked kidney beans | 1 TBS thyme |
| ¼ cup chopped sage | 3 TBS olive oil |
| 1 medium-size yellow onion, finely diced | Ground mace, ground cloves, and salt and pepper to taste |
| ¼ cup dried figs, finely chopped | |
| ¼ cup chopped parsley | |

In a mixing bowl, combine and thoroughly integrate the beans, sage, onion, figs, parsley, and thyme. Heat the olive oil in a frying pan and add the bean mixture, gently pressing it into a pancake. When it is heated through and holds its shape, slip it out of the pan onto a platter and sprinkle with the mace, cloves, salt, and pepper as desired.

---

# TO MAKE A MEAT OF YOUNG BEANES WITH FLESH OR OTHERWISE

*Epulario, 1598*

E. Dromio:  A man may break a word with your sir, and words
             are but winde: aye, and break it in your face, so he
             break it not behinde. (*The Comedy of Errors* 3.1.74–76)

*Before the sixteenth century, the only bean available in England (or elsewhere in Europe) was the broad bean. However, by the time Shakespeare was born, new varieties of beans had been introduced from the Americas, including navy beans, green beans, and kidney beans. Among the upper classes, beans were usually consumed without their shells—or "cods" as they were then called—but eating them unshelled was not unknown and may have been the usual practice among the poor. James Hart, for example, in his 1633 Klinike, noted that "the fruit and cods of Kidney Beanes boiled together before they be ripe,*

*and buttered, and so eaten with their cods, are exceeding delicate meat." Dietary author-
ities of the day also concurred in recommending that beans be eaten with mint, as in this
recipe, because it diminished their "windiness."*

Take Beanes and blanch them with whot water like almonds, then set them to
boile, and when they are boiled, put to them a little Parsely, and Mints well beaten,
and seeth them with salt Beefe or Bacon, let it be somewhat green and it is the better. The like may be done with pease and other fruits when they are greene.

---

 ## MODERN RECIPE                                    Makeability: 1

2 cups of broad or white kidney beans          2 TBS chopped mint

1/4 cup chopped parsley                         6 strips of bacon, chopped

Place the beans into a saucepan of boiling water and cook until desired tenderness is achieved (5 to
10 minutes). Drain the beans in a colander and return to the saucepan, stirring in the remaining
ingredients until heated through.

---

# TO SEETH GOURDES AFTER THE CATALONIAN FASHION

*Epulario, 1598*

Oberon: Fetch me that flower; the hearb I shew'd thee once,
The juyce of it, on sleeping eye-lids laid,
Will make or man or woman madly dote
Upon the next live creature that it sees.
Fetch me this hearbe, and be thou heere againe,
Ere the Leviathan can swim a league. (*A Midsummer Night's Dream* 2.1.169–174)

Take the juice of the Gourd and make it very clean, then put it into a pipkin with
good larde or oyle, and set the pipkin on the coales upon a soft fire, and make it to
boile, stirring it with a spoone: it should seeth for the space of foure houres, then
take fat broth coloured with saffron, & put into the Gourdes, adding thereto sugar,
spice, and a little Verjuice according to the tast. You may also put to it a few yolkes
of egges beaten together with a little old cheese.

---

 ## MODERN RECIPE                                    Makeability: 2

2 cups pumpkin, cubed                          1 pinch of saffron

1/4 cup lard or olive oil                      1 TBS sugar

2 cups beef or chicken stock

1 tsp of mixed cinnamon, mace, cloves, ginger, and pepper

2 TBS verjuice (see Appendix 1)

3 beaten egg yolks

1/4 cup hard white cheese, finely grated

In a casserole dish, cook the squash and olive oil or lard on a gentle simmer for 30 to 40 minutes, or until the pumpkin is just tender. Add the stock, sugar, spice mixture, and verjuice. Mix the eggs and cheese and pour into the pumpkin. Combine and heat thoroughly before serving.

# TO FRY GOURDES OR POMPEONS

*Epulario, 1598*

Hotspur:                    O, he is as tedious
            As a tyred Horse, a rayling Wife,
            Worse than a smoakie House. I had rather live
            With Cheese and Garlick in a Windmill farre,
            Than feede on Cates, and have him talke to me,
            In any Summer-House in Christendome. (*1 Henry IV* 3.1.155–160)

Take Gourdes and make them very cleane, then cut them in thinne peeces, and let them boile one waume, then take them out and dry them and salt them, rouling them in floure, that done, fry them in good oile, then take them off the fire, and take a little Garlike and crummes of bread and stampe them together with a little Verjuice, then straine it, and put this sauce upon the Gourds, it will be good if you put nothing but Verjuice, Fennel seed, and a little basill: and if you will have it yellow, cast saffron into it.

 ## MODERN RECIPE                                    Makeability: 2

2 cups pumpkin, cut in sticks 2 inches long by 1/2-inch thick

1 TBS salt

1 cup flour for dredging

1/2 cup olive oil for frying

1 clove of minced garlic

1/2 cup bread crumbs

2 TBS verjuice (see Appendix 1)

1 tsp fennel seeds

6 basil leaves, chopped

1 pinch saffron

Bring a large saucepan of water to a boil. Add the squash and return to a boil. Drain the squash in a colander and pat dry with a clean kitchen towel. Sprinkle the squash with salt and dredge it with flour. Heat the olive oil, as needed, in a large frying pan and fry the squash pieces until golden brown. Fry in small batches to allow for sufficient space for even cooking. Keep the cooked pieces warm. In a mixing bowl, combine the minced garlic, bread crumbs, verjuice, fennel seeds, basil, and saffron. Place the pumpkin on a platter, sprinkle generously with the bread crumb mixture, and serve.

# 9

# EGGS AND DAIRY

Prince:        What men?
Sheriff:       One of them is well known, my gracious lord, A gross fat man.
First Carrier: As fat as butter. (*1 Henry IV* 2.4.504–506)

For rural households in Shakespeare's England, owning a milk cow meant easy access to a nutritious foodstuff that could be consumed in a variety of forms. As a poor husbandman says in a 1594 treatise entitled *A Looking Glass for London and England*, "my Cow is a Common-wealth to me, for first, sir, she allowes me, my wife and sonne, for to banquet ourselves withal, Butter, Cheese, Whay, Curds, Creame, sod milk, raw-milke, sower-milke, sweete-milk, and butter-milke." (His second reason for treasuring his cow, as he goes on to say, is that she alerts him to impending storms by raising her tail.) In London and other large centers, access to fresh milk was more difficult or at least more problematic: cow milk (as well as some goat milk and sheep milk) was sold in the street by the pailful, but it was often watered down or contaminated by whatever had fallen into it as the milkmaid trudged along her route. Moreover, the challenge of keeping it fresh, especially in the summer, meant that most of the milk that was produced was turned into longer-lasting products like cheese and butter or was added to beer or wine to make a caudle, rather than being drunk straight as a beverage. Indeed, fresh milk was not considered healthy for everyone: Andrew Boorde, for example, asserted in his *Compendyous Regyment* that it was not good for people who have "gurgulacyons in the belly," or for people with sanguine temperaments. He did acknowledge, though, that both cow's milk and ewe's milk could be good for "olde men & chyldren specyally if it be sodden, addynge to it a lytell suger." He added, too, that "mylke of a woman, & the mylke of a goate … be good for them that be in a consumpcyone." A further hazard, according to Boorde, was fresh or "raw" cream. Strawberries and cream, he says, is a farmer's banquet, but "such banquettes hath put men in jeoperdy of theyr lyves." Other milk-related dangers were caused by human error. Thomas Tusser advised using poison or "bane" to kill rodents in the cattle barn—"In dayry no cat, / Lay bane for Rat"—but urged the husbandman to be careful where he put it: "Take heede how thou layest, the bane for the rats, / for poisoning servant, thy selfe and thy brats."

Butter was sometimes eaten as a dish in its own right, much as we now eat ice cream or yogurt. *A Propre New Booke of Cokery*, for example, includes butter as one of the dishes served at dinner on a fish day. (Because butter and other dairy products were not considered meat, they could be eaten on fish days and during Lent). Likewise, Gervase Markham, in *The English Husbandman*, notes that "sage with sweet Butter is a most excellent breakfast," a fact affirmed by Hugh Plat in *The Jewell House of Art and Nature*, where he writes that "in month of May, it is very usuall with us to eat some of the smallest, and youngest sage leaves with butter in a morning." Plat adds that he once delighted his friends by serving them butter flavored with cinnamon, mace, and even cloves, but this appears to be an innovation devised by Plat rather than a common practice. Thomas Cogan, in his 1584 *Haven of Health*, also affirmed that brown bread and butter made a "good breakfast for a countryman" (he adds that "more gently-bred stomachs" need fine white manchet). Butter was sometimes salted and packed into earthenware pots to help preserve it; if it was unsalted, it was known as sweet butter. High-quality butter had a natural yellow hue, which was sometimes counterfeited in butter of lesser quality by coloring it with carrot juice. As for the buttermilk that remained after the butter had been churned, William Bullein wrote that it was "very holsome to be dronke in the morning or evening … if it be eaten with Sugar, and new white bread."

Cheeses, according to Andrew Boorde in his 1547 *Compendyous Regyment*, were produced in four varieties: soft, hard, spermyse (which was flavored with the juice of herbs), and green (with "green" referring not to the color, but to the perceived freshness of the cheese, which was achieved by leaving in some of the whey). Throughout England, regional specialties of cheese were well known. Banbury was renowned for producing a very thin cheese, which is probably why Bardolph exclaims "You Banbury cheese!" to Master Slender in *The Merry Wives of Windsor*. Worcester cheeses, according to Fynes Moryson, were the most highly esteemed of English cheeses, but Cheshire and Suffolk produced greater quanitities of cheese, which they exported to the London markets. Surprisingly, perhaps, the village of Cheddar did not become known for its cheese until the mid-seventeenth century, well after Shakespeare had died.

In making cheese, the milk was first curdled by adding to it rennet, which was usually derived from the stomach of an unweaned calf, but sometimes from lambs or even from hares or chickens. Other substances were also used to curdle milk, including the sap of a fig tree, the flowers of wild thistle, the leaves of artichoke, and the eggs of pike fish. Gervase Markham advised that the young dairy maids who made cheese should be cleanly, scab-free, and "farre from being troubled with their tearmes"—that is, not menstruating. Markham added that the dairy maids, after pressing the whey from the cheese, could use that viscous substance for the "feeding of the Hogs and Dogs, as also in the time of Dearth for sustenance for the Familie." After cheeses had been pressed and wrapped in cloth, they were buried in a pile of linseed that, according to Markham, would "keepe them fresh and coole in the hotest times, and hot in the coldest times."

Considering that they boiled or roasted anything that had feathers, it is hard to believe that Shakespeare's contemporaries were choosey about what kinds of eggs they ate, but that is exactly what Andrew Boorde claims in his *Compendyous Regyment*: "In Englande there is no egges used to be eaten but henne egges." Thomas Twyne, writing three decades later in 1576, essentially echoes Boorde's claim, though he does allow that partridge eggs are also a good source of nutrition. Gervase Markham, in his 1614 *Cheap and Good Husbandry*, says of turkeys that "their egges are exceeding wholesome to eate," but the very fact that he feels the need to make such a comment suggests that they were not commonly served to the table. The dietary authorities of the time concur in saying that duck eggs and goose eggs are unfit for human consumption, and indeed none of the 538 recipes of this period that call for eggs specify anything other than those of chickens. Surely, however, things were different in rural areas, where occasional dearths would have made even the lowliest egg a toothsome prize.

# TO MAKE A CREAME CALLED A FOOLE

*Elinor Fettiplace's Receipt Book*, 1604

Thersites: Why, thou picture of what thou seemest,
and idol of idiot worshippers, here's a letter for thee.
Achilles: From whence, fragment?
Thersites: Why, thou full dish of fool, from Troy. (*Troilus and Cressida* 5.1.6–9)

*This dish is so simple that it might have been called "simpleton." Instead, someone named it "fool," which is much the same thing. Indeed, the phrase "simple fool" appears frequently in sixteenth- and seventeenth-century literature: "Come hyther thou simple foole," says a woman in a 1586 dialogue by Ulpian Fulwell. One might even say that this dish is so simple that it is foolproof.*

Take thicke creame and boile it with some sugar & a nutmeg sliced when it hath boiled a prettie while, put in the yelks of fower eggs well beaten, & stirre it about, & then take it from the fire, & put in two or three spoonfulls of rose water, then stirre it till it bee almost cold, then have sippets, cut in a dish and wet them through with sack, & then poure the creame to them, and when it is cold put some sugar & nutmeg smale sliced upon it, and so serve it.

---

 ## MODERN RECIPE                                         Makeability: 3

1 cup 35% cream

2 TBS sugar

1 tsp nutmeg

4 egg yolks

2 TBS rosewater

1 cup dry sherry

4 slices of lightly toasted 60% whole wheat bread for sippets

Sugar and nutmeg for garnish

In a saucepan, bring to a gentle boil the cream, sugar, and nutmeg. Reduce to a simmer and allow to cook about 10 minutes before removing from the heat. Whisk the egg yolks and slowly add some of the cream to temper them. Pour the egg mixture into the saucepan of cream and stir. Add the rosewater and stir until the liquid cools. Cut the sippets and soak them with dry sherry before arranging them on a platter. Pour the cream over the sippets and sprinkle with sugar and nutmeg.

---

# A FREGESEY OF EGGES

*A New Booke of Cookerie, 1615*

Amiens: It will make you melancholly Monsieur Jaques.
Jaques:   I thanke it: More, I prethee more, I can sucke
          melancholly out of a song, As a Weazel suckes egges:
          More, I pri'thee more. (*As You Like It* 2.5.10–13)

Beat a dozen of Egs with Creame, Sugar, Nutmeg, Mace, Rosewater, and a Pome-water cut overthwart in slices: put them into the Frying-pan with sweet Butter, and the Apples first: when they be almost enough take them up, and cleanse your Pan: put in sweet Butter, and make it hot: put in halfe the Egges and Creame at one time: stirre it with a Sawcer, or such a thing. Take it out, and put it in a Dish, put in the rest of the Egges and Creame, like the former, and then put in your Apples round about the batter. Then cast on the other side on the top of it, and keepe it from burning with sweet Butter. When it is fryed on both sides enough wring on the juyce of an Orenge, and serve it in.

---

 ## MODERN RECIPE                                      Makeability: 3

| | |
|---|---|
| 12 eggs | 2 TBS rosewater |
| $^1/_2$ cup cream | 1 apple, cored and cut into quarter-inch slices |
| 2 TBS sugar | 6 TBS unsalted butter |
| $^1/_2$ tsp nutmeg | Juice of 1 orange |
| $^1/_2$ tsp ground mace | |

Beat together the eggs, cream, sugar, nutmeg, mace, and rosewater. In a large frying pan melt 2 tablespoons of the butter and fry the apples, leaving them just a bit crisp. Set aside and keep warm. Wipe out the pan, add 2 tablespoons of butter, and pour in half of the egg mixture. Stir gently. When the eggs have set and are slightly firm, slip them out of the dish and onto a platter. Add the remaining butter and cook the remaining eggs. While the second batch of eggs is cooking, arrange the apple slices on the first batch of eggs. Cover with the second batch to create a "sandwich" with the apple slices in the middle. Pour on the orange juice and serve.

---

# TO BUTTER EGGES OF THE BEST FASHION

*A Delightfull Daily Exercise for Ladies and Gentlewomen, 1621*

Falstaff: Indeed you come neere me now Hal, for we
          that take Purses, go by the Moone and seven Starres,
          and not by Phoebus hee, that wand'ring Knight so
          faire. And I prythee sweet Wagge, when thou art King,

as God save thy Grace, Majesty I should say, for
Grace thou wilte have none.
Prince: What, none?
Falstaff: No, not so much as will serve to be Prologue to an
Egge and Butter. (*1 Henry IV* 1.2.13–21)

*In the quotation from 1 Henry IV, Falstaff means that the grace that one says before snacking on an egg and butter is very small and that the Prince lacks even that amount of grace. In Shakespeare's England, it was common to say grace both before and after eating. Even when dining alone, an individual would begin the meal with a prayer, such as this short one that Thomas Vicars proposes as appropriate for one person: "Lord blesse these good creatures of thine to my use, and sanctifie mee ever to thy holy service, through Jesus Christ my Lord and onely saviour."*

Boyle your Egges very hard, and then blanch them in cold water, then slice them as thinne as wafers then you may take sweete butter drawne thicke with faire water, then season your Egges with a little grose Pepper, and salt and then put them into your thicke butter, and so set them upon a Chafindish of char-coales, now and then tossing and turning them upside downe, then you may dish them up in very fayre dish, and prick fryed toastes about them: and strew on them a little grose pepper and salt, and so you may serve them to the Table hot.

---

 ## MODERN RECIPE                                         Makeability: 2

8 hard-boiled eggs                          Salt and fresh-cracked pepper to taste
4 TBS unsalted butter                       4 slices fried toast

Thoroughly cool the hard-boiled eggs before slicing with a very sharp knife to about quarter-inch thickness. Sprinkle with salt and pepper. Melt the butter in a frying pan and heat the egg slices. Frying in several small batches, allow them to cook thoroughly to make turning them over easier. Season with a bit more salt and pepper and serve with the slices of fried toast.

---

# TO MAKE CAST CREAME ANOTHER WAY

*The Good Huswifes Handmaide for the Kitchin, 1594*

Westmoreland: 'Faith, Sir John, 'tis more than time that
I were there, and you too: but my Powers are there
alreadie. The King, I can tell you, lookes for us all:
we must away all to Night.
Falstaff: Tut, never feare me, I am as vigilant as a Cat, to
steale Creame.
Prince: I thinke to steale Creame indeed, for thy theft hath
alreadie made thee Butter. (*1 Henry IV* 4.2.53–60)

Take the milk that is milked over night, and scum off the Cream: then take the milk and sixe whites of Egs, straine them together, and two yolks of Egs mingled together, and boyle them altogether untill they turne to a Curde, then put therto a quantitie of Vergious, and then it will turne: then take the same, and put it in a linnen cloth, and hang it upon a pin a litle while, and let the whey run from it. Then take it downe and straine it into a platter, and season it with a litle Rosewater and Sugar, and so serve it.

---

 ## MODERN RECIPE                                   Makeability: 3

| | |
|---|---|
| 1 quart whole milk | 2 TBS verjuice (see Appendix 1) |
| 6 egg whites | 1 tsp rosewater |
| 2 egg yolks | 2 tsp sugar |

Mix together the milk and eggs and bring to a boil. Add the verjuice. Let cool and strain through a clean kitchen towel and sieve. When the whey has been drained, add the rosewater and sugar and stir.

---

# TO MAKE PANPERDY

*The English Huswife, 1615*

Sir Toby: Out o' tune sir, ye lye: Art any more than a
Steward? Dost thou thinke because thou art vertuous,
there shall be no more Cakes and Ale?
Feste: Yes by Saint Anne, and Ginger shall bee hotte in the
mouth too.
Sir Toby: Th'art i'th right. Goe sir, rub your Chaine
with crums. A stoope of Wine, Maria. (*Twelfth Night* 2.3.113–119)

*The name "panperdy" derives from the French "pain perdu," meaning "lost bread," because the bread that was used to make the dish was often stale and dried out. As for the Feste's comment that "ginger shall be hot i' the mouth," he is probably alluding to the fact that ale was sometimes spiced with ginger, and that ginger, as John Gerard affirmed, was well known for "provoking venerie."*

To make the best Panperdy, take a dozen egges, and breake them and beat them very well, then put unto them cloves, mace, cinamon, nutmeg, and good store of suger, with as much salt as shall season it: then take a manchet and cut it into thicke slices like tostes; which done take your frying pan and put into it good store of sweet butter, and being melted lay in your slices of bread, then powre upon them one halfe of your egges, then when that is fried with a dish turn your slices of bread upward, and then powre on them the other halfe of your egges, and so turne them till both sides be browne: then dish it up and serve it with suger strowed upon it.

## MODERN RECIPE                                          Makeability: 2

| | |
|---|---|
| 9 to 12 whole eggs | 1 TBS sugar (plus 1 tsp sugar for garnish) |
| 1/4 tsp cloves | 1 tsp salt or to taste |
| 1/4 tsp mace | Slices of white bread cut three-quarter-inch thick |
| 1/4 tsp cinnamon | |
| 1/4 tsp nutmeg | 3 TBS unsalted butter |

Beat the eggs vigorously and whisk in the spices, sugar, and salt. In a large frying pan, melt 2 table-spoons of butter over medium heat and arrange in it the slices of bread. Pour half of the egg mixture over the bread and cook for 4 to 5 minutes, or until the eggs are just set. Slide the bread and eggs out of the pan onto a platter. Add the remaining tablespoon of butter. Set a second platter on top of the platter of bread and eggs and flip it over. Slide the panperdy back into the pan and pour over the second half of the eggs. Cook until both sides are brown. Slip it out of the pan and sprinkle with sugar.

# TO BAKE SMALL MEATS

*A Book of Cookrye*, 1591

| | |
|---|---|
| Pandarus: | Troilus! Why, he esteems her no more than I esteem an addle egg. |
| Cressida: | If you love an addle egg as well as you love an idle head, you would eat chickens i' th' shell. (*Troilus and Cressida* 1.2.132–135) |

*The word "meat," in Shakespeare's England, meant both flesh and food in general, as in this recipe where the "small meats" are the boiled eggs.*

Take Egges and seethe them hard, then take the yolkes out of them and braye them in the morter, and temper them with Creme, and then straine them, and put to them Pepper, Saffron, Cloves, Mace, small raisins, Almonds blanched and small shred and grated bread.

## MODERN RECIPE                                          Makeability: 2

| | |
|---|---|
| 6 hard-boiled eggs | 2 blades of whole mace |
| 1/2 cup 35% cream | 2 TBS raisins |
| 1/4 tsp pepper | 1 TBS blanched almonds, finely chopped |
| 1 pinch saffron | 2 TBS bread crumbs |
| 1/4 tsp ground cloves | |

Carefully cut the hard-boiled eggs in half. Gently remove the yolk keeping the white intact. In a mixing bowl (or mortar and pestle), mash the egg yolks and add the cream, a little at a time to make a paste. Add the remaining ingredients and mix together. Stuff the egg whites with the mixture.

# TO MAKE THE BEST TANSEY

*The English Huswife*, 1615

| Courtezan: | Your man and you are marvailous merrie sir. |
|---|---|
| | Will you goe with me, wee'll mend our dinner here? |
| S. Dromio: | Master, if you do, expect spoon-meate, or bespeake |
| | a long spoone. |
| S. Antipholus: | Why Dromio? |
| S. Dro.: | Marrie he must have a long spoone that must eate |
| | with the divell. (*The Comedy of Errors* 4.3.56–62) |

*A tansy, which is essentially a kind of omelet, takes its name from the herb that was originally used to flavor it. Over time, however, the nature of the dish evolved so that the herb tansy became an optional ingredient (as in this recipe) or was removed entirely, even as the name of the dish stayed the same. Those recipes that removed the tansy from the tansy were prescient: it is now known that the herb contains thujone, which can cause convulsions. As for the quotation from* The Comedy of Errors, *Dromio's reference to spoon-meat implies that he is afraid that Antipholus will meet with misfortune if he dines with the courtesan: spoon-meat was food prepared for invalids, which is what Antipholus will supposedly become at the hands of the courtesan. Dromio's subsequent reference to a long spoon is less obscure: it simply means that one should keep one's distance from the devil.*

First then for making the best Tansey, you shall take a certaine number of Egges, according to the bignesse of your frying-panne, and breake them into a dish, abating ever the white of every third egge: then with a spoone you shall cleanse awaie the little white chickin knots which sticke to the yelkes, then with a little creame beate them exceedingly together; then take of greene wheate blades, Violet leaves, Strawbery leaves, Spinage and Succory of each a like quantity, and a few Wall-nut buds, chop and beate all these very well, and then straine out the juice, and mixing it with a little more creame, put it to the egges and stirre all well together, then put in a fewe crummes of bread, fine grated bread, Cinamon, Nutmegge and salt; then put some sweet butter into the frying-panne, and so soone as it is melted put in the Tansey and frie it browne without burning, and with a dish turne it in the panne as occasion shall serve; then serve it up having strewed good store of sugar upon it, for to put in sugar before will make it heavie: some use to put of the hearbe Tansey into it, but the Wall-nut tree buds do give the better taste; therefore when you please to use the one doe not use the other.

MODERN RECIPE Makeability: 3

4 eggs

2 egg yolks

1/4 cup 35% cream

1/2 cup wheat blades or pea shoots

1 TBS violet leaves (if available)

1/4 cup chopped spinach

1/4 cup chopped succory (also known as chicory, radicchio, and endive)

2 TBS walnut buds (if available)

1/4 cup bread crumbs

1/2 tsp cinnamon

1/2 tsp nutmeg

1/4 tsp salt

2 TBS unsalted butter

2 TBS sugar for garnish

In a large mixing bowl, beat the eggs and cream together well. Roughly chop together the herbs, drain any liquid, and mix with a dash of cream before combining with the egg mixture. Stir in the bread crumbs, cinnamon, nutmeg, and salt. Melt half the butter in a large frying pan, pour in the tansy mixture, and cook until the edges turn dark yellow and have set. Slide the tansy onto a large plate, add the remaining butter, and gently flip the tansy to cook the other side briefly. Remove the tansy, sprinkle with sugar, and garnish with a bit of chicory or pea shoots.

# TO BAKE A CUSTARDE OR DOWSET

*The English Huswife*, 1615

Parolles: I know not how I have deserved to run into
my Lords displeasure.
Lafeu: You have made shift to run into't, bootes and
spurres and all: like him that leapt into the Custard, and
out of it you'le runne againe, rather than suffer question
for your residence. (*All's Well That Ends Well* 2.5.35–40)

*As the name of this recipe implies, dowsets were synonymous with custards. The name is a diminutive of the French "douce" meaning "sweet." The word was also used to refer to testicles, as in Francis Beaumont's 1620 play* Phylaster, *where a soldier says of a captured Spanish prince, "let's geld him, and send his dowsets for a dish to the bordello."*

To bake an excellent Custarde or Dowset; you shall take good store of eggs, and putting awaie one quarter of the whites beate them exceeding well in a bason, and then mix with them the sweetest and thickest creame you can get, for if it be any thing thinne the Custard will be wheyish, then season it with salt, sugar, cinamon, cloves, mace, and a little Nutmegge, which done raise your coffins of good tough wheate paste, being the second sort before spoke of, and if you please raise it in pretty workes or angular formes, which you may do by fixing the upper part of the crust to the nether with the yelks of eggs; then when the coffins are ready, strowe the bottomes a good thicknesse over with Currants and Sugar, then set them into the Oven and fill them up with the confection before blended, and so drawing them adorne all the toppes with Carraway Cumfets, and the slices of Dates prickt right up, and so serve them up to the table.

---

 MODERN RECIPE                                          Makeability: 3

3 whole eggs

1 egg yolk

2 cups cream

1/8 tsp salt

1/2 cup sugar

1/2 tsp cinnamon

1/4 tsp ground cloves

1/4 tsp ground mace

1/4 tsp nutmeg

1/2 cup currants mixed with 1 TBS sugar

Pastry recipe "To make fine paste" on page 214, or buy premade pastry.

1 tsp candied caraway (see recipe for "How to candie Ginger, Nutmegs, or any Roote or flowers" on page 247)

4 sliced dates

Prepare 4 pastry shells, each about as big as a large muffin. Preheat oven to 300°F. Beat the eggs well and mix them with the cream, adding the salt, sugar, cinnamon, cloves, mace, and nutmeg. In the bottom of the pastry shells, spoon a layer of currants and sugar. Pour the custard mix into the pastry shells and bake until the center of the custard is just set. Garnish the custards with caraway or orange comfets and slices of date and serve.

---

# TO MAKE A TRIFLE

*The Good Huswifes Jewell, 1596*

Egeus: Thou hast by Moone-light at her window sung,
With faining voice, verses of faining love,
And stolne the impression of her fantasie,
With bracelets of thy haire, rings, gawdes, conceits,
Knackes, trifles, Nose-gaies, sweet meats (messengers
Of strong prevailment in unhardned youth). (*A Midsummer Night's Dream* 1.1.30–35)

*According to the Oxford English Dictionary, the name "trifle" was first bestowed on a cream-based dessert in 1598. This recipe, though, was published in 1596, which means that the Oxford English Dictionary is off by at least two years. The "trifle" that Egeus refers to in the quotation from A Midsummer Night's Dream is even older: it was used to mean "a thing of no importance" since the thirteenth century. Trifles of the dessert kind were also known as "fools," as in the recipe "To make a creame called a foole."*

Take a pinte of thicke Creame, and season it with Sugar and Ginger, and Rose-water, so stirre it as you would them have it, and make it luke warme in a dish on a Chafingdishe and coales, and after put it into a silver peece or a bowle, and so serve it to the boorde.

## MODERN RECIPE                                         Makeability: 2

2 cups 35% cream

3 TBS sugar

1 TBS minced ginger

2 TBS rosewater

Gently heat to lukewarm but do not boil the cream, sugar, ginger, and rosewater. Allow to cool slightly and whisk vigorously to create a mousse-like cream.

# TO POTCHE EGGES IN BROTH

*The Widowes Treasure, 1588*

Westmoreland:  But there's a saying very old and true,
     "If that you will France win,
     then with Scotland first begin."
     For once the Eagle England being in prey,
     To her unguarded Nest, the Weazell Scot
     Comes sneaking, and so sucks her Princely Egges,
     Playing the Mouse in absence of the Cat,
     To tame and havocke more than she can eate. (*Henry V* 1.2.166–173)

Take Vergis and Faire water, and a dish of new Yest: and put therein Cloves, Mace, Currans, Suger, sweete Butter, a handfull of Spinage, and let them boyle a good while: then having potched your egges in faire Water that is seething: then laye your Egges in broth and serve them foorth with hearbs laide over them.

## MODERN RECIPE                                         Makeability: 3

6 eggs

1 TBS verjuice (see Appendix 1)

1 packet active dry yeast

1/4 tsp cloves

2 blades of whole mace

2 TBS currants

1 TBS sugar

2 TBS unsalted butter

1 cup spinach

1 cup chicken broth

1 spring thyme, rosemary, and parsley for garnish

Add the verjuice and yeast to the saucepan of water and bring to a gentle boil. Add the cloves, mace, currants, sugar, butter, and spinach. In another saucepan, bring water to a gentle boil and poach the eggs two or three at a time for a few minutes, depending on desired softness of the yolks. In a deep-sided dish, pour out the verjuice-broth mixture and add the poached eggs. Garnish with fresh herbs and serve.

# TO DRESSE AND FILL EGGES

*Epulario, 1598*

Third Servant:  Goe thou, I'le fetch some flaxe and whites of egges
To apply to his bleeding face, now heaven helpe him. (*King Lear* 3.7.109–110)

*The saffron that this recipe calls for (to color the mixture of yolks, currants, and spices) would probably have been locally grown, the saffron crocus having been introduced to England from the Mediterranean in the Middle Ages. William Harrison, who lived just a few miles from Saffron Walden (so named because of the saffron that was grown there in large quantities), noted in his 1586* Description of England *that an acre of land could produce up to twenty pounds of dried saffron, which, at twenty shillings a pound, amounted to 400 shillings, roughly the annual wages of a skilled worker such as a carpenter. The labor required to harvest saffron was, however, significant: an acre of land could sustain about a million and a half flowers, each of which needed to have its delicate thread-like stigmas manually removed by workers known as crokers. Saffron was used not just in culinary preparations, but in medical remedies as well: a 1596 handbook called* A Rich StoreHouse or Treasury for the Diseased *calls for saffron in remedies for back pain, jaundice, piles, small pox, and "the burning & intollerable heate of urine."*

Seeth new Egs in water untill they be hard, then peele them and cut them in the middle, and take out the yolks, and doe not break the white, and stampe some part of those yolks with a few Currans, Parsley, Margerum and Mint, chopped very small, with two or three whites of Egs, with what spice you thinke good. And when they are mixed together colour it with Saffron, and fill the Egges therewith, and frie them in oyle: and for sauce take a few of those yolkes which remain unstamped with a few Currans, and stampe them well together, and temper them with a little Verjuice, and straine them, putting thereto Sugar, Cloves, and good store of Sinamon, let this sauce boyle a little, and when you will send the Egges to the Table, put this sauce upon them.

---

 ## MODERN RECIPE                                          Makeability: 4

| | |
|---|---|
| 6 hard-boiled eggs | For the sauce |
| 1 TBS chopped currants | 6 hard-boiled egg yolks |
| 1 TBS finely chopped parsley | 1 tsp currants |
| 1 tsp finely chopped marjoram | 3 TBS verjuice (see Appendix 1) |
| 1 TBS finely chopped mint | 1/2 tsp sugar |
| 3 finely chopped hard egg whites | 1/4 tsp cloves |
| 1 pinch saffron | 1 tsp cinnamon |
| Olive oil or lard as needed for frying | |

*Continued on next page*

*Continued from previous page*

Cut the hard-boiled eggs in half, being careful to not break the whites. Remove the yolks and mash them. Mix the yolks with the currants, parsley, marjoram, mint, egg whites, and the saffron. Fill the hard-boiled egg whites with the yolk paste. Heat oil in a small pan and gently fry the eggs. Arrange the eggs close together to prop them up while cooking. To make the sauce, mash the six hard-boiled egg yolks and mix with the currants. Add the remaining ingredients. Heat the sauce in a saucepan and spoon it over the fried, dressed eggs.

# TO MAKE A DISH OF SNOW

*A Book of Cookrye, 1591*

Camillo:                                       He tels her something
That makes her blood looke on't: Good sooth she is
The Queene of Curds and Creame. (*The Winter's Tale* 4.4.159–161)

*During the so-called "little ice age" that gripped the Northern Hemisphere from the six-teenth century to the mid-nineteenth century, England experienced noticeably cooler win-ters. In London, the Thames would occasionally freeze solid, and people would gather on the ice to chat and play games. When this occurred in 1564 (the year Shakespeare was born), the impromptu gatherings turned into a full-blown "frost fair," a festive event that would occur for centuries afterward, whenever the river froze over. When the Thames froze again in 1599, Shakespeare and his company took the opportunity to dismantle their theatre and haul its timbers across the ice to cheaper property on the other side of the river. There, they reassembled the building and renamed it The Globe. In this recipe the creamy "snow" that is cast upon the rosemary branches no doubt reminded some of Shakespeare's contemporaries of those cold but festive days when they could walk upon their river.*

Take a pottle of sweet thick Cream, and the white of eight Egs, and beate them altogither with a spooone, then put them into your Creme with a dish full of Rose-water and a dish full of Sugar withall, then take a stick and make it clean, and then cut it in the end four square, and therwith beat all the aforesaid things togither, and ever as it ariseth, take it off, and put it into a Cullender, this doon, take a platter and set an Apple in the midst of it, and stick a thick bush of Rosemary in the Apple. Then cast your Snow upon the Rosemary & fill your platter therwith, and if you have wafers, cast some withall, and so serve them foorth.

 ## MODERN RECIPE                                       Makeability: 3

2 cups whipping cream, at least 35%            1 large bright red apple

1 TBS rosewater                                1 large rosemary sprig

2 TBS sugar                                    Wafers for garnish

8 egg whites

Whip the cream to form soft peaks, slowly adding the rosewater and sugar (for best results, chill the mixing bowl and the whisk for an hour or so before whipping the cream). Whisk the egg whites to airy, glossy peaks. In small batches, very gently fold the whipped cream into the egg whites with a spatula. With a skewer drive a hole into the core of the apple where the stalk was. Insert the rosemary into the apple and place it in the center of a platter. With the spatula, spoon out the "snow" around the apple and cover the platter. Put small dollops of snow in the branches of the rosemary. Place a few wafers around the edges of the platter.

# TO MAKE EGGES IN MONESHINE

*A Propre New Booke of Cokery,* 1545

Edgar:  Had'st thou beene ought But Gozemore, Feathers, Ayre,
    (So many fathome downe precipitating)
    Thou'dst shiver'd like an Egge: but thou do'st breath:
    Hast heavy substance, bleed'st not, speak'st, art sound,
    Ten Masts at each, make not the altitude
    Which thou hast perpendicularly fell.
    Thy life's a Myracle. Speake yet againe. (*King Lear* 4.6.49–55)

*The quaint name of this recipe comes from the resemblance of a yellow egg yolk to the full moon. Nowadays, in contrast, we think of an unbroken egg yolk as being "sunny-side up" (though we continue to associate eggs with the moon through Easter, which is a lunar holiday). In* A Midsummer Night's Dream, *one of the "rude mechanicals" is named "Moonshine" because that is what he represents in the bumbling play that they perform for the reconciled lovers. "This lanthorn," he tells them, "doth the horned moon present; / Myself the man i' the moon do seem to be." Shakespeare, incidentally, didn't invent the word "moonshine," but he is recorded as the first author to use the word "moonbeam."*

Take a disshe of rose water and a dissh full of suger and set them upon a chafyng-disshe & let them boyle, than take the yelkes of eight or nyne egges new layde and put them thereto every one from other, and so let them harden a litel, and so after this maner serve them foarth and cast a lytell Sinamon and Suger upon them.

 MODERN RECIPE                                    Makeability: 3

| 1 cup rosewater | 8 egg yolks |
| 1 cup sugar | Cinnamon and sugar for garnish |

Bring the rosewater and sugar to a boil in a large saucepan. Have ready the 8 egg yolks. Reduce the water to a gentle boil and slip in the egg yolks gently one at a time. Allow each egg to cook 2 to 3 minutes (or longer if a harder yolk is desired). With a slotted spoon, remove the eggs, allow to drain, and place on a plate. Sprinkle with the cinnamon and sugar to taste.

# 10

# FRITTERS, FRICASSEES, AND PUDDINGS

It was the day whereon both rich and poore,
Are chiefely feasted with the selfe same dish,
When every Paunch till it can hold no more,
Is Fritter-filled, as well as heart can wish,
And every man and maide doe take their turne,
And tosse their Pancakes up for feare they burne,
And all the Kitchin doth with laughter sound,
To see the Pancakes fall upon the ground.

—William Fennor, *Pasquils Palinodia*, 1619

We now think of a fritter as anything fried in batter, but for Shakespeare and his contemporaries the term sometimes stretched to encompass anything that was fried in oil. The recipe entitled "To make fritters of Figges," for example, contains no milk, no eggs, and no flour—in other words, no batter. Similarly, we now think of a fricassee as a dish of fried or stewed meat that is served with a sauce, but in the sixteenth and seventeenth centuries the word "fricassee" (or "frycase," as it was sometimes spelled) had a broader application. For example, the recipe called "To make a Frycase of colde Mutton or Veale" doesn't really have a sauce to speak of, while the recipe called "To make any Quelquechose" refers to itself as a "fry-case," but really employs something more like a batter than a sauce. All in all, it is probably safe to follow the lead of Gervase Markham who, in *Countrey Contentments, or The English Huswife*, uses the terms almost interchangeably.

As for the word "pudding," the current North American usage of that word is a far cry from the way it was used in Shakespeare's England. For us, a pudding is a sweet dessert made of sugar, milk, flavoring, and a thickening agent such as cornstarch, rice, or tapioca. For Shakespeare's contemporaries, a pudding was typically a mixture of chopped ingredients that was stuffed into an intestine and then boiled, roasted, or fried. Such a composition was clearly similar to what we now call a sausage. Some puddings, however, were cooked in a cloth bag (as with "A Cambridge pudding") rather than in an intestine, some were cooked inside a cavity formed in another food (as with "How to make a Pudding in a Turnep root"), and some were cooked without being encased at all (as with "To make an Italian pudding"). Many puddings contained meat, but some did not. With some pudding recipes, it is difficult to see why the dish is called a pudding rather than a fritter, as with a recipe found in John Murrell's *Book of Cookrye* called "To make a Pudding in a Frying-panne." To complicate things further, the various kinds of puddings described above were also, in Shakespeare's England, known as "sausages" and "isings."

As with cheeses, different kinds of regional puddings developed, with different towns or shires coming to be associated with different types of puddings. John Taylor, for example, in a 1630 pamphlet called *The Great Eater of Kent*, alluded to "the Bag-puddings of Gloucestershire, the Blacke-puddings of Worcestershire, the Pan puddings of Shropshire, the White puddings of Somersetshire, the Hasty-puddings of Hamp-shire, and the Pudding-pyes of any shire." As a culinary technique, puddings—at least the ones that are encased in a bag or intestine or casing—may owe something to the ancient Roman practice of "engastration," whereby a small animal was stuffed inside a larger animal, which was then stuffed inside a still larger animal, which was then stuffed inside an even larger animal, and so on, all of which were then cooked and served. The stuffing that we still put into a Christmas turkey, or the mixture that we spoon into the hollow of a deviled egg, are perhaps vestiges of these practices.

# TO MAKE ISING PUDDINGS

*The Good Huswifes Handmaide for the Kitchin, 1594*

Petruchio: Grumio, my horse.
Grumio:   Aye sir, they be ready, the Oates have eaten
         the horses. (*The Taming of the Shrew* 3.2.204–206)

Take a platter full of Otemeale grotes clean picked, and put thereto of the best Creame sodden that ye can get, blood warme, as much as shall cover the grotes, and so let them lie and soake three houres, or somewhat more, till they have drunke up the Cream, and the grotes swollen and soft withall. Then take six Egges whites and yolkes, and straine them faire into your grotes: then take one platterfull and a half of beefe suet, the skin cleane pulled from it, and as small minced as is possible. So that when ye have minced it, you muste largelie have one platterfull and a halfe, & rather more than lesse: then mingle these wel among your grotes then season them with some salt and some Saffron: & if ye will put in Cloves and Mace: then fill your Puddings, but not too ful, and see they be faire washed and sweet, and beware yee pull not away too much of the fat within, for the fatter they be within, the better it is for the Puddings: also if ye finde too much Creame left among the grotes, after they have lyne foure houres: then put out part of it, and so seeth up your puddings.

---

## MODERN RECIPE                                  Makeability: 3

| | |
|---|---|
| 1 cup oatmeal groats | 6 eggs |
| 2 cups 35% warm cream | 1 cup minced suet |

*Continued on next page*

*Continued from previous page*

| | |
|---|---|
| 1 tsp salt | 3 blades of mace |
| 1 pinch saffron | Sausage casings (if available) |
| $1/2$ tsp ground cloves | |

Preheat oven to 350°F. Soak the groats in the cream for about three hours. Drain the cream, put the groats in a mixing bowl, and add the eggs, suet, salt, saffron, cloves, and mace. Pour the pudding mixture into sausage casings and bake for 40 to 45 minutes, or until set in the middle. If sausage casings are not available, bake the ising pudding in a small casserole dish until set.

# TO FARSE ALL THINGS

*The Second Part of the Good Hus-wives Jewell, 1597*

Grumio: Where's the Cooke, is supper ready, the house
trim'd, rushes strew'd, cobwebs swept, the servingmen
in their new fustian, the white stockings, and
every officer his wedding garment on? Be the Jackes
faire within, the Gils faire without, the Carpets laide, and
everie thing in order? (*The Taming of the Shrew* 4.1.40–45)

*"Farse"—or rather "farce"—means "to stuff," which is exactly what is to be done with this mixture of eggs, bread, and seasonings. You might, for example, try this stuffing or "farcemeat" when you next roast a chicken. Curiously, the "farce" that denotes a slap-stick comedy is the same word as the culinary "farce": a farce was originally a short, hu-morous piece that was "stuffed" between the more serious scenes of a religious drama.*

Take a good handful of tyme, Isope, Parselye, and three or foure yolkes of Egges hard rosted, and choppe them with hearbes small, then take white bread grated and raw egs with sweet butter, a few small Raisons, or Barberies, seasoning it with Pepper, cloves, Mace, Sinamon and Ginger, working it altogether as paste, and then may you stuffe with it what you will.

## MODERN RECIPE                                    Makeability: 1

| | |
|---|---|
| 3 cups bread crumbs | $1/3$ cup finely chopped basil |
| 3 eggs | $1/4$ cup thyme |
| 4 hard-boiled egg yolks | $1/3$ cup hyssop (see Appendix 1) |
| $1/2$ cup of raisins | $1/3$ cup finely chopped parsley |
| $1/4$ barberries (see Appendix 1) | 1 tsp cinnamon |
| $1/3$ cup of butter | 1 tsp ginger |

$^1/_2$ tsp ground mace                           $^1/_2$ tsp pepper

$^1/_2$ tsp cloves

Mix ingredients together in a bowl and work them until they become a paste. Use the mixture to stuff meats and poultry.

# TO MAKE FRITTERS OF SPINNEDGE

*The Good Huswifes Jewell, 1596*

Olivia:  O you are sicke of selfe-love Malvolio, and taste
         with a distemper'd appetite. (*Twelfth Night* 1.5.87–88)

*Philip Moore, in a 1564 work entitled* The Hope of Health, *warned his readers not to consume the water in which spinach was boiled because "it is unprofitable to the stomake, causing vomet, & engendring wynde." Similarly, this recipe also advises the reader to "let the water runne" from the boiled spinach.*

Take a good deale of Spinnedge, and washe it cleane, then boyle it in faire water, and when it is boyled, then take it forth and let the water runne from it, then chop it with the backe of a knife, and then put in some egges and grated Bread, and season it with suger, sinamon, ginger, and pepper, dates minced fine, and currans, and rowle them like a ball, and dippe them in Batter made of Ale and flower.

## MODERN RECIPE                                    Makeability: 4

For the spinach fritters:                     1 TBS minced dates

4 cups spinach                                1 TBS currants

2 eggs

1 cup bread crumbs                            For the batter:

1 TBS sugar                                   1$^1/_4$ cups ale

1 tsp cinnamon                                1$^1/_3$ cups all-purpose flour

$^1/_2$ tsp ginger                            Lard or beef suet as needed for frying (at least

$^1/_4$ tsp pepper                            1$^1/_2$ to 3 inches deep) to 365°F.

Put the flour into a mixing bowl. Gradually stir in the ale and whisk into a batter. Wash the spinach if needed and boil for a few minutes. Drain it and chop roughly. In another mixing bowl, combine the spinach, eggs, bread crumbs, and remaining ingredients. Roll the mixture into golf ball-sized pieces and dip into the batter, covering thoroughly. In a deep pot, fry the spinach fritters in the lard until heated through and golden, approximately 3 to 4 minutes.

# HOW TO MAKE A PUDDING IN A TURNEP ROOT

*A Book of Cookrye*, 1591

Prince:                                          Why do'st thou converse
with that Trunke of Humors, that Boulting-
Hutch of Beastlinesse, that swolne Parcell of Dropsies,
that huge Bombard of Sacke, that stuft Cloakebagge of
Guts, that rosted Manning Tree Oxe with the Pudding in
his Belly, that reverend Vice, that grey iniquitie, that
Father Ruffian, that Vanitie in yeeres? wherein is he good,
but to taste Sacke, and drinke it? wherein neat and
cleanly, but to carve a Capon, and eat it? (*1 Henry IV* 2.4.443–451)

*In the sixteenth century, the words "turnip," "rape," and "navet" all referred to the same root vegetable. Turnip, however, appears to have outstripped the other two words around the middle of the century and to have taken the lead rather suddenly: in 1548 William Turner, in his treatise entitled* The Names of Herbes, *wrote, "I have hearde some call it in englishe a turnep," which seems imply that the word "turnip," though known, was not common. Just three years later, however, in a book called* A New Herbal, *Turner referred to "the great round rape called commonly a turnepe," suggesting that "turnip" was now the most familiar name. Whatever it was called, turnips were a staple food of the poor, especially in Wales, where they were often eaten raw. John Gerard, in his 1597* Herball, *noted that there were both wild turnips and garden turnips, "some with round roots globe fashion, other ovall or peare-fashion; and another sort longish or somewhat like a Radish."*

Take your Turnep root, and wash it fair in warm water, and scrape it faire and make it hollow as you doo a Carret roote, and make your stuffe of grated bread, and Apples chopt fine, then take Corance, and hard Egs, and season it with Sugar Sinamon, and Ginger, and yolks of hard egs and so temper your stuffe, and put it into the Turnep, then take faire water, and set it on the fire, and let it boyle or ever you put in your Turneps, then put in a good peece of sweet Butter, and Claret Wine, and a little Vinagre, and Rosemarye, and whole Mace, Sugar, and Corance, and Dates quartered, and when they are boyled inough, then will they be tender, then serve it in.

---

 MODERN RECIPE                                          Makeability: 4

| | |
|---|---|
| 4 white turnips | 1/2 tsp minced ginger |
| 1 cup bread crumbs | |
| 1/2 cup diced apple | For the liquor: |
| 1 TBS currants | 2 TBS unsalted butter |
| 2 hard-boiled egg yolks, chopped | 1 cup red Bordeaux wine |
| 1 tsp sugar | 2 TBS vinegar |
| 1/2 tsp cinnamon | 1 sprig rosemary |

| | |
|---|---|
| 1 blade of whole mace | 1 TBS currants |
| 1 TBS sugar | 1 TBS chopped dates |

Clean and cut away the outer waxy skin of the turnips. Cut off the top inch or so and hollow out the turnips. In a bowl, stir together the bread crumbs, apple, currants, egg yolks, sugar, cinnamon, and ginger. Stuff the turnips with the bread crumb and apple mixture. Place the turnips into a small pot of boiling water but keep the water below the top of the turnip. Add the butter, wine, vinegar, and remaining ingredients and simmer gently for 45 minutes, or until the stuffing is heated through. Arrange the turnips on a platter and spoon over them some of the liquor from the pot.

# TO MAKE PANCAKES

*The Good Huswifes Handmaide for the Kitchin, 1594*

| | |
|---|---|
| Celia: | Were you made the messenger? |
| Touchstone: | No by mine honor, but I was bid |
| | to come for you. |
| Rosalind: | Where learned you that oath foole? |
| Touchstone: | Of a certaine Knight, that swore by his |
| | Honour they were good Pan-cakes, and swore by his |
| | Honor the Mustard was naught: Now I'le stand to it, the |
| | Pancakes were naught, and the Mustard was good, |
| | and yet was not the Knight forsworne. |
| Celia: | How prove you that in the great heape of your |
| | knowledge? |
| Rosalind: | Aye marry, now unmuzzle your wisedome. |
| Touchstone: | Stand you both forth now: stroke your |
| | chinnes, and sweare by your beards that I am a knave. |
| Celia: | By our beards (if we had them) thou art. |
| Touchstone: | By my knaverie (if I had it) then I were: but if you sweare by that that is |
| | not, you are not |
| | forsworn: no more was this knight swearing by his |
| | Honor, for he never had anie; or if he had, |
| | he had sworne it away, before ever he saw those Pancakes, |
| | or that Mustard. (*As You Like It* 1.2.57–76) |

*Pancakes enjoyed special status in Shakespeare's England because of Pancake Tuesday, also known as Shrove Tuesday or Mardi Gras. Falling on the day before Lent (the forty-day period when everyone was required to stop eating meat), Pancake Tuesday became for many people a day of riotous consumption, as they steeled themselves against the long and dreary fast to come. John Taylor, in his 1620* Jack a Lent, *reported that the unbridled gourmandizing began at 9:00* A.M.:

*There is a Bell rung, call'd The Pancake Bell, the sound whereof makes thousands of people distracted, and forgetfull eyther of manners or humanitie: then there is a thing called wheaten flowre, which the sulphory Necromanticke Cookes doe mingle with water, Egges, Spice, and other tragicall magicall inchantments, and then they put it by little and little, into a Frying pan of boyling Suet, where it makes a confused dismall hissing (like the Learnean Snakes in the*

*Reeds of Acheron, Stix, or Phlegeton) untill at the last by the skill of the Cookes, it is trans-form'd into the forme of a flap-jack, which in our translation is call'd a Pancake, which omi-nous incantation the ignorant people doe devoure very greedily (having for the most part well dined before) but they have no sooner swallowed that sweet candyed baite, but straight their wits forsake them, and they runne starke mad assembling in routs and throngs numberless of ungoverned numbers, with uncivill civill commotions.*

Taylor added that after the pancakes, the revellers moved on to various meat dishes, with "*such boyling and broyling, such roasting and toasting, such stewing and brewing, such baking, frying, mincing, cutting, carving, devouring, and gorbellyed gurmondizing, that a man would thinke people did take in two moneths provision at once into their paunches, or that they did ballast their bellies with meate for a voyage to Constantinople, or the West-Indies.*"

Take new thicke Creame a pinte, foure or five yolks of egs, a good handful of flower and two or three spoonefuls of ale, strain them together into a faire platter, and sea-son it with a good handfull of sugar, a spoonefull of synamon, and a little Ginger: then take a frying pan, and put in a litle peece of Butter, as big as your thumbe, and when it is molten brown, cast it out of your pan, and with a ladle put to the further side of your pan some of your stuffe, and hold your pan aslope, so that your stuffe may run abroad over all the pan as thin as may be: then set it to the fire, and let the fyre be verie soft, and when the one side is baked, then turn the other, and bake them as dry as ye can without burning.

---

 ## MODERN RECIPE                                    Makeability: 2

| | |
|---|---|
| 2 cups 35% cream | 3 TBS sugar |
| 4 egg yolks | 1 tsp cinnamon |
| 1³/₄ cups all-purpose flour | 1/4 tsp ginger |
| 2 TBS ale | 2 TBS unsalted butter |

Combine the ingredients, except for the butter, in a mixing bowl. In large frying pan, melt the butter and add a ladleful of batter to one side of the pan. Hold the pan on a steep angle allowing the batter to run to the other side. Continue until the batter has covered the pan in a quarter-inch thickness. When the pancake has set, turn it over and cook the other side.

---

# TO MAKE PESCODS ANOTHER

*The Good Huswifes Handmaide for the Kitchin, 1594*

Olivia:    Of what personage, and yeeres is he?
Malvolio:  Not yet old enough for a man, nor yong
           enough for a boy: as a squash is before tis a pescod,
           or a Codling when tis almost an Apple: Tis with him in
           standing water, betweene boy and man. (*Twelfth Night* 1.5.152–156)

*What Shakespeare and his contemporaries called "peascods," we call "peapods." The "cod" of "peasecod" meant "pouch," and can also be found in "codpiece," an accoutrement that men in Shakespeare's England attached to the front of their breeches to cover their "privie members." A 1583 collection of humorous anecdotes, called* The Mirrour of Mirth, *relates a story about a vicar who, on his way to church, bought a live carp for dinner, which he then tied to his codpiece and covered with his gown. Shortly thereafter, as he walked down the aisle of his church to collect offerings, the dying carp began to wriggle about, causing the Vicar's gown to bob up and down in a manner that caused great consternation among the congregation.*

Take Apples, and mince them small, take figs, Dates, Corrans, great Raisons, sinamon, Ginger, and Sugar, mince them, and put them all together, and make them in litle flat peeces, and frie them in Butter and Oyle.

---

 ## MODERN RECIPE                                        Makeability: 3

2 apples, peeled, cored, and finely chopped

4 dried figs, minced

4 dates, minced

1 TBS currants

1 TBS raisins

1 tsp cinnamon

$^{1}/_{2}$ tsp minced ginger

1 TBS sugar

Butter and lard for frying

For the batter:

1$^{1}/_{3}$ cups all-purpose flour

1 tsp salt

$^{1}/_{4}$ tsp pepper

1 TBS lard or melted butter

3 egg yolks

$^{1}/_{2}$ cup of flat ale

Combine the flour, salt, pepper, lard, and egg yolks. Slowly add the ale. Add the fruit, spices, and sugar together and form into dollops the size and shape of peapods. In a deep pot, heat the lard (2$^{1}/_{2}$ to 3 inches deep) to 365°F and set in a few dollops, to cook for 3 to 4 minutes, making sure they are not crowded too close to one another. Remove to a kitchen towel to drain. Repeat until all the mixture is cooked.

---

# FRITTERS ON THE COURT FASHION

*A New Booke of Cookerie, 1615*

King Henry:  And to conclude, the Shepherds homely Curds,
            His cold thinne drinke out of his Leather Bottle,
            His wonted sleepe, under a fresh trees shade,
            All which secure, and sweetly he enjoyes,
            Is farre beyond a Princes Delicates:
            His Viands sparkling in a Golden Cup,
            His bodie couched in a curious bed,
            When Care, Mistrust, and Treason waits on him. (*3 Henry VI* 2.5.47–54)

Take the Curdes of a Sacke Posset, the yolkes of six new layd Egges, and the whites of two of them, fine flower, and make thicke batter: cut a Pomewater in small pieces: season it with Nutmeg, and a little Pepper, put in a little strong Ale, warme Milke: mingle all togethrr, and put them into Lard, neither too hot nor too colde. If your Batter swimme, it is good temper.

---

 ## MODERN RECIPE                                        Makeability: 3

For the batter:

1 cup of sacke posset curdes (see "To make a good posset curde" on page 270)

6 egg yolks

2 egg whites

1 TBS ale

1 TBS warm whole milk

1 1/2 cup all-purpose flour

For the apple:

1 moist apple cored and cut in small chunks

1 tsp nutmeg

1/4 tsp pepper lard or beef suet for frying as needed

Heat the lard (at least 1 1/2 to 3 inches deep) to 365°F. Mix the posset curdes, eggs, ale, milk, and flour into a thick batter. In a separate bowl, mix together the apple, nutmeg, and pepper and fold into the batter. Spoon the batter into a deep pot of heated lard. Fry the apple in several small batches to ensure even cooking, about three to four minutes. Drain on kitchen towels.

---

# THE BEST FRITTERS

*The English Huswife, 1615*

Falstaff: Have I laid my braine in the Sun, and dri'de it,
    that it wants matter to prevent so grosse ore-reaching as
    this? Am I ridden with a Welsh Goate too? Shal I have
    a Coxcombe of Frize? Tis time I were choak'd with a
    peece of toasted Cheese.

Evans: Seese is not good to give putter; your belly
    is all putter.

Falstaff: Seese, and Putter? Have I liv'd to stand
    at the taunt of one that makes Fritters of English? (*The Merry Wives of Windsor* 5.5.134–142)

*Nowadays, we sometimes express bewilderment by saying, "It's all Greek to me." In Shakespeare's England, they were more likely to say, "It's all Welsh to me," because that language was not formally studied (as Greek and Latin were) and in fact was deemed strange and barbarous. Thus, when Hotspur says of Glendower in 1 Henry IV that "no man speaks better Welsh" (3.1.48), he means that no one speaks more gibberish. The Welsh accent was also sometimes disparaged, as in the quotation from The Merry Wives of Windsor where Falstaff mocks Evans for saying "seese and putter" instead of "cheese and butter."*

To make the best Fritters, take a pinte of creame and warme it, then take eight egges, only abate fowre of the whites and beate them well in a dish, and so mixe them with the creame, then put in a little Cloves, Mace, Nutmegge and Saffron and stirre them well together: then put in two spoonefull of the best ale-barme and a little salt and stirre it againe, then make it thicke according to your pleasure with wheate flowere, which done, set it within the aire of the fire that it may rise and swell; which when it doth you shall beate it in once or twice, then put into it a penny pot of sacke: all this being done, you shal take a pound or two of sweet seame and put it into a panne, and set it over the fire, and when it is moulten and begins to bubble, you shall take the fritter batter, and setting it by you, put thicke slices of well pared Apples into the batter: And then taking the Apples and batter out together with a spoone put it into the boiling seame, and boile your fritters crispe and browne: and when you finde the strength of your seame decay, you shall renew it with more seame, and of all sorts of seame, that which is made of the beefe suet is the best and strongest: when your fritters are made strow good store of sugar and cinamon upon them being faire disht, and so serve them up.

---

 ## MODERN RECIPE                                    Makeability: 4

2 cups 35% cream

4 egg yolks

4 whole eggs

$1/2$ tsp ground cloves

$1/2$ tsp ground mace

1 tsp nutmeg

2 pinches saffron

1 packet active dry yeast

$1/2$ tsp salt

$1 1/2$ cups all-purpose flour

$1/4$ cup dry sherry

4 apples, peeled, cored, and cut into quarter-inch slices

Sugar and cinnamon for garnish

Lard or beef suet for frying as needed

Warm the cream slightly. In a large mixing bowl, combine the cream, eggs, spices, yeast, and salt. Whisk in the flour to a batter-like consistency. Cover the bowl and place it on a warm oven, allowing mixture to rise, about two hours. Whisk in the sherry. Heat the lard (at least $1 1/2$ to 3 inches deep) to 365°F. Coat the apple slices in the batter and fry in the oil until golden brown. Remove the fritters and drain on a kitchen towel. Sprinkle with sugar and cinnamon while still hot.

---

# TO MAKE ANY QUELQUECHOSE

*The English Huswife*, 1615

Some Pigeons, Davy, a couple of short-legg'd Hennes:
a joynt of Mutton, and any pretty little tiny Kickshawes,
tell William Cooke. (*2 Henry IV* 5.1. 21–23)

The French word "quelquechose" means "something," an appropriate name for a dish which is, as Gervase Markham says, "a mixture of many things together." In English, a variant of "quelquechose" also arose—"kickshaws," as in the passage from 2 Henry IV—thanks to the tendency of Shakespeare's contemporaries to blithely pronounce foreign words as if they were were not foreign. (A case in point is the name "Jacques"—as in the cynical character from As You Like It—which they pronounced "jay-kweez.") In nonculinary contexts, the word "kick-shaws" was also used to mean "a fancy trick." For example, in Twelfth Night, Sir Andrew claims to be able to do tricky dance moves, which prompts Sir Toby to ask, "Art thou good at these kickshawses, knight?" As for the recipe, the "fry-case" to which it refers is not a pan or vessel, but simply a variant spelling of "fricassee"; in other words, the mixture of eggs, cream, currants, and so on is a fricassee into which the pig's pettitoes are put.

To make a Quelquechose which is a mixture of many things together: take egges and breake them, and doe away one halfe of the whites, and after they are beaten, put to them a good quantity of sweet Creame, Currants, Cinnamon, Cloves, mace, Salt, and a little Ginger, spinage, endive, and marygold flowers grossely chopt, and beat them all very well together; Then take pigges pettitoes slic't and grossely chopt, and mix them with the egges, and with your hand stirre them exceeding well together: then put sweet butter in your frying pan, and being melted, put in all the rest, and frie it browne without burning, ever and anon turning it till it be fried enough: then dish it up upon a flat plate, and cover it with suger, and so serve it foorth. Onely herein is to be observed that your petitoes must be very well boiled before you put them into the fry-case. And in this manner as you make this Quel-quechose, so you may make any other, whether it be of flesh, smal birds, sweet rootes, oisters, muskles, cockles, giblets, lemmons, orenges, or any fruit, pulse, or other sallet herbe whatsoever: of which to speak severally were a labour infinite, because they vary with mens opinions.

---

 **MODERN RECIPE**                                        Makeability: 4

| | |
|---|---|
| 4 whole eggs | 1/4 tsp ginger |
| 4 egg yolks | 2 cups chopped spinach |
| 1/4 cup 35% cream | 1 cup chopped endive |
| 1 TBS currants | 1/4 cup edible flowers |
| 1/2 tsp cinnamon | 4 pig trotters, cooked and roughly chopped (or substitute another meat) |
| 1/2 tsp ground cloves | |
| 1/4 tsp ground mace | 1/4 cup unsalted butter for frying |
| 1 tsp salt | Sugar for garnish |

Beat together in a large mixing bowl the eggs, cream, spices, spinach, and herbs. Add the chopped pig trotters and combine. In a large frying pan, melt the butter, pour in the mixture, and stir to a consistency similar to scrambled eggs. Spoon the quelquechose onto a serving platter and sprinkle with sugar.

# TO MAKE FRITTERS OF ALMONDS, WITH THE BRAWNE OR FLESH OF A HENNE

*Epulario, 1598*

Touchstone: Sweetest nut, hath sowrest rinde,
     such a nut is Rosalinde. (*As You Like It* 3.2.107–108)

*The favorite nut in Shakespeare's England was the almond: of the 2,100 recipes that were published in this period, 173 of them call for almonds, versus nine that call for pine nuts, six for walnuts, three for pistachios, two for chestnuts, and none for hazelnuts or filberts. Walnuts, in fact, are mentioned more often as indications of the size of other ingredients than they are as ingredients in their own right: phrases such as "take a lumpe of butter of the bigness of a walnut" are not uncommon. Ironically, walnuts are also mentioned in a recipe that explains how to create an artificial walnut by pressing pastry into a walnut-shaped mold.*

Take Almonds and stampe them with Rosewater and a little milke and straine them, then take the brawne or flesh of the brest of a Pullet, boyle it and stampe it apart from the Almonds, then take a little flower and whites of Egges according to the quantity you will make, and a little Sugar, mingle all this together, and make your fritters in what quantity you will, and frie them in Suet or Butter, and let them not be overmuch baked.

---

 ## MODERN RECIPE      Makeability: 3

1/2 cup blanched almonds, finely minced

1 tsp rosewater (see Appendix 1)

1/2 cup whole milk or as needed

2 boiled chicken breasts with meat removed and finely shredded

1 1/2 cups all-purpose flour

1 TBS sugar

1 cup of beef suet or 1/2 lb unsalted butter for frying, as needed

Combine the ingredients in a large mixing bowl until you have a batter-like consistency. Add more fluid or flour as needed. Into a skillet of hot suet or butter, place spoonfuls of the chicken and almond fritters and cook until just golden brown on both sides. Remove and drain on kitchen towels.

---

# TO MAKE FRITTERS OF FIGGES

*Epulario, 1598*

Soothsayer: You shall out-live the Lady whom you serve.
Charmian:  Oh excellent, I love long life better than Figs. (*Antony and Cleopatra* 1.2.33–34)

*This recipe calls for both figs and almonds, perhaps in accordance with sixteenth-century dietary theory. Andrew Boorde, for example, claimed that "fygges doth nurysshe mervelously, when they be eaten with blanched almons." Curiously, figs were also thought to cause lice. Boorde in 1547 noted that they "provoke a man to sweate: wherfore they do ingender lyce"; Joannes de Mediolano in 1607 claimed that "by figs are by lice engendred"; and Michael Scot in 1633 suggested that figs cause corrupt humors to rise to "the uppermost part of the skinne; and out of such humors are Lice ingendred." A sure-fire remedy, according to Gervase Markham, was to rub the afflicted scalp with "oyle of Radish" and "lard of bacon."*

Take a few Almonds and pine kernels, as many as you will and stampe them, let them bee very white, adding thereunto two drie figges and Currans with Spice, and if this stuffe be too thick put a little Rosewater to it, then take Figs and make a hole in ech Figge hard by the stalke, and fil them with this stuffe, then frie them in oyle and cast Sugar on them.

---

 ## MODERN RECIPE                                        Makeability: 4

| | |
|---|---|
| 1/4 cup almonds | 1/2 tsp nutmeg |
| 1/4 cup pine nuts | 1 TBS rosewater (see Appendix 1) |
| 2 dried figs, minced | 12 fresh figs |
| 1 TBS currants, minced | Lard for frying as needed |
| 1/2 tsp cinnamon | 2 TBS sugar for garnish |

In a mortar and pestle crush the almonds and pine nuts. Work in the minced figs, currants, and spices. Add rosewater as needed to thin out the stuffing. Cut off the top of the figs and scoop out most of the inside. Fill the figs with the almond stuffing and pinch closed. In a pot, heat the lard (at least 1 1/2 to 3 inches deep) to 365°F. Carefully put the figs into the lard and fry until cooked through. Remove the fritters and drain on kitchen towels before arranging on a serving platter and sprinkle with sugar.

---

# TO MAKE AN ITALIAN PUDDING

*A New Booke of Cookerie, 1615*

> Roderigo: I cannot beleeve that in her, she's full of
> most bless'd condition.
> Iago: Bless'd figges-end. The Wine she drinkes is made of
> grapes. If shee had beene bless'd, shee would never have
> lov'd the Moore. Bless'd pudding. Didst thou not see her
> paddle with the palme of his hand? Didst not marke
> that? (*Othello* 2.1.251–257)

*Why the author of this recipe considered it an appropriate dish for dinner, but not supper, is puzzling. None of the other 2,100 recipes that were published in this period limit themselves to one meal or the other. Perhaps the mealtime injunction in this recipe was out of consideration for two of its ingredients, rosewater and nutmeg, both of which are also found in a medicinal recipe entitled "To provoke sleep." Did the author fear that eating this dish too close to bedtime might result in drowsy dinner guests? As for the quotation from* Othello, *Iago's "Blessed pudding," like his "Blessed fig's end," is intended to belittle Desdemona, whom Roderigo has just described as being of "blessed condition." Desdemona, scoffs Iago, is no more full of blessedness than the tip of a fig or a boiled pudding.*

Take a Penny white Loafe, pare off the crust, and cut it in square pieces like unto great Dyes, mince a pound of Beefe Suit small: take halfe a pound of Razins of the Sunne, stone them and mingle them together, and season them with Sugar, Rosewater, and Nutmegge, wet these things in foure Egges, and stirre them very tenderly for breaking the Bread: then put it into a Dish, and pricke three or foure pieces of Marrow, and some sliced Dates: put it into an Oven hot enough for a Chewet: if your Oven be too hot, it will burne: if too colde, it will be heavy: when it is bakte scrape on Sugar, and serve it hot at dinner, but not at Supper.

---

 ## MODERN RECIPE                                          Makeability: 3

1/2 loaf white bread, crust removed and cut into 1-inch cubes

1 lb beef suet, minced

1/2 lb raisins

1/2 cup sugar

1 TBS rosewater (see Appendix 1)

1 tsp nutmeg

4 eggs

6 pieces marrow (see Appendix 1)

6 dates, sliced

2 TBS sugar for garnish

Preheat oven to 350°F. In a large mixing bowl, combine the beef suet, raisins, sugar, rosewater, nutmeg, and eggs. Add the bread cubes and gently stir together, avoiding breaking up the bread. Spoon the mixture into a casserole dish and top with the marrow and dates. Cover and bake for 40 minutes, or until the center of pudding is just slightly firm. Remove from the oven, sprinkle with sugar, and bake for a further 10 minutes uncovered.

---

# A CAMBRIDGE PUDDING

*A New Booke of Cookerie, 1615*

Mistress Page:  Why Sir John, do you thinke though wee
would have thrust vertue out of our hearts by the head
and shoulders, and have given our selves without scruple
to hell, that ever the devill could have made you our delight?
Ford:              What, a hodge-pudding? A bag of flax?
Mistress Page:  A puft man?

| | |
|---|---|
| Page: | Old, cold, wither'd, and of intollerable entrailes? |
| Ford: | And one that is as slanderous as Sathan? |
| Mistress Page: | And as poore as Job? |
| Ford: | And as wicked as his wife? |
| Evan: | And given to Fornications, and to Tavernes, and Sacke, and Wine, and Metheglins, and to drinkings and swearings, and starings? Pribles and prables? (*The Merry Wives of Windsor* 5.5.145–158) |

*A hodge-pudding, which is one of the things Falstaff is called in the quotation from* The Merry Wives of Windsor, *was a sausage made from a medley of ingredients. The "hodge" part of the name derives from the French "hocher," meaning "to shake together," and is also found in the word "hodge-podge."*

Searce grated Bread through a Cullinder, mince it with Flower, minst Dates, Currins, Nutmeg, Sinamon, and Pepper, minst Suit, new Milke warme, fine Sugar, and Egges: take away some of their whites, worke all together. Take halfe the Pudding on the one side, and the other on the other side, and make it round like a loafe. Then take Butter, and put it in the middest of the Pudding, and the other halfe aloft. Let your liquour boyle, and throw your Pudding in, being tyed in a faire cloth: when it is boyled enough cut it in the middest, and so serve it in.

---

 ## MODERN RECIPE                                      Makeability: 4

| | |
|---|---|
| 1 cup dry bread crumbs | 1 cup beef suet, finely chopped |
| 2 cups sifted all-purpose flour | 1 cup warm whole milk |
| 1/2 cup finely chopped dates | 1 cup sugar |
| 1/2 cup currants | 2 whole eggs |
| 1/4 tsp nutmeg | 3 egg yolks |
| 1/4 tsp cinnamon | 2 TBS butter |
| 1/4 tsp pepper | |

In a large mixing bowl, combine the ingredients. Add more flour if the mixture is too loose. Divide the pudding mixture into two equal portions and form into round "loaves." Put bits of butter on top of one half and set the other half on the buttered loaf. Secure the pudding in cheesecloth and place it in a large pot of boiling water. Simmer for 1 to 1 1/2 hours, or until the pudding is set in the middle.

---

# A SWANNE OR GOOSE PUDDING

*A New Booke of Cookerie, 1615*

Sweet Swan of Avon! what a sight it were
To see thee in our waters yet appeare,
And make those flights upon the bankes of Thames,
That so did take Eliza, and our James. (Ben Jonson's commendatory poem
  in memory of Shakespeare)

*The preceding quotation is not by Shakespeare but about him: Ben Jonson wrote the lines in memory of his friend (and rival playwright), and they were published along with commendatory poems by several other authors at the beginning of the 1623 First Folio edition of Shakespeare's works. The Eliza and James that Jonson refers to in his verse were, of course, Queen Elizabeth and King James, who frequently traveled up and down the Thames by barge.*

Stirre the bloud of a Swanne, or Goose, steepe fine Oatmeale in milke, Nutmeg, Pepper, sweet Hearbes, minst Suit: mingle all together with Rosewater, Lemmon pils minst fine, Coriander seeds, a little quantitie thereof.

---

## MODERN RECIPE                                        Makeability: 5

1 1/2 cup swan's blood

1/3 cup milk

1/2 cup fine oatmeal (oatmeal flour)

1/4 tsp nutmeg

1/4 tsp pepper

1/2 tsp marjoram

1/4 tsp thyme

2 TBS beef suet

1 tsp rosewater

1 tsp minced lemon zest

1/2 tsp coriander seeds, minced

Stir the swan's blood into the milk and oatmeal and add the remaining ingredients. In a saucepan, bring to a boil and simmer gently until thick.

# 11

# BROTHS, POTTAGE, AND SOPS

And this same last hard pinching yeere, 1630, some in this same towne, ate the flesh
of cats, and made good pottage thereof.

—James Hart, *Klinike*, 1633

For Shakespeare, a stew was not a food but a place, specifically a brothel, so called
because brothels contained hot tubs where people sat and tried (vainly) to sweat
out their venereal diseases. In fact, the use of the word "stew" to denote a dish
made by simmering meat and vegetables didn't develop until well after Shakespeare died, as did the word "soup." Shakespeare and his contemporaries often
referred to such culinary concoctions as "pottages," the name deriving simply from
the pot in which the foodstuff was cooked. Easily made and hearty, pottages were
a staple of the English diet. The poor probably ate pottage daily, and the wealthy
featured pottages among the many dishes that were served to their tables. Thomas
Dawson, for one, included "pottage or stewed broth" in a sample menu for a first
course in *The Good Huswifes Jewell*. So popular was pottage that Andrew Boorde,
in his 1547 *Compendyous Regyment*, claimed that "potage is not so much used in
all christendom as it is used in Englande." Boorde added that "potage is made of
the liquor in the which flesshe is sodden in, with puttynge to chopped herbes, and
oatmell," but by the late sixteenth century oatmeal was not an ingredient in most
printed recipes for pottages. (Incidentally, Boorde also cautioned that in times of
plague, pottage should be made without herbs, because "the corrupcion of the
ayer" infected the leaves.)

Broths (which have no connection with brothels) were very similar to pottages, as
is suggested by Dawson's reference to "pottage or stewed broth." We now tend to think
of broths as being thin liquids, the meat and vegetables having been strained out. In
Shakespeare's England, however, broths were usually not strained, and were sometimes
made even thicker by the addition of eggs, crushed almonds, cream, or bread crumbs.
In fact, the only real difference between broth and pottage was that the latter could
include meat-free concoctions, such as "pottage of lettuce," "pottage of beanes," and
"pottage of cherries." Broths, in contrast, almost always contained flesh of some sort.

Sops (also known as sippets) were slices of bread used to soak up the liquid of a
pottage or broth. They were usually placed on the bottom of a dish or trencher,

and then smothered with the other boiled foodstuff, much as we now do with potatoes or rice. Many recipes from the sixteenth and early seventeenth centuries called for the slices of bread to be lightly toasted before being placed in the dish: "have manchet cut like tostes and tost them brown," says a recipe called "To Make Court Sops." Sops were a culinary staple in Shakespeare's England, and this is reflected in the fact that thirty-six of the recipes included in this book direct the cook to serve the dish upon sops. This popularity was reinforced by the dietary belief that bread was the natural complement to flesh: as Gervase Markham asserted in 1616, "bread by its owne good nature doth correct the faults that are in other meates."

# TO BOYLE YONG PEASON OR BEANES

*A Book of Cookrye, 1591*

Second Carrier:   Pease and Beanes are as danke here as a
        Dog, and this is the next way to give poore Jades the
        Bottes: This house is turned upside downe since Robin
        the Ostler dyed.
First Carrier:   Poore fellow never joy'd since the price
        of oats rose, it was the death of him.
Second Carrier:   I thinke this is the most villanous
        house in al London rode for Fleas: I am stung like
        a Tench.
First Carrier:   Like a Tench? There is ne're a King
        in Christendome, could be better bit, then I
        have beene since the first Cocke.
Second Carrier:   Why, you will allow us ne're a Jorden,
        and then we leake in your Chimney: and your Chamber-
        lye breeds Fleas like a Loach.
First Carrier:   What Ostler, come away, and be hangd:
        come away.
Second Carrier:   I have a Gammon of Bacon, and two
        razes of Ginger, to be delivered as farre as Charing-crosse.
First Carrier:   The Turkies in my Pannier are quite starved. (*1 Henry IV* 2.1.8–28)

*The original plural of "pea" was "peason," much as "oxen" is still the plural of "ox." Slowly, however, "peas" developed as an alternative plural, and both forms were in existence during Shakespeare's lifetime. Thus, this recipe refers to "peason," while the passage from Shakespeare alludes to "peas." The carriers in this passage—whose job was to transport goods from rural areas to cities like London—are complaining that the peas and beans that are fed to their horses by the ostler (a caretaker of horses) are dank, which leads to mildew, which can give horses a parasite known as the bots. The goods being transported by these carriers are not out of the ordinary: a big chunk of bacon, some whole roots of ginger, and some live turkeys.*

First shale them and seethe them in faire water, then take them out of the water and put them into boyling milk, then take the yolks of Egs with crums of bread, and ginger, and straine them thorow a strainer with the said milk, then take chopped percely, Saffron and Salt, and serve it foorth for Pottage.

---

 ## MODERN RECIPE                                        Makeability: 2

2 cups sweet or sugar-snap peas        1 tsp minced ginger

2 cups milk                                          $1/2$ cup chopped parsley

2 hard-boiled egg yolks                       1 pinch saffron

$1/2$ cup bread crumbs                         $1/4$ tsp salt

Shell the peas and blanch them in boiling water. Remove the peas to a saucepan of hot milk and add the egg yolks, bread crumbs, and ginger. Force through a fine-meshed sieve into a bowl and add the parsley, saffron, and salt. Stir together and serve.

---

# TO MAKE GALLANTINE

*The Good Huswifes Handmaide for the Kitchin, 1594*

Salanio:                                               Now by two-headed
Janus, Nature hath fram'd strange fellowes in her time:
Some that will evermore peepe through their eyes,
And laugh like Parrats at a bag-piper.
And other of such vineger aspect,
That they'll not shew their teeth in way of smile,
Though Nestor sweare the jest be laughable. (*The Merchant of Venice*
1.1.50–56)

*In the early fifteenth century, a galantine was a sauce for fish and fowl, but by the six-teenth century it could also be a dish (as in this recipe) of bread soaked in some sort of seasoned liquid. The vinegar called for in the recipe was probably white wine vinegar. Less affluent households would make do with malt vinegar, made by fermenting ale rather than wine (and thus its other name, alegar). Vinegar was reputed to have many potent properties: according to Thomas Lupton in his 1579 book* A Thousand Notable Things, *Hannibal once made a passage through the Alps by burning the rocks that stood in his way and then pouring vinegar upon them—doing so "made them so softe, that they might fall easily in peeces." In the passage from* The Merchant of Venice, *the astringent nature of vinegar is equated with individuals whose sour expression never gives way to a smile.*

Take tostes of white bread, boyle them on a chafingdish of coales, with vinigar, when it hath soked afore in the vinegar, and in the boyling put in a brance of Rose-mary, Sugar, Synamon and Ginger, straine it, and serve it.

## MODERN RECIPE

Makeability: 1

| | |
|---|---|
| 6 slices white bread | 1 tsp sugar |
| 1/2 cup white vinegar | 1/2 tsp cinnamon |
| 1 sprig rosemary | 1 tsp chopped ginger |

Lightly toast the bread and simmer in water and vinegar, adding the rosemary, sugar, cinnamon, and ginger.

# TO MAKE ORDINARY STEW'D BROTH

*The English Hus-wife*, 1615

| | |
|---|---|
| Belarius: | This youth, howe're distrest, appears he hath had Good Ancestors. |
| Arviragus: | How Angell-like he sings! |
| Guiderius: | But his neate Cookerie! |
| Arviragus: | He cut our Rootes in Charracters, |
| | And sawc'st our Brothes, as Juno had bin sicke, |
| | And he her Dieter. (*Cymbeline* 4.2.48–53) |

*In the quotation from Cymbeline, the gentlemen are praising Imogen for his fancy culinary techniques (he carves root vegetables into letters or "characters") and for the restorative powers of his cooking: he sauces his broths so well that they would not be beneath an ailing goddess, such as Juno.*

*The powdered wood of the sandalwood tree—known in Shakespeare's time as saunders—was used in this recipe to give the broth a reddish hue. Other substances that were used to alter the color of foods included saffron for yellow, spinach juice for green, and turnsole for blue. Blood was sometimes used, too, when saunders was in short supply, and sauces were sometimes blackened with crumbs of burnt toast. In this recipe, we've substituted beet root for the hard-to-get powdered sandalwood.*

To make ordinary stew'd broth, you shall take a neck of Veal, or a legg, or marrow-bone of Beef, or a Pullet, or Mutton, and after the meat is washt, put it into a pot with fair water, and being ready to boyl, scum it well; then you shall take a couple of Manchets, and pairing away the crust, cut it into thick slices, and lay them in a dish and cover them with hot broth out of the pot; when they are steept, put them and some of the broth into a strainer and strain it, and then put it into a pot: then take half a pound of Prunes, half a pound of Raisins, and a quarter of a pound of Currants clean pickt and washt, with a little whole Mace, and two or three bruised cloves, and put them into the pot, and stir all well together, and so let them boyl till the meat be enough, then if you will alter the colour of the broth, put in a little Turnsoyl or red Sanders, and so serve it upon sippets, and the fruit uppermost.

---

 MODERN RECIPE                                    Makeability: 3

6 lb beef stock bones

4 quarts water

3 slices white bread, crusts removed

1/4 cup chopped prunes

1 TBS raisins

1 TBS currants

1 blade of whole mace

1 whole clove

1 cup beets, finely diced

Slices of lightly toasted 60% whole wheat bread

In a stock pot, cover the beef bones in water and bring to the boil. Reduce to a simmer and skim as needed. Place a ladle of hot broth into a dish and soak the bread slices. With a fine-meshed sieve, strain the bread and broth back into the stock pot. Add the prunes, raisins, currants, and spices and stir. If you desire a deeper color, add diced beets. Simmer the broth gently, partly covered, for 3 to 4 hours. Arrange the sippets on a platter and pour some broth onto them. Top with the prunes, raisins, and currants.

---

# TO MAKE POTTAGE OF CHERRIES

*A Book of Cookrye*, 1591

Helena:  We, Hermia, like two Artificiall gods,
         Have with our needles, created both one flower,
         Both on one sampler, sitting on one cushion,
         Both warbling of one song, both in one key:
         As if our hands, our sides, voices, and mindes
         Had beene incorporate. So we grew together,
         Like to a double cherry, seeming parted,
         But yet a union in partition,
         Two lovely berries molded on one stem,
         So with two seeming bodies, but one heart,
         Two of the first life coats in Heraldry,
         Due but to one and crowned with one crest. (A *Midsummer Night's Dream*
           3.2.203–214)

Fry white bread in butter til it be brown and so put it into a dish, then take Cherries and take out the stones and frye them where you fried the bread then put thereto Sugar, Ginger, and Sinamon, for lacke of broth, take White or Claret Wine, boyle these togither, and that doon, serve them upon your Tostes.

MODERN RECIPE                                              Makeability: 2

| | |
|---|---|
| 6 slices white bread | 1/2 tsp minced ginger |
| Unsalted butter for frying as needed | 1/2 tsp cinnamon |
| 2 cups pitted cherries | 1/2 cup red Bordeaux wine |
| 1 tsp sugar | |

Fry each slice of bread in butter until just brown. Remove, set aside, and keep warm. Sauté the cherries in butter and add the sugar, ginger, and cinnamon. Add the wine and simmer until the mixture thickens nicely. Arrange the fried bread on a platter and spoon on the cherry pottage.

# TO MAKE THE OLDE BROATH

*A Delightfull Daily Exercise for Ladies and Gentlewomen, 1621*

Salerio: My winde cooling my broth,
   Would blow me to an Ague, when I thought
   What harme a winde too great might doe at sea.
   I should not see the sandie houre-glasse runne,
   But I should thinke of shallows, and of flats,
   And see my wealthy Andrew docks in sand,
   Vailing her high top lower then her ribs
   To kisse her buriall; should I goe to Church
   And see the holy edifice of stone,
   And not bethinke me straight of dangerous rocks,
   Which touching but my gentle Vessels side
   Would scatter all her spices on the streame,
   Enrobe the roring waters with my silkes,
   And in a word, but even now worth this,
   And now worth nothing. (*The Merchant of Venice* 1.1.22–36)

*Four hundred years ago, things went in and out of fashion just as they do nowadays. When Malvolio, in* Twelfth Night, *appears "cross-gartered"—that is, with the garters on each leg crossing over one another like shoelaces—the other members of the household mock him for being ridiculously out of style. Likewise, John Murrell, when he published this recipe in 1621, felt he needed to describe it as "old," though presumably he intended the positive connotations of yesteryear that we associate with "the good old days." In contrast, other recipes from the period advertise their novelty, such as "To make Almond butter after the best and newest manner" and "To make a new dish called Tomascella." As for the quotation from* The Merchant of Venice, *Salerio is suggesting that if he had invested all his wealth in a ship carrying spices back from the East, everything would remind him of the hazards that could bring him to ruin. Blowing on his hot broth would make him think of tempests, and seeing sand run through an hour-glass would evoke the fear that his ship had run aground in shallow waters.*

Take a peece of freshe beefe and slice it in very thinne slices as broad as two fingers, then set it on to the fire with as much faire water as will cover it over, and when you have skummed it well, season it with a little beaten Cloves and Mace, and Ginger, a litle salt, and six slist Onions, a litle Ale-yeist, a handfull of Currance, a halfe-penny-white loafe cut in very thinne slices, a handfull of Parsley, halfe a handfull of Savory, and Time stript, and shred, stewe all these together till it bee halfe stewed away, then dish it up and strowe salt round about it, and when you have done it very neately, then serve it to the table hot.

---

 ## MODERN RECIPE    Makeability: 2

| | |
|---|---|
| 2 lb stewing beef | $^{1}/_{2}$ cup currants |
| 1 tsp ground cloves | 6 slices thinly sliced white bread |
| 2 blades of whole mace | $^{1}/_{2}$ cup chopped parsley |
| 1 tsp ground ginger | $^{1}/_{4}$ cup chopped savory |
| $^{1}/_{2}$ tsp salt | $^{1}/_{4}$ cup thyme |
| 3 small onions, sliced | Salt to taste |
| 1 packet active dry yeast | |

In a large saucepan, cover the beef with water and bring to a boil, skimming as needed. Add the remaining ingredients and simmer the mixture slowly until it has reduced by half. Pour the mixture onto a platter, sprinkle with salt, and serve.

---

# TO MAKE FINE RICE POTTAGE

*The Treasure of Commodious Conceits, 1591*

Ferdinand:  Sir, I will pronounce your sentence: You shall fast
a Weeke with Branne and water.
Costard:    I had rather pray a Moneth with Mutton and Porridge. (*Love's Labour's Lost* 1.1.291–293)

*Despite the odd inclusion of oak bark, this recipe is remarkably bland: unlike all the other recipes published in this era, this one contains no spices whatsoever. After experiencing a few spoonfuls of the pottage in its authentic form, a guest may want to embellish the dish slightly by sprinkling on a bit of sugar and cinnamon, nutmeg, or ginger.*

Take halfe a pound of Jorden Almondes, and halfe a pound of Rice, and a gallon of running water, and a handfull of Oke barke, and let the barke be boyled in the running water, and the Almondes beaten with the hulles and all on, and so strained to make the Rice Porredge withall.

## MODERN RECIPE                                    Makeability: 2

½ lb ground almonds                ½ cup oak bark (if available)
½ lb cooked rice

In a saucepan, boil the oak bark in the water for an hour or until very soft. Force the almonds, rice, and oak bark through a fine-meshed sieve and into a bowl.

# TO MAKE SOPS FOR A CAPON

*A Book of Cookrye*, 1591

Ulysses:   Take but degree away, untune that string,
           And hark what discord follows! Each thing melts
           In mere oppugnancy: the bounded waters
           Should lift their bosoms higher than the shores,
           And make a sop of all this solid globe. (*Troilus and Cressida* 1.3.109–113)

Take Tostes of Bread, Butter, Claret wine and slices of Orenges, and lay them upon the Tostes and Sinamon Sugar and Ginger.

## MODERN RECIPE                                    Makeability: 2

6 ½-inch slices of toasted 60% whole wheat       ½ tsp cinnamon
bread
                                                 1 tsp sugar
4 TBS melted unsalted butter
                                                 ½ tsp minced ginger
½ cup red Bordeaux wine

1 orange, sliced

Lightly toast the bread on an open flame. Combine the butter, wine, and oranges and spoon onto the toasts. Mix together the cinnamon, sugar, and ginger and sprinkle over the sops.

# EISANDS WITH OTEMEALE GROTES

*A Book of Cookrye*, 1591

Titania:   Or say sweete Love, what thou desirest to eat.
Bottom:    Truly a pecke of Provender; I could munch
           your good dry Oates. Me-thinkes I have a great desire to
           a bottle of hay: good hay, sweete hay hath no fellow.

> Titania: I have a venturous Fairy, That shall seeke
> the Squirrels hoard, And fetch thee new Nuts.
> Bottom: I had rather have a handfull or two of dried pease. (*A Midsummer Night's Dream* 4.1.30–36)

*Groats are hulled grain of various sorts, such as oats, barley, or wheat. Shakespeare refers to groats in his plays, but usually he means another kind of groat, namely, a small coin worth four pence. For example, in 2 Henry IV, Falstaff discovers that he is essentially broke, with only "Seven groats and two pence" in his possession. As for the other unusual word in this recipe's title, "eisands," it may be a variant of the word "isings," which denoted a mixture that was stuffed into what used to be called a "pudding," but what we would now call a sausage casing (see, for example, the recipe "To make Ising puddings" in the "Fritters and Puddings" chapter). This recipe for "Eisands with Otemeal grotes," however, seems more like a pottage than a stuffing, which is why we've placed it in this chapter. A further odd word appears in the foregoing quotation from Shakespeare. Bottom, with his head now transformed into that of an ass, announces that he would like a "bottle" of hay. This "bottle" is not related to the "bottle" that we keep beverages in, but rather is a distinct word meaning "bundle."*

Take a pinte of Creame and seethe it, and when it is hot, put therto a pinte of Ote-meale grotes, and let them soke in it all night, and put therto viii yolks of egs, and a little Pepper, Cloves, mace, and saffron, and a good deale of Suet of beefe, and small Raisins and Dates, and a little Sugar.

---

 ## MODERN RECIPE                                         Makeability: 3

| | |
|---|---|
| 2 cups 18% cream | 1 pinch saffron |
| 1 cup buckwheat groats | 1/2 cup suet |
| 8 egg yolks | 2 TBS small raisins |
| 1/4 tsp freshly ground pepper | 1 TBS chopped dates |
| 1/4 tsp ground cloves | 1 TBS sugar |
| 1 blade of mace | |

Scald the cream, add the groats, and let them soak over night. Next day, stir in the remaining ingredients, heat, and serve.

---

# HOW TO MAKE SOPS OF ALMAIN

*A Book of Cookrye*, 1591

> Antonio: Content your self, God knows I lov'd my neece,
> And she is dead, slander'd to death by villaines,

That dare as well answer a man indeede,
As I dare take a serpent by the tongue.
Boyes, apes, braggarts, Iackes, milke-sops. (*Much Ado About Nothing* 5.1.87–91)

Take white wine with Beere or Ale, and put crums of white bread, yolks of Egs sugar and sinamon, with Salt and saffron, strain these and boile them a little togither then cut white bread into your dishe, and put the pottage to it, and so serve it foorth.

---

 ## MODERN RECIPE                                                  Makeability: 2

| | |
|---|---|
| 1 cup white wine | $1/2$ tsp cinnamon |
| 1 cup ale | $1/2$ tsp salt |
| 1 cup bread crumbs | 1 pinch saffron |
| 2 hard-boiled egg yolks | 6 slices lightly toasted white bread |
| 1 tsp sugar | |

Pour the wine and ale into a mixing bowl and add the bread crumbs, egg yolks, sugar, cinnamon, salt, and saffron. Force the mixture through a fine-meshed sieve into a saucepan and bring to a boil. Cut the bread into triangle shapes and arrange on a platter. Pour the pottage over the bread.

---

# FOR TO MAKE FRUMENTE

*Wyl Bucke His Testament*, 1560

Bassanio: Gratiano speakes an infinite deale of nothing,
more than any man in all Venice. His reasons are as two
graines of wheate hid in two bushels of chaffe: you shall
seeke all day ere you finde them, & when you
have them they are not worth the search. (*The Merchant of Venice* 1.1.114–118)

*Frumenty is a pottage that takes its name from "frumentum," the Latin word for "grain." The "lyer" that is referred to in the recipe is a lear, that is, a thickening sauce, in this case probably made from beef and mutton broth mixed with bread. Frumenty was sometimes served with venison.*

Take fayre whete that is faire picked and clene and pile him well and washe him in many waters & cast in a pot of hote sethinge water and let him sethe tyl they be tender, and then take them up, and caste him in another faire pot and caste therto lyer of befe and Moton, and caste therto swete milke & set him ouer the fire and stere them to the boyle, and then sete them downe & let them sethe, & loke they be thicke ynough of his owne kinde, and cast therin saffron and salte, when it is ynough serve them forth in faire disshes.

MODERN RECIPE                                          Makeability: 2

1 cup whole grain wheat                        1 cup whole milk

3½ cups water                                  2 pinches saffron

½ cup beef broth mixed with bread crusts to    ½ tsp salt
thicken

Add the wheat to the water and boil until tender (45 minutes or longer). Remove the wheat to another pot and add the beef broth and crusts and the milk. Return to a boil and reduce to a simmer. Stir in the saffron and salt and serve.

# TO MAKE A CAWDLE OF OTE MEALE

*The Second Part of the Good Hus-wives Jewell, 1597*

Captain:  I cannot draw a cart, Nor eate dride oats;
          If it bee mans worke I'le do't. (*King Lear* 5.3.39–40)

*Caudles were warm drinks served either to individuals confined to bed (especially women who had recently given birth) or to their visitors and well-wishers. This recipe calls for the caudle to be used as a sauce for sippets, but it could just as easily be gulped down as a nourishing beverage at breakfast or bedtime. The word "caudle" derives from the Latin "calidus," meaning "warm."*

Take two handful or more of great otemeal, and beat it in a Stone Morter wel, then put it into a quart of ale, and set it on the fire, and stirre it, season it with Cloves, mace, and Suger beaten and let it boile til it be enough, then serve it forth upon Soppes.

 MODERN RECIPE                                          Makeability: 2

2 cups rolled oats                             1 TBS superfine sugar

4 cups ale                                     Slices of lightly toasted 60% whole wheat
                                               bread for sippets
½ tsp each ground cloves and mace

Grind the oatmeal in a mortar and pestle. In a saucepan, stir the oatmeal into the ale and bring to a boil. Reduce to a simmer and add the cloves, mace, and sugar. Continue to cook for 30 to 35 minutes, stirring frequently. Serve upon sippets.

# TO MAKE LENTHEN HAGGESSE WITH POCHED EGGES

*The Second Part of the Good Hus-wives Jewell, 1597*

Falstaff: Marry, there is another Indictment upon thee,
for suffering flesh to bee eaten in thy house, contrary to
the Law, for the which I thinke thou wilt howle.
Hostess: All Victuallers doe so: What is a Joynt of Mutton,
or two, in a whole Lent? (*2 Henry IV* 2.4.343–345)

*We now think of haggis as a traditional Scottish dish, made by stuffing various minced ingredients into an animal's stomach and then boiling it. In Shakespeare's time, however, haggis was as much an English dish as a Scottish one, made by mincing or shredding ingredients, which might or might not be subsequently encased in an animal's stomach. In this recipe, the haggis is essentially a pottage, which is poured over the poached eggs after they've been placed on sippets. The absence of meat in this recipe is what makes it "Lenthen," that is a dish that could be legally eaten during Lent. However, as the quotation from 2 Henry IV suggests, the laws pertaining to Lent and other "fish days" were not always observed.*

Take a Skillet of a pinte, and fill it half with vergious, and halfe with water, and then take Margerome, Wintersaverie, Peniroyall, mince, Time, of eche six crops, wash them and take foure Egges, hard rosted, and shred them as fine as you can, & put the hearbes thus into the broth, then put a great handfull of currants, and the crummes of a quarter of a Manchet, and so let it seeth til it be thicke, then season it with Suger, Sinamon, Salt, and a good peece of Butter, and three or foure spoonefulles of Rosewater, then poch seaven Egges and lay them on sippets, and poure the Haggesse on them, with Sinamon and Sugar strewed on them.

---

 ## MODERN RECIPE                                    Makeability: 2

| | |
|---|---|
| 1 cup verjuice (see Appendix 1) | 1 cup bread crumbs |
| 1 cup water | 1 tsp sugar |
| 4 hard-boiled eggs, finely chopped | 1 tsp cinnamon |
| 1/4 cup chopped marjoram | 1 tsp salt |
| 1/2 cup chopped savory | 2 TBS unsalted butter |
| 1/2 cup chopped mint | 4 TBS rosewater (see Appendix 1) |
| 1/4 cup thyme | 7 eggs |
| 1/2 cup currants | 7 slices lightly toasted 60% whole wheat bread |

Pour the verjuice and water into a 12-inch skillet and add the eggs. Stir in the spices, currants, and bread crumbs until the mixture thickens. Season with the sugar, cinnamon, and salt along with the butter and rosewater. Continue to cook, allowing the mixture to thicken further. Meanwhile, in a large pot of gently boiling water, poach the 7 eggs to preference. Arrange the sippets on a platter and top each with a poached egg. Pour the verjuice-herb broth over the platter. Sprinkle with a little sugar and cinnamon and serve.

# 12

# BREADS, WAFERS, AND PASTRY SHELLS

Now of all other food or nourishment, bread is the most noble.... The excellency of bread may from hence also be collected, that no meale is ordinarily without bread, if it may be had.

—James Hart, *Klinike*, 1633

The vast majority of households in Shakespeare's London didn't have an oven, which meant that most people had to make bread either by frying it (as was common in the north of England) or by using a baking pan (a lidded vessel onto which embers would be heaped). Alternatively, bread could be bought from a baker's stall at market or, in a center such as London, could be delivered to one's house by a woman known as a huckster. Hucksters worked for the bakers, who gave them an extra loaf for every twelve loaves that they sold. This thirteenth loaf, which the hucksters were entitled to sell for their own profit, gave rise to the term "a baker's dozen," first recorded in print in 1599.

Bakers were required to sell several different kinds of bread, which varied according to their weight, price, and quality. At the top of these commercially produced breads was wastel, a loaf made of fine white flour. Wastel bread was also known as manchet or court bread, so named because it was the bread served to the members of the royal court. Another kind of loaf, known as simnel, was also made of fine white flour, but it was boiled before it was baked (much like modern bagels). Both wastel and simnel sold for one farthing per loaf. Of somewhat lesser quality was white loaf; this, too, was made of white flour, though of a less fine variety than with wastel bread or simnel bread. A small white loaf sold for a farthing, and a large white loaf for a halfpenny. White loaf was also known as temse bread or cocket. Next came wheaten loaf, which was essentially made from whole wheat, that is, unsifted grain meal. A small wheaten loaf sold for a halfpenny and a large wheaten loaf for a penny. Wheaten loaf was also known as cheat bread, ravel bread, yeoman's bread, or cribble bread. Finally, near the bottom, was a bread known as household loaf, which was a coarse brown bread made from a mixture of grains such as wheat, rye, and barley. It sold for a halfpenny.

The price of all of these commercially made breads was fixed: a penny loaf of wheaten bread always cost a penny. The size of the loaf, however, varied according

*The Assize of Bread*, John Powel, 1608. This series of woodcuts, which appeared at the top of every page in *The Assize of Bread* as a kind of running header, depicts the process of making bread: grinding the grain into flour, sifting the flour, kneading the flour into dough, forming the dough into lumps and weighing them, kneading the lumps of dough, shaping the lumps of dough into round loaves, marking the loaves with the baker's "seal," and finally placing the loaves in the oven. © British Library Board. All Rights Reserved C.40.d.7 pg 12.

to the price of grain. A statute known as the Assize of Bread and Ale, dating back to the thirteenth century, set out how much the various loaves had to weigh in relation to the current price of grain. For example, when a quarter (that is, eight bushels) of wheat cost 13 shillings and six pence, then a halfpenny household loaf in London was to weigh 29 ounces; but if a quarter of wheat cost 17 shillings, then a halfpenny household loaf in London was to weigh 24 ounces. The weight of the various loaves changed every time the cost of wheat went up or down by six pence.

Bakers also had to abide by other rules set out in the Assize of Bread and Ale. For example, every baker had a unique seal that had to be impressed upon every loaf before it was sold, so that the authorities could track down the baker if a loaf turned out to be too light or contained adulterated flour. Bakers were also prohibited from making "fancy" breads, such as spiced breads, buns, or biscuits, unless those products were needed for a funeral or for special holidays such as Christmas and Easter Friday. They were also forbidden to reuse their stale bread by chopping it up, soaking it in water, and kneading it back into other dough. Bakers had to apprentice for seven years before they were allowed to open up their own bakehouse. Any baker who failed to observe the laws of the Assize was fined or put into the pillory.

In times of dearth, the poor sometimes had to resort to less palatable kinds of bread, such as that made from oats. Peas and beans, too, were dried and milled into flour, which was then baked into sour-tasting loaves. Gervase Markham in a 1616 edition of *Maison Rustique*, commented that during famines he had even seen people eating breads made of bran, acorns, chestnuts, and fern roots. Some of these breads would have been less tasty and less nutritional than horse-breads, which were fed to the horses of gentlemen who stopped for a night at an inn. As with most things in Shakespeare's England, bread was understood to be bound up with social rank. The finest bread, according to Gervase Markham, was "good for idle and unlaboured persons, such as are students, monks, canons and other fine and daintie persons, which stand in neede to be fed with food of light and easie digestion." Whole wheat bread, he added, was most appropriate for "workefolkes, as delvers, porters, and such other persons as are in continuall travell, because they have neede of such like food, as consisteth of a grosse, thicke, and clammie juice." Finally, rye bread was "fit to be eaten of the countrie people and poore inhabitants of the land, but not for men of note and birth living at their ease."

Pastry dough was called "paste" in Shakespeare's England and was used, in the words of Gervase Markham, for "containing of all manner of baked meates, whether it be flesh, fish, rootes, hearbes, fruits, or other composition whatsoever." These pastes varied according to their purpose. Often, they were used to help preserve the food that was to be baked within them, in which case they were usually made of stiff rye flour that was molded into a thick-walled "coffin" (as the molded paste was called). These shells were so tough and sturdy that they were often free-standing, that is, unsupported by any vessel or baking dish. A meat baked in a sealed coffin made of thick rye paste might last for several weeks. Generally, when food baked in this kind of paste was served, the paste itself was not eaten, or at least not by people of refinement. Indeed, "pie-crust eater" was used as a term of disparagement, as in Thomas Dekkers' 1599 comedy *The Shoemaker's Holiday*, where it is applied to menial servants. Other pastes, made of fine wheat flower, were used to enclose baked meats that were brought straight from the oven to the table. Because this kind of paste was more delicate, it usually had to be supported by an earthenware vessel or, alternatively, by a coffin made of the thick and sturdy rye paste—in other words, one pastry shell was placed inside another pastry shell. Recipes for these finer pastes often call for sugar and spices, which affirms that they were eaten along with whatever baked contents they enclosed.

# TO MAKE LEAVENED BREAD

*The Good Huswifes Handmaide for the Kitchin, 1594*

Vincentio:                        Lord Angelo is precise,
              Stands at a guard with Envie: scarce confesses
              That his blood flowes: or that his appetite
              Is more to bread than stone. (*Measure for Measure* 1.3.50–53)

*The dietary authorities in Shakespeare's England warned that bread should not be eaten straight out of the oven but rather should be allowed to sit for one day in the summer and three days in the winter. They also believed that eating the crust of bread was unhealthy, not because it sometimes had ash from the oven baked into its surface but because the crust was dry and therefore engendered choler and melancholy. Accordingly, as Gervase*

Markham notes, "great personages" would "chip their bread," meaning that they, or one of their servants, would chisel off the crust.

Take six yolkes of Egs, and a litle peece of Butter as big as a Walnut, one handfull of verie fine flower, and make al these in paste, and all to beat it with a rolling pin, till it be as thin as a paper leafe, then take sweet Butter and melt it, and rub over all your paste therewith, with a feather: then roll up your paste softly as ye would roll up a scroll of paper, then cut them in peeces of three inches long, and make them flat with your hands, and lay them upon a sheet of cleane paper, and bake them in an Oven or panne, but the Oven may not bee too hot, and they must bake halfe an howre, then take some sweete butter and melt it, and put that into your paste when it commeth out of the Oven, and when they are verie wet, so that they be not drie, take them out of your butter, and lay them in a faire dish, and cast upon them a litle Sugar, and if you please, Synamon and Ginger, and serve them foorth.

---

 ## MODERN RECIPE            Makeability: 4

| | |
|---|---|
| 6 egg yolks | 1 cup all-purpose flour |
| 1 TBS unsalted butter (plus $1/2$ cup melted butter) | Blend of 1 tsp sugar, $1/2$ tsp cinnamon, $1/2$ tsp minced ginger |

Preheat oven to 325°F. On a clean work surface, work the eggs, 1 TBS butter, and flour into a dough. With a rolling pin, roll out the dough to a $1/8$-inch thickness. With a feather (though a modern pastry brush works just as well), brush on the melted butter, covering thoroughly, reserving about half of the butter. Roll up the dough like a scroll and cut into three-inch pieces. Flatten the pieces gently and taper the ends slightly. Place the small loaves on parchment paper on a baking sheet and bake 30 to 40 minutes. Remove from the oven and place on a platter, brushing with the remaining melted butter. Sprinkle with the sugar, cinnamon, and ginger mixture and serve.

---

# THE MAKING OF MANCHETS AFTER MY LADIE GRAIES USE

*The Good Huswifes Handmaide for the Kitchin, 1594*

Demetrius:                 Easie it is
       Of a cut loafe to steale a shive. (*Titus Andronicus* 2.1.86–87)

*Manchets were small loaves made from the finest wheat flour, each loaf weighing about eight ounces before it went into the oven and six ounces after it came out. The origin of the name is uncertain, though it may be connected with the French "manche," meaning "sleeve," which the loaf may have resembled in size and shape. Manchets were also known as "paindemain," which derives from the Latin "panis dominicus" meaning "bread of the master," and also as "wastel," which derives from a French source* meaning "cake." As for the quotation from Titus Andronicus, Demetrius is invoking a proverb that would have been well known in Shakespeare's England. The proverb literally means that once a loaf of bread has been cut, it is easy to cut off another slice (or shive) without anyone knowing the difference. Figuratively, though, Demetrius means that now that Lavinia is married (and no longer a virgin), there will be no physical evidence if he and Bassianus sexually assault her.

Take two peckes of fine flower, which must be twice boulted, if you will have your manchet verie faire: Then lay it in a place where ye doe use to lay your dowe for your bread, and make a litle hole in it, and put in that water as much leaven as a crab, or a pretie big apple, and as much white salt as will into an Egshell, and all to breake your leaven in the water, and put into your flower halfe a pinte of good Ale yeast, and so stir this liquor among a litle of your flower, so that ye must make it but thin at the first meeting, and then cover it with flowre, and if it be in the winter, ye must keepe it verie warm, and in summer it shall not need so much heate, for in the Winter it will not rise without warmeth. Thus let it lie two howers and a halfe: then at the second opening take more liquor as ye thinke will serve to wet al the flower. Then put in a pinte and a halfe of good yest, and so all to breake it in short peeces, after yee have well laboured it, till it come to a smoothe paste, and be well ware at the second opening that yee put not in too much liquor sodenlie, for then it wil run, and if ye take a litle it will be stiffe, and after the second working it must lie a good quarter of an hower, and keep it warme: then take it up to the moulding board, and with as much speede as is possible to be made, molde it up, and set it into the Oven, of one pecke of flower ye make ten caste of Manchets faire and good.

---

 **MODERN RECIPE** Makeability: 3

2½ cups whole wheat flour

1 cup all-purpose flour

1 cup lukewarm water

1 tsp salt

1 cup good ale yeast (or 1 packet active dry yeast)

3 TBS unsalted butter (optional)

Preheat oven to 350°F. Activate the yeast in ½ cup of the warm water, according to package directions. In a mixing bowl, sift the flours and the salt. Place the flour mixture onto a clean work surface, make a "well," and pour in the water (if butter is desired, mix it in). With your hands, gradually work in all the flour, drawing from the inside of the well. Knead the dough for 10 to 15 minutes, adding more flour if it becomes too sticky. Put the dough in a buttered bowl and cover, letting it rise in a warm place for 2 hours. Punch the dough down and turn it out onto a clean surface. Shape the dough into several round flat loaves and let it rise again, about 20 to 40 minutes, or until it doubles in size. Shape again into round, flat loaves and score the tops with a sharp knife if desired. Bake for 30 to 40 minutes, or until the bottom of the loaf sounds hollow when tapped.

# TO MAKE PUFFE PASTE

*Delightes for Ladies, 1609*

Titus: I will grind your bones to dust,
    And with your blood and it, Ile make a Paste,
    And of the Paste a Coffin I will reare,
    And make two Pasties of your shamefull Heads,
    And bid that strumpet your unhallowed Dam,
    Like to the earth swallow her increase. (*Titus Andronicus* 5.2.186–191)

Take a quart of the finest flower, and the whites of three egges, and the yolkes of two, and a little colde water, and so make it into perfect paste, then drive it with a rouling pin abroad, then put on small peeces of butter, as big as Nuts uppon it, then fold it over, then drive it abroad againe, then put small peeces of butter upon it as you did before, doe this ten times, alwaies folding the paste and putting butter betweene everie fold. You may convay any prettie forced dish, as Florentine, Cherry tart, rice, or pippins, &c, betweene two sheets of that paste.

---

 ## MODERN RECIPE                          Makeability: 4

4 cups all-purpose flour

3 egg whites

2 egg yolks

1/4 cup ice water

1 lb unsalted butter (cut in peanut-sized chunks and refrigerated)

Preheat oven to 475°F. Pour the flour onto a clean, cool work surface. Make a hole or "well" in the middle of the flour and pour in the eggs. With your hand draw in the flour to mix with the eggs and knead it into a soft dough. Use the ice water as needed. Refrigerate for 20 minutes. Sprinkle a bit of flour on the work surface and with a rolling pin roll out the dough into a rectangle (about a third of an inch thick). On one half of the dough, place pieces of butter and then cover by folding over the other half. Roll out the dough into a rectangle again. And once again add pieces of butter to one half, covering with the other half and rolling it into a rectangle. Repeat for 10 folds. When all the "turns" have been made, refrigerate the dough for several hours before baking. Trim the edges of the puff paste with a sharp knife and cut it into shapes if desired. Now roll out the dough to just less than a quarter-inch thick. Sprinkle with a bit of water before placing in a 475°F oven for 5 minutes. Turn the heat to 375°F and bake a further 20 to 30 minutes (depending on the size of the puff pastry).

# TO MAKE WAFERS

*The English Huswife, 1615*

Pistol:                                    Trust none:
      for Oathes are Strawes, mens Faiths are Wafer-Cakes,
      and hold-fast is the onely Dogge, my Ducke. (*Henry V* 2.3.50–51)

*In a 1616 translation of a French text called* Maison Rustique, *Gervase Markham distinguishes the different kinds and qualities of meal that are produced when grinding grain. "The finest part of the meale," he writes, "is called the flower of meale … whereof the pasterers or cookes for pastrie doe make wafers, and such like daintie knackes." He adds that none of the grain goes to waste: even the mill-dust, which was too fine to be used in baking, was collected and sold to printers, who used it to make glue for binding books.*

To make the best Wafers, take the finest Wheate flower you can get and mixe it with Creame, the yelkes of egges, Rose water, sugar and cinamon till it be a little thicker, than Pan-cake batter; and then warming your wafer Irons on a Char-cole fire annoint them first with sweet butter, and then lay on your butter and presse it, and bake it white or browne at your pleasure.

---

 ## MODERN RECIPE                                    Makeability: 2

1½ cups whole wheat flour                 3 TBS sugar

1 cup 35% cream                           2 tsp cinnamon

2 egg yolks                               Unsalted butter

1 tsp rosewater (see Appendix 1)

Preheat your wafer iron (check with a camping or outdoor supply store for cast iron molds that can be used over a camp fire). Mix the flour, cream, egg yolks, rosewater, sugar, and cinnamon into a batter. Coat the "wafer irons" with butter, pour in the batter, and cook until white or brown as desired.

---

# TO MAKE FINE PASTE

*The Second Part of the Good Hus-wives Jewell, 1597*

Lafeu: No, no, no, your sonne was misled with a
      snipt taffata fellow there, whose villanous saffron
      would have made all the unbak'd and dowy youth
      of a nation in his colour. (*All's Well That Ends Well* 4.5.1–4)

Take faire flower and wheate, & the yolkes of egges with sweet Butter, melted, mixing all these together with your hands, til it be brought dowe paste, & then make your coffins whether it be for pyes or tartes, then you may put Saffron and suger if you wil have it a sweet paste, having respect to the true seasoning some use to put to their paste Beefe or Mutton broth, and some Creame.

---

 ## MODERN RECIPE                                      Makeability: 4

2 cups all-purpose flour                    1/2 cup unsalted butter

2 egg yolks                                 1/4 cup ice water as needed

Pour the flour onto a clean, cool work surface, creating a "well" in the middle, into which the eggs and butter are placed. With your hands, work the flour into a dough to bring it together. Add ice water as needed. It will be crumbly at first. Flatten the dough into a disk about 6 inches in diameter and 1 1/2 inches thick. Wrap with plastic wrap and chill it before rolling out for "coffins" for pies or tarts. For a sweeter pastry, add saffron and a couple tablespoons of sugar.

# 13

# SALADS

May it please your grace, to take note of a gentleman, well read, deepely learned, and
throughly grounded in the hidden knowledge of all sallets and pothearbs whatsoever.
—Francis Beaumont, *The Woman Hater*, 1607

In *Countrey Contentments, or The English Huswife*, Gervase Markham distinguishes
between simple and compound salads, or as they were then called, "sallets." Simple
salads, according to Markham, are made from a single "salad herb" dressed with vinegar and oil, and sugar or pepper. Such salads can be prepared, he adds, from chives,
scallions, radishes, carrots, turnips, lettuce, asparagus, cucumbers, beans, or "a world
of others, too tedious to nominate." Compound salads, on the other hand, are made
by mixing together "all manner of wholesome Herbs," dressed again with vinegar
and oil, and sugar or pepper. The actual recipe for a compound salad that Markham
provides is even more elaborate, at least in so far as it incorporates not just "salad
herbs," but a variety of dried fruits, nuts, and even olives and capers. Other salad
recipes go still further afield, calling for flowers such as roses, carnations, and violets
and for seafood such as shrimp, pickled herring, and salmon. Even things that we
would perhaps never dream of eating, such as the leaves of the gooseberry bush,
made their way into the salads of the sixteenth and early seventeenth centuries. On
the other hand, several items that we now consider salad staples—such as tomatoes
and celery—were unavailable in Shakespeare's England.

We may find it peculiar that Shakespeare's contemporaries sometimes boiled salads, a practice that was inspired in part by the belief that the temperament of some
vegetables (and fruits) could be "corrected" by heat. John Gerard, for example,
observed that "lettuce maketh a pleasant sallad, being eaten raw with vineger, oyle,
and a little salt: but if it be boyled it is sooner digested, and nourisheth more." Salads
were not usually included in the sample dinner menus that sometimes appeared in
the cookery books of this period, probably because they were considered a kind of
"preamble" to the meal proper. For example, John Gerard notes that salads are served
"in the beginning of supper, and eaten first before any other meate." Likewise, Markham, while advising on the order in which dishes should be brought to the table,
instructed the huswife to "first marshall her sallets, delivering the grand Sallet first,
which is ever more compound; then greene Sallets, then boyld Sallets, then some

smaller compound Sallets." The salads were then to be followed by a parade of fried, roasted, baked, and boiled meats. This initial placement probably reflected the belief that many "salad herbs," such as radishes, stimulated the appetite.

Curiously, Markham also notes that some salads are "for show only." Such ornamental salads might be made of carrots that had been dyed "sundry colours" and "cut into many shapes and proportions, as some into knots, some in the manner of scutchions and arms, some like birds, and some like wild beasts." Whether these remained on the table throughout the meal, or were removed after guests had an opportunity to behold them, is unclear.

# AN EXCELLENT BOYLED SALLET

*The English Huswife*, 1615

Edgar: Poore Tom, that eates the swimming Frog, the
　　　Toad, the Tad-pole, the wall-Neut, and the water: that in
　　　the furie of his heart, when the foule Fiend rages, eats
　　　Cow-dung for Sallets; swallowes the old Rat, and the
　　　ditch-Dogge; drinkes the green Mantle of the standing
　　　Poole: who is whipt from Tything to Tything, and
　　　stockt, punish'd, and imprison'd. (*King Lear* 3.4.128–134)

To make an excellent compound boil'd Sallat: take of Spinage well washt two or three handfulls, and put it into faire water and boile it till it bee exceeding soft and tender as pappe; then put it into a Cullander and draine the water from it, which done, with the backside of your Chopping-knife chop it and bruise it as small as may bee: then put it into a Pipkin with a good lump of sweet butter and boile it over againe; then take a good handfull of Currants cleane washt and put to it, and stirre them well together, then put to as much Vinegar as will make it reasonable tart, and then with sugar season it according to the taste of the Master of the house, and so serve it upon sippets.

---

 MODERN RECIPE　　　　　　　　　　　　　　　　　　　Makeability: 2

4 cups spinach

4 TBS unsalted butter

1/2 cup currants

1/4 cup red wine vinegar

3 TBS sugar

1/2-inch slices of 60% toasted whole wheat bread for sippets

Rinse the spinach and then boil it in water until soft. Drain the spinach in a colander and then crush it with the back side of a chef's knife. Melt butter in a saucepan and add the spinach. Add currants, red wine vinegar, and sugar. Stir together and heat through. Serve spinach salad on sippets.

# ANOTHER COMPOUND SALLET

### The English Huswife, 1615

Jack Cade: Fye on Ambitions: fie on my selfe, that have a
sword, and yet am ready to famish. These five daies
have I hid me in these Woods, and durst not peepe out,
for all the Country is laid for me: but now am I so
hungry, that if I might have a Lease of my life for a
thousand yeares, I could stay no longer. Wherefore on
a Bricke wall have I climb'd into this Garden, to see if I
can eate Grasse, or picke a Sallet another while, which is
not amisse to coole a mans stomacke this hot weather. (*2 Henry VI* 4.10.1–15)

*This "excellent sallat" contains a bevy of herbs and vegetables, all of which were reputed to have properties that directly affected a person's health or appearance. Lettuce, for example, was widely believed to cause one's sight to dim. But lettuce also had the power—according to John Gerard in his 1597 Herbal—to "keepe away drunkennesse." Cucumbers, Gerard added, could cure "copper face," a vascular disease characterized by a red nose and caused by chronic alcoholism. Sometimes more dubious benefits were assured: a 1565 translation of* The Secretes of the Reverend Maister Alexis of Piemont *promised that washing your hair with a distillation of capers would turn it green. But why would someone in sixteenth-century England want green hair?*

To compound an excellent sallat, and which indeede is usual at great feasts, and upon Princes tables: Take a good quantity of blanch't Almonds, and with your shredding knife cut them grosly; then take as manie Raisyns of the sunne clean washt, and the stones pick't out, as many Figges shred like the Almonds, as many Capers, twice so many Olives, and as manie Currants as all the rest, cleane washt: a good handfull of the small tender leaves of red Sage and Spinage: mix all these well together with a good store of Sugar and lay them in the bottome of a great dish, then put unto them Vinegar and Oyle, and scrape more Suger over all; then take Orenges and Lemons, and paring away the outward pills, cut them into thinne slices, then with those slices cover the Sallet all over; which done, take the thinne leafe of the red Coleflowre, and with them cover the Orenges and Lemmons all over; then over those Red leaves lay another course of old Olives, & the slices of well pickld Coucumbers, together with the very inward hart of Cabbage Lettice cut into slices, then adorn the sides of the dish and the top of the Sallet with mo slices of Lemons and Orenges and so serve it up.

 ## MODERN RECIPE                    Makeability: 2

| | |
|---|---|
| 1/2 cup blanched almonds, rough-chopped | 1 cup pitted green olives plus a second cup for another layer |
| 1/2 cup raisins, rough-chopped | 3 cups currants |
| 1/2 cup dried figs, rough-chopped | 1 cup red sage |
| 1/2 cup capers, rough-chopped | 1 cup spinach |

2 tsp sugar

2 large peeled oranges, sliced

1 large peeled lemon, sliced

1 cup red cauliflower leaves (substitute red cabbage)

4 large dill pickles, sliced lengthwise

1 cup cabbage hearts, shredded

For the salad dressing

3 tsp sugar

2 tsp olive oil

Vinegar to taste

In a mixing bowl, stir together almonds, raisins, figs, capers, 1 cup olives, currants, red sage, spinach, and sugar. Place the mixture in the bottom of a 9 × 12-inch dish and drizzle with oil and vinegar to taste. Peel orange and lemon, slice thin, and lay them on top of almond mixture. Add a layer of cauliflower leaves, followed by a layer of olives and slices of pickle. Add a layer of cabbage. Garnish with a few slices of oranges and lemons and serve.

# A SALLET OF ROSE-BUDS, AND CLOVE GILLY-FLOWERS

*A New Booke of Cookerie, 1615*

Lafeu:   Twas a good Lady, 'twas a good Lady. Wee may
         picke a thousand sallets ere wee light on such another
         hearbe.
Clowne:  Indeed sir she was the sweete Margerom
         of the sallet, or rather the hearbe of grace.
Lafeu:   They are not hearbes, you knave, they are
         nose-hearbes.
Clowne:  I am no great Nabuchadnezar sir, I have
         not much skill in grass. (*All's Well That Ends Well* 4.5.13–21)

*In the quotation from* All's Well That Ends Well, *Lafeu praises the supposedly deceased Helena by comparing her to a rare and precious herb, one whose equal would scarcely be found even if herbs for a thousand salads were plucked. The Clown then tries to extend the metaphor but gets it somewhat wrong: he compares her to marjoram and then to rue (also known as herb-of-grace), both of which, according to Lafeu, are herbs used for making aromatic pot-pourris rather than salads. The Clown then excuses himself by acknowledging that he is no Nebuchadnezzar, the ancient Babylonian king who became a grass expert when God transformed him into a beast of the field. As for the clove gilly-flowers that appear in the recipe title but not in the recipe, they are a kind of clove-scented carnation.*

Picke Rosebuds, and put them into an earthen Pipkin, with white Wine-vineger, and Sugar: so may you use Cowslippes, Violets, or Rosemary-flowers.

 ## MODERN RECIPE                                           Makeability: 1

4 cups assorted rosebuds, violets and nasturtiums

White wine vinegar to taste

Sugar to taste

Put the assorted flowers into an earthenware pot. Toss with vinegar and sugar to taste.

# SALLATS FOR FISH DAIES, ANOTHER

*The Second Part of the Good Hus-wives Jewell, 1597*

The forward violet thus did I chide,
Sweet thief, whence didst thou steal thy sweet that smells,
If not from my love's breath? The purple pride
Which on thy soft check for complexion dwells,
In my love's veins thou hast too grossly dyed. (Sonnet 99, 1–5)

*Nowadays, we rarely eat flowers (with the exception of capers, which are the pickled buds of a Mediterranean shrub). In Shakespeare's England, however, the petals of violets, roses, carnations, marigolds, borages, and elders often made their way into various dishes. In fact, few flowers seem to have been exempted, as is suggested by the almost-poetic opening sentence of a recipe devoted to candying flowers: "Gather what flowers you please, in the heate of the day, when the dew is off them."*

Salmon cut long waies, with slices of onions laid upon it, and upon that to cast violets, oyle and vineger.

---

 ## MODERN RECIPE                                      Makeability: 1

1 side cooked or cured salmon          Oil and vinegar to taste

1 red onion                            Violets for garnish

Arrange the salmon on a platter. Slice red onions paper thin and lay them on the salmon. Drizzle with oil and vinegar to taste and garnish with violets.

---

# SALLATS FOR FISH DAIES, ANOTHER

*The Second Part of the Good Hus-wives Jewell, 1597*

Sir Toby: 'Tis a Gentleman heere. A plague
o' these pickle herring: How now Sot? (*Twelfth Night* 1.5.117–118)

*In this quotation from* Twelfth Night, *Sir Toby begins to announce the arrival of a gentleman and then makes an abrupt reference to pickled herring. The reference makes sense if we presume that it is preceded by a loud belch, one that he attributes to a recent fishy snack. As for the recipe, the rundles to which it refers are simply circular shapes into which the strips of pickled herring are formed. The "tawney" that is used as a garnish is probably the herb tansy.*

Take pickeeld herring cut long waies and lay them in rundles with onions and parsley chopped, and other herringes the bones being taken out to bee chopped together and laid in the roundles with a long piece laide betwixt the rundles like the proportion of a snake, garnished with Tawney long cut, with vinegar and oile.

### MODERN RECIPE                                    Makeability: 3

1 jar pickled herring fillets

1 cup chopped onion

1/2 cup chopped parsley

2 TBS chopped tansy (see Appendix 1)

Oil and vinegar to taste

Arrange half the fillets in circles in a dish. Chop the remaining fillets (reserving four of them) and mix with the onion and parsley. Spoon the mixture into the center of the herring circles. Take the remaining four fillets and run them between the herring circles to look like snakes.

## SALLATS FOR FISH DAIES, AN OTHER

*The Second Part of the Good Hus-wives Jewell, 1597*

Countess:  Alas, this is a Child, a silly Dwarfe:
It cannot be, this weake and writhled shrimpe
Should strike such terror to his Enemies. (*1 Henry VI* 2.3.22–24)

Carret rootes being minced, and then made in the dish, after the proportion of a flowerdeluce, then picke Shrimps and lay upon it with oyle and vinegar.

### MODERN RECIPE                                    Makeability: 1

4 medium carrots

1/2 lb cooked shrimp

1/4 cup olive oil

3 TBS red wine vinegar

Grate carrots into bowl. Add olive oil and vinegar, reserving enough for the shrimp. Plate the grated carrot in the shape of a fleur-de-lis. Toss the shrimp in the remaining oil and vinegar and arrange on the fleur-de-lis of carrot.

## TO MAKE A SALLET OF LEMMONS

*The Good Huswifes Jewell, 1596*

Emilia:                        Let Husbands know,
Their wives have sense like them: They see, and smell,

And have their Palats both for sweet, and sowre,
As Husbands have. (*Othello* 4.3.95–98)

Cut out slices of the peele of the Lemmons long waies, a quarter of an inche one peece from an other, and then slice the Lemmon very thinne and lay him in a dish crosse, and the peeles about the Lemmons, and scrape a good deale of suger upon them, and so serve them.

 ## MODERN RECIPE

Makeability: 2

3 lemons                                    1 TBS sugar

Wash the lemons well. Cut quarter-inch strips along the length leaving a quarter inch between cuts. Julienne the strips and reserve for garnish. Slice the lemons very thinly, removing any pips. Arrange the slices on a plate and sprinkle generously with sugar. Garnish the lemon slices with the julienned strips of peel. Serve immediately, before the sugar dissolves.

# SALLATS FOR FISH DAIES, AN OTHER

*The Second Part of the Good Hus-wives Jewell, 1597*

Cleopatra:                                   My Sallad dayes,
When I was greene in iudgement, cold in blood,
To say, as I saide then. (*Antony and Cleopatra* 1.5.76–78)

*The olives in this recipe were probably green rather than black. Fynes Moryson, in his 1617 Itinerary, commented that he was unfamiliar with the black variety until he visited Italy: "I remember wee had blacke Olives, which I had never seene before, and they were of a most pleasant taste."*

Olives and Capers in one dish, with vineger and oyle.

 ## MODERN RECIPE

Makeability: 1

2 cups green olives                         4 TBS olive oil
2 TBS capers                                2 TBS red wine vinegar

Combine olives and capers in a large mixing bowl. Whisk together olive oil and red wine vinegar and combine with olives and capers. Toss and serve.

# 14

# PIES AND TARTS

King Richard:  Our Lands, our Lives, and all are Bullingbrookes,
 And nothing can we call our owne, but Death,
 And that small Modell of the barren Earth,
 Which serves as Paste, and Cover to our Bones. (*Richard II* 3.2.151–154)

The popularity of pies and tarts in Shakespeare's England is attested to in several ways. For one thing, the 2,100 recipes that were published in the period include 99 recipes that call themselves "tarts" (which was applied primarily to fruit-based pastries) and another 31 that call themselves "pies" (which was applied to both fruit- and meat-based pastries). As well, the variety of tarts and pies—even if we limit ourselves to the nonmeat variety—is extensive. There are recipes for almond tarts, apple tarts, barberry tarts, bean tarts, borage flower tarts, briar hip tarts, cheese tarts, cherry tarts, chestnut tarts, cowslip tarts, damson tarts, date tarts, egg tarts, eglantine berry tarts, elderflower tarts, gooseberry tarts, grapevine tarts, marigold tarts, pear tarts, pea tarts, primrose tarts, prune tarts, pumpkin tarts, quince tarts, raspberry tarts, rice tarts, spinach tarts, strawberry tarts, turnip tarts, and warden tarts. As a final piece of evidence attesting to the role of pies and tarts in Shakespeare's England, consider that in the quotation that begins this chapter King Richard, as he contemplates his overthrow by Bolingbroke, compares himself to a pie, with the earth of his grave serving as a pastry cover for his bones. The metaphor, of course, suggests that he sees his defeat as a kind of cannibalism, as if Bolingbroke is about to consume him—but still, only a pie-loving nation could take his comparison seriously.

## TO MAKE A TART OF GOOSEBERRIES

*The Good Huswifes Handmaide for the Kitchin, 1594*

First Soldier:  He calles for the tortures,
 what will you say without em?
Parolles:  I will confesse what I know without constraint.
 If ye pinch me like a Pasty, I can say no more. (*All's Well That Ends Well* 4.3.120–123)

Take Goseberies, and perboyle them in white or Claret Wine, or strong Ale, and withall boyle a litle white bread: then take them up, & draw them through a strainer as thick as you can with yokes of six Eggs, then season it up with Sugar, and halfe a dish of Butter, and so bake it.

---

 ## MODERN RECIPE                                   Makeability: 2

2 cups gooseberries

3 cups white wine (substitute red wine or strong ale)

$^{1}/_{2}$ cup white bread crumbs

6 egg yolks

$^{1}/_{2}$ cup sugar

1 cup butter

Pastry recipe "To make fine paste" on page 214, or buy premade pastry.

Preheat the oven to 350°F. Prepare a pastry shell and top. Precook the shell for 10 minutes, or just until it begins to brown. Parboil the gooseberries and bread crumbs in the wine. Force these ingredients and the egg yolks through a fine-meshed strainer and into a mixing bowl. Season with the sugar and butter, pour the mixture into the pastry shell, and cover with the pastry top. Bake for 35 to 40 minutes, or until the crust is golden brown.

---

# TO MAKE LUMDARDY TARTES

*The Good Huswifes Handmaide for the Kitchin, 1594*

Nym:  My name is Corporall Nim: I speak, and I avouch;
'tis true: my name is Nim: and Falstaffe loves your wife:
adieu, I love not the humour of bread and cheese:
adieu. (*The Merry Wifes of Windsor* 2.1.127–130)

*The beets called for in this recipe are probably the beet greens rather than the beet root. Other recipes, for example, also specify beets, but in a context that makes it fairly clear that the greens are intended. The recipe called "A Pudding in a Tench," for example, instructs the cook to "take beets boiled, or spinage," and clearly the greens of a beet are more similar to spinach than the root. Further evidence may be found in John Gerard's 1597 Herball, where he writes "the greater red Beet or Roman Beet, boyled and eaten with oyle, vineger and pepper, is a most excellent and delicate sallad: but what might be made of the red and beautifull root (which is to be preferred before the leaves, as well in beauty as in goodnesse) I refer unto the curious and cunning cooke." Similarly, James Hart in his 1633 Klinike notes that beets are "commonly used for pot-herbs" and then adds in an offhand manner that "in some places they make sallets of the red-beet root," which again implies that the beet was primarily seen as a leafy vegetable rather than a root vegetable. As for the quotation from The Merry Wives of Windsor, when Nym says that he does not love "the humour of bread and cheese," he means that he feels no loyalty to Falstaff because he receives only humble food from him.*

Take Beets, chop them small, and put to them grated bread and cheese, and mingle them wel in the chopping, take a few Corrans, and a dish of sweet Butter, & melt it then stir al these in the Butter, together with three yolks of Eggs, Synamon, ginger, and sugar, and make your Tart as large as you will, and fill it with the stuff, bake it and serve it in.

 ## MODERN RECIPE                                        Makeability: 2

8 cups finely chopped beet greens (thick stalks removed)

1 cup bread crumbs

1 cup grated cheese (any white English cheese that can be grated)

2 TBS currants

1/4 cup melted unsalted butter

3 egg yolks

1/2 tsp cinnamon

1/4 tsp minced ginger

1/4 cup sugar

Pastry recipe "To make fine paste" on page 214, or buy premade pastry.

Prepare a pastry shell. Preheat oven to 350°F. Combine the beet greens, bread crumbs, and cheese and mix well. Add the currants, butter, egg yolks, cinnamon, ginger, and sugar, stirring them well. Pour into the pastry shell and bake for 35 to 40 minutes, or until the filling has set.

# TO MAKE A TART OF RYCE

*The Good Huswifes Jewell,* 1596

| Sir Toby: | A false conclusion: I hate it as an unfill'd Canne. To be up after midnight, and to go to bed then is early: so that to go to bed after midnight, is to goe to bed betimes. Does not our lives consist of the foure Elements? |
| Sir Andrew: | Faith so they say, but I thinke it rather consists of eating and drinking. |
| Sir Toby: | Th'art a scholler; let us therefore eate and drinke. (*Twelfth Night* 2.3.6–14) |

Boyle your Rice, and put in the yolkes of two or three Egges into the Rice, and when it is boyled, put it into a dish, and season it with Suger, Sinamon and Ginger, and butter, and the juyce of two or three Orenges, and set it on the fire againe.

 ## MODERN RECIPE                                        Makeability: 2

1 cup white rice

2 cups water

3 egg yolks

2 TBS sugar

1 tsp cinnamon

1 tsp minced ginger

*Continued on next page*

*Continued from previous page*

2 TBS unsalted butter

juice from 2 oranges

Pastry recipe "To make fine paste" on page 214, or buy premade pastry.

Prepare a pastry shell and top. Preheat oven to 350°F. Cook the rice in the water until just tender. Transfer the rice to a large frying pan, add the remaining ingredients, and heat thoroughly. Pour the mixture into the pastry shell and bake until the crust is golden brown, about 40 minutes.

# A WARDEN PIE

*The English Huswife, 1623*

Petruchio: You lye infaith, for you are call'd plaine Kate,
And bonny Kate, and sometimes Kate the curst:
But Kate, the prettiest Kate in Christendome,
Kate of Kate-hall, my super-daintie Kate,
For dainties are all Kates, and therefore Kate. (*The Taming of the Shrew* 2.1.185–189)

*From a nutritional point of view, wardens were considered by dietary handbooks of the period to be the best variety of pear. Those handbooks also cautioned, however, that wardens were not to be eaten raw, but rather should be baked or roasted. James Hart, in his* Klinike, *especially commended the custom of sticking cloves and cinnamon into wardens before baking them, in order to further "correct" their temperament. As for the passage from* The Taming of the Shrew, *Petruchio's punning hinges on the fact that Kate's name is a homonym with "cate," which denoted any sort of sweet or dainty foodstuff, such as pies, custards, or marzipan. Nowadays, caterers serve cates.*

Take of the fairest and best Wardens, and pare them, and take out the hard cores on the top, and cut the sharp ends at the bottome flat; then boyle them in Whitewine and suger, untill the sirrup grow thick: then take the Wardens from the sirrup into a cleane dish, & let them cool; then set them into the coffin, and prick cloves in the tops, with whole sticks of cinamon, and great store of suger as for Pippins; then cover it, and onely reserve a vent-hole, so set it in the oven and bake it: when it is bak'd, draw it forth, and take the first sirrup in which the Wardens were boyld, and taste it, and if it be not sweet enough, then put in more suger, and some rosewater, & boile it againe a little, then powre it in at the vent-hole, and shake the pie well; then take sweet Butter, and rose-water melted, and with it anoynt the pye-lid all over, and then strow on it store of Sugar, and so set it into the oven again a little space, and then serve it up And in this manner you may also bake Quinces.

MODERN RECIPE                                      Makeability: 3

| | |
|---|---|
| 4 large, firm Bartlett pears, cut in quarters | Pastry recipe "To make fine paste" on page 214, or buy premade pastry. |
| 2 cups white wine | |
| 1 cup sugar | For the glaze and garnish: |
| 1/4 cup whole cloves, as needed | 3 TBS unsalted butter |
| 2 cinnamon sticks | 1 TBS rosewater (see Appendix 1) |
| 1/4 cup sugar | 2 TBS sugar |

Prepare a pastry shell and top. Preheat the oven to 350°F. Boil the pears in the wine and sugar until they soften slightly and the liquid thickens. Remove the pears to a dish and allow them to cool. Insert two cloves into each pear quarter. Arrange the pears in the pastry shell and add the cinnamon sticks. Cover the pie with pastry, cut a 1-inch diameter hole in the center, and bake for 30 minutes. Meanwhile, heat the wine and sugar mixture and test for sweetness. Add more sugar if desired. Melt the butter, add the rosewater, and keep warm. After the pie has baked for 30 minutes, remove it and pour a few tablespoons of the liquid into the pie through the vent hole. Rock the pie back and forth gently to distribute the liquid. Brush the top crust with the butter and rosewater and sprinkle it with the sugar. Bake for the remaining 15 minutes, or until golden brown.

# A QUARTER TART OF PIPPINS

*A New Booke of Cookerie*, 1615

Petruchio:  Thy gowne, why aye: come Tailor let us see't.
Oh mercie God, what masking stuffe is heere?
Whats this? a sleeve? 'tis like demi cannon,
What, up and downe carv'd like an apple Tart? (*The Taming of the Shrew*
4.3.86–89)

Quarter them, and lay them betweene two sheetes of Paste: put in a piece of whole Sinamon, two or three bruised Cloves, a little sliced Ginger, Orrengado, or onely the yellow outside of the Orenge, a bit of sweet Butter about the bignesse of an Egge, good store of Sugar: sprinkle on a little Rosewater. Then close your Tart, and bake it: Ice it before it goe to the Boord, serve it hot. This Tart you may make of any puft-paste, or short paste that will not holde the raising. If you bake it in any of these kindes of pastes, then you must first boyle your Pippins in Claret Wine and Sugar, or else your Apples will be hard, when your Crust will be burnt and dryed away. Besides, the Wine giveth them a pleasant colour, and a good taste also. Though you boyle your Pippins tender, take heed you breake not the quarters, but bake them whole.

## MODERN RECIPE                                          Makeability: 2

6 firm apples suitable for baking, peeled, cored, and cut in quarters

1½ cups Bordeaux wine

½ cup sugar

1 cinnamon stick

3 bruised cloves

1 TBS sliced ginger

1 TBS orange zest (or 1 tsp oregano)

2 TBS unsalted butter

2 TBS sugar

1 TBS rosewater (see Appendix 1)

Puff pastry recipe "To make puffe paste" on page 214, or buy premade puff pastry.

2 lightly beaten eggs with a tablespoon of water for the pastry

Prepare two triangular-shaped sheets of puff pastry. Preheat the oven to 350°F. Poach the apple quarters in the wine and sugar until the apples begin to soften. Remove the apples from the wine. Place a sheet of puff pastry on a cookie sheet and arrange the apples on the pastry, leaving an edge of 1 inch. Distribute the cinnamon stick, cloves, orange zest, dollops of butter, and rosewater over the apples. Brush the edge with the egg and water wash and cover with a second sheet of puff pastry. Press the edges together firmly. If desired, brush the top of the crust with any remaining egg wash. Bake for 30 minutes.

# TO BAKE A CITRON PIE

*The Second Part of the Good Hus-wives Jewell, 1597*

Bolingbroke: Loe, as at English Feasts, so I regreete
The daintiest last, to make the end most sweet. (*Richard II* 1.3.67–68)

*The word "citron," in this period, was used to denote the lemon as well as other lemon-like fruits, such as the lime or cedrat. As for the quotation from Richard II, Bolingbroke's comment probably implies a contrast between English feasts, which concluded with highly sugared "banquetting stuffe," and French feasts, which tended to close with savory items such as cheese.*

Take your citron, pare it and slice it in peeces, and boile it with grose pepper and Ginger, and so lay it in your Paste with butter, and when it is almost baked put thereto Vineger, Butter, and Suger, and let it stande in the Oven a while and soke.

## MODERN RECIPE                                          Makeability: 2

3 large lemons

¼ tsp fresh-cracked black pepper

1 TBS minced ginger

⅔ cup unsalted butter

1 tsp vinegar

1 tsp butter

2 tsp sugar

Pastry recipe "To make fine paste" on page 214, or buy premade pastry.

Preheat the oven to 350°F. Prepare a pastry shell and top and precook the shell for 10 minutes. Peel the lemons and cut them into pieces. Remove the seeds. Slip the lemon into a pot of boiling water with pepper and ginger and cook for 2 or 3 minutes. Remove the lemon from the water, drain, and arrange in the pastry. Place a few dollops of butter on the lemon. Cover with pastry, cut a small vent hole, and bake for 25 minutes. Meanwhile, mix together the vinegar, the remaining butter, and sugar. After the pie has baked for 25 minutes, remove from the oven, pour the vinegar mixture into the vent hole, and return to the oven to bake for 10 more minutes.

# TO MAKE A TARTE OF STRAWBERIES

*The Good Huswifes Jewell, 1596*

Ely: The Strawberry growes underneath the Nettle,
And holesome Berryes thrive and ripen best,
Neighbour'd by Fruit of baser qualitie:
And so the Prince obscur'd his Contemplation
Under the Veyle of Wildnesse, which (no doubt)
Grew like the Summer Grasse, fastest by Night,
Unseene, yet cressive in his facultie. (*Henry V* 1.1.61–67)

*James Hart, in his 1633* Klinike, *remarks that strawberries with cream "is a dish wherein our Gentlewomen doe much delight" even though it is "not so agreeable to their constitution of body." More preferable, he adds, is to eat them "with a little claret wine and sugar." As for the word "endore," which appears in the recipe, it means "to apply a yellow glaze."*

Take Strawberies and washe them in claret wine, thicke and temper them with rose-water, and season them with sinamon, suger and ginger, and spread it on the Tarte, and endore the sides with butter, and cast on Suger and biskettes, and serve them so.

 MODERN RECIPE                                          Makeability: 2

4 cups hulled strawberries

1/2 cup red Bordeaux wine

1 TBS rosewater (see Appendix 1)

1/2 tsp cinnamon

1 cup sugar (plus sugar for garnish)

1/4 tsp minced ginger

1/4 cup melted unsalted butter for glazing pastry

Pastry recipe "To make fine paste" on page 214, or buy premade pastry.

Biskets (see recipe for "To make English Bisket" on page 237, or substitute a dry gingersnap cookie)

*Continued on next page*

*Continued from previous page*

Preheat the oven to 350°F. Prepare a pastry shell and precook it for 10 minutes or just until it begins to brown. In a mixing bowl, gently stir the wine into the strawberries and let marinate for 15 minutes before pouring off the liquid. Take half of the strawberries, mash them gently, and return them to a mixing bowl with the whole berries. Stir in the rosewater, add the cinnamon, sugar, and ginger, and spoon it into the pastry shell. Brush the edges of the crust with butter. Bake for 35 to 40 minutes, or until the filling has set and the crust is golden brown. Remove it from oven and sprinkle sugar and crumbled "biskets" on top.

# TO MAKE A CLOSE TARTE OF CHERRIES

*The Good Huswifes Jewell,* 1596

| King: | Now by thy lookes |
| | I gesse thy Message. Is the Queene deliver'd? |
| | Say aye, and of a boy. |
| Lady: | Aye, aye, my Liege, |
| | And of a lovely Boy: the God of Heaven |
| | Both now, and ever blesse her: 'Tis a Gyrle |
| | Promises Boyes heereafter. Sir, your Queen |
| | Desires your Visitation, and to be |
| | Acquainted with this stranger. 'Tis as like you, |
| | As Cherry, is to Cherry. (*Henry VIII* 5.1.161–169) |

*A ''close'' tart is one with a pastry cover. The charger in which the pitted cherries are laid is a large platter, one that can be filled just as a battery is filled or ''charged'' with electricity. Damask water is rosewater, named after a variety of rose that was thought to have originated in Damascus.*

Take out the stones, and laye them as whole as you can in a Charger, and put Mustard in, synamon and ginger to them, and laye them in a Tarte whole, and close them, and let them stand three quarters of an houre in the Oven, then take a sirrope of Muscadine, and damask water and suger, and serve it.

 ## MODERN RECIPE                                     Makeability: 3

4 cups of cherries, stones removed

3 TBS prepared mustard (see recipe on page 265)

1 TBS cinnamon

1 tsp minced ginger

1/4 cup melted unsalted butter for glaze

2 TBS muscadine syrup

1 tsp rosewater (see Appendix 1)

2 TBS sugar

Pastry recipe "To make fine paste" on page 214, or buy premade pastry.

For the muscadine syrup:
1 1/4 cups of sweet white wine

1 3/4 cups sugar
1 1/2 TBS lemon juice

Preheat the oven to 350°F. Prepare the muscadine syrup by boiling the wine, sugar, and lemon juice until thick. Prepare a pastry shell and top and precook the shell for 10 minutes or just until it begins to brown. Mix the cherries with the other ingredients and pour them into the pastry shell. Cover with pastry and brush lightly with butter. Make a small vent hole in the center of the crust and bake for 45 minutes, or until filling has set and pastry is golden brown. Remove the tart from the oven, pour the muscadine syrup, rosewater, and sugar into the tart, and rock it gently to distribute the fluid.

# TO MAKE A TART OF POMPEONS

*Epulario, 1598*

So are you to my thoughts as food to life,
Or as sweet season'd showers are to the ground;
And for the peace of you I hold such strife,
As twixt a miser and his wealth is found.
Now proud as an injoyer, and anon
Doubting the filching age will steale his treasure,
Now counting best to be with you alone,
Then betterd that the world may see my pleasure,
Some-time all ful with feasting on your sight,
And by and by cleane starved for a looke,
Possessing or pursuing no delight
Save what is had, or must from you be tooke.
Thus do I pine and surfet day by day,
Or gluttoning on all, or all away. (Sonnet 75)

*John Gerard, in his 1597 Herball, warns that pumpkins are "utterly unwholesome for such as live idlely; but unto robustious and rustick people nothing hurteth that filleth the belly." Before serving this dish to dinner guests, you may want to apprise them of Gerard's caveat, so that they can decide for themselves whether or not they can eat it with impunity.*

Take Pompeons and make them cleane and grate them as you doe Cheese, and boile them a little in broth or in milk, then take as much new Cheese as aforesaid, adde to it also a little old Cheese, take also a pound of the panch of a Hogge, or a Cowes Udder well sodden and chopped small, and if you will you may use Butter in stead of those two thinges aforesaid, or suet, adding unto it halfe a pound of Sugar, a little Saffron and Sinamon with a quart of milk, and Egges, as need requireth. And when you thinke the Pompeons are sodden take them up and straine them, and colour it with a little Saffron, then making a crust of past under it, put it in a pan, and make a soft fire both under and over it, and being halfe baked, cover it with Wafers or such like stuffe instead of an upper crust, and being thorow baked, straw it with Sugar and Rosewater.

## MODERN RECIPE                                           Makeability: 4

2 cups grated pumpkin (or 1¹/₂ cups canned unseasoned pumpkin)

1¹/₂ cups whole milk

1¹/₂ cups cottage cheese (drained of fluid)

¹/₄ cup grated hard cheese

¹/₂ lb pig tripe or 1 lb udder, finely chopped (see Appendix 1)

¹/₂ cup sugar

2 pinches saffron

1 TBS cinnamon

2 eggs

Wafers (see "To make waffers" on page 214)

sugar

Rosewater (see Appendix 1)

Pastry recipe "To make fine paste" on page 214, or buy premade pastry.

Prepare a pastry shell. Preheat oven to 350°F. Cook the pumpkin in the milk until tender and drain. In a bowl combine the pumpkin, cheeses, udder, sugar, saffron, cinnamon, and eggs. Mash the mixture and pour it into the pastry shell. Bake for 50 to 60 minutes. After 30 minutes, remove the tart and cover it with wafers. Bake for the remaining time and until the filling has just set. Remove from the oven and garnish with sugar and rosewater.

# TO MAKE A TARTE OF MEDLERS

*The Good Huswifes Jewell, 1596*

Lucio: Nay tarrie, I'le go along with thee, I can tel thee
pretty tales of the Duke.
Duke: You have told me too many of him already sir if
they be true: if not true, none were enough.
Lucio: I was once before him for getting a Wench with childe.
Duke: Did you such a thing?
Lucio: Yes marrie did I; but I was faine to forswear it,
They would else have married me to the rotten Medler.
(*Measure for Measure* 4.3.164–171)

*As the following recipe affirms, the fruit of the medlar tree becomes palatable only after it has been allowed to begin rotting, a process with horticulturalists refer to as bletting. In Shakespeare's England, the medlar was also referred to as "open arse," so called because one end of the fruit is deeply indented. The word "medlar" was also used as a slang name for a prostitute, as in the quotation from Measure for Measure. The usage was prompted not only by the view that many prostitutes were "rotten" with venereal disease, but also by the coincidental resemblance of "medlar" to "meddler," that is, to someone who meddles or messes around.*

Take medlers that be rotten, and stamp them, then set them on a chafing dish and coales, and beate in two yolkes of egges boyling it till it be somewhat thick, then season them with suger, sinamon, and ginger, and lay it in a paste.

## MODERN RECIPE                                    Makeability: 3

6 cups extremely ripe medlars (substitute crab apples, peeled and finely chopped)

2 egg yolks

1 cup sugar

2 TBS ground cinnamon

1 TBS minced ginger

Pastry recipe "To make fine paste" on page 214, or buy premade pastry.

Prepare two pastry shells and tops. Preheat oven to 350°F. In a large saucepan, bring the apples to a simmer. In a mixing bowl, lightly beat the egg yolks and add a few tablespoons of the hot apple mixture and stir together. Pour the egg and apple mixture into the saucepan of apples and stir, adding the sugar, cinnamon, and ginger and heat thoroughly. Pour the mixture into the pastry shell, cover and prick the top pastry, and bake for 50 to 55 minutes, or until golden brown.

*Medlers*

*To make a Tart of Medlers.*

Take *Medlers* that be rotten, and ſtamp them, and ſet them upon a chafin-diſh with coales, and beat in two yolks of Eggs, boyling till it be ſomewhat thick, then ſeaſon it with *Sugar*, *Cinamon*, and *Ginger*, and lay it in paſte.

*A Book of Fruits & Flowers*, Anonymous, 1653. As the recipe below this woodcut suggests, the fruit of the medlar tree becomes edible only after it has become "rotten," which is often achieved by not harvesting until it has suffered a frost. Shakespeare alludes to medlars in four different plays, usually in reference to their rottenness, as in *Measure for Measure* where Lucio refers to a prostitute as a "rotten medlar" (4.3.164–172). © British Library Board. All Rights Reserved E.690[13] pg 24.

# TO MAKE A TARTE THAT IS COURAGE TO A MAN OR WOMAN

*The Good Huswifes Jewell*, 1596

Mrs. Ford:  Sir John? Art thou there, my Deere? My male-Deere?
Falstaff:    My Doe, with the blacke Scut? Let the skie raine
             Potatoes: let it thunder, to the tune of Greenesleeves,
             haile-kissing Comfits, and snow Eringoes: Let there
             come a tempest of provocation, I will shelter mee heere. (*The Merry Wives
             of Windsor* 5.5.16–21)

*The potato that Falstaff calls down from the skies and that is employed in this recipe is the sweet potato, which was introduced to England from South America in the last half of the sixteenth century. The other potato—known as the Virginia potato or the white potato—was known to horticulturalists like John Gerard in Shakespeare's time but wasn't cultivated in England, except as a curiosity, until the eighteenth century. (Yams, from Africa, are sometimes confused with sweet potatoes, but they are a distinct species.) Falstaff invokes potatoes, as well as kissing-comfits and eringoes (both of which are sugary confections), because they were thought to provoke sexual desire: essentially, he is assuring Mrs. Ford that even if he were pelted with aphrodisiacs he would remain secure in her arms alone. William Harrison, in his 1587* Description of England, *announced that he would not spend time writing about the sweet potato because it was a "venerous root," good only for provoking lust.*

Take twoo Quinces, and twoo or three Burre rootes, and a potaton, and pare your Potaton, and scrape your rootes and put them into a quart of wine, and let them boyle till they bee tender, & put in an ounce of Dates, and when they be boyled tender, Drawe them through a strainer, wine and all, and then put in the yolkes of eight Egges, and the braynes of three or foure cocke Sparrowes, and straine them into the other, and a little Rose water, and seeth them all with suger, Cinamon and Gynger, and Cloves and mace, and put in a little sweet butter, and set it upon a chafingdish of coles beteene two platters, and so let it boyle till it be something bigge.

 ## MODERN RECIPE                                        Makeability: 3

2 quinces, peeled and chopped (substitute pears)

2 burdock roots, peeled and chopped (see Appendix 1)

1 sweet potato, peeled and chopped

4 cups white wine

6 chopped dates

8 egg yolks

4 cock sparrow brains (substitute 4 tsp Spam)

2 TBS rosewater (see Appendix 1)

1/2 cup sugar

1 tsp cinnamon

1/2 tsp minced ginger

1/4 tsp ground cloves

1/2 tsp ground mace

3 TBS unsalted butter

Pastry recipe "To make fine paste" on page 214, or buy premade pastry

Prepare a pastry shell. Preheat oven to 350°F. Soak the burdock roots for 10 minutes and discard the water. Place the quinces, burdock roots, sweet potato, and dates in a large saucepan, cover with wine, and bring to a boil. Pour the mixture through a strainer to remove the fluid. Add the egg yolks and sparrow brains and force the mixture through a fine-meshed sieve. Add the rosewater and simmer the mixture in a large skillet, adding the spices and butter. Pour the tart filling into the pastry shell and bake for 40 to 45 minutes, or until the crust is golden brown.

# TO MAKE TARTES OF THE SMALL GREENE THRIDS THAT WIND ABOVE VINE BRANCHES

*Epulario*, 1598

Lear: To thee, and thine hereditarie ever,
      Remaine this ample third of our faire Kingdome,
      No lesse in space, validitie, and pleasure
      Than that conferr'd on Gonerill. Now our Joy,
      Although our last and least; to whose yong love,
      The Vines of France, and Milke of Burgundie,
      Strive to be interest. What can you say, to draw
      A third, more opilent than your Sisters? Speake. (*King Lear* 1.1.79–86)

Take these Thrids about the vines and boile and choppe them with a knife, and the like may bee done with the red, then take good new Cheese and a Cowes udder well sodden, and stamp them together, and if you will in stead of the Cowes Udder you may use Suet or Butter, adding thereto ginger, Sinamon, and a good quantity of sugar, put this into a frying or baking pan, with paste both under and above, & when it is almost baked, pricke the upper crust full of holes: being baked, straw Sugar and Rosewater upon it.

---

 ## MODERN RECIPE                                    Makeability: 5

3 cups chopped grape vine tendrils (substitute thin strips of celery cut along the length or parsley stalks)

1 cup cottage cheese (fluid drained)

1 cup chopped udder (see Appendix 1)

1 tsp minced ginger

1 tsp cinnamon

1/2 cup sugar

Rosewater (see Appendix 1)

Pastry recipe "To make fine paste" on page 214, or buy premade pastry.

Prepare a pastry shell and top. Preheat oven to 350°F. Mix the grape vine threads, cottage cheese, udder, spices, and sugar and pour into the pastry shell. Cover the pie with the pastry top and bake for 35 minutes. Remove the pie, prick the top crust with holes, and bake for another 15 minutes. Remove it from the oven and sprinkle with sugar and rosewater.

# 15

# BISCUITS AND SPICED BREADS

Jacques:                                    And in his braine,
            Which is as drie as the remainder bisket
            After a voyage: He hath strange places cram'd
            With observation, the which he vents
            In mangled formes. (*As You Like It* 2.7.38–42)

In Shakespeare's England a strict line was drawn between ordinary breads and spiced breads (which were also known as spiced cakes). The former—which included various-sized loaves of white bread, whole wheat bread, and brown bread—were regulated by the Assize of Bread, which determined the price that a baker could charge for them. The latter—which included breads or cakes sweetened with sugar and spiced with aniseed, caraway, nutmeg, ginger, fennel, cloves, or cinnamon—were not regulated by the Assize of Bread. This, paradoxically, did not mean that bakers could make and sell spiced breads willy-nilly, but rather that they were forbidden to make them at all (except for special occasions, such as funerals and Christmas). Most spiced breads, therefore, would have been made at home and only by those who had access to an oven and could afford the expensive spices. An ounce of cloves, for example, cost as much as an ordinary laborer earned in two days.

Biscuits were popular in Shakespeare's England because they could be kept for a long time. This was usually achieved by boiling or baking them once, letting them cool, and then baking them again (in fact, the word "biscuit" derives from a French source that means "twice cooked"). Some recipes, however, instruct the cook to bake the biscuits once and then dry them further in the open air. Biscuits made of grains such as rye, barley, or oats were a staple of sailors, who packed them into water-tight barrels and took them aboard their ships. Gervase Markham likewise noted that biscuits were a good food for anyone who was "besieged within some fort or holde." Fancy biscuits—made of fine flour, sugar, butter, and various spices—were popular among the gentry. Thirty recipes for such biscuits were published in this period, with elegant names such as "Prince Bisquet," "French Bisket," "Naples Bisket," and "Fine Bisket." Other baked goods—such as cracknels, resbones, and jumbals—were not actually called biscuits, but they were made in much the same way. One way that biscuits were used in Shakespeare's England that may not be familiar to the modern cook was as a kind of sweet garnish. For example, the recipe called "To make a tarte of strawberies" instructs the cook to cover the outside of the tart with butter and then "cast on Suger and biskettes." The biscuits that were cast onto the tart were probably small bits of biscuit that were either sliced up before they went into the oven or flakes that were scraped off a whole biscuit after it came out of the oven.

# TO MAKE ENGLISH BISKET

*A Delightfull Daily Exercise for Ladies and Gentlewomen, 1621*

Thersites:  Thou shouldst strike him.
Ajax:       Cobloaf!
Thersites:  He would pun thee into shivers with his fist,
            as a sailor breaks a biscuit. (*Troilus and Cressida* 2.1.36–39)

*When Ajax calls Thersites a cobloaf, he has in mind a small and probably misshapen loaf of bread, probably made from the last bit of dough after the other full loaves have been formed.*

Take eight new layd egges, taking away the whites of foure of them, beat the eight yoalks and the other foure whites in a faire bowle the fourth part of an houre, then take a pound of fine flower being dryed in an earthen pot close covered: then take eight ounces of hard sugar beaten fine, and beate them into your egges with the end of a rowling pin, and beate it so very hard for the space of an houre, but by no meanes let it not stand still, always beating it, then have an Oven as hot as for manchet ready cleane, having some saucers of flat plates, or little tyn Coffins buttered over with a feather as thinne as you can strike it over, then put into your foresaid paste Colianderseede, sweete Fennell seede, and Caroway seed, of each the fourth part of an ounce, when you have beaten these into your paste, put it into your saucers, and set them presently into the Oven, and when you see it rise up and looke white, you may take downe your lid, and in a quarter of an houre they will be made, then box it up and keepe it all the yeare.

---

 ## MODERN RECIPE                                          Makeability: 3

| | |
|---|---|
| 8 egg yolks | 1 tsp coriander seeds |
| 4 egg whites | 1 tsp fennel |
| 4 cups all-purpose flour | 1 tsp caraway |
| 1 cup superfine sugar | 2 TBS unsalted butter for the baking tins |

Preheat oven to 350°F. Beat the eggs vigorously for 15 minutes. Add the flour in small batches while stirring. Add the spices and beat vigorously for one hour (unless you have boundless energy and lots of time, use an electric stand mixer). Butter the baking tins lightly and put in the dough. Put the tins in the oven. When the dough begins to rise and look white, bake for approximately another 15 minutes.

# TO MAKE BREAD CALLED THE ITALIAN CRUST

*A Delightfull Daily Exercise for Ladies and Gentlewomen, 1621*

| | |
|---|---|
| Pandarus: | Well, I have told you enough of this; for my part, I'll not meddle nor make no farther. He that will have a cake out of the wheat must needs tarry the grinding. |
| Troilus: | Have I not tarried? |
| Pandarus: | Ay, the grinding; but you must tarry the bolting. |
| Troilus: | Have I not tarried? |
| Pandarus: | Ay, the bolting; but you must tarry the leavening. |
| Troilus: | Still have I tarried. |
| Pandarus: | Ay, to the leavening; but here's yet in the word 'hereafter' the kneading, the making of the cake, the heating of the oven, and the baking; nay, you must stay the cooling too, or you may chance to burn your lips. (*Troilus and Cressida* 1.1.13–24) |

*In North America, recipes tend to measure flour and sugar by the cup, a volume that was standarized (at half a pint) in the mid-nineteenth century. In England, such ingredients are usually measured by weight, which was also the usual practice in Shakespeare's time. A pound was supposed to weigh the equivalent of 7,000 grains of barley, but in order to ensure that its weight did not shift over time, or from place to place, official brass weights were made, with one set being deposited in London's Exchequer, and other sets being sent out to cities and towns across England. The brass weights that Queen Elizabeth issued in 1588 (to correct some flaws that afflicted earlier sets of official weights) were so accurate that they remained England's national standard until 1824.*

Take sixteene ounces of fine flower dryed in an oven, eight ounces of fine sugar beaten and cearst, one Nutmeg, a race of Ginger finely beaten, a graine of Muske, a thimble-full of the powder of an Oring-peele: worke all these into past, with foure ounces of butter, and the whites of foure new laide Egges, and worke them into small rowles as long as your finger, like a bakers rowle, then set them upon a white paper being buttered and pricke them very thicke with a needle, then washe them over with the white of an egge, and strewe them all over with Sugar carowayes then set them into an oven as hot as for manchet, and when you see them looke white, take down your lid and in a quarter of an houre they will be backt, and box them and keepe them dry for your use.

---

 ## MODERN RECIPE                                     Makeability: 3

| | |
|---|---|
| 2 cups all-purpose flour | 1 grain of musk (see Appendix 1) |
| 1 cup superfine sugar | 1/2 tsp powdered orange peel |
| 1 tsp nutmeg | 1/2 cup unsalted butter |
| 1 TBS minced ginger | 4 egg whites (plus 2 more for egg wash) |

2 TBS candied caraway seeds (see "How to candie Ginger, Nutmegs, or any Roote or flowers" on page 247)

Preheat oven to 350°F. Combine flour, sugar, nutmeg, ginger, musk, and orange peel powder. Add the butter and four egg whites and work into a dough. Shape the dough into small loaves about 5 inches long and 2 inches in diameter. Prick with a fork, wash with two egg whites, and sprinkle sugared caraway seeds on top. Bake for 25 to 30 minutes and remove while the loaves are still white.

# TO MAKE FINE CRACKNELS

*The Good Huswifes Jewell, 1596*

Nathaniel: Sir hee hath never fed of the dainties that are bred
in a booke. He hath not eate paper as it were: He hath not
drunke inke. His intellect is not replenished, hee is onely
an animall, onely sensible in the duller parts.
(*Love's Labour's Lost* 4.2.24–27)

*Cracknels, which take their name from the cracking sound they make when bitten, are a kind of biscuit in that they are first boiled and then baked ("biscuit" means "twice cooked"). Rather quaintly, they make an appearance in the 1611* King James Bible, *where Jeroboam tells his wife to flee to Shiloh, "and take with thee ten loaves, and cracknels, and a cruse of honie" (1 Kings 14:3). Dainties, to which Nathaniel alludes in the quotation from* Love's Labour's Lost, *also appear in the* King James Bible: *"Let mee not eate of their dainties," says King David in reference to the temptations of wicked men (Psalm 141:4).*

Take fine flower and a good quantitie of egges and many as wil supply the flowre, then take as muche suger as will sweeten the past, as if you will not bee at the cost to rayse it with egges, and put thereto sweete water, Cynamon and a good quantitie of Nutmegges and mace, according to your bread, take a good quantitie of Annis seede, and let all this bee blended with your flower, and the putting in of your egges or other moysture, then sette on your water and lette it bee at seething, before you put your Cracknelles in it they will goe to the bottome and at their rising take them out and drie them with a cloth then bake them.

 ## MODERN RECIPE                                       Makeability: 2

2 cups flour

4 eggs

1 cup sugar

2 eggs

1 TBS rosewater with a pinch of cloves and mace (see Appendix 1)

*Continued on next page*

*Continued from previous page*

$^1/_2$ tsp cinnamon                                        1 TBS aniseed

$^1/_2$ tsp each nutmeg and mace

Bring a large pot of water to boil. Preheat oven to 325°F. Mix into a paste the flour, eggs, sugar, and rosewater. Add the spices and work into the dough. Roll it out to quarter-inch thickness and cut in the desired shapes. A few at a time, slip the pieces of cracknels into the water. Remove them as they rise to the surface. Dry them gently with kitchen towels, place them on a baking sheet with parchment paper, and bake them until crisp 20 to 30 minutes.

# TO MAKE GOOD RESBONES

*The Good Huswifes Jewell, 1596*

Venus:  Torches are made to light, jewels to wear,
        Dainties to taste, fresh beauty for the use,
        Herbs for their smell, and sappy plants to bear. (*Venus and Adonis* 163–165)

*The popularity of this recipe is attested to by the fact that it appears not only in* The Good Huswifes Jewell, *but also in the 1594 edition of* A Good Huswifes Handmaide for the Kitchin, *and the 1620 and 1629 editions of* A Book of Cookerie. *The 1594 version of the recipe, however, is called "To make good Restons," which is probably closer to the original name of this spice cake. In turn, "restons" probably derives from "raston," which in the fifteenth century was the name of a kind of tart.*

Take a quart of fine flower, lay it upon a faire boord and make a hoale in the midd-est of the flower with your hande, and put a spoonefull of Ale yeast thereon, and ten yolkes of egges, & two spoonefuls of cinamon and one of ginger, and one of cloves and mace, and a quarterne of suger finelye beaten, and a little saffron, & halfe a spoonefull of salt, then take a dishe full of butter, melt it and put it into your flower, and therewithall make your paste as it were for mancheat, and mould it a good while, & cutte it in peeces of the bigness of Ducks egges, and so mould everie peece as a mancheat, & make them after the fashion of an inkhorn broad above and narrow beneath, then sette them in the Oven, and let them bake three quarters of an houre, then take two dishes of butter and clarifie it upon a soft fire, then draw it out of the oven, and scrape the bottome of them faire and cleane, and cut them overthwart in foure peeces, and put them in a faire charger, and put your clarified butter uppon them, and have cinamon and ginger readie by you, and suger beaten verie small, and mingle altogether, and ever as you set your peeces together, cast some of your suger, cinamon and ginger upon them, when you have set them all up, lay them in a faire platter & put a litle butter upon them, & cast a little suger on them, & so serve them.

**MODERN RECIPE**                                    Makeability: 4

4 cups all-purpose flour

1/4 cup ale yeast (substitute active dry yeast and follow package instructions)

10 egg yolks

2 TBS cinnamon

1 tsp each of ginger, cloves, and mace

1/2 cup sugar

2 pinches saffron

1 tsp salt

4 TBS melted unsalted butter

1/2 cup clarified unsalted butter

Cinnamon, superfine sugar, and ginger for garnish

Preheat oven to 350°F. Pour the flour into a mound on a clean, cool working surface. Make a hole or "well" in the center of the mound and pour in the yeast, egg yolks (lightly beaten), spices, salt, and butter. Work into a dough and knead it for 10 minutes. Cut the dough into egg-sized pieces and mould them into horn-shaped cones. Set the loaves on parchment paper on a cookie sheet and bake for 35 to 40 minutes, or until done. When just cool enough, cut into four quarters and arrange in a platter. Pour over the clarified butter and sprinkle with the cinnamon, sugar, and ginger.

# TO MAKE SPICE CAKES

*The English Huswife*, 1615

Clown:      Then fare thee well, I must go buy Spices for
            our sheepe-shearing.
Autolycus:  Prosper you sweet sir. Your purse is not
            hot enough to purchase your Spice. (*The Winter's Tale* 4.3.114–117)

*The leavening agent in this recipe is "ale barme," which is the yeasty froth that forms on ale as it ferments. Andrew Boorde, in his 1542* Compendyous Regyment, *indicates that barm was also called godesgood, that is, "God's good." A fifteenth-century brewing manual explained that this name was bestowed in recognition that barm was not invented by humans but rather "cometh of the grete grace of God."*

To make excellent spice Cakes, take halfe a pecke of very fine wheate flower, take almost one pound of sweet butter, and some good milke and creame mixt together, set it on the fire, and put in your butter and a good deale of suger, and let it melt together: then straine Saffron into your milke a good quantity; then take seaven or eight spoonefull of good Ale barme, and eight egges with two yelkes and mix them together, then put your milke to it when it is somewhat cold, and into your flower put salt, Aniseedes bruised, Cloves and Mace and a good deale of Cinamon: then worke all together good and stiffe that you need not worke in any flower after; then put in a little rosewater cold, then rub it well in the thing you knead it in, and worke it throughly: if it be not sweet enough scrape in a little more suger, and pull it all in peeces, and hurle in a good quantity of currants, and so worke all together againe, and bake your Cake as you see cause in a gentle warme oven.

## MODERN RECIPE                    Makeability: 4

2/3 cup whole milk

1/4 cup 35% cream

3/4 cup unsalted butter

1 1/2 cups sifted sugar

2 pinches saffron

8 TBS ale barme (substitute 1 envelope active dry yeast)

8 whole eggs

2 yolks

2 1/3 cups sifted all-purpose flour

3/4 tsp salt

2 TBS aniseed, lightly bruised to release oils

3/4 tsp ground cloves

1/2 tsp ground mace

1 TBS cinnamon

1 TBS rosewater (see Appendix 1)

2 TBS currants

Preheat oven to 350°F and bring all ingredients to room temperature. Gently heat the milk and cream in a large saucepan. Add the butter and sugar and allow to melt before adding the saffron. Stir well and remove from the heat. Add the ale barme if available. Beat the eggs, temper them with some of the milk and cream mixture, and combine, but do not let them scramble. Mix together the salt, flour, and spices. Mix the milk and cream mixture with the flour and work together, kneading it well. Rub the dough with the rosewater and add the currants, kneading them together. Taste for sweetness and add more sugar if desired. Cut the dough into smaller pieces, shape into rounded cakes, and bake for 50 minutes.

# TO MAKE PRINCE-BISKET BREAD

*A Closet for Ladies and Gentlewomen, 1627*

York: Marry (they say) my unkle grew so fast,
     That he could gnaw a crust at two houres old,
     'Twas full two yeares ere I could get a tooth.
     Grandam, this would have beene a byting Jest. (*Richard III* 2.4.27–30)

*Bisket bread, according to Tobias Venner in his* Via Recta ad Vitam Longam, *is good for those "that desire to grow leane." Venner's comment is unusual because dietary handbooks rarely counselled their readers on how to lose weight. Their lack of interest in promoting weight loss may reflect the fact that everyone in Shakespeare's England had experienced or witnessed the effects of famine. Bad harvests led to severe dearths such as one that lasted from 1594 to 1598, which prompted Hugh Plat to write* Sundrie New and Artificiall Remedies Against Famine, *in which he proposed that bread might be made from pumpkins and that "a fresh turf or clod of earth, applyed every daie unto the stomach of a man,* will preserve him from famishing for some smal number of daies.'' Another grain shortage that struck in 1607 may have influenced Shakespeare's Coriolanus, which opens with citizens rioting because grain is being withheld from them. Even when harvests were good, many people lacked sufficient food, which prompted Thomas Tusser to remind successful husbandmen to be generous: "Remember those children whose parents be poore, / which hunger yet dare not to crave at thy doore." The great girth achieved by Henry VIII in his final decades or by Falstaff, "the fat knight with the great belly-doublet" (Henry V 4.7.47) was all the more notable because it was uncommon.

Take a pound of very fine Flower, as much Sugar thorowly searced, one ounce of Anniseeds cleane pickt, take eight Egges, and a spoonfull of Muskadine, and beat all into batter as thick as for Fritters: beat it thus in a Bowle one houre: then put it into your coffins of plate, or frames of wood, and set it in an Oven, and let it remaine there one houre: you may slice some of them when they bee a day old, and dry them againe upon a hurdle of Wicker: you may also take one of your loaves, and wash it over with the yolke of an Egge beaten with a little Rose-water, and while it is greene, cast Biskets and Carrowaies on it, and a little white Candy, and it will shew as if it did haile on it: then spot it with gold, and give it to whom you please.

---

 ## MODERN RECIPE                                   Makeability: 3

3 cups all-purpose flour

2 cups sifted sugar

1 TBS aniseed

8 eggs

1 TBS muscadine or other sweet red wine

2 TBS unsalted butter for loaf pans

1 egg yolk and 1 tsp rosewater for egg wash (see Appendix 1)

Biskets (see "To make English Bisket" on page 237, or substitute a dry gingersnap cookie)

2 TBS caraway seeds

2 TBS sugar

Gold flakes

Preheat oven to 350°F. Combine the flour, sugar, aniseed, eggs, and muscadine into a thick batter. Beat for one hour (easiest, of course, if an electric stand mixer is employed). Place the dough into lightly buttered loaf pans and bake one hour, or until a knife inserted into the center of the loaf comes out dry or check by removing the loaf and tapping on the bottom of the bread: it should produce a hollow sound. If desired, decorate the loaf with a wash of egg and rosewater, garnish with crumbled "biskets," caraway seeds, sugar, or gold flakes.

---

# TO MAKE BISKET BREAD, OTHERWISE CALLED FRENCH BISKET

*Delightes for Ladies*, 1609

Doll Tearsheet: Sirrha, what humor is the Prince of?

Falstaff:        A good shallow young fellow: hee would have made a good Pantler, hee would have chipp'd Bread well. (*2 Henry IV* 2.4.235–237)

*In this quotation from 2 Henry IV, Falstaff mocks the Prince by insisting that he is only fit to be a pantler, that is, a servant who looked after the household bread and whose tasks included chipping the crusts from loaves before they were served to the table. There were several reasons why bread was chipped. For one thing, it removed the bits of ash that had settled onto the the bread and that stuck to its surface as it baked in the coal or wood-fired oven. As well, dentistry was as yet a rudimentary profession and, given the popularity of sugar among the gentry, many people were afflicted with tooth decay that made chewing crunchy food an unpleasant task. Additionally, the crust was thought to dry up the moisture of the human body, which exacerbated health problems associated with certain temperaments. As Tobias Venner advised in his Via Recta ad Vitam Longam, "let the utmost and harder part of the crust be chipped away, of which let such as are by nature cholericke and melancholicke have speciall care."*

Take halfe a pecke of fine flower, two ounces of coriander seedes, one ounce of annis seedes, the whites of foure egges, half a pinte of Ale yeast, and as much water as will make it up into stiffe paste, your water must be but blood warme, then bake it in a long roll as big as your thigh, let it stay in the oven but one houre, and when it is a day olde, pare it and slice it overthwart, then sugar it over with fine poudred sugar, and so dry it in an oven again, and being drie, take it out & sugar it again, then boxe it, and so you may keepe it all the yeare.

---

 ## MODERN RECIPE                                        Makeability: 4

3 cups all-purpose flour

1 tsp coriander seeds

1/2 tsp aniseed

4 egg whites

1/2 cup ale yeast (subsitute 1 packet active dry yeast)

2 cups warm water

1 cup confectioner's (powdered) sugar

Preheat oven to 350°F. In a large mixing bowl, combine the flour, seeds, and egg whites. Mix the yeast in the water and let dissolve for a few minutes. Gradually pour the water and yeast into the flour mixture and work into a dough. Turn it out onto a clean work surface and knead it for 10 minutes. Cover and let rise in a warm place until the dough has doubled in size, about one hour. Punch down the dough and shape into a long roll. Place the dough on a baking sheet or in a large loaf pan. Cover and let rise a second time, again to double size. Bake for one hour and then remove. The next day, trim off the crust, slice it thinly across its width, and sprinkle with sugar. Dry it in the oven and sprinkle with more sugar.

---

# TO MAKE JOMBILS A HUNDRED

*The Second Part of the Good Hus-wives Jewell, 1597*

Tribune: Sorrow concealed, like an Oven stopt,
            doth burne the hart to Cinders where it is. (*Titus Andronicus* 2.4.36–37)

*This recipe instructs the cook to make jombils (also known as "jumbals") by tying the rolled dough into knots, which provides a clue as to the origin of their name. They were presumably named after gimbals, which in the sixteenth century were linked metal rings, rather like the five interlinking rings that now represent the Olympics and that might have found use on a ship or in a livery stable.*

Take twenty Egges put them into a pot both the yolkes and the white, beat them wel, then take a pound of beaten suger and put to them, and stirre them wel together, then put to it a quarter of a peck of flower, and make a hard paste thereof, and then with Anniseede moulde it well, and make it in little rowles beeing long, and tye them in knots, and wet the ends in Rosewaterr, then put them into a pan of seething water, but even in one waum, then take them out with a Skimmer and lay them in a cloth to drie, this being doon lay them in a tart panne, the bottome being oyled, then put them into a temperat Oven for one howre, turning them often in the Oven.

---

 ## MODERN RECIPE                                   Makeability: 4

| | |
|---|---|
| 3 eggs | 2 TBS bruised aniseed |
| 1 cup superfine sugar | 1/4 cup rosewater (see Appendix 1) |
| 2 cups all-purpose flour | lard for greasing a baking sheet |

Preheat oven to 350°F. Beat the eggs well and stir in the sugar until it is incorporated. Add the flour and aniseed and work into a "hard paste." Roll out the dough into a long "rope" about half an inch thick. Cut the rope into pieces and tie it into knots. Dab the ends with the rosewater. Bring a large pot of water to the boil. Slip in gently a few jombils at a time and allow to cook about two minutes, or until they rise to the surface. Remove with a slotted spoon, drain and dry gently with a kitchen towel, and place on a greased baking sheet. Bake for 30 to 35 minutes, or until done, turning often.

# 16

# STEWED FRUITS, CANDIED SPICES, AND SUGAR PLATE

Doll Tearsheet: You a Captaine? you slave, for what? for tearing
a poore Whores Ruffe in a Bawdy-house? Hee a Captaine?
hang him Rogue, hee lives upon mouldie stew'd-Prunes,
and dry'de Cakes. (*2 Henry IV* 2.4.143–146)

The dishes featured in this chapter would have been served at the conclusion of a formal meal (that is, at the end of the second course) or as part of a separate dessert "banquet," one that might have been hosted in a different room than the meal that preceded it or, weather permitting, outside in a garden or arbor. In a sense, these banquetting dishes are the logical extension of the dishes that belong to the other courses: they take the ingredients that characterize the other dishes and then zero in on them. Those ingredients are sugar (which appears in more than half of the 2,100 recipes published in this period), fruit (especially apples, pears, prunes, and currants, which have supporting roles even in the meat and fish dishes), nuts (specifically, almonds), and spices (such as ginger and nutmeg). The stewed fruit dishes, for example, are little more than boiled fruit and sugar; the candied spices—or comfits, as they were then called—are essentially sugar-coated bits of ginger, nutmeg, and other spices; and the sugar plate (epitomized by marzipan, or marchpane as it was then called) consists primarily of sugar and almonds, molded into various shapes and forms. These sugar-laden banquet treats were apparently so popular that guests sometimes sneaked them home in what we might now call a doggy bag, as is described by a character named Sugar who appears in a 1629 allegory called *Wine, Beer, and Ale, Together by the Eares.* Sugar first brags that women adore him: "They are the best friends I have, for I am alwaies in their mouthes." He then adds that "If I come to a banquet ... every woman bestowes a handkerchef upon mee, and strives to carry me away in their cleanest linen." Indeed, for some women a linen napkin is too small, and they "would bring whole sheets for me to lie in" if modesty didn't prevent them.

# HOW TO CANDIE GINGER, NUTMEGS, OR ANY ROOTE OR FLOWERS

*Delightes for Ladies*, 1609

Pompey: I am as well acquainted heere, as I was in our
house of profession: one would thinke it were Mistris
Overdons owne house, for heere be manie of her olde
Customers. First, here's yong Mr Rash, hee's in for a
commoditie of browne paper, and olde Ginger, nine
score and seventeene pounds, of which hee made five
Markes readie money: marrie then, Ginger was not much in request, for the
olde Women were all dead. (*Measure for Measure* 4.3.1–9)

*In the sixteenth and seventeenth centuries, a seed, root, or flower that was coated with layers
of congealed sugar was called a condite. Thomas Cogan, in his 1584* Haven of Health, *noted that "ginger Condite, is better for students: for being well made, if it be taken in the
morning fasting, it comforteth much the stomacke and head, and quickneth remembrance."
In the quotation from* Measure for Measure, *Pompey is visiting a prison, where he recognizes
Master Rash, who has been jailed for usury. It was illegal to lend money for interest in Shakespeare's England (Shakespeare's father was charged with that offense in 1570), so lenders
would try to circumvent the law by "buying" from their client some worthless goods in
exchange for a large sum of money. In the case of Master Rash, the worthless goods were
"brown paper and old ginger," the ginger being worthless not only because it was old but
because the elderly women, who would usually make and enjoy candied ginger, were all dead.*

Take a quarter of a pounde of the best refined sugar, or sugar candie which you can
get, powder it, put thereto two spoonfulls of Rosewater, dip therein your Nutmegs,
ginger, rootes, &c being first sodden in faire water till they bee soft and tender, the
oftener you dip them in sirrup, the thicker the candie will bee, but it will be the
longer in candying: your sirup must be of such stiffenesse, as that a drop thereof
being let fall upon a pewter dish, may congeale and harden beeing cold. You must
make your sirrup in a chafingdish of coales, keeping a gentle fire: after your sirup is
once at his full height, then put them upon papers presently into a stove or in
dishes, continue fire some ten or twelve daies, till you finde the candie hard and
glistering like diamonds; you must dippe the red rose, the gillow flower, the marigold, the borrage flower, and all other flowers but once.

---

 ## MODERN RECIPE                                            Makeability: 4

2 cups of confectioner's sugar

2 cups of water

2 TBS rosewater (see Appendix 1)

Assortment of caraway seeds, nutmegs, ginger,
parsnips, and other roots

Assortment of roses, wild carnations (clove
pinks), marigolds, and zucchini flowers (if
available)

*Continued on next page*

*Continued from previous page*

Wash the roots and soak in water 24 hours. Peel and dry. In a large pot, bring the water and sugar to the soft-ball candy stage (234°F on a candy thermometer) and in it cook the roots for 20 minutes. Remove, drain (reserving the syrup), and store the roots on a wire rack in a dark place for four days. For the flowers, dip them once into the syrup and place them on parchment paper.

# TO MAKE GINGER BREAD

*Delightes for Ladies*, 1609

Hotspur: Sweare me, Kate, like a Lady, as thou art,
          A good mouth-filling Oath: and leave "In sooth,"
          And such protest of Pepper Ginger-bread,
          To Velvet-Guards, and Sunday-Citizens. (*1 Henry IV* 3.1.251–254)

*The royal court, under Queen Elizabeth and later under King James, was a place of political intrigue, infighting, and occasional poisonings. It is comforting, therefore, to learn that the members of court, as this recipe suggests, could at least agree on a favorite gingerbread. Their gingerbread, however, was rather different from what we are used to: it was boiled rather than baked, and the final product was more like a confection than a cookie or bread. Etymologically, this isn't surprising: the word "gingerbread" is a corruption of the Old French "gingembras," which simply meant "preserved ginger": that is, the "bread" part arose only when fourteenth-century Anglophones mispronounced the last syllable of "gingembras." In Shakespeare's England, gingerbread was often sold at fairs in the form of gingerbread men and women. Puritans, however, sometimes complained that it was sinful to sell and eat confections shaped like people. In Ben Jonson's* Bartholomew Fair, *a Puritan named Busy calls them an "idolatrous grove of images" and overturns the table from which they are being sold.*

Take three stale Manchets, and grate them: drie them, and sift them through a fine sieve: then adde unto them one ounce of ginger beeing beaten, and as much Cinamon, one ounce of liquorice and anniseeds being beaten together and searced, halfe a pound of sugar, then boile all these together in a posnet, with a quart of claret wine, till they come to a stiffe paste with often stirring of it; and when it is stiffe, mold it on a table, and so drive it thin, and put it in your moldes: dust your moldes with Cinamon, Ginger, and liquorice, beeing mixed together in fine powder. This is your Ginger bread used at the Court, and in all Gentlemens houses at festival times. It is otherwise called drie Leach.

 MODERN RECIPE                                      Makeability: 3

4 cups dry bread crumbs forced through a fine-meshed sieve

1 oz finely minced ginger

1 oz cinnamon

½ oz ground and sifted aniseed

$^{1}/_{2}$ oz ground and sifted licorice root (or substitute ground fennel seeds)

$1^{1}/_{4}$ cup sugar

4 cups Bordeaux wine cinnamon, ginger, and licorice powder for dusting pans or molds

Preheat oven to 350°F. In a mixing bowl, combine the bread crumbs, ginger, cinnamon, aniseed, licorice, and sugar. Pour the mixture into a large saucepan with the wine and stir into a stiff paste. Add more bread crumbs if needed. Put the dough on a clean work space and allow it to cool before rolling it out thin. Dust the molds with the cinnamon powder and put in the gingerbread. Bake for 8 to 10 minutes, depending on thickness.

# TO MAKE MANUS CHRISTI

*The Good Huswifes Jewell*, 1596

Audrey: Would you not have me honest?
Clown: No truly, unlesse thou wert hard favour'd:
for honestie coupled to beautie, is to have
Honie a sawce to Sugar. (*As You Like It* 3.3.26–29)

*The name "manus Christi" means "hand of Christ" and probably reflects the belief that this confection (which originated in the early fifteenth century) had healing properties. Sugar was believed by many to be a wonder drug and was so used by apothecaries. Thomas Lupton, for one, in his 1579 treatise entitled* A Thousand Notable Things, *affirmed that if one puts sugar into a wound it "doth not onely clense all corruption from it, and consumes all superfluous flesh or matter in it: but also heales it marvelously." The ground pearl and gold leaf that the recipe calls for were likewise considered to have pharmaceutical benefits. The medicinal nature of this confection also makes it more likely that the "Rie" flour that it calls for is actually rice flour rather than rye flour: rice, by virtue of its relative rarity, was deemed to have greater healing properties than humble rye. A similar printer's error occurs in a recipe called "To make fine rise porredge" where the spellings "rise" and "ryce" occur at the beginning of the recipe, followed by a single instance of "rie" near the end of the recipe.*

Take five spoonefull of Rosewater, and graines of Ambergreece, and 4 grains of Pearle beaten very fine, put these three together in a Saucer and cover it close, and let it stande covered one houre, then take foure ounces of very fine Suger, and beate it small, and search it through a fine search, then take a little earthen pot glased, and put into it a spoonefull of Suger, and a quarter of a spoonefull of Rosewater, and let the Suger and the Rosewater boyle together softelye, till it doe rise and fall againe three times. Then take fine Rie flower, and sifte on a smooth borde, and with a spoone take of the Suger, and the Rosewater, and first make it all into a roundcake and then after into little Cakes, and when they be halfe colde, wet them over with the same Rosewater, and then laye on your golde, and so shall you make very good Manus Christi.

## MODERN RECIPE

Makeability: 5

$^1/_2$ cup rosewater (see Appendix 1)

$^1/_{120}$ oz ambergris

$^1/_{120}$ oz powdered pearl (substitute any other calcium carbonate, such as chalk)

$^1/_2$ cup sugar

$^1/_2$ cup rice flour

Gold leaf, as desired

Combine the rosewater, ambergris, and powdered pearl in a dish. Wait one hour. (If you don't have ambergris and powdered pearl, don't wait one hour.) Add the sugar to the mixture of rosewater, ambergris, and powdered pearl and bring it to a gentle boil for two minutes. Sift the rice flour onto a mixing board, and drop spoonfuls of the rosewater mixture onto the rice flour. Mold each spoonful into a small ball or "cake," wet them with more of the rosewater mixture, and apply gold leaf to each one.

# TO ROUGH-CANDIE SPRIGS OF ROSEMARIE

*A Daily Exercise for Ladies and Gentlewomen, 1617*

> Friar Laurence:  Drie up your teares, and sticke your Rosemarie
> On this faire Corse, and as the custome is,
> And in her best array beare her to Church. (*Romeo and Juliet* 4.5.79–81)

*Rosemary was a traditional symbol of memory and immortality and was therefore associated with both weddings and funerals, which is why Friar Laurence, in the quotation from* Romeo and Juliet, *instructs Juliet's family to strew her body with that herb. The comparison of the powdered sugar to sparks of diamonds is one of the many lovely metaphors found in recipes of this period.*

Lay your Rosemarie branches one by one upon a faire sheete of paper, then take Sugar-candie beaten smal like sparks of diamonds, and wet it in a little Rose-water in a silver spoone, and lay it as even as you can upon every branch, and set them a drying a good way off from the fire, and in one houre they will be dry, then turne them, and candie the other side, and when both sides be throughly dry, box them & keepe them all the yeere: they wil appeare to the eye in their natural colour, and seeme to be covered with sparks of diamonds.

## MODERN RECIPE

Makeability: 2

6 rosemary branches

3 cups sugar

$^3/_4$ cup rosewater (see Appendix 1)

Arrange the rosemary branches on a sheet of parchment paper. Mix the sugar and rosewater and thoroughly wet the rosemary. Let the branches dry in a warm place. Turn the branches and coat the other side.

# TO BAKE SMALL MEATS

*A Book of Cookrye*, 1591

Prince: But sweet Ned, to sweeten which name of Ned, I
give thee this peniworth of Sugar, clapt even now
into my hand by an under Skinker, one that never
spake other English in his life, then "Eight shillings
and six pence," and, "You are welcome:" with this
shrill addition, "Anon, Anon sir, Score a Pint of
Bastard in the Halfe Moone, or so." (*1 Henry IV* 2.4.21–27)

*This recipe contains a trio of words—"bray," "bastard," and "coffin"—that you might
expect to find in a Mickey Spillane crime novel. In a sixteenth-century culinary context,
however, "bray" simply denoted the act of crushing an ingredient with a mortar and pestle.
"Bastard" was a sweet Spanish wine, similar to muscatel in flavor and may have aquired
its name because it was sometimes adulterated or articificially sweetened with honey.
"Coffin" was what a pastry crust was called, a usage that persisted until the eighteenth
century. Somewhat oddly, the culinary sense of "coffin" and the funereal sense of "coffin"
overlapped throughout the sixteenth and seventeenth centuries. A further peculiar word
appears in the quotation from 1 Henry IV: a skinker was a tapster or bartender, and an
under-skinker was a young man who was apprenticing in that trade.*

Take Peares also sodden in Ale, and bray and straine them with the same Licour,
and put therto Bastard and Honny, and put it into a pan and stir it on the fire til it
be wel sodden, then make little coffins and set them in the Oven til they be hard,
and then take them out againe, and put the foresaid licour into them and so serve
them forth.

---

 ## MODERN RECIPE                                Makeability: 3

6 Bartlett pears, peeled, cored, and cut in
small pieces

1 cup ale

1 cup sweet Spanish white wine

1/4 cup honey

Pastry recipe "To make fine paste" on page
214, or buy premade pastry.

Prepare 6 pastry shells, each about the size of a large muffin. Preheat oven to 350°F. Boil the pears
in the ale, wine, and honey until soft. Pass the pear mixture through a fine-meshed sieve and pour
into small pie shells. Bake for 25 minutes, remove from the oven, and pour in 2 TBS of the liquor.
Bake for another 10 minutes.

# HOW TO MAKE POMAGES

*A Book of Cookrye, 1591*

Fool: Shalt see thy other Daughter will use thee kindly,
      for though she's as like this, as a Crabbe's like an Apple,
      yet I can tell what I can tell.
Lear: What can'st tell Boy?
Fool: She will taste as like this as, a Crabbe do's to a Crab:
      thou canst tell why ones nose stands i' th' middle on's face?
Lear: No.
Fool: Why to keepe ones eyes of either side's nose, that what a man
      cannot smell out, he may spy into. (*King Lear* 1.5.14–22)

Take a quart of red wine or sweet wine, and v or vi well watrishe Apples, pare them and cut them in peeces and cast away the cores, then put the apples with the wine into a pot and boyle them on the fire till they be tender, and take a manchet lofe and cut it in thin peeces and cast it into the pot, then when the apples be tender, put to them, a quarter of a pound of Sugar, but draw them through a strainer before, and also an ounce of Sinamon, halfe a quarter of an ounce of ginger, and boyle al these togither in a chafer or a pot, and then take them out again, and put them into a faire bason or in a charger, then make a dredge of sinamon, sugar and Ginger, but most of Sugar, and dresse your Pomages in faire dishes, then cast in your dredge and serve it out hot or colde.

---

 ## MODERN RECIPE       Makeability: 2

4 cups red wine

6 apples suitable for eating, peeled, cored, and chopped

6 thin slices white bread

1/2 cup sugar

1 TBS cinnamon

1 tsp minced ginger

For the dredge:

1/2 cup sugar

2 TBS cinnamon

1 tsp minced ginger

Bring to a boil the red wine and apple pieces. When tender, add the bread. Force the apple and bread mixture through a fine-meshed sieve into a saucepan and stir in the sugar, cinnamon, and ginger. Bring to a gentle simmer. Pour the mixture onto a platter and sprinkle on the dredging mixture. Serve hot or cold.

# TO MAKE MEAT OF QUINCES

*Epulario*, 1598

Pompey:   Sir, she came in great with childe: and longing
             (saving your honors reverence) for stewd prunes; sir,
             we had but two in the house, which at that very
             distant time stood, as it were in a fruit dish (a
             dish of some three pence; your honours have seene such
             dishes) they are not China-dishes, but very good dishes.

Escalus:   Go to, go to, no matter for the dish, sir.

Pompey:   No indeede, sir, not of a pin; you are therein
             in the right: but, to the point: As I say, this Mistris
             Elbow, being (as I say) with childe, and being great
             bellied, and longing (as I said) for prunes: and having
             but two in the dish (as I said) Master Froth here, this
             very man, having eaten the rest (as I said) and (as I say)
             paying for them very honestly: for, as you know
             Master Froth, I could not give you three pence againe.

Froth:   No indeede.

Pompey:   Very well: you being then (if you be
             remembred) cracking the stones of the foresaid prunes.

Froth:   Aye, so I did indeede.

Pompey:   Why, very well: I telling you then (if you be
             remembred) that such a one, and such a one, were
             past cure of the thing you wot of, unlesse they kept
             very good diet, as I told you.

Froth:   All this is true.

Pompey:   Why very well then.

Escalus:   Come: you are a tedious foole. (*Measure for Measure* 2.1.89–117)

*Nowadays, quinces are rarely used in cookery, at least in North America. In the United States, for example, fewer than 200 acres of land are devoted to commercially grown quince. In Shakespeare's England, however, this relative of the pear and apple appeared in more recipes than any other fruit, ranging from tarts and pies to succades and preserves. Marmalades, which originated as a kind of preserve, were an especially popular way of using quinces: 16 of the 2,100 recipes published in this period are for quince marmalade. The word "marmalade," in fact, derives from the Portuguese name for the quince, "marmelo." As for the stewed prunes that Pompey and Master Froth fixate on in the quotation from* Measure for Measure, *no recipe with that name appears among the 2,100 from this period, but there is one entitled "To make Prunes in sirrope," which stews the prunes in a mixture of wine and sugar.*

Seeth thy Quinces in broth of leane flesh, then stampe them and temper them with Almond milk, made with broth of Pullets or flesh, and if time serve straine them, and put them into a pipkin with sugar, ginger, sinamon, and a little saffron, & set them to boile on a soft fire, because it should not smell of the smoke, and stirre them with a spoone. And it shall be the better if you put a little fresh butter into it, and when they are boiled cast spice upon them.

## MODERN RECIPE                                    Makeability: 2

| | |
|---|---|
| 3 quinces, peeled, cored, and chopped | 1 tsp cinnamon |
| 3 cups chicken broth | 2 pinches saffron |
| ¼ cup almond milk (see page 276) | 2 TBS unsalted butter |
| ½ cup sugar | 1 tsp ground nutmeg for garnish |
| 1 TBS minced ginger | 1 tsp ground cloves for garnish |

Boil the quinces in chicken broth until tender. Mash the quinces with almond milk, force them through a fine-meshed sieve, and transfer to a saucepan. Add the sugar, ginger, cinnamon, and saffron and bring to a gentle boil stirring frequently. Stir in the butter, spoon the quince mixture into a serving dish, and sprinkle it with nutmeg and cloves.

# TO MAKE THE BEST MARCHPANE

*The English Huswife, 1615*

First Servant:    Where's Potpan, that he helpes not
                  to take away? He shift a Trencher? he scrape a Trencher?
Second Servant: When good manners shall lie all in one
                  or two mens hands, and they unwasht too, 'tis a foule thing.
First Servant:    Away with the joyntstooles, remove
                  the Court cubbord, looke to the Plate: good thou,
                  save mee a piece of Marchpane. (*Romeo and Juliet* 1.5.1–8)

*Marchpane, or what we now call marzipan, was an almond-based confection central to the dessert banquets that concluded formal meals and feasts in Shakespeare's England. The sticky consistency of marchpane meant that it could be sculpted into interesting shapes or "printed" by pressing a pattern onto its surface. In this recipe, the "cumfets" that adorn the marchpane are comfits, that is, candied nuts or spices.*

To make the best March-pane; take the best Jordan almonds & blaunch them in warm water, then put them into a stone morter, and with a wodden pestell beat them to pappe, then take of the finest refined sugar well searst, and with it and Damaske rose-water beate it to a good stiffe paste, allowing almost every Jordan almond three spoonful of sugar; then when it is brought thus to a paste lay it upon a faire table, and strowing searst sugar under it moulde it like leaven, then with a roling-pinne role it forth and lay it upon wafers washt with Rose-water; then pinch it about the sides and put it into what forme you please, then strow searst sugar all over it, which done wash it over with Rose-water and sugar mixt together, for that will make the Ice, then adorne it with Cumfets, guilding, or whatsoever devises you please and so set it into a hot stove, and there bake it crispy and so serve it forth. Some use to mix with the paste Cinamon and Ginger finely searst, but I referre that to your particular taste.

MODERN RECIPE                                    Makeability: 3

1 lb blanched almonds finely ground

2 cups superfine sugar

1 cup water

1 tsp rosewater (see Appendix 1)

1/2 tsp cinnamon

1/2 tsp minced ginger

1/4 cup sugar wafers (see "To make waffers" on page 214) washed with rosewater (see Appendix 1)

Orange comfets (see "To make orange comfets" below)

Preheat oven to 325°F. Blend the ground almonds, sugar, and rosewater into a paste. Sprinkle a clean work surface with sugar and roll out the marchpane with a rolling pin. Wet the wafers with rosewater and lay the marchpane on the wafers. Pinch the marchpane over the edges of wafers, add a few orange comfets, and bake them until crispy.

# TO MAKE ORENGE COMFETS

*The Treasurie of Hidden Secrets*, 1600

Menenius: You know neither mee, your selves, nor any thing:
you are ambitious, for poore knaves cappes and legges:
you weare out a good wholesome Forenoone, in hearing
a cause beteene an Orenge wife, and a Forfetseller,
and then rejourne the Controversie of three-pence
to a second day of Audience. (*Coriolanus* 2.1.67–72)

*Comfits were confections made by coating spices, seeds, nuts, or pieces of fruit with layers of melted sugar. A comfit such as this might be used to adorn the marchpane whose recipe also appears in this chapter.*

Take Orenge pillings, lay them in faire water a day and a night, then seeth them in white wine: then take them out of the wine, and put them in an earthen pot, & put therein Suger, Sinamon, Cloves, and Mace whole, and seeth them together without any other liquor, and so it is made.

 MODERN RECIPE                                    Makeability: 3

1 cup orange zests

1 cup white wine

3/4 cup sugar

1 cinnamon stick

6 bruised cloves

4 blades of mace

*Continued on next page*

*Continued from previous page*

Wash the oranges thoroughly. Zest the oranges in long threads and soak in a bowl of water for 24 hours. Remove the zests from the water and pat dry. In a medium saucepan, combine the zests and the white wine, bring to the boil, and cook for 15 minutes. Remove the zests to another saucepan, adding the sugar, cinnamon, cloves, and mace. Gently cook over medium-low heat until the zests are candied. Cool on a piece of parchment paper.

# TO BUTTER GOOSEBERRIES

*Elinor Fettiplace's Receipt Book, 1604*

Falstaff:                                            Vertue is of so little
regard in these Costermongers times, that true
valor is turn'd Beare-heard. Pregnancie is made a
Tapster, and hath his quicke wit wasted in giving
Recknings: all the other gifts appertinent to
man (as the malice of this Age shapes them) are
not woorth a Gooseberry. (*2 Henry IV* 1.2.167–173)

*James Hart, in his 1633* Klinike, *comments that gooseberries were unknown "in ancient times" (by which he means the ancient Greeks and Romans), but that they are "now with us, in frequent use." The 2,100 recipes printed in this period confirm Hart's claim, as gooseberries make an appearance in 38 of them. Hart adds that cooks often use gooseberries in place of verjuice, a substitution that John Gerard, in his 1597* Herball, *also affirms to be a common practice.*

Take your gooseberries before they are ripe, & put them in a dish with a good piece of sweet butter, cover them close & let them boyle till they begin to break, then stirre them till they bee all broken, then put in some sugar to them & rosewater & the Yelks of two eggs beaten, so stirre it alltogether, & serve it upon sippets.

 ## MODERN RECIPE                                      Makeability: 2

1 cup gooseberries

$^{1}/_{2}$ cup unsalted butter

$^{1}/_{4}$ cup sugar

1 TBS rosewater (see Appendix 1)

2 egg yolks

6 slices lightly toasted 60% whole wheat bread for sippets

Melt the butter in a saucepan and add the gooseberries. Cook them until they begin to break, stirring frequently. Add the sugar and rosewater; beat the eggs yolks and add them. Stir the mixture and cook for about 10 minutes. Arrange the sippets on a platter and pour the buttered gooseberries over.

# TO MAKE DATE-LEACH

*The English Huswife, 1615*

Parolles:                                    Virginitie like
an olde Courtier, weares her cap out of fashion, richly
suted, but unsuteable, just like the brooch & the
tooth-pick, which were not now: your Date is better in
your Pye and your Porredge, than in your cheeke: and
your virginity, your old virginity, is like one of our
French wither'd peares, it looks ill, it eates drily, marry
'tis a wither'd peare: it was formerly better, marry
yet 'tis a wither'd peare: Will you any thing with it?
(*All's Well That Ends Well* 1.1.156–164)

*There were two kinds of "leach" in Shakespeare's England. One was a sweet dish made from ingredients such as milk, almonds, eggs, and sugar that was often thickened with isinglass, which is a gelatin extracted from the air-bladders of certain fish. The other, which this recipe is an example of, was known as dry leach and was made by mixing sugar and finely chopped fruit or nuts into a paste, and then letting it dry. This recipe invites the cook to "print" the leach-paste, which means pressing it with a metal form or mold so that it acquires a desired shape. Popular molds, as another recipe indicates, were letters of the alphabet, coats of arms, and knots, as well as "beasts, birds, and other fancies." Incidentally, the name of this dish derives from the Old French "lesche" meaning "to lick." As for the quotation from All's Well That Ends Well, Parolles—who is trying to convince Helena that her virginity is not worth keeping—puns on the word "date": it is better to have a pie that's dated (that is, filled with dates) than a face that's dated (that is, dated with old age).*

To make an excellent date Leache take Dates and take out the stones and the white rinde, and beate them with Sugar Cinamon and Ginger very finely: then worke it as you would worke a peece of Past, and then print them as you please.

---

 ## MODERN RECIPE                                    Makeability: 2

| | |
|---|---|
| 1 cup dried dates, minced | 2 tsp minced ginger |
| ½ cup sugar | Water as needed |
| 3 tsp cinnamon | Sugar for garnish |

Mince the dates as finely as possible. In a mixing bowl, work the dates, sugar, cinnamon, and ginger into a paste that will hold together. Add drops of water as needed. Shape and mold the date-leach as desired and let dry.

# TO BOILE CITRONS

*The Second Part of the Good Hus-wives Jewell, 1597*

Witches:  Double, double, toile and trouble;
Fire burne, and Cauldron bubble. (*Macbeth* 4.1.10–11)

When your Citrons be boiled, pared and sliced, seeth them with water and wine, and put to them butter, small Raysons, and Barberies, suger, sinamon and Ginger, and let them seeth till your citrons be tender.

---

 ## MODERN RECIPE                                    Makeability: 2

3 lemons, peeled and sliced to a quarter-inch thickness

1/2 cup water

1/2 cup white wine

1/2 cup unsalted butter

2 TBS raisins

1 TBS barberries (see Appendix 1)

1/4 cup sugar

1 tsp cinnamon

1 tsp minced ginger

In a saucepan, combine the ingredients and bring to a gentle boil. Simmer over medium heat until the lemons are tender. Stir frequently.

---

# 17

# SAUCES AND POWDERS

Cassius:  This rudeness is a sauce to his good wit,
        Which gives men stomach to digest his words
        With better appetite. (*Julius Caesar* 1.2.300–302)

Tobias Venner, in his 1620 dietary treatise called *Via Recta ad Vitam Longam*, asserted that "the best and most common of all sauces is salt." His comment may strike us as puzzling, since we now think of sauces as liquid concoctions. Etymologically, however, Venner had a point: the word "sauce" derives from the Latin "salsus" meaning "salted" (as do the words "saucer," which originally denoted a vessel for holding sauce, and "salad," which in ancient times was a dish of salted vegetables). In fact, Shakespeare's contemporaries tended to think of sauces not in terms of their composition but rather in terms of their function: anything that was supposed to increase appetite, whether it was wet or dry, was a sauce. For this reason, Venner also named vinegar, verjuice, mustard, lemons, olives, capers, honey, and sugar as common sauces. Other authorities, such as Michael Scot, also cited anchovies and radishes as sauces because they too "sharpen the appetite." In *Macbeth*, Malcolm uses the word "sauce" in this way when he pretends to confess that gaining power would lead him to want more power: "my more-having would be as a sauce / To make me hunger more."

Tobias Venner also referred to "divers kinds of mixt sauces devised and composed by the skill of Cookes," by which he meant sauces as we now conceive of them. According to Venner, these "compound sauces," as he calls them in one passage, or "confused sauces," as he describes them elsewhere, were esteemed by "ingurgitating belly-gods." Prudent individuals needed to use such sauces with caution, because they tended to encourage gluttonous overeating. Judging from the recipes of the time, some of these compound sauces were specific to certain dishes (such as the red wine sauce in the recipe called "To dresse a hare"), some were associated with certain kinds of meat (such as "A sauce for veal"), and some were intended for use with all kinds of foods (such as "To make good garlike sauce").

Dishes in Shakespeare's England were also flavored or enhanced with powders, that is, with ready-made mixtures of ground spices, much as the now-familiar curry powder is a mixture of turmeric, coriander, cumin, and so on. In the Middle Ages, three spice mixtures had been popular: blanch powder (named after the white sugar it contained), powder douce (a sweet mixture, containing spices such as cinnamon and ginger), and powder fort (a hotter or more savory mixture, containing spices such as pepper, mace, and galingale). By the sixteenth century, only blanch powder continued to appear in cookery books and is in fact called for by two of the recipes included in this book. Such powders, to the extent that they were intended to increase appetite, were also considered sauces. Thomas Cogan, for instance, in his 1584 *Haven of Health*, provides instructions for making "a very good blanch powder" to "sauce a hen."

# BLANCH POWDER

*The Haven of Health*, 1584

Prince:   I did never see such pittifull Rascals.
Falstaff: Tut, tut, good enough to tosse: foode for Powder,
          foode for Powder: they'le fill a Pit, as well as better:
          tush man, mortall men, mortall men. (*1 Henry IV* 4.2.63–66)

*As its name suggests, blanch powder was a whitish powder—made from sugar and various spices—that was strewn on food just before it was served to the table. The powder to which Falstaff refers, in the quotation from* 1 Henry IV, *is quite different: he means gun powder and is alluding to the fact that the decrepit men he has conscripted for battle will serve as cannon fodder just as well as healthy men. Incidentally, two recipes in this book specifically call for blanch powder, namely, "To make a tarte of spinnage" and "A Troute baked or minced."*

With two ounces of sugar, a quarter of an ounce of ginger, & half a quarter of an ounce of Cinnamon, al beaten smal into powder, you may make a very good blanch powder to strow upon roasted apples, Quinces or Wardens, or to sauce a hen.

---

 ## MODERN RECIPE                                    Makeability: 1

$^1/_4$ cup sugar                                    1 tsp 6 cinnamon powder
1 TBS ginger power

Mix together well the sugar, ginger, and cinnamon. The blanch powder is suitable for sprinkling on roasted apples, quinces or wardens, or roasted or baked poultry.

---

# PIGGESAUCE

*The Good Houswives Treasure*, 1588

Sir Andrew: Heere's the Challenge, reade it: I warrant
            there's vinegar and pepper in't.
Fabian:     Is't so sawcy?
Sir Andrew: Aye, is't? I warrant him: do but read. (*Twelfth Night* 3.4.145–148)

Take halfe Vineger, and halfe Vergis, a handfull of percely and Sage chopte very small, a Pomewater shredde very small, then take the gravie of the Pigge, with Suger and Pepper and boyle them together.

## MODERN RECIPE — Makeability: 2

1/4 cup white vinegar

1/4 cup cup verjuice (see Appendix 1)

1/2 cup parsley, finely chopped

1/2 cup sage, finely chopped

1 tart apple, finely diced

1 cup pan gravy from roast pork

1 tsp sugar

1/4 tsp fresh-cracked pepper

In a saucepan, whisk together all the ingredients and bring to a boil. Simmer until the sauce reduces and thickens slightly.

# SAUCE FOR A HENNE OR PULLET

*The English Huswife, 1615*

Benedick: By my sword Beatrice thou lov'st me.
Beatrice: Doe not sweare by it and eat it.
Benedick: I will sweare by it that you love mee, and I will make him eat it that sayes I love not you.
Beatrice: Will you not eat your word?
Benedick: With no sawce that can be devised to it. I protest I love thee. (*Much Ado About Nothing* 4.1.273–279)

Take a good quantitie of beere and salt, and mixe them well together with a fewe fine bread crummes, and boile them on a chafing dish and coles, then take the yelkes of three or fowre hard egges, and being shred put it in to the beere and boile it also: then the Hen being almost enough, take three or fowre spoonfull of the gravy which comes from her and put it to also, and boile all together to an indifferent thicknes, which done, suffer it to boile no more, but only keepe it warme on the fire, and put into it the juice of two or three Orenges, and the slices of Lemmon pils all shred small, and the slices of Orenges also having the upper rind taken away: then the Henne being broken up, take the brawnnes thereof and shredding them small put it into the sauce also, and stirring all well together put it hot into a cleane warme dish, & lay the Hen (broke up) in the same.

## MODERN RECIPE — Makeability: 3

1 1/2 cups beer

1 TBS salt

1/4 cup fine bread crumbs

3 hard-boiled egg yolks

1/4 cup pan juices from a roast chicken (or 1/4 cup chicken stock)

*Continued on next page*

*Continued from previous page*

3 oranges, sliced                            2 cooked chicken thighs

1 lemon peel, sliced

Stir together in a saucepan the beer, salt, and bread crumbs and bring to a boil. Mince the egg yolks finely and add to the beer along with the chicken pan juice, orange juice, lemon peel, and orange slices. Simmer gently, allowing the sauce to thicken. Mince the chicken thighs and add to the sauce, stirring the ingredients together. Pour the sauce onto a large warm platter and add the chicken pieces.

## TO MAKE A SAUCE FOR MUTTON

*The Good Huswifes Handmaide for the Kitchin, 1594*

Host:  They shall have my horses, but I'le make them
pay: I'le sauce them, they have had my houses a week
at commaund: I have turn'd away my other guests, they must
come off, I'le sawce them, come. (*The Merry Wives of Windsor* 4.3.8–11)

Take Onions, slice them, boyle them in Vergious, cut a peece of lean Mutton that is almost rosted, mince it very small, put it to your sauce, let it boile altogether a good while, when you serve your mutton in, poure that upon it.

---

 MODERN RECIPE                                      Makeability: 2

1 large yellow onion                         ½ cup lamb pieces taken from a partially
                                             roasted leg
1 cup verjuice (see Appendix 1)

Slice the onion thinly and boil in the verjuice. Mince the pieces of lamb meat, adding it to the verjuice and onion. Let the sauce simmer gently and reduce for about 30 minutes. When you serve the mutton, pour the sauce upon it.

---

## TO MAKE GOOD GARLIKE SAUCE

*Epulario, 1598*

Like as to make our appetite more keene
With eager compounds we our pallat urge,
As to prevent our malladies unseene,
We sicken to shun sicknesse when we purge.

Even so being full of your nere-cloying sweetnesse,
To bitter sawces did I frame my feeding;
And sicke of wel-fare found a kind of meetnesse,
To be diseas'd ere that there was true needing.
Thus pollicie in love t' anticipate
The ills that were not, grew to faults assured,
And brought to medicine a healthfull state
Which rancke of goodnesse would by ill be cured.
But thence I learne and find the lesson true,
Drugs poyson him that so fell sicke of you. (Sonnet 118)

Take blanched almonds well stamped, and being halfe beaten, put as much garlike to them as you think good, and stampe them together, tempering them with water least it bee oiley. Then take crummes of white bread what quantity you will, and soke it either in leane broth of flesh or fish as time serveth: this sauce you may keepe & use with all meats, fat or leane as you think good.

---

 ## MODERN RECIPE                                        Makeability: 2

1 cup blanched almonds, chopped          1/4 cup bread crumbs

5 cloves chopped garlic                  1 cup chicken stock

1/4 cup water as needed

In a mortar and pestle (or blender), pound the almonds to a coarse consistency. Add the garlic and combine using drops of water to create a paste. Heat the chicken stock and whisk in the bread crumbs and almond mixture. Simmer until the sauce reduces and thickens. Use the sauce with any meat.

---

# TO MAKE GALLANTINE FOR FLESH OR FISH

*The Second Part of the Good Hus-wives Jewell, 1597*

Malcolm:                          With this, there growes
            In my most ill-composed Affection, such
            A stanchlesse Avarice, that were I King,
            I should cut off the Nobles for their Lands,
            Desire his Jewels, and this others House,
            And my more-having, would be as a Sawce
            To make me hunger more, that I should forge
            Quarrels unjust against the Good and Loyall,
            Destroying them for wealth. (*Macbeth* 4.3.77–85)

*A galantine was originally a sauce for fish, but it also developed into a stand-alone dish made of sopped bread and spices. This recipe, as is implied by the instruction to "serve it in*

saucers," is probably intended to be a dipping sauce. Its most unusual feature is the burnt toast, which places it within a tradition of "black sauces" that date back to the Middle Ages.

Take browne bread and burne it black in the tosting of it, then take them and lay them in a litle wine and vineger, and when they have soked a while, then strain them, seasoning it with sinamon, ginger, Pepper and salte, then set it on a chafing dish with coales, and let it boyle till it bee thick, and then serve it in saucers.

---

 ## MODERN RECIPE                                    Makeability: 2

10 quarter-inch thick slices 100% whole wheat bread, crusts removed

2 cups white wine

1/2 cup red wine vinegar

1/2 tsp cinnamon

1 tsp chopped ginger

1/4 tsp fresh-cracked black pepper

1/2 tsp salt

Toast the bread to a black color and immerse in the wine and vinegar mixture. Pass the soaked bread through a fine-meshed sieve into a mixing bowl and season with the cinnamon, ginger, pepper, and salt. Simmer in a saucepan until it thickens. Serve in saucers.

---

# A SAUCE FOR VEAL

*The English Huswife, 1615*

Friar Laurence:  O mickle is the powerfull grace that lies
In Plants, Hearbs, stones, and their true qualities:
For nought so vile, that on earth doth live,
But to the earth some speciall good doth give.
Nor ought so good, but strain'd from that faire use,
Revolts from true birth, stumbling on abuse. (*Romeo and Juliet* 2.3.15–20)

*This recipe calls for a "good store of currants," which is in keeping with the inordinate fondness that Shakespeare's contemporaries had for that dried fruit. Fynes Moryson, in his 1617 Itinerary, remarked that currants were "so frequent in all places, and with all persons in England, as the very Greekes that sell them, wonder what we doe with such great quantities thereof, and know not how we should spend them, except we use them for dyeing, or to feede Hogges."*

To make sauce for a joint of Veale, take all kind of sweet pot hearbes, and chopping them very small with the yelkes of two or three egges boyle them in Vinegar and Butter, with a fewe bread crummes and good store of currants; then season it with

Sugar and Cinnamon, and a Clove or two crusht, and so powr it upon the veale, with the slices of Orenges and Lemmons about the Dish.

---

 ## MODERN RECIPE                                    Makeability: 3

| | |
|---|---|
| 1 cup chopped spinach | 3 TBS currants |
| 1/2 cup carrots, finely diced | 1 tsp sugar |
| 1/2 cup parsnips, finely diced | 1/4 tsp cinnamon |
| 3 beaten egg yolks | 2 crushed cloves |
| 1/2 cup vinegar | 1 orange, sliced (for garnish) |
| 4 TBS unsalted butter | 1 lemon, sliced (for garnish) |
| 2 TBS bread crumbs | |

On low heat, combine spinach, carrots, parsnips, and vinegar in a saucepan. Take a few spoonfuls of the vinegar mixture from the saucepan and whisk into the egg yolks. Pour the tempered yolks back into the saucepan. Season with sugar, cinnamon, and cloves and heat thoroughly. Pour over the veal and garnish with orange and lemon slices.

---

# FOR TO MAKE MUSTARD

*Maison Rustique, Or the Countrey Farme, 1616*

Doll Tearsheet:  They say Poines hath a good Wit.
Falstaff:        Hee a good Wit? hang him Baboone, his Wit is
                 as thicke as Tewksburie Mustard: there is no more conceit
                 in him, than is in a Mallet. (*2 Henry IV* 2.4.2383–241)

*John Gerard, in his 1597 Herball, says that "the seed of Mustard pound with vinger, is an excellent sauce, good to be eaten with any grosse meates either fish or flesh." Numerous recipes for mustard-based condiments existed, ranging from a simple pork sauce made from mustard, vinegar, sugar, and pepper, to a complex paste made from mustard, grapes, cinnamon, cloves, vinegar, verjuice, and wine. Tewkesbury mustard, which Falstaff alludes to in the quotation from 2 Henry IV, included horseradish in its composition. Many dishes also included ground mustard seed as a seasoning, including recipes for a cherry tart, stewed herring, fried tripe, and boiled ox tongue. Sixteenth-century dietary authorities commended the use of mustard, including William Bullein who wrote that "nothinge doth pierce more swifter into the brayne than it doth."*

The most ordinarie way for the making of your Mustard, is, only to wash the seed verie cleane, then put it into your Mustard Quernes, and grind it either with strong vineger (which is the best) or with good Beere or Ale, or with Butter-milke.

## MODERN RECIPE

Makeability: 1

1 cup mustard seeds, yellow, white, brown, or a mix thereof

¹/₂ cup white vinegar (and as needed for consistency)

Soak the mustard seeds in clean water overnight and pick clean. Crush the seeds in a mortar and pestle to the desired consistency. Add the vinegar and mix into a paste. Beer, ale, or buttermilk can be used instead of vinegar. If you want to incorporate an ingredient from other mustard recipes, add 2 TBS of honey.

# 18

# BEVERAGES

Sir Toby: Come, come, I'll go burn some sack; 'tis too
late to go to bed now; come, knight; come, knight. (*Twelfth Night* 2.3.189–190)

Coffee and tea were not available in England until the mid-seventeenth century. This meant that Shakespeare had to write 37 plays and 144 sonnets without the benefit of caffeine. In fact, considering that most people washed down their breakfast with a pint of ale and continued to quaff various alcoholic beverages throughout the day, Shakespeare may very well have composed the greatest works of English literature while slightly drunk. It is probably not even an exaggeration to say that pretty much everyone in the sixteenth and seventeenth centuries was in a continuous state of mild inebriation. A Berkshire farmer named Robert Loder, for example, kept accounts from 1611 to 1618 showing that each person in his household drank, on average, between 1 and $1\frac{1}{2}$ gallons of beer a day. Likwise, during Elizabeth's reign, the royal household consumed approximately 600,000 gallons of beer annually. That household supported between 1,000 and 1,500 aristocrats and servants, meaning that each person tossed back between 400 and 600 gallons a year, or about 1 to $1\frac{1}{2}$ gallons a day. This included children. Dietary handbooks did not debate whether children should drink alcohol but only how much. Richard West, in his 1619 *Schoole of Vertue*, was typical: "Let not a childe drinke above twice or thrice at the most at one meale, and that gently, and not without reason: who bestoweth wine and beere on his childe beyond reason, defameth and abuseth him."

The reason for all this tippling was that nonalcoholic alternatives such as water and milk were considered insalubrius. Andrew Boorde, for example, in his 1547 *Compendyous Regyment*, wrote "water is not holsome sole by itselfe for an Englysshe man." Similarly, James Hart, in his 1633 *Klinike*, warned his readers not to drink water derived from snow or hail. The reasons given by Boorde, Hart, and others for eschewing water were of course incorrect: they thought that the cold and sluggish temperament of water made it hard to digest, when in reality it was microbes and impurities that made it dangerous to drink. The process of turning water into a fermented beverage, however, helped to remove those impurities and pathogens, making ale, beer, or wine a heathier choice than water or milk.

### SKELTONS
#### GHOST.

TO all Tapſters and Tiplers,
And all Ale-houſe Vitlers,
Inne-keepers, and Cookes,
That for pot-ſale lookes,
And will not giue meaſure,
But at your owne pleaſure,
Contrary to Law,
Scant meaſure will draw,
In Pot, and in Canne,
To cozen a Man
Of his full Quart a penny,
Of you there's to many:
For in King *Harry's* time,
When I made this Rime
Of *Elynor Rumming*,
With her good Ale tunning;
Our Pots were full quarted,
We were not thus thwarted,
With froth-Canne and nick-pot,
And ſuch nimble quick-ſhot,

A 2      That

*Elynour Rummin, the Famous Alewife*, John Skelton, 1624. In Shakespeare's England, women were sometimes allowed to own and operate an inn or tavern, usually coming into its possession when their husbands died without heirs. According to this verse (which was actually written long before it was published in 1624), Elynour Rummin was one such woman, although judging from her appearance in this woodcut, it was an occupation that took a toll on her. In Shakespeare's plays, women who manage their own establishments include the Hostess who appears in *1 Henry IV*, *2 Henry IV*, and *The Merry Wives of Windsor*, as well as Madame Overdone, who operates a brothel in *Measure for Measure*. Courtesy of Henry E. The Huntington Library, Rare Books, 69463.

Wine was much more expensive than ale or beer (27 pence for a gallon of claret wine versus 2 pence for a gallon of ale), which made it a drink of the upper classes. Wine was sometimes diluted with water and sometimes it was boiled or "burned" with spices to make a beverage called "hippocras"—when Sir Toby departs to "burn some sack," he is making hippocras. It was also common for sugar to be added to wine, a practice that Fynes Moryson in his 1617 travelogue said he "never observed in any other place or Kingdome." It is for this reason that Poins, in *1 Henry IV*, refers to Falstaff as "Sir John Sack and Sugar." Wine was believed to have a uniquely invigorating power. Andrew Boorde, for example, asserted that wine "doth quycken a mans wyttes, it doth comfort the heart, … it doth rejoyce all the powers of man, and dothe nuryshe them, it dothe ingendre good bloude, it doth comforte and doth nurysshe the brayne and all the body." Boorde's comendation of wine was echoed half a century later by Falstaff in *2 Henry IV*:

> A good sherris-sacke hath a twofold
> operation in it. It ascendes me into the braine; dries me
> there all the foolish and dull and crudy vapors which
> environe it; makes it apprehensive, quicke, forgetive,
> full of nimble fiery and delectable shapes; which,
> delivered o'er to the voyce, the tongue, which is the birth,
> becomes excellent wit. The second property of your
> excellent sherris is, the warming of the blood, which
> before (cold and setled) left the lyver white and pale,
> which is the badge of pusillanimitie and cowardize;
> but the sherris warmes it and makes it course from the
> inwards to the partes extreames. (4.3.95–106)

Unlike wine, which was primarily imported from Europe and parts of Africa, ale was a domestically produced potation. Ale had a long history in England. In English, the earliest written references to ale date back to the tenth century, and it was certainly brewed long before that. Andrew Boorde even claimed that "ale for an englysh man is a natural drynke," a sentiment echoed in *The Winter's Tale* where Autolycus says, "a quart of ale is a dish for a King" (4.3.8). Not surprisingly, therefore, there was some resentment when brewers, in the early sixteenth century, began to meddle with the age-old recipe for ale by adding hop flowers. Thanks to this innovation, the new beverage, known as beer, lasted longer but its flavor was altered, prompting Henry VIII to rail against the "wicked weed called hoppes." By the late sixteenth century, however, beer-making was well established in England, and indeed English beer was so highly regarded on the continent that, according to Fynes Moryson, taverns in Holland and Germany were forbidden to sell it, for fear it would undermine their domestic product. Ale and beer were made in a variety of strengths, ranging from "small ale" to "double ale" and even to "double double." Specific kinds of ale and beer were dubbed with imaginative names such as Angels Food, Dragons Milke, Mad Dogge, Stride Wide, Lift Leg, Huffecap, Father Whoreson, and Go By The Wall. The taverns in Shakespeare's England were likewise vividly named, including The Boars Head, The Bull Head, The Three Cranes, The Swan, The Mermaid, The Red Lion, The Wind Mill, The Kings Head, The Ship, and The Three Tuns. A painted sign outside each establishment would depict whatever animal or object was featured in the tavern's name, so that the illiterate masses would be able to tell whether the tavern they were standing in front of was The Swan or The Wind Mill. Usually the sign would also depict a bush, which was the traditional symbol of taverns. The bush probably represented ivy, the sacred plant of Bacchus, god of wine. The Epilogue of *As You Like It* alludes to this customary depiction: "If it be true that good wine needs / no bush, 'tis true that a good play needs no/epilogue."

Taverns could be rough and tumble places. Owners sometimes adulterated the beverages with substances ranging from water (to make a barrel last longer) to calcium oxide (that is, lime, which made a flat beverage sparkle—"You rogue, here's lime in this sacke," complains Falstaff in *1 Henry IV* [2.4.121]). As Richard Rawlidge noted in his 1628 treatise called *A Monster Late Found Out*, tavern owners also fed their patrons "pickeld herring, salt beefe, and anchoves" in order to "cause them to take their liquor the more freely." The patrons, in turn, were often boorish and rowdy. Phillip Stubbes, in his 1583 *Anatomie of Abuses*, described how customers would sit in taverns for a week at a time, "swilling, gulling, and carowsing" until they "stammer, stagger & reele to & fro, like madmen, some vomiting spewing & disgorging their filthie stomacks, other some pissing under the boord as they sit." Finding a place to urinate was also a problem for the carriers in *1 Henry IV*: because the owner of the inn where they are spending the night will not trust them with chamber pots, they have to "leake in your Chimney" (2.1.21). The crown tried to exert some control over taverns by licensing them, limiting their numbers, and hiring "ale conners" to ensure that the price and quality of ale and beer were appropriate. Shakespeare's father, for example, was made an ale conner in Stratford in 1557.

In addition to ale, beer, and wine, Shakespeare's contemporaries also produced and consumed other alcoholic beverages, including cider (made from apples), perry (made from pears), and raspis (made from raspberries). Mead and metheglin were brewed from honey, though they had declined in popularity since the Middle Ages, except in Wales. Spirits were also distilled, such as aquavitae and absinthe. Mixtures of drinks were also in vogue, including posset (hot milk curdled with wine or ale), caudle (gruel, spices, ale or wine, and sometimes eggs), syllabub (milk, sugar, and wine or cider), and balderdash (an undefined mixture of whatever dregs were left over). Oddly, tobacco—which had been introduced by Walter Raleigh—was also seen as a kind of beverage, as the smoke was said to be "drunk" rather than inhaled. A 1620 pamphlet entitled *A Discourse and Discovery of New-Found-Land*, for example, alludes to men who have been "much accustomed to drinke Tobacco, strong Ale, double Beere."

# TO MAKE A GOOD POSSET CURDE

*The Widowes Treasure, 1588*

Lady Macbeth: The Doores are open: And the surfeted Groomes
doe mock their charge With Snores. I have drugg'd
their Possets, That Death and Nature doe contend
about them, Whether they live, or dye. (*Macbeth* 2.2.5–8)

*Possets were warm beverages usually made of milk, eggs, wine or ale (or both), and herbs or spices such as ginger, knotgrass, marigold, fennel, bugloss, and carduus benedictus. Some posset recipes also included vinegar, to help curdle the milk, whereas others boiled the mixture until it became so thick that it was eaten with a spoon. Possets were often served as remedies for various ailments, including the ague, kidney stones, and colic. This recipe is somewhat unusual in that it doesn't contain alcohol.*

Firste take the Milke and seethe it on the fire, and before it seeth put in your Egges according to the quantitye of your Milke, but see that your Egges be tempered with some of your Milke that standeth on the fier, and you must stirre it still untill it seethe, and beginneth to rise, then take it from the fire, and have your drinke ready in a faire Bason on a chafing dishe of coales, and put your Milk into the bason as it standeth, and cover it, and let it stande a while, then take it up, and cast on ginger and sinamon.

**MODERN RECIPE** Makeability: 2

2 quarts whole milk

8 eggs

1 tsp minced ginger

1 tsp ground cinnamon

3 cups sherry or port wine (or to taste)

In a saucepan, heat the milk slowly. In a mixing bowl, whisk 1/2 cup of warm milk into the beaten eggs to temper them. Then slowly pour this egg mixture into the milk. Stir continuously and bring to a gentle boil. Have at the ready a bowl of sherry or port wine and pour the milk and egg mixture into it. Cover and let stand for 10 minutes. Sprinkle with cinnamon and ginger when serving.

# TO MAKE WATER IMPERIALL

*Elinor Fettiplace's Receipt Book, 1604*

Ford:                                    I will rather trust a
Fleming with my butter, Parson Hugh the Welshman
with my Cheese, an Irish-man with my Aqua-vitae bottle,
or a Theefe to walke my ambling gelding, than my
wife with her selfe. (*The Merry Wives of Windsor* 2.2.289–293)

*This recipe calls for aquavitae, an alcoholic spirit whose name means "water of life." In England, aquavitae was usually made by distilling the lees of wine (that is, the dregs that are left over after the fermentation process has been completed). In this regard, brandy— whose name literally means "burnt wine"—is a kind of aquavitae. The rhubarb that is called for by this recipe was probably included for medicinal rather than culinary purposes: until the mid-seventeenth century, rhubarb was used by apothecaries rather than cooks, as is suggested by Macbeth's question about "What rhubarb, cyme, or what purgative drug,/ Would scour these English hence?" The "lawne" that the recipe refers to is a piece of linen, used like a tea bag to enclose certain ingredients.*

Take two quarts of strong aquavitae, a pound of white sugar, a few reasins of the Sun, the stones pulled out, one ounce of large mace, half a quarter of an ounce of Cynamon unbeaten, put all this into a pipkin, so let it stand 24 howers, then boile it till a pinte bee consumed, then take it from the fire, & put in a little rubarb, then let it stand till it bee cold, & straine into a glas, then hang some musk & amber greece in the glas in a peece of Lawne.

 **MODERN RECIPE** Makeability: 1

8 cups clear brandy

2 cups sugar

1/2 cup raisins

4 blades of mace

*Continued on next page*

*Continued from previous page*

| | |
|---|---|
| 1 TBS of roughly chopped cinnamon stick | Musk (see Appendix 1) |
| 1 cup chopped rhubarb stalks | Ambergris (see Appendix 1) |

Combine the ingredients in covered saucepan for 24 hours. Uncover the saucepan and boil the ingredients until they have reduced by 2 cups. Remove from the heat and allow to come to room temperature. Strain through cheesecloth or a clean kitchen towel into a glass bowl.

The firſt maner is, when we diſtill any liquide ſubſtance oʒ flowers in the Sunne by foʒce of his heate. The ſeconde, when the Diſtillation is done, by foʒce of the heate of fire. The thirde is perfourmed by the heate, which conſiſteth in putrified and rotten matters oʒ ſubſtaunces, of which particularlye, and by oʒder, we ſhall after intreat.

Firſt, the Diſtillation that is done in the Sunne, when the veſſell oʒ Lymbecke of Glaſſe filled with the matter, which a man woulde diſtill, is ſet fully in the hote Sunne on

*The Newe Jewell of Health*, Konrad Gesner, 1576. Fermented beverages such as wine were turned into spirits through distillation, a process that could involve heating a liquid over a flame or simply setting it in the heat of the sun, which in this woodcut is cunningly intensified through the use of a mirror. As the "spirit" of the liquid evaporated, it was captured by a tube at the top of the vessel, where it condensed and dripped down into another vessel. Aquavitae, whose name means "water of life," was produced by this means in Shakespeare's England. Courtesy of Henry E. The Huntington Library, Rare Books, 59956.

## TO MAKE EPOCRAS

*A Way to Get Wealth, 1625*

> Falstaff: If Sacke and Sugar bee a fault, Heaven helpe
> the Wicked. (*1 Henry IV* 2.4.465–466)

*Epocras (or hippocras, as it was usually known) was named after the "hippocras bag" through which the beverage was filtered. This filter, in turn, took its name from*

*Hippocrates, the ancient Greek physician who ostensibly advocated its use. Today, Hippocrates is best remembered for the Hippocratic oath that physicians promise to observe when practicing medicine.*

Take a gallon of Clarret or White-wine, and put therin foure ounces of Ginger, an ounce and a halfe of Nutmegs, of Cloves one quarter, of Suger foure pound: let all this stand together in a pot at least twelve houres, then take it, and put it into a cleane bagge made for the purpose, so that the wine may come with good leasure from the spices.

## MODERN RECIPE                                    Makeability: 2

8 cups red or white wine               1/2 TBS ground cloves

4 TBS minced ginger                    4 cups sugar

1/2 TBS chopped nutmeg

In a large mixing bowl, combine the ingredients and stir. Cover and let stand 12 hours. Strain through cheese cloth or a clean kitchen towel.

# CIDER OR PERRY

*The English Husbandman, 1613*

Richard:  And that I love the tree from whence thou sprang'st:
Witnesse the loving kisse I give the Fruite. (3 *Henry VI* 5.7.31–32)

Bruise or crush the Apples or Peares in peeces, & so remove them into other cleane vessells, till all the fruit be bruised: then take a bagge of hayre-cloath, made at least a yard, or three quarters, square, and filling it full of the crusht fruit, put it in a presse of woode, made for the purpose, and presse out all the juyce and moisture out of the fruit, turning and tossing the bagge up and downe, untill there be no more moisture to runne forth, and so baggefull after baggefull cease not untill you have prest all: wherein you are especially to observe, that your vessells into which you straine your fruit be exceeding neate, sweet, and cleane, and there be no place of ill savour, or annoyance neare them, for the liquour is most apt, especially Cyder, to take any infection. As soone as your liquour is prest forth and hath stoode to settle, about twelve houres, you shall then turne it up into sweet hogsheads, as those which have had in them last, either White-wine or Clarret, as for the Sacke vessell it is tollerable, but not excellent: you may also if you please make a small long bagge of fine linnen cloath, and filling it full of the powder of Cloves, Mace, Cynamon, Ginger, and the dry pils of Lemons, and hang it with a string at the bung-hole into the vessell, and it will make either the Cyder, or Perry, to tast as pleasantly as if it were Renish-wine.

## MODERN RECIPE                                    Makeability: 1

15 juicy apples or pears

1 tsp whole cloves

2 blades of whole mace

1 cinnamon stick

$^{1}/_{2}$ tsp minced ginger

1 TBS dry lemon peels

1 cup dry sherry (optional)

Peel, core, chop, and crush the apples or pears into a mash. Place the mash in a cheesecloth, thin kitchen towel, or new nylon and allow the juice to drip through into a pot, squeezing the mash occasionally (you should be able to extract about 6 cups of juice from 15 apples). After you have extracted the juice, let it settle and then pour it into another container, leaving any sediment behind. In another piece of cheese cloth, bundle the spices and lemon peels, tie tightly with kitchen string, and immerse it in the cider or perry for a day or more.

# TO MAKE A CAUDLE TO COMFORT THE STOMACKE, GOOD FOR AN OLDE MAN

*The Good Huswife's Jewell, 1596*

Camillo:                         I am his Cup-bearer.
If from me he have wholesome Beveridge,
Account me not your Servant. (*The Winter's Tale* 1.2.344–346)

*Caudles, like possets, were intended to be wholesome beverages, the kind of restoring drink that one imbibed first thing in the morning or upon going to bed. They were also served to the feeble and to women who were recovering from childbirth. The muscadine that this recipe calls for was probably a sweet, white, Italian wine.*

Take a pinte of good Muscadine, and as much of good stale ale, mingle them together, then take the yolkes of twelve or thirteene Egges newe laide, beat well the Egges first by themselves, with the wine and ale, and so boyle it together, and put thereto a quarterne of Suger, and a fewe whole Mace, and so stirre it well, til it seeth a good while, and when it is well sod, put therin a few slices of bread if you will, and so let it soke a while, and it will be right good and wholsome.

## MODERN RECIPE                                    Makeability: 2

2 cups muscadine or sweetish white wine

2 cups ale (let it sit overnight to become flat)

12 egg yolks

$^{1}/_{2}$ cup sugar

3 blades of mace

3 slices of lightly toasted 60% whole wheat bread

Mix together the wine and ale. Beat the egg yolks and add to the juice and ale. Beat again. Bring the mixture to a boil in a saucepan and add the sugar and mace, stirring well. Simmer for 15 minutes before adding the bread and allowing them to soak. Stir well.

# TO MAKE BUTTERED BEERE

*The Good Huswifes Handmaide for the Kitchin, 1594*

Berowne: White handed Mistris, one sweet word with thee.
Princess: Honey, and Milke, and Suger: there is three.
Berowne: Nay then two treyes, an if you grow so nice
    Methegline, Wort, and Malmsey; well runne dice:
    There's halfe a dozen sweets.
Princess: Seventh sweet adue,
    Since you can cogg, Ile play no more with you.
Berowne: One word in secret.
Princess:        Let it not be sweet.
Berowne: Thou greev'st my gall.
Princess:        Gall, bitter.
Berowne: Therefore meete. *(Love's Labour's Lost 5.2.231–238)*

*In the quotation from* Love's Labour's Lost, *the Princess deflects Berowne's request by pretending to take it literally: he has asked for "one sweet word" so she names three sweet things—honey, milk, and sugar. Berowne then matches her by naming three sweet drinks: metheglin (made from honey), wort (a sweet, unfermented beer), and malmsey (a sweet Mediterranean wine). The Princess then tops him by adding a seventh word that she finds sweet: saying goodbye to him.*

Take three pintes of Beere, put five yolkes of Egges to it, straine them together, and set it in a pewter pot to the fyre, and put to it halfe a pound of Sugar, one penniworth of Nutmegs beaten, one penniworth of Cloves beaten, and a halfepenniworth of Ginger beaten, and when it is all in, take another pewter pot and brewe them together, and set it to the fire againe, and when it is readie to boyle, take it from the fire, and put a dish of sweet butter into it, and brewe them together out of one pot into an other.

---

 ## MODERN RECIPE         Makeability: 2

6 cups beer

5 egg yolks

1 cup sugar

1/4 tsp nutmeg

1/4 tsp ground cloves

1 dash minced ginger

1/4 cup unsalted butter (or to taste)

*Continued on next page*

*Continued from previous page*

Whisk the egg yolks, combine with the beer, and force through a fine-meshed sieve into a large saucepan. On medium-high heat, add the sugar, nutmeg, cloves, ginger, and butter and bring to the boil. Just as it boils, put in the butter and pour the mixture into another pot. Bring it to a boil and pour it back into the original pot. Perform the transfer a few times and serve.

# HOW TO MAKE ALMOND MILKE

*The Good Houswives Treasure*, 1588

Thersites: Would I could meet that rogue Diomed!
I would croak like a raven; I would bode, I would bode.
Patroclus will give me anything for the intelligence of
this whore; the parrot will not do more for an almond
than he for a commodious drab. (*Troilus and Cressida* 5.2.194–198)

Take a peece of the screge end of a neck of mutton, a good handful of huld barly a good handfull of colde hearbs, a litle salt then take a handful of almonds & blanche them and grinde them in a stone morter, and straine the licour through a faire bolter, then put in a little Suger, and so give it to drinke.

 ## MODERN RECIPE                                    Makeability: 1

| | |
|---|---|
| 1 lb neck piece of mutton | 1 cup rosemary |
| 3/4 cup hulled barley | 1 tsp salt |
| 1 cup sage | 1 cup blanched almonds, crushed |
| 1 cup thyme | 1/4 cup sugar |

Add to 2 quarts of water the mutton neck, barley, herbs, salt, almonds, and bring to a boil. Strain the mixture through a cheesecloth (or a clean kitchen towel) and add the sugar.

# TO MAKE A TYSSAN

*The Good Huswifes Handmaide for the Kitchin*, 1594

Constable: Dieu de Battailes, where have they this mettell?
Is not their Clymate foggy, raw, and dull?
On whom, as in despight, the Sunne lookes pale,
Killing their Fruit with frownes. Can sodden Water,
A Drench for sur-reyn'd Jades, their Barly broth,
Decoct their cold blood to such valiant heat?

And shall our quick blood, spirited with Wine,
Seeme frostie? (*Henry V* 3.5.15–22)

*In the quotation from* Henry V, *the Constable is surprised that the English soldiers, who supposedly drink barley broth, are overcoming the French soldiers, who have the ostensible advantage of being wine drinkers. The Constable's consternation is founded on the belief, common at the time, that wine is akin to blood in nature. As Michael Scot affirmed in* The Philosophers Banquet, *wine "is the most easie converted into blood, spirituall and naturall heat." What the Constable apparently does not appreciate is that barley broth, which is a kind of "tyssan" or tisane, was also thought to be nourishing and restorative. In this recipe, the addition of the eggshells is intended to contribute to the medicinal qualities of the tisane, but you can omit them if you prefer.*

Take a pinte of Barley beeing picked, sprinkled with faire water, so put it in a faire stone morter, and with your pestell rub the barley, and that will make it tuske, then picke out the barley from the huskes, and set your barley on the fyre in a gallon of faire wter, so let it seeth til it come to a pottel. Then put into your water, Succory, Endive, Cinkefoyle, Violet leaves, of each one handfull, one ounce of Anniseed, one ounce of Liquoris bruised, and thirtie great raisons, so let all this geare seeth till it come to a quart: then take it off, let it stand and settle, and so take of the clearest of it, and let it be strained, and when you have strained the clearest of it, then let it stand a good pretie while. Then put in foure whites of Egs al to beaten, shels and all, then stir it well together, so set it on the fyre againe, so let it seeth, and ever as the scum doeth rise take it off, and so let it seeth a while: then let it run through a strainer or an Ipocras bagge, and drinke of it in the morning warme.

 MODERN RECIPE                                Makeability: 3

4 quarts water

2 cups pearl barley

1 cup succory (also known as chicory, radi-cchio, and endive)

$^1/_2$ cup cinkefoyle (see Appendix 1)

$^1/_2$ cup violet leaves (if available)

2 TBS aniseed

2 TBS licorice root (if available or substitute with another 2 TBS aniseed)

30 large raisins

4 egg whites and shells (washed)

Boil the barley in the water until it reduces by half. Add the remaining ingredients (except for the eggs) and reduce to one quart. Remove from the heat and let the mixture cool and settle. When it has settled, strain the clearest of the liquid into a saucepan through cheesecloth or a clean kitchen towel. Let it stand and settle for one hour. Stir in the eggs and shells and bring the tisane to a boil. Skim off the shells and impurities that rise. Strain once again and drink in the morning warm.

## A MONSTER LATE FOVND OVT AND DISCOVERED.

*Or*

The scourging of Tiplers, the ruine of *Bacchus*, and the bane of Tapsters.

*wherein is plainly set forth all the lawes of the Kingdome, that be now in force against Ale-house keepers, Drunkards, and haunters of Ale-houses, with all the paines and penalties in the same lawes.*

With sundry of their cunning inventions, hatched out of the Divells store-house, and daily practised by Ale-house-keepers, Tapsters, &c. With an easie way to reforme all such disorders.

Compiled by *R. R.*

Isa: 5. 11. *Woe be to them that rise vp early to follow drunkennesse, &c.*

Imprinted at *Amsterdam* Anno 1628.

*A Monster Late Found Out and Discovered*, Richard Rawlidge, 1628. In this woodcut, a homespun figure of temperance pulls two "tiplers"—that is, drunkards—toward reformation and sobriety. She leads them, like cattle, by means of cords through their noses. Any resemblance to the authors of this book is coincidental. Courtesy of Henry E. The Huntington Library, Rare Books, 51778.

# APPENDIX 1
# HARD TO FIND INGREDIENTS

AMBERGRIS This aromatic substance, which is vomited forth by sperm whales and then harvested from shores or from the surface of the sea, is not procurable, unless you are a perfume manufacturer. To our knowledge, there is no culinary substitute for ambergris, so you will have to omit it from the few recipes that call for it.

BARBERRIES These tart red berries are often available in Persian food markets. If unavailable, you can substitute red currants or, as a last resort, dried cranberries or goose berries.

BURDOCK The root of this thistle is available in Asian food markets. The Japanese name of the root is *gobo*. Artichoke can be substituted for burdock, to which it is related. Burdock root can also be purchased ready for use from the Monterey Bay Spice Company: http://www.herbco.com. If you would like to grow your own, seeds can be purchased from The Thyme Garden Herb Company: http://www.thymegarden.com.

CINQUEFOIL This perennial herb is native to Europe but was introduced to North America where it now grows wild in arid regions. It can also be purchased ready for use from the Monterey Bay Spice Company: http://www.herbco.com. If you would like to grow your own, seeds can be purchased from The Thyme Garden Herb Company: http://www.thymegarden.com.

CLARY This perennial herb, a member of the mint family, is fairly common in Europe, but may be difficult to procure in North America. It can be purchased ready for use from the Monterey Bay Spice Company: http://www.herbco.com. If you would like to grow your own, seeds can be purchased from The Thyme Garden Herb Company: http://www.thymegarden.com. You can also substitute sage leaves (clary and sage are closely related), but increase the number of sage leaves because they are smaller than clary leaves.

HYSSOP This perennial herb, a member of the mint family, is native to Europe but was introduced to North America where it now grows wild throughout much of the continent. It can also be purchased ready for use from the Monterey Bay Spice Company: http://www.herbco.com. If you would like to grow your own, seeds can be purchased from The Thyme Garden Herb Company: http://www.thymegarden.com. If you are unable to locate or grow hyssop, substitute thyme or lavender.

ISINGLASS This gelatin, made from the air-bladder of sturgeon, cod, and carp, is sometimes sold by beer- and wine-making stores (brewers and vintners use it as a clarifying agent). For culinary recipes, plain gelatin works just as well.

MARROW This substance, derived from the inside of bones, might be available from an "old-fashioned" butcher, or you might be able to find a butcher who will cut open some large bones so that you can scrape it out yourself. Alternatively, you can substitute butter or suet, but cut the amount in half.

MUSK This highly aromatic substance, which is derived from a gland found in the abdomen of the male musk deer, is not procurable. You can substitute a leaf or two of the musk mallow plant, which grows wild in much of North America, or use a drop or two of musk mallow oil, which you may find in an herbal store.

ROSEWATER This scented water, which is infused with rose petals, is available in Eastern European, Middle Eastern, and Indian food markets. You may also be able to locate rose syrup, but you would need to dilute it with water. You can also make your own rosewater: take five or six handfuls of rose petals, crush them slightly, put them into a pot with just enough distilled water to cover them, put a lid on the pot, heat the water for an hour or more (but don't bring it to a boil), and then strain out the petals. Alternatively, you can put the rose petals in a glass jar with distilled water, set the jar in the sun for two weeks, and then strain out the petals. Make sure that the roses you use have not been sprayed with insecticide or fungicide.

TANSY This very bitter perennial herb is now known to contain the toxin thujone and therefore should not be eaten. Substitutes include other bitter herbs, such as rue, feverfew, endive, and dandelion leaves.

UDDER This part of cow is nearly impossible to procure. You can substitute tripe.

VERJUICE This tart juice, pressed from unripe fruit such as grapes or apples, is available from a limited number of suppliers. Grape-based verjuice can be ordered and shipped from igourmet (www.igourmet.com), Navarro Vineyards (www.navarrowine.com), or Crown Bench Estates in Canada (www.crownbenchestates.com). If you are searching for the product on-line, bear in mind that some companies spell it "verjuice" and others "verjus." If you have access to grapevines or an apple tree, you can harvest the fruit while it is still green and press the juice yourself (make sure to refrigerate it afterward, or you will end up with wine or vinegar). Alternatively, you can approximate grape verjuice by taking leftover white wine and gently boiling the alcohol off. Juice pressed from gooseberries (even ripe ones) also makes a passable verjuice, as does juice pressed from ripe (but sour) crab apples: crush the fruit (or run it through a blender), add some water, let it sit for few hours, and then strain it through a cloth. As a last resort, you can substitute unsweetened apple juice or grape juice, mixed with a bit of vinegar or lemon juice. In Shakespeare's England, verjuice made from apples would have been more common than that made from grapes, so if possible use the apple-based variety.

# APPENDIX 2
# WAGES AND PRICES

Money in Shakespeare's England was counted using various units, most notably pennies, shillings, and pounds: there were 12 pennies (or pence) in a shilling, and 20 shillings in a pound. For example, a pound of mace, in the 1590s, cost 1 pound 4 shillings 3 pence, which would usually be rendered as 1 £, 4 s, 3 d. However, because North American readers are not familiar with pounds and shillings, we've converted wages and prices (in the charts below) to just pence in order to make it easier to compare the cost of one item to another. Thus, we can render the cost of a pound of mace in the 1590s as 291 pence.

    The first chart below indicates the daily income associated with various occupations or roles. Thus, a soldier earned a wage of about 5 pence a day, whereas a nobleman's annual income (from rents and sinecures) averaged out to about 1,600 pence a day. The second chart provides the cost of various items. Together, the two charts give some indication of what goods were and were not within the reach of individuals of various occupations. For example, one lemon would cost a ploughman half of his daily wage; one turkey cost almost three days of wages for a carpenter. A nobleman, with the income he received in one day, could buy 3,200 pounds of herring if he wanted to—enough to feed about 5,000 people.

| Pence/day | Job/Title/Role |
| --- | --- |
| 1½ | Ordinary domestic servant |
| 4 | Ploughman (in addition to his wage, he also received his daily food) |
| 4 | Women's "ordinary" work (such as hoeing and weeding) |
| 5 | Soldier |
| 6 | Skilled rural laborer (e.g., a thatcher) |
| 7 | Prized domestic servant |
| 12 | Craftsman |
| 12 | Actor in a theater company |
| 12 | Carpenter |
| 12 | Mason |

| Pence/day | Job/Title/Role |
| --- | --- |
| 13 | Minor Parson |
| 15 | Plumber |
| 500 | Esquire |
| 1,000 | Knight |
| 1,600 | Nobleman |

| Cost in Pence | Item |
| --- | --- |
| $^1/_2$ | 1 pound of herring |
| $^1/_2$ | 1 pound of salt |
| 1 | Standing room admission to the Globe |
| 1 | 1 broadside ballad |
| 1 | 1 orange |
| 1 | 1 loaf of bread |
| $1^1/_4$ | 1 pound of pork |
| $1^3/_4$ | 1 pigeon |
| 2 | 1 lemon |
| 2 | 1 gallon of ale |
| 2 | 1 pound of beef |
| 2 | 1 pound of mutton |
| 2 | The fine exacted by Sir John Harrington from any servant who was late for dinner |
| 2 | 1 ordinary drinking glass |
| $2^1/_2$ | 1 pound of cheese |
| $2^3/_4$ | 1 pound of bacon |
| 3 | 1 small saucer |
| 3 | 1 mustard pot |
| $3^1/_2$ | 1 pound of prunes |
| $3^3/_4$ | 10 pounds of oysters |
| 4 | 1 pound of figs |
| 4 | 1 pound of suet |
| 4 | 1 pound of candles |
| 4 | 1 pen and inkhorn |
| 4 | 1 kitchen knife |
| 4 | 1 gallon of malt vinegar |
| $4^1/_2$ | 1 rabbit |
| $4^1/_2$ | 1 pound of butter |
| $4^1/_2$ | 1 dozen eggs |
| 5 | 1 pound of raisins |
| 5 | 1 pound of dates |
| 5 | A public meal at an inn |
| 6 | 1 pound of currants |
| 6 | 1 pound of rice |
| 6 | 1 mousetrap |
| $7^1/_2$ | 1 table fork |

| Cost in Pence | Item |
| --- | --- |
| 12 | 1 hen |
| 12 | 1 lobster |
| 12 | 1 pomegranate |
| 12 | 1 pair of spectacles |
| 15 | 1 pound of coarse sugar |
| 16 | 1 gallon of wine vinegar |
| 17 | 1 bushel of oats (about 32 pounds by weight) |
| 18 | 1 chafing dish |
| 19 | 1 pound refined sugar |
| 19 | 1 pair of stockings for a dwarf |
| 20 | 1 frying pan |
| 24 | 1 capon |
| 24 | A private meal at an inn |
| 27 | 1 gallon of claret (wine) |
| 29 | 1 bushel of barley (about 48 pounds by weight) |
| 29 | 1 bushel of beans (about 30 pounds by weight) |
| 29 | 1 bushel of peas (about 30 pounds by weight) |
| 32 | 1 pair of Spanish (fancy) shoes |
| 33 | 1 pound of ginger |
| 34 | 1 turkey |
| 36 | 1 shirt |
| 41 | 1 gallon of sack (wine) |
| 44 | 1 gallon of muscatel (wine) |
| 46 | 1 pound of pepper |
| 48 | 1 boy's hat |
| 52 | 1 bushel of wheat (about 60 pounds by weight) |
| 54 | 1 Book of Common Prayer |
| 60 | 1 pound of cinnamon |
| 67 | 1 pound nutmeg |
| 96 | 1 pound of cloves |
| 120 | 1 rapier and dagger |
| 144 | 1 large copper kettle |
| 156 | 1 fresh salmon |
| 168 | 1 servant's blanket |
| 192 | 1 pair of fancy gloves |
| 240 | The fine for eating flesh on a fish day |
| 240 | 1 pound of saffron |
| 291 | 1 pound of mace |
| 492 | 1 Church Bible |
| 840 | 1 watch |
| 2,400 | 1 chiming clock |
| 2,856 | 1 saddle horse or coach horse |

# APPENDIX 3
# THE FIRST COURSE AND THE SECOND COURSE FOR FISH DAYS

Two courses from a sample menu for flesh days are given on page 53. Here, the corresponding courses for fish days are provided.

SERVICE FOR FISH DAIES  Butter; A Sallet with hard Egs; Pottage of sand Eles and Lampernes, red Herring, greene broyled and strewed upon White Herring; Ling Haburdine, sauce Mustard; Salt salmon minced, sauce Mustard and vergious, and a litle Sugar; Powdered Conger, Shad, Mackerell, sauce Vinigar; Whiting, sauce, with the liver and Mustard or vergious; Thornback, sauce, liver, and mustard, pepper and salt strowed upon, after that it is bruised; Fresh Codde, sauce Greene sauce; Dace, Mullet, Eeles upon sops; Roche upon sops; Perch; Pike in Pike sauce; Trout upon sops; Tench in Gellie or Gresyll; Custard.

THE SECOND COURSE  Flounders or Floukes, Pike sauce; Fresh Salmon; Fresh Conger; Bret; Turbut; Halibut, sawce Vinegar; Breame upon sops; Carpe upon sops; Soles, or any other fishes fryed; Rosted Eele, Sauce the dripping; Rosted Lampernes; Rosted Porpos; fresh Sturgion, sauce Galentine; Crevis, Crab, Shrimps, sauce Vinegar; Baked Lampray; Tart; Figs; Apples; Almonds blanched; Cheese; Raisins; Peares.

*Source:* From *The Good Huswifes Handmaide for the Kitchin*, 1594.

# APPENDIX 4
# "DIALOGUE FOR TABLETALKE"

Pierre Erondelle, a French schoolmaster, fled his homeland to avoid the religious persecution that he faced as a Protestant. After settling in London, he began to teach French. An avid educator, Erondelle wrote his own language texts, including *The French Garden for English Ladyes*, published in 1605, which included dialogues written in English on one page and in French on the facing page. In this one, called "Dialogue for Tabletalke," we sometimes get the impression that "The Lady" is trying to cram as many nouns and verbs into her speech as possible, but it nevertheless captures how a formal dinner might have unfolded in Shakespeare's England.

*The Lady. The Butler (called Diligent Soing). The Lady Beau Se-Jour. Mrs. DuPont Gaillard. The two Gentlemen (Du Vault-L'Amour & De Petit-Sens). The Ladies Daughters.*

*Lady:* Diligent Soing, where have you covered the table for dinner?

*Diligent Soing:* Madame, I have covered it in the great chamber.

*Lady:* Now Sirs, Ladies, Gentlewomen, will it please you to goe up? I will be bolde to bid you most welcome in my Lord Ry-Mellaines absence, who is now at Court. Madame, and you Mistris, are you not weary to have trotted so much with me?

*Lady Beau Se-Jour:* Weary? For what should we be so? We have almost gone nothing, but a little about the Exchange.

*Lady:* Diligent Soing, why have you not covered with the tablecloth & napkins of damaske? You have not plate trenchers enough. Set at every trencher plate a knife, a spoone, and a silver forke. Take away the saltsellers cover. Are the silver plates upon the cup boord? Goe fetch another basen and ewer, for these two be too fewe for us all to wash. See that every basen hath his towell. Take away the knives case, set the golden cup in the midst of the cupboard. All the sliver gilt cuppes are not there. Is there wine in those silver pottes? You have forgotten the silver chafingdish. I praye yee see that the drinking glasses be cleane. Put cleane and fresh water in the tubbes, that of copper, and the other of wood, the one to keepe the drinke fresh, and the other to refresh the glasses and cuppes, to the end we may drinke fresh, for it is very hotte. Is the pepper boxe on the table? See that the little silver bottle be full of vineger of roses. Go to, let us wash handes, but let us have our oysters first, for we should be forced to wash againe. Set the round table in the midst of the chamber. Goe fetch some browne bread, white bread, some stale bread, some newe bread, sawcers and vineger, with onyons and pepper. Madame, will it please you to eat any oysters? You shall have some opened.

*Lady Beau Se-Jour:* Truely, Madame, I never eate any.

*Lady:* I will none then. Take them away, for indeed it is too hot to eat of them. We are yet in the dog dayes, when it is naught to eat meates over hotte, and the phisitians holde, that there is nothing hotter than shell-fish. But aske first of those Gentlemen and Gentlewomen, if they will eat anye.

*Gentlemen & Gentlewomen:* No, Madame, not for this time.

*Lady:* Give us then to wash. Mistriss DuPont Gaillard, bring your cousin Du Vault-L'Amour with you and come, wash with my Lady and me. We may wash well foure in a basen.

*Mrs. DuPont Gaillard:* Pardon me, Madame, we will wash after you.

*Lady:* Go to, go to. Be not so mannerly. Draw nere both of you without any ceremony. As for my cousin De Petit-Sens, I will give him leave to wash with the maydens, for he is not yet married. Page, why how now cock-braine? Where be your eyes? Fling the towell. Go to, let us sit downe. My Lady Beau Se-Jour, will it please you to take your place in this chayre? And you Mistris, sit you there. Give a stoole and a cushen to Master Du Vault-L'Amour, neere his Cousin. And you cousin De Petit-Sens, knowe you not where to place your self? Now let one praise God. Rene, you must be our chaplaine, in the absence of Master Almeners: say Grace.

*Rene:* O Lord, which giv'st thy creatures for our food, hearbs, beastes, birds, fish, & other giftes of thine, blesse these giftes, that they may doe us good and we may live, to praise thy name divine. And when the time is come this life to end, vouchsafe our soules to heaven may ascend.

*Lady:* What wil it please you to eat Madame? Sup up a little broth, you shall finde it of a reasonable taste. Take the white of this boyled capon. Will you have some of this hen boyled with leekes or else of that with rice?

*Lady Beau Se-Jour:* I pray you give me some salte. What manner of turneps be these?

*Lady:* They are of our owne growth, but the seed thereof was sent me from Cane in Normandie, where groweth the best Turneps in France. They be not as our English turneps, which be big and round, but these are smaller and longer, and of much better taste. Taste some.

*Lady Beau Se-Jour:* Verily they are very good: but I pray you sister cut me a little of that powder beefe, the sight of it maketh one longe to eat of it. It is no wonder if the beefe of England is so much esteemed, for I beleeve that we have better than any other countrye that is.

*Master De Petit-Sens:* Aye, but Madame, you must take it with his appurtenances, which is musterd, otherwise you doe disgrace it: for even as a rich stone hath not so much grace as when it is set in golde, so the powdred beefe is (as it were) naked, without musterd.

*Lady Beau Se-Jour:* Truely, it is well reasoned of you. If I were a musterd-maker, I would be thankefull unto you with a whole rundlet of musterd, and you should chuse of that which you should like best, either of that of Tewkesbury, or of that of Dyjon, for your wise reason, because that if your reason be of force, even as the stone is put in the golde, so the piece of beefe should be put in musterd, of all sides (saving a little of the top) which would make musterd much deerer, whereby the musterd makers should thereby become richer.

*Lady:* Go to, you are so busie in prating, that you eat nothing at all. Take away this boyld meat. Let some tostes be made in the marrowe. What say you of this roste beefe? It is English meate too. Will you eat of this veale? Or of this legge of mutton with a gallandine sauce? But I beleeve that you are so fine that you cannot eat such grosse meates. Give me a draught of white wine. My Lady Beau Se-Jour, and you Mistris Du Pont-Gaillard, I salute your good grace.

*Master Du Vault-L'Amour:* I drink to you with all my hart. And my cousin De Petit-Sens, you are put in the cup too.

*The Company:* We most humblye thanke you, good Madame.

*Lady:* What wine will it please you to drinke? Claret wine, Orleans wine, Spanish wine, Greeke wine? But those two are too strong to drinke this hotte weather. I pray you taste of the wine of the soyle of [illegible] and you shall finde it verye delicate.

*Mrs. DuPont Gaillard:* I pray you give me some of it and bring some water: Powre more.

*Lady:* Truly Mistris, you drinke your wine like a good Christian, you baptize well your wine. How can you judge of the goodness of it?

*Mrs. DuPont Gaillard:* Mistris Fleurimonde and Charlote, wil you give me leave to drinke to you, & to all at the lower end?

*Master De Petit-Sens:* Mistris, the lower end is readye to doe you reason.

*Mrs. DuPont Gaillard:* Right reason cannot but be well taken, sir. Mistris Fleurimonde, give me some small beere, for the double beere is too strong.

*Lady Beau Se-Jour:* Mistris Fleurimonde, drinke some wine. That will not marre your mariage.

*Lady:* She should drinke water rather, for that will make her the fayrer. Truly the custome of France is praise-worthy, where maids never (or seldome) drinke any wine. Yea also the maryed women doe drinke none without water, unlesse they be somewhat aged.

*Master Du Vault-L'Amour:* Yet so it is, Madame, that I have seen Frenchwomen in this country drinke wine wel enough without water, without any great intreatie for it.

*Lady:* You knowe that it is more easie to imitate the vices, than the good manners of a countrye, and specially if there be any delectation in it: Alexander the Great (a Prince of his nature most temperate) suffered himselfe well to be caried away to the Persians sensualities, & to make himself worshipt as a God, which was wholy contrary to the manners of the Macedonians. So the Frenchwomen have learned of us to drinke wine without water. But you Master Du Vault-L'Amour, I have not yet sene you drinke. Showe us how you will drinke it.

*Master Du Vault-L'Amour:* Verily, Madame, I am altogether contrary to the French gentlewomen, for either I drink it pure, or if I make any mixture, I do be-wine the water, & not water the wine, for it is better to mend a thing, than to make a good thing to be woorse.

*Master De Petit-Sens:* There is yet another reason sir: it is, that the worthiest thing ought alwayes to be uppermost, and the inferiour under.

*Lady Beau Se-Jour:* Master De Petit-Sens, I believe you have eaten pidgions, you speake somwhat grosse.

*Master De Petit-Sens:* Madame, it is the speaker that must expound his speech. I meane but well. I knowe not if you do otherwise.

*Lady:* But now you talk of pidgions, bring the second messe, take away these pyes, for you eat none of them, but leave that of artichokes, for we will eat of it anon. Will you have of this turkye baked? Or of this peacocke? The cooke hath well shewed that the spyces are good cheape, for he hath put to it enough of pepper, of ginger, of cloves, of maces, of nutmegs, of sinamon, of saffron, and of suger. Cut some of that wilde bore-pig, it is better than our tame pigs. Sir, cut me a slice of that dryed neates-tongue.

*Mrs. DuPont Gaillard:* From whence had you this wilde pig, Madame? For there is no wilde Bores in England.

*Lady:* There is a gentleman in France, which hath taken a wilde sow alive and all her litter, in his toilles, and hath sent two of them to my Lord of Ry-mellaine. I have presented one to a good friend of mine, and reserved the other for ourselves. Master Du Vault-L'Amour, I will make you deserve your dinner: As you have taken paine this morning to be our gentleman usher, so you must be our carver. Cut me some lambe, some kid, cut those greene geese, that cignet, this ducke, these pidgions. Give us some of those partriges, of that fesant, of the quailes, to everyone a larke. Set these chickens lower, and these rabet-suckers. This leveret should be tender, for it was well hunted, and it is but young. Give the wood-cockes to the maydes, and give us the Snites. These wood pidgions are not well larded. Madame, eat of that rayle, it is very fat. Mistris, shall I give you of these teales? It is so long since I did eat any young storkes nor bittor. What say you of this herne? You need not feare that it tasteth of the sea, for they are brought us alive, and we feed them in the house. Take away these greene pease, for they be colde, but we leave the best meate. Give me a legge of that caponet to make a carbonado. Page, bid the cooke broyle that well, and put to it a little wine, salte, and pepper. We name in English this quarter, the legge of a capon, but if you should aske a French-man the legge of a capon, he would give you simply the legge and not the thigh where the meate is:

therefore it seemeth unto me, that they speake in that, more properly than we. See how fat that caponet was. Take a winge of it. Give heere some Oranges. Shall I give you an olive? Take away these capers. Set those cucumbers lower, and that sallet of crompe lettice. Heere, maydens, eat of those sallets of spinage, of endive, of burrage flowers, of buglose, of sage, of rosemary, of violet buds. We have eaten yet not venison. It is very fat. Some beyond the sea do mervaile much how the Englishmen could eat their capons without oranges: but we should mervaile much more how they can eat their oranges without capons? Do you love fish? Set some fresh vineger in the saucers. There is some fresh sammon, sturgion. Let this Lobster be broken. Will you have some Crevis? Take some shrimps. This sole is very great and thick. Did you ever see a fayrer gurnet? Give me some turbut. There be fayre smelts, they smell very well. Oh, what a fayre whiting! I beleeve you care not for fresh fish, for that of the sea is better. Carye away then this pyke, that carpe, this breame, this tench, and the eele also, for it is too muddy. But what? There is no body that eateth any thing. Have you no stomackes? I beseech you all, if you will doe me a pleasure, to make good cheere and to be merry, for truely you are as welcome, as in your owne houses.

*Lady Beau Se-Jour:* Master De Petit-Sens, why doe you not tell my Lady that eating and drinking hath taken away all our stomackes. In truth, I have not seene of a long time (at once) so much poultre nor foule, nor so good fish. You have good caters.

*Lady:* Come on, let me give you some of this quince pye, of this tarte of almonds, of that of cherrie, of gooseberries, of prunes.

*Mrs. DuPont Gaillard:* Certainly madame, I know not how we should eat any more, unlesse we should borrowe other bellyes.

*Lady:* Take away then all this, and bring us the fruite. Do you love cheese? There is Holland cheese, some angelot, auvergne cheese, parmesan. Will you have some grated cheese with sage and suger? If you find the same too strong, take some of that Banbury cheese, for it is milder in taste (to the mouth). Take of that which you like best, for many doe love strong cheese and tarte, and specially the good tiplers, for they taste wine the better. Will it please you to eat some creame, strawberryes, or raspberries? Be not these bigge peaches? What say you of these apricoks? They be from our owne garden. Doe you love any plummes, peares, apples? Eate some of those green wal-nuts. Crack some of the smal nuts. Why have we no chest-nuts? But what? Me thinketh that we are tyred in so fayre a waye. Then take away, and give us to wash. Is there any rose-water or sweet water within the ewer? Rene, give God thankes first.

*Rene:* O Lord our god, we yield thee prayse, for this thy gracious store, praying that we may have the grace to keep thy lawes and lore. And when this life shall flitte away, graunt us to live with thee for aye.

*Lady:* Much good may it doe you every body. But let us not rise yet. It is good to sit a while after dinner, as saith the English proverbe: after dinner sit a while, after supper walk a mile.

*Rene:* Madame, there is beneath, Master Ouyt-Aign, and Master Chere-Lie, which are come to see you.

*Lady:* They be most welcome, pray them to come up. You are welcome Gentlemen, is it afore dinner?

*Master De Chere Lie:* How, after dinner Madame! It will be anone supper time.

*Lady:* You jest, but in good earnest what is it a clock? We doe but rise from table.

*Master De Chere Lie:* It is past two a clocke. We have dyned at my Lady of Bon-Maintiens house, which doth expect your company at supper.

*Lady:* I will not break with her God willing. No one but your comming will make us change purpose, and we will take a walke, under the oaken wood leaves or in the orchard under the vine bower. And if we be weary of walking, we will rest us under the arboures. Doe you like it so?

*The Company:* As it shall please you Madame.

# GLOSSARY

The following words appear in the original recipes included in this book and may be unfamiliar to many readers. We provide only the relevant culinary meanings that were current in Shakespeare's England, many of which differ from our modern usage. "Pudding," for example, tended to denote a savory dish (sometimes in a casing, like a sausage) rather than a sweet, milk-based dessert. When variant spellings of a word are significantly different—such as "fregesey" and "frycase"—we include all those variants as headwords.

**Abate**  To remove, as in "take eight egges, only abate fowre of the whites."

**Abroad**  To make flat, to spread over a surface, as in "hold your pan aslope, so that your stuffe may run abroad over all the pan as thin as may be."

**Alloes, allowes**  See *Olave*.

**Ambergreece, ambergris**  An aromatic secretion vomited forth by sperm whales and used as a flavoring agent, as in the recipe "To make Manus Christi."

**Anoynt**  To brush or smear one thing onto another, as in "take sweet Butter, and rose-water melted, and with it anoynt the pye-lid all over."

**Barberry**  A berry that grows on a shrub (*Berberis vulgaris*), somewhat similar to red currants in appearance and flavor.

**Barm**  Yeast.

**Bastard**  A sweet Spanish wine, somewhat similar to muscatel in flavor.

**Bayes, baies**  Bay leaf.

**Beaumanger**  A dish made of fowl, mixed with other "white" ingredients such as cream, rice, almonds, and sugar.

**Belly**  The inner cavity of an eviscerated creature, as in "boyle your chickens in faire water, with a little whole mace, put into their bellies a little parsley."

**Blade**  In reference to mace, a blade is the dried sheath that is removed from the nutmeg that it encases. It looks rather like a little yellowish-brown or reddish-brown squid, with a surface area of about a square inch.

**Bleaw manger** See *Beaumanger*.

**Boord** The "board" or table where meals were eaten, as in "put it into a silver peece or a bowle, and so serve it to the boorde."

**Borage** A plant (*Borago officinalis*) whose flower has five blue or pink petals. The flower has a honey-like flavor, and the leaves a cucumber-like flavor.

**Boult** To sift flour, as in "Take two peckes of fine flower, which must be twice boulted."

**Box** To preserve something by putting it into a tightly closed wooden box, as in "box them and keepe them dry for your use."

**Brance, branch** A sprig, as in "two branches of rosemary or sage."

**Brawne** Usually the meat of a boar, but sometimes flesh of other animals.

**Bray** To crush in a mortar, as in "take the yolkes out of them and braye them in the morter."

**Break** To come apart, as in "boyle till they [the gooseberries] begin to break, then stirre them till they bee all broken."

**Breame** A fresh-water fish (*Abramis brama*).

**Brimmes** The edges of a leaf, as in "make a round hole in your cabbadge, as much as will receive your farsing meat, take heede you breake not the brimmes."

**Broche** A kind of spit or skewer, as in "larde him and roast him on a broche."

**Brue** To cook together, as in "take as much thicke butter being drawne, with a little vineger and a sliced lemmon, and brue them together."

**Bruise** To crush, as in "with the backside of your chopping-knife chop it [spinach] and bruise it as small as may bee."

**Burre** The burdock plant (*Arctium lappa*).

**Butchers prick** A kind of wooden skewer, as in "pare your turnepes as you would pare a pippin then cut them in square pieces, an inch and a halfe long and as thicke as a butchers pricke or skewet."

**But-end** The rear of a carcass, as in "take the flesh out at the but-end."

**Cabadge, cabbedge** Cabbage.

**Canel** Cinnamon.

**Capon** A castrated rooster.

**Carbonado** A strip of meat broiled on a gridiron.

**Card** An instrument with metal teeth, usually used for combing wool, but sometimes for pulling meat into small strands, as in "parboyle the braune … then take a payre of cardes and carde him as small as is possyble."

**Cast** To sprinkle, as in "let it stande a while, then take it up, and cast on ginger and sinamon."

**Cast** Thickened or turned to curds, as in "to make cast Creame."

Caste An ordinary quantity of bread or ale, as in "of one pecke of flour ye make ten caste of manchets faire and good."

Caudle, cawdle A warm drink, made of gruel, ale or wine, spices, and sometimes eggs.

Cearse See *Searce*.

Ceason Another spelling of "season."

Certaine An undefined quantity, as in "put in a certaine of fine biskets well serced."

Chafer A chafing dish.

Chafing dish An iron basin containing hot coals, used for simmering food or keeping it warm.

Charger A platter, as in "dish it up on great chargers or long spanish dishes made in the fashion of our english wooden trayes."

Cheat Variation of "mancheat" or "manchet," as in "lette it into the oven, your oven beeing so whot as it were for cheat bread."

Chewet Small, round pastries.

Cinkefoyle Cinquefoil, a five-leafed plant (*Potentilla reptans*).

Citron The lemon itself, or a lemon-like fruit.

Clap To wrap, as in "clap it round-wise about a spit."

Claret A wine of a yellowish color, distinct from both white and red.

Close Tightly, as in "the cabbadge must be stopped close with his cover in the time of his boyling."

Cockle A kind of mollusk (*Cardium edule*).

Coffin A pie or pastry crust.

Coleflowre Cauliflower.

Colianderseede Coriander.

Collar A piece of meat tied up into a roll.

Comfet, cumfet Comfit, a confection made by coating a piece of fruit, a seed, or a nut with melted sugar.

Conceit A fancy or "made" dish with numerous ingredients.

Coney A rabbit.

Congar A kind of eel.

Consumed Boiled away, as in "seethe them upon a softe fier of coales, tyll the water be consumed."

Corance, corrans, currance, currins Currants, also known as Raisins of Corance or Raisins of Corinth.

Couch To lay, as in "couch three peeces or foure in one coffin of the veale."

Cowslip A plant with aromatic yellow flowers (*Primula veris*).

**Cracknelles** A crunchy, spiced biscuit.

**Crop** The head of an herb or flower, as in "take Margerome, Wintersaverie, Peniroyall, mince, Time, of eche sixe crops."

**Damask** A species of rose, once thought to have originated in Damascus.

**Damson** A kind of juicy, bluish-black plum.

**Dowset** A sweet dish of eggs, cream, sugar, and seasoning.

**Draw** To pull forth, as from an oven or fireplace.

**Dredging** A coating made of various crushed or powdered ingredients, such as sugar, flour, and spices.

**Dress** To ready a dish for presentation at the table.

**Drive** To push, press, or flatten, as in "make it into perfect paste, then drive it with a rouling pin abroad, then put on small peeces of butter."

**Drop** The release of juices from a joint of roasting meat, as in "spit it and give it halfe a dozen turnes before the fire, then drawe it when it beginnes to droppe, and presse it between two dishes and save the gravie."

**Eisand** More commonly *ising*, a kind of pudding or what we would now call a sausage.

**Endore** To apply a yellow glaze of butter or egg yolk, as in "endore the sides [of the tart] with butter."

**Faggot** A bunch or bundle, as in "put into your pot a faggot of rosemary and time."

**Faire, fayre** Clean, as in "set it on to the fire with as much faire water as will cover it over."

**Farce** To stuff, as in "take your meate and with these oisters and hearbes farce or stop it, leaving no place empty."

**Fast** Tightly attached, as in the "cabbadge must be stopped close with his cover in the time of his boyling, and bound fast round about for breaking."

**Flay, flea** To remove the skin, as in "take your Pig and flea it."

**Florentine** Meat baked in a pot with a pastry cover, as in the recipe called "A florentine of veale."

**Foole** A kind of custard.

**Forced** A dish in which one thing (such as a pastry shell) contains another thing, as in "you may convay any prettie forced dish, as florentine, cherry tart, rice, or pippins, &c, betweene two sheets of that paste."

**Fregesey, frycase** A fricassee, that is, a dish of meat stewed in a sauce, like a ragout.

**Fridayes** A dish to be eaten on a fish day as in the recipe called "A Fridayes pye."

**Fritter** A dish of meat, vegetables, or fruit fried alone or in batter.

**Galantine**  A sauce for fish; also, a dish made of sopped bread and spices.

**Gammon**  The lower part of a side of bacon.

**Geare**  Stuff or things, as in "put into your water, succory, endive, cinkefoyle, violet leaves, of each one handfull, one ounce of anniseed, one ounce of liquoris bruised, and thirtie great raisons, so let all this geare seeth till it come to a quart."

**Giblets**  The liver, gizzard, and other "innards" of poultry.

**Gilly-flowers**  A carnation with a clove-like scent and flavor (*Dianthus caryophyllus*).

**Grain**  A very small unit of weight, as in "put in two or three graines of bezar." There are 7,000 grains in a pound.

**Grose, grosse**  Whole or unbroken, as in "season your egges with a little grose pepper." It can also denote large pieces of something, as in "marygold flowers grossely chopt."

**Grotes**  Groats, that is, hulled and crushed oats, wheat, or barley.

**Guise**  Fashion or style, as in "to make a stew after the guise of beyonde the sea."

**Haggesse**  A haggis, made by boiling a mixture of seasoned ingredients until it thickens.

**Hash**  To slice into small pieces, as in "take your meat off the spit, and hash it into a pewter dish."

**Height**  A method of determining the viscosity of a syrup by pouring a small amount of it from a spoon held at a certain height: the diameter of the vertical strand that stretches from the spoon indicates how thick the syrup is, as in "boyle them together to such an height, as that dropping some thereof out of a spoone, the sirup doe rope and run into the smalnesse of an haire."

**Hippocras**  Wine flavored with spices.

**Hippocras bag**  A cone-shaped bag of cotton or linen used to filter spices from wine.

**Hope**  The flower of the hop-plant (*Humulus lupulus*), better known as hops.

**Hurdle**  A framework, upon which something can be set to dry, as in "you may slice some of them when they bee a day old, and dry them againe upon a hurdle of wicker."

**Hurle**  To throw or put, as in "hurle in a good quantity of currants."

**Hutchpot**  A dish made of a mixture of ingredients.

**Hysope**  Hyssop, a plant (*Hyssopus officinalis*) whose leaves have a somewhat bitter minty flavor.

**Ice**  A sugar glaze, as in "wash it over with rose-water and sugar mixt together, for that will make the ice."

**Ipocras**  See *Hippocras*.

Ising  A kind of pudding, or what we would now call a sausage.

Isinglasse  A gelatin extracted from the air bladders of certain fresh-water fish.

Isope  See *Hysope*.

Jambales, jombils, jumbals  A kind of flavored biscuit.

Lap  To cover or roll, as in "lap them in floure and fry them in Butter" or "lap them up like allowes."

Lard  To insert extra fat into a joint of meat before cooking it, as in "if it [the venison] be leane you shall larde it either with Mutton lard, or pork larde."

Lawne  Linen fabric, used for straining liquids.

Leach, leache, leiche  A sweet dish made from ingredients such as milk, almonds, eggs, sugar, and often thickened with isinglass. Another dish, known as dry leach, was made by mixing sugar and finely chopped fruit or nuts into a paste, and then letting it dry.

Liquor, licour  The juice or fluid exuded by a meat as it cooks.

Lightes  The lungs of an animal.

List  To prefer, as in "garnish your dish as you list."

Made  A dish composed of many ingredients, as in "a made dish of sheepes tongues."

Manchet, mancheat  A small loaf of fine, white bread.

Marchpane  Marzipan, an almond-based confection.

Marie  Marrow, the substance found within the cavities of bones.

Medlar  A fruit resembling a small, brown apple.

Meat  Food of any kind, flesh or otherwise, as in "To make a fried meat of Turneps."

Mo  More.

Moyse  A dish of stewed fruit.

Mullet  A fish belonging to the family *Mugilidae*.

Muscadine  A sweet, white, Italian wine.

Musk  An aromatic substance extracted from a gland found in the abdomen of the male musk deer.

Navon  A kind of turnip, more commonly known as navet.

Neate  An ox.

Olaves, olives  Slices of meat rolled up with seasoning and stewed in a sauce, as in "to roast olaves of veal." The name has no connection to the fruit of the olive tree and is sometimes spelled alloes, allowes, or aloes.

Orrengado  Oregano.

Overthwart  Crosswise, as in "cut it overthwart in round peeces of the bignesse of your hand."

**Panch**  The stomach.

**Pap**  Semi-liquid food.

**Paste**  The kneaded and flattened dough used to encase foodstuffs before they are baked; a pastry shell.

**Peascod**  A pea pod.

**Peason**  Peas.

**Peniriall**  Pennyroyal, a kind of mint (*Mentha pulegium*).

**Pennyworth**  As much as a penny will buy, as in "put to it halfe a pound of sugar, one penniworth of Nutmegs beaten, one penniworth of Cloves beaten, and a halfepenniworth of Ginger beaten."

**Perywinckel**  Periwinkle, a bivalve mollusk (*Littorina littorea*).

**Pettitoes**  The feet of an animal, especially the pig.

**Pill**  The peel of a fruit, as in "a little of an orenge pill."

**Pippin**  A kind of sweet apple.

**Pipkin**  A small earthenware vessel with a lid.

**Poch**  To poach, that is, to simmer in water, as in "poch seaven Egges and lay them on sippets."

**Pomages**  A dish of stewed apples.

**Pomewater**  A juicy, sharp-flavored kind of apple.

**Pompeon**  A pumpkin.

**Posnet**  A pot with a handle and three feet.

**Posset**  A spiced drink of hot milk curdled with wine or ale.

**Potche**  See *Poch*.

**Pottle**  A measure of four pints.

**Presently**  Immediately.

**Print**  To press a shape or pattern onto a foodstuff, such as marzipan.

**Proynes**  Prunes.

**Pudding**  A mixture of chopped ingredients, often stuffed into a casing such as an intestine and then cooked, similar to what we would now call a sausage (as with the recipe called "To make Ising puddings"). Some puddings, however, were cooked in a cloth bag (as with "A Cambridge pudding"), some were cooked inside a cavity formed in another food (as with "How to make a Pudding in a Turnep root"), and some were cooked without being encased (as with "To make an Italian pudding").

**Pullet**  A young hen.

**Pulse**  Legumes, such as peas, beans, and lentils.

**Purtenance**  The edible "innards" of an animal, such as the heart, liver, and lungs.

**Quailing** To curdle or thicken, as in "set your broth no more on the fire for quailing, and serve it without sippets."

**Quarterne** A quarter of a measure, as in "two spoonefuls of cinamon and one of ginger, and one of cloves and mace, and a quarterne of suger finelye beaten."

**Quelquechose** A fancy dish of many ingredients. The name means "something" in French.

**Quince** A yellowish, pear-shaped fruit (*Pyrus cydonia*).

**Race** A root, as in "put into your broth ten beaten cloves, a race of ginger."

**Raise** To construct or build up a pastry shell, as in "raise your coffins of good tough wheate paste."

**Raisins of Corance** See *Corance*.

**Relisht** Flavored, as in "chop them small with two or three well relisht ripe apples."

**Rosewater** Water infused with the flavor and scent of rose petals.

**Rundle** A circular shape, as in "take pickeeld herring cut long waies and lay them in rundles with onions and parsley chopped."

**Sack** Used to denote sherry or other fortified white wines. The word derives from the Spanish "sacar," meaning "to export."

**Sallat, sallet** Salad.

**Saunders** Red sandalwood, used for food coloring.

**Score** Twenty.

**Screge** The neck of an animal.

**Seame, seeme** Fat or lard, as in "of all sorts of seame, that which is made of the beefe suet is the best and strongest."

**Searce** To sift, as in "take a pound of very fine Flower, as much Sugar thorowly searced."

**Seeth** To boil.

**Severall** Different or distinct, as in "take your ducke boyled or roasted, and put them into two severall pipkins."

**Shog** To mix by shaking something back and forth in a pot, as in "boyle all these together on a chafing-dish of Coales, and put it into your Pye: shog it well together, and serve it to the Table."

**Sinamon, sinamond, synamon** Cinnamon.

**Sippets** Synonymous with "sops," which are slices of bread, often slightly toasted, used to soak up the juice or broth of a dish.

**Skewet** A kind of skewer, as in "pare your turnepes as you would pare a pippin then cut them in square pieces, an inch and a halfe long and as thicke as a butchers pricke or skewet."

**Skimmer** A perforated ladle for removing effluent from liquids.

**Slip** To remove the leaves (or similar appendages) from the stem or stalk of a plant, as in "small raisons and suger, time and rosemary, slipped."

**Smoore, smore** To cook in a lidded vessel, as in the recipe called "For the fillets of a Veale, smoored in a Frying-panne."

**Soft** In reference to a fire, a gentle flame, as in "let them stue very easily upon a soft fire."

**Sod** To boil, as in "the Capon must bee sodden in faire water."

**Sop** A slice of bread, often slightly toasted, used to soak up the juice or broth of a dish.

**Sowce** To preserve something by pickling it in brine or vinegar.

**Sparagus** Asparagus.

**Splette** To split, as in "take your Pike and pull out all hys guttes, and doo not splette your Pyke."

**Stale** Not fresh, as in "take three stale Manchets, and grate them."

**Stamp** To mix by pounding together, as in "take blanched almonds well stamped, and being halfe beaten, put as much garlike to them as you think good, and stampe them together."

**Stop** To close, to put a lid on.

**Strain** The verb "strain" can mean several things depending on the context. First, it can denote, as it still does, the separating of one substance (especially a liquid) from another, as in "seeth the gourdes in water, then presse the water out of them and straine them." Second, it can mean to mix two or more ingredients together by pressing them through a strainer or sieve as in "straine the yolkes with the rosewater and the suger." In the recipes of the period, the latter sense is more common.

**Straw** To strew or sprinkle.

**Succory** Also known as chicory, endive, or radicchio (*Cichorium intybus*). The leaves of the plant, used in salads, have a slightly bitter flavor.

**Suet, sewet, suit** Solid fat found around the kidneys of cattle and sheep.

**Swimme** To float on top, as in "if your butter swimme, it is good temper."

**Tansy** An omelet flavored with juice or leaves of the tansy plant (*Tanacetum vulgare*).

**Tawney** The tansy plant (*Tanacetum vulgare*).

**Tenches** A freshwater fish (*Tinca vulgaris*), similar to a carp.

**Toase** To pull apart fibers, as in "take the brawne of a capon, toase it like wool."

**Trencher** A square of wood with a plate-sized hollow in the center, and a smaller depression in the upper right corner for holding salt.

**Trifle** A kind of custard.

**Trusse** To tie up, as in "trusse and scald your Chickens."

**Tuske** To remove grain from its husk.

**Tyssan** Tisane, a beverage made by steeping barley and other ingredients in boiling water.

**Vaunts** A seasoned pastry containing fruit and meat.

**Vent-hole** A small hole in the middle of pastry lid allowing steam to escape and through which liquids (such as butter or verjuice) can be added after baking.

**Vergice, vergious, vergis, verjuice** The juice extracted by pressing unripe fruit. In England verjuice tended to be made from apples, but elsewhere (such as France and Italy) from grapes. The name literally means "green juice."

**Wallop** The action of bringing something to a rolling boil and then letting it subside, as in "set it on the fire and faire scum it, and when it seetheth a full wallop, put in your Shrimpes faire washed." Sometimes several "wallops" would be required, as in a recipe for Manus Christi that says, "let the Suger and the Rosewater boyle together softelye, till it doe rise and fall againe three times." A wallop was synonymous with a "waume" or "walm."

**Warden** A kind of pear.

**Waume** See *Wallop.*

**Waxe** To become, to grow, as in "seeth them in that liquor tyll it waxe somewhat thick."

**Whiting** A highly prized fish with white flesh.

**Widgen, widgin** The widgeon, a kind of duck.

**Withal** In some contexts, this word means "along with the rest," as in "put them into your Creme with a dish full of Rosewater and a dish full of Sugar withall." In other contexts, it means "entirely," as in "take a very litle saffron to collour your batter withall."

**Yest** Yeast

# BIBLIOGRAPHY

When quoting Shakespeare, we have drawn on an original-spelling edition of his complete works (edited by Stanley Wells and Gary Taylor, and published by Clarendon Press), so that quotations from his plays and poems retain the late sixteenth- and early seventeenth-century "feel" that characterizes the other period texts that we have quoted. However, in order to assist readers in finding those passages in a readily available edition of Shakespeare's works, we have cited those quotations using the act, scene, and line numbering system of David Bevington's modernized-spelling edition (published by Longman).

## SOURCES OF ORIGINAL RECIPES

Anonymous. *A Closet for Ladies and Gentlewomen. Or, the Art of Preserving, Conserving, and Candying with the Manner How to Make Divers Kinds of Sirups, and All Kinde of Banqueting Stuffes. Also Divers Soveraigne Medicines and Salves for Sundry Diseases.* London, 1627. Early English Books Online. Folger Shakespeare Library (reel 590) and the British Library (reel 1773).

Anonymous. *The Good Hous-Wives Treasurie Beeing a Verye Necessarie Booke Instructing to the Dressing of Meates. Hereunto Is also Annexed Sundrie Holsome Medicines for Divers Diseases.* London, 1588. Early English Books Online. British Library.

Anonymous. *A Good Huswifes Handmaide for the Kitchin Containing Manie Principall Pointes of Cookerie, aswell How to Dresse Meates, After Sundrie the Best Fashions Used in England and Other Countries, with Their Apt and Proper Sawces, Both for Flesh and Fish, as also the Orderly Serving of The Same to the Table. Hereunto are Annexed, Sundrie Necessarie Conceits for the Preservation of Health. Verie Meete to be Adjoned to The Good Huswifes Closet of Provision for Her Houshold.* London, 1594. Early English Books Online. Bodleian Library.

Anonymous. *A Propre New Booke of Cokery Declaryng What Maner of Meates bee Best in Ceason for All Tymes of the Yere and How Thes Ought to bee Dressed and Served at the Table Bothe for Fleshe Daies and Fisshe Daies: With a Newe Addicion, Veri Necessarye for All Them that Delighteth in Cokery.* London, 1545. Early English Books Online. University of Glasgow Library.

A.W. *A Book of Cookrye Very Necessary for All Such as Delight Therin.* London, 1591. Early English Books Online. Bodleian Library.

Dawson, Thomas. *The Good Huswifes Jewell Wherein is to be Found Most Excellent and Rare Devises for Conceites in Cookery, Found out by the Practise of Thomas Dawson. Whereunto is Adjoyned Sundry Approved Receits for Many Soveraine Oyles, and the Way to Distill Many Precious Waters, with Divers Approved Medicines for Many Diseases. Also Certain Approved Points of Husbandry, Very Necessary for All Husbandmen to Know.* London, 1596. Early English Books Online. Henry E. Huntington Library and Art Gallery.

Dawson, Thomas. *The Second Part of the Good Hus-Wives Jewell Where is to be Found Most Apt and Readiest Wayes to Distill Many Wholsome and Sweet Waters. In Which Likewise is Shewed the Best Maner in Preserving of Divers Sorts of Fruits, & Making of Sirrops. With Divers Conceits in Cookerie with The Booke of Carving.* London, 1597. Early English Books Online. Henry E. Huntington Library and Art Gallery.

Fettiplace, Elinor. *The Complete Receipt Book of Ladie Elynor Fettiplace.* 1604–1647. Reprint, Bristol: Stuart Press, 1999.

Lacy, John. *Wyl Bucke His Testament.* London, 1560. Early English Books Online. Bodleian Library.

Markham, Gervase. *Countrey Contentments, in Two Bookes the First, Containing the Whole Art of Riding Great Horses in Very Short Time, with the Breeding, Breaking, Dyeting and Ordring of Them, and of Running, Hunting and Ambling Horses, with The Manner How to Use Them in Their Travell. Likewise in Two Newe Treatises the Arts of Hunting, Hawking, Coursing of Grey-Hounds with the Lawes of the Leash, Shooting, Bowling, Tennis, Baloone &C. By G.M. The Second Intituled, The English Huswife: Containing the Inward and Outward Vertues which Ought to be in a Compleate Woman: As Her Phisicke, Cookery, Banqueting-Stuffe, Distillation, Perfumes, Wooll, Hemp, Flaxe, Dairies, Brewing, Baking, and All Other Things Belonging to an Houshold. A Worke Very Profitable and Necessary for the Generall Good of this Kingdome.* London, 1615. Early English Books Online. British Library.

Markham, Gervase. *Countrey Contentments, or The English Huswife Containing the Inward and Outward Vertues which Ought to be in a Compleate Woman. As Her Skill in Physicke, Surgerie, Extraction of Oyles, Banqueting-Stuffe, Ordering of Great Feasts, Preserving of All Sorts of Wines, Conceited Secrets, Distillations, Perfumes, Ordering of Wooll, Hempe, Flax, Making Cloth, Dying, The Knowledge of Dayries, Office of Malting, Oats, Their Excellent Uses in a Family, Brewing, Baking, and All Other Things Belonging to an Houshold. A Worke Generally Approved, and Now Much Augmented, Purged and Made Most Profitable and Necessarie for All Men, and Dedicated to The Honour of The Noble House Of Exceter, and the Generall Good Of this Kingdome.* London, 1623. Early English Books Online. British Library.

Markham, Gervase. *The English Husbandman. The First Part: Contayning the Knowledge of the True Nature of Every Soyle Within this Kingdome: How to Plow It; And the Manner of the Plough, And other Instruments Belonging Thereto. Together with the Art of Planting, Grafting, and Gardening After Our Latest and Rarest Fashion. A Worke Never Written Before by Any Author: And Now Newly Compiled for the*

*Benefit of this Kingdome.* London, 1613. Early English Books Online. Henry E. Huntington Library and Art Gallery.

Murrell, John. *A Daily Exercise for Ladies and Gentlewomen Whereby They May Learne and Practice the Whole Art of Making Pastes, Preserves, Marmalades, Conserves, Tartstuffes, Gellies, Breads, Sucket Candies, Cordiall waters, Conceits in Sugar-Workes of Severall Kindes. As also to Dry Lemonds, Orenges, or Other Fruits. Newly Set Forth, According to the Now Approved Receipts, Used Both by Honourable and Worshipfull Personages.* London, 1617. Early English Books Online. British Library.

Murrell, John. *A Delightfull Daily Exercise for Ladies and Gentlewomen Whereby is Set Foorth the Secrete Misteries of The Purest Preservings in Glasses and Other Confrictionaries, as Making of Breads, Pastes, Preserves, Suckets, Marmalates, Tartstuffes, Rough Candies, with Many Other Things Never before in Print. Whereto is Added a Booke Of Cookery.* London, 1621. Early English Books Online. British Library.

Murrell, John. *A New Booke of Cookerie Wherein is Set Forth The Newest And Most Commendable Fashion for Dressing or Sowcing, eyther Flesh, Fish, or Fowle. Together with Making of all Sorts of Jellyes, and Other Made-Dishes for Service; Both to Beautifie and Adorne Eyther Nobleman or Gentlemans Table. Hereunto also is Added the Most Exquisite London Cookerie.* London, 1615. Early English Books Online. Bodleian Library.

Partridge, John. *The Treasurie of Commodious Conceits, & Hidden Secrets and may be Called, The Huswives Closet, of Healthfull Provision. Mete and Necessarie For the Profitable Use of all Estates Both Men and Women: and also Pleasaunt for Recreation, with A Necessary Table of all Things Herein Contayned. Gathered out of Sundrye Experiments Lately Practised by Men of Great Knowledge.* London, 1573. Early English Books Online. Henry E. Huntington Library and Art Gallery.

Partridge, John. *The Treasurie of Commodious Conceits, and Hidden Secretes Commonlie Called The Good Huswives Closet of Provision, For the Health of Her Houshold. Meete And Necessarie for the Profitable Use of all Estates. Gathered out of Sundry Experiments, Lately Practised by Men of Great Knowledge: And Now Newly Corrected, and Inlarged, With Divers Necessary Phisicke Helpes, Not Impertinent to Every Good Huswife to Use in Her House Amongst Her Own Famelie.* London, 1591. Early English Books Online. Bodleian Library.

Partridge, John. *The Treasurie of Hidden Secrets. Commonlie Called, The Good-Huswives Closet Of Provision, For The Health Of Her Houshold Gathered out of Sundrie Experiments, Lately Practised by Men of Great Knowledge: And Now Newly Enlarged With Divers Necessary Phisicke Helpes, and Knowledge of the Names and Naturall Disposition of Diseases, that Most Commonly Happen to Men and Women. Not Impertinent for Every Good Huswife To Use in Her House, Amongst Her Owne Familie.* London, 1600. Early English Books Online. British Library.

Partridge, John. *The Widowes Treasure Plentifully Furnished with Sundry Precious and Approved Secretes in Phisicke and Chirurgery for the Health and Pleasure of Mankinde: Hereunto are Adjoyned, Sundry Pretie Practises and Conclusions of Cookerie: With Many Profitable and Holesome Medicines for Sundrie Diseases in Cattell.* London, 1588. Early English Books Online. Harvard University Library.

Plat, Hugh. *Delightes for Ladies to Adorne their Persons, Tables, Closets, and Distillatories: with Beauties, Banquets, Perfumes & Waters.* London, 1609. Early English Books Online. Henry E. Huntington Library and Art Gallery.

Rosselli, Giovanni. *Epulario, or The Italian Banquet Wherein is Shewed the Maner How to Dresse and Prepare All Kind of Flesh, Foules or Fishes. As also How to Make Sauces, Tartes, Pies, &C. After the Maner of all Countries. With an Addition of Many Other Profitable and Necessary Things.* London, 1598. Early English Books Online. Henry E. Huntington Library and Art Gallery. A translation of a 1516 Italian work entitled *Opera Nova Chiamata Epulario.*

## OTHER CITED WORKS

Alley, Hugh. *Hugh Alley's Caveat.* Ed. Ian Archer, Caroline Barron, and Vanessa Harding. London: London Topographical Society, 1988.

Anonymous. *A Briefe Note of the Benefits that Grow to This Realme, by the Observation of Fish-Daies with a Reason and Cause Wherefore the Law in that Behalfe Made, is Ordained.* London, 1627. Early English Books Online. Bodleian Library.

A.T. *A Rich Store-House or Treasury for the Diseased.* London, 1596. Early English Books Online. Henry E. Huntington Library and Art Gallery.

Beaumont, Francis. *The Woman Hater.* London, 1607. Early English Books Online. Durham University Library.

Boorde, Andrew. *A Compendyous Regyment.* London, 1547. Early English Books Online. British Library.

Bradwell, Stephen. *Helps for Suddain Accidents Endangering Life.* London, 1633. Early English Books Online. Folger Shakespeare Library.

Breton, Nicholas. *Fantasticks Serving for a Perpetuall Prognostication.* London, 1626. Early English Books Online. Folger Shakespeare Library.

Breton, Nicholas. *Pasquils Mad-Cap And His Message.* London, 1600. Early English Books Online. Bodleian Library.

Bullein, William. *Bulleins Bulwarke of Defence.* London, 1562. Early English Books Online. Henry E. Huntington Library and Art Gallery.

Cockeram, Henry. *The English Dictionarie.* London, 1623. Early English Books Online. Folger Shakespeare Library.

Cogan, Thomas. The *Haven of Health.* London, 1584. Early English Books Online. Henry E. Huntington Library and Art Gallery.

Cokayne, Thomas. A *Short Treatise of Hunting.* London, 1591. Early English Books Online.

Darell, Walter. A *Short Discourse of the Life of Servingmen.* London, 1578. Early English Books Online. Henry E. Huntington Library and Art Gallery.

Dekker, Thomas. The *Seven Deadly Sinnes of London.* London, 1606. Early English Books Online. British Library.

Des Périers, Bonaventure. *The Mirrour of Mirth and Pleasant Conceits.* London, 1583. Early English Books Online. Trinity College (University of Cambridge) Library.

Earle, John. *Micro-Cosmographie.* London, 1628. Early English Books Online. British Library.

Erasmus, Desiderius. *A Lytell Booke of Good Maners for Chyldren.* London, 1532. Early English Books Online. British Library.

Fulwell, Ulpian. *The First Parte, of the Eyghth Liberall Science.* London, 1579. Early English Books Online. British Library.

F.W. A *Treatise of Warm Beer*. London, 1641. Early English Books Online. Cambridge University Library.

Gerard, John. *The Herball Or Generall Historie of Plantes*. London, 1597. Early English Books Online. Henry E. Huntington Library and Art Gallery.

Harrison, William. *The Description of England*. In: *The First and Second Volumes of Chronicles*. London, 1587. Early English Books Online. Henry E. Huntington Library and Art Gallery.

Hart, James. *Klinike, Or the Diet of the Diseased*. London, 1633. Early English Books Online. Henry E. Huntington Library and Art Gallery.

Here Beginneth the Booke, Named the Assize of Bread. London, 1580. Early English Books Online. British Library.

Heywood, Thomas. *How a Man May Chuse a Good Wife From a Bad*. London, 1602. Early English Books Online. Eton College Library.

Hill, Thomas. *The Gardeners Labyrinth*. London, 1577. Early English Books Online. Bodleian Library.

Hill, Thomas. *The Profitable Arte of Gardening*, London, 1593. Early English Books Online. Arnold Arboretum (Harvard University) Library.

Innocent III, Pope. *The Mirror of Mans Lyfe*. London, 1576. Early English Books Online. Folger Shakespeare Library.

J.B. *An English Expositor*. London, 1621. Early English Books Online. Bodleian Library.

Jeninges, Edward. *A Briefe Discovery of the Damages that Happen to This Realme by Disordered and Unlawfull Diet*. London, 1590. Early English Books Online. Henry E. Huntington Library and Art Gallery.

Joannes, De Mediolano. *The Englishmans Doctor*. London, 1608. Early English Books Online. British Library.

Jonson, Ben. *The Complete Poems*. Harmondsworth: Penguin Education, 1975.

Johnson, Thomas. *Cornucopiae*. London, 1596. Early English Books Online. Henry E. Huntington Library and Art Gallery.

Langton, Christopher. *An Introduction Into Phisycke Wyth an Universal Dyet*. London, 1545. Early English Books Online. British Library.

Lupton, Thomas. *A Thousand Notable Things*. London, 1579. Early English Books Online. British Library.

Lyly, John. *Euphues and His England*. London, 1580. Early English Books Online. Bodleian Library.

Machyn, Henry. *The Diary of Henry Machyn*. London: The Camden Society, 1848.

Magno, Alessandro. "The London Journal of Alessandro Magno, 1562." Caroline Barron, Christopher Coleman, Claire Gobbi, eds. *London Journal* 9 (1983), pp. 136–52.

Markham, Gervase. *A Way to Get Wealth*. London, 1625. Early English Books Online. Folger Shakespeare Library.

Markham, Gervase. *Cheape and Good Husbandry*. 1614. Early English Books Online. British Library.

Markham, Gervase. *Maison Rustique, Or the Countrey Farme*. London, 1616. Early English Books Online. British Library.

Middleton, Thomas. *A Critical Edition of Thomas Middleton's The Witch*. Ed. Edward J. Esche. New York: Garland, 1993.

Moore, Philip. *The Hope of Health*. London, 1564. Early English Books Online. Henry E. Huntington Library and Art Gallery.

Moryson, Fynes. *An Itinerary*. London, 1617. Early English Books Online. British Library.

Nashe, Thomas. *Nashes Lenten Stuffe*. London, 1599. Early English Books Online. Henry E. Huntington Library and Art Gallery.

Nashe, Thomas. *Pierce Penilesse His Supplication to the Divell*. London, 1592. Early English Books Online. Henry E. Huntington Library and Art Gallery.

Nichols, John B. *The Progresses and Public Processions of Queen Elizabeth*. 3 vols. London: J. Nichols and Son, 1823.

Norden, John. *The Surveyors Dialogue*. London, 1607. Early English Books Online. Bodleian Library.

Phiston, William. *The Schoole of Good Manners*. London, 1609. Early English Books Online. Harvard University Library.

Plat, Hugh. *Sundrie New and Artificiall Remedies Against Famine*. London, 1596. Early English Books Online. Henry E. Huntington Library and Art Gallery.

Plat, Hugh. The *Jewell House of Art and Nature*. London, 1594. Early English Books Online. Henry E. Huntington Library and Art Gallery.

Powel, John. *The Assize of Bread Newly Corrected and Enlarged*. London, 1608. Early English Books Online. British Library.

Purchas, Samuel. *Purchas His Pilgrimes in Five Bookes*. London, 1625. Early English Books Online. University of Illinois (Urbana-Champaign Campus).

Rawlidge, Richard. *A Monster Late Found Out and Discovered*. London, 1628. Early English Books Online. Henry E. Huntington Library and Art Gallery.

R.C. *A Wonder in Kent of the Admirable Stomacke of One Nicholas Wood*. London, 1630. Early English Books Online. Pepys Library.

Scot, Michael. *The Philosophers Banquet*. London, 1633. Early English Books Online. Newberry Library.

Shakespeare, William. *The Complete Works*. Ed. Stanley Wells and Gary Taylor. Oxford: Clarendon Press, 1986.

Shakespeare, William. *The Complete Works of Shakespeare*. Ed. David Bevington. New York: Longman, 1997.

Spenser, Edmund. *The Faerie Queene*. Ed. A.C. Hamilton. London: Longman, 1977.

Stephens, John. *Essayes and Characters, Ironicall, and Instructive*. London, 1615. Early English Books Online. Henry E. Huntington Library and Art Gallery.

Stow, John. *A Survay of London*. London, 1598. Early English Books Online. Henry E. Huntington Library and Art Gallery.

Stubbes, Phillip. *The Anatomie of Abuses*. London, 1583. Early English Books Online. Henry E. Huntington Library and Art Gallery.

Taylor, John. *The Great Eater of Kent*. London, 1630. Early English Books Online. Henry E. Huntington Library and Art Gallery.

Taylor, John. *Jack a Lent, His Beginning and Entertainment*. London, 1620. Early English Books Online. British Library.

Taylor, John. *The Praise of Hemp-Seed*. London, 1620. Early English Books Online. Henry E. Huntington Library and Art Gallery.

Tilney, Edmund. *A Briefe and Pleasant Discourse of Duties in Mariage*. London, 1571. Early English Books Online. Bodleian Library.

Turner, William. *The Names of Herbes in Greke, Latin, Englishe, Duche and Frenche*. London, 1548. Early English Books Online. British Library.

Turner, William. *A New Herball*. London, 1551. Early English Books Online. Library of Congress.

Topsell, Edward. *The Historie of Foure-Footed Beastes*. London, 1607. Early English Books Online. British Library.

Tusser, Thomas. *Five Hundredth Pointes of Good Husbandry*. London, 1577. Early English Books Online. Folger Shakespeare Library.

Twyne, Thomas. *The Schoolemaster, Or Teacher of Table Philosophie*. London, 1576. Early English Books Online. Harvard University Library.

Vicars, Thomas. *The Grounds of that Doctrine Which is According to Godlinesse*. London, 1630. Early English Books Online. Durham University (Durham, England) Library.

West, Richard. *The Schoole of Vertue*. London, 1619. Early English Books Online. British Library.

Whitbourne, Richard. *A Discourse and Discovery of New-Found-Land*. London, 1620. Early English Books Online. Henry E. Huntington Library and Art Gallery.

## OTHER RESOURCES

Albala, Ken and Lisa Cooperman. *Cooking in Europe, 1250–1650*. Westport, Connecticut: Greenwood Press, 2006.

Albala, Ken. *Eating Right in the Renaissance*. Berkeley: University of California Press, 2002.

Ayrton, Elisabeth. *The Cookery of England*. London: Penguin Books, 1989.

Ball, Mia. *Worshipful Company of Brewers: A Short History*. London: Hutchinson Benham, 1977.

Beebe, Ruth Anne. *Sallets, Humbles and Shrewsbury Cakes: A Collection of Elizabethan Recipes Adapted for the Modern Kitchen*. Boston: David R. Godine, 1976.

Bessunger, Bernard N. *Recipes of Old England: Three Centuries of English Cooking, 1580–1850*. Newton Abbot: David & Charles, 1973.

Best, Michael. "A Lost Cookery Book of the Sixteenth Century." *The Library*, Series 5, vol. 32, no. 1(1977): 156–60.

Best, Michael R. Introduction. *The English Housewife*. 1615. By Gervase Markham. Kingston and Montreal: McGill-Queen's University Press, 1986.

Beveridge, William Henry. *Prices and Wages in England from the Twelfth to the Nineteenth Century*. London: F. Cass, 1965.

Black, Maggie, ed. *A Taste of History: 10,000 Years of Food in Britain*. London: British Museum Press, 1993.

Brears, Peter. *All the King's Cooks: The Tudor Kitchens of King Henry VIII at Hampton Court Palace*. London: Souvenir Press, 1999.

Brears, Peter, and Pamela Sambrook. *The Country House Kitchen, 1650–1900: Skills and Equipment for Food Provisioning*. Vol. 8. Phoenix Mill, Far Thrupp, Stroud, Gloucestershire: A. Sutton Pub. in association with the National Trust, 1996.

Brears, Peter. *Food and Cooking in 16th Century Britain: History and Recipes*. England: Historic Buildings and Monuments Commission for England, 1985.

Brears, Peter. *Food and Cooking in 17th Century Britain: History and Recipes*. England: Historic Buildings and Monuments Commission for England, 1985.

Caton, Mary Anne, Joan Thirsk, and Folger Shakespeare Library. *Fooles and Fricassees: Food in Shakespeare's England.* Washington, D.C.: Folger Shakespeare Library, 1999.

Cornett, Patricia L. "Some Poetic and Dramatic Uses of Cookery in Shakespeare's Plays." *Shakespeare Yearbook* 8(1997): 383–94.

Drummond, J.C., and A. Wilbraham. *The Englishman's Food: Five Centuries of English Diet.* London: Random House, 1992.

Emerson, Kathy Lynn. *Wives and Daughters: Women of Sixteenth Century England.* Troy, N.Y.: Whitston, 1984.

Flandrin, Jean Louis, Massimo Montanari, and Albert Sonnenfeld. *Food: A Culinary History from Antiquity to the Present.* New York: Columbia University Press, 1999.

Goody, Jack. *Cooking, Cuisine, and Class: A Study in Comparative Sociology.* Cambridge Cambridgeshire: Cambridge University Press, 1982.

Hole, Christina. *The English Housewife in the Seventeenth Century.* London: Chatto & Windus, 1953.

Hollyband, Claudius, Pierre Erondelle, and M. St. Clare Byrne. *Elizabethan Home, Discovered in Two Dialogues by Claudius Hollyband and Peter Erondell, and Edited by M. St. Clare Byrne.* ed. London, Methuen, 1949.

Honan, Park. *Shakespeare: A Life.* Oxford: Oxford University Press, 1999.

Laurence, Anne. *Women in England, 1500–1760: A Social History.* New York: St. Martin's Press, 1994.

Le Fanu, T.P. "Some Seventeenth-Century Recipes." *The Journal of the Royal Society of Antiquaries of Ireland*, Series 5, vol. 3, no. 4, alt. no. 23, (1893): 422–24.

Lorwin, Madge. *Dining with William Shakespeare.* New York: Atheneum, 1976.

MacDonald, Russ. *The Bedford Companion to Shakespeare: An Introduction with Documents.* New York: Bedford-St. Martin's, 2001.

Markham, Gervase, and Michael R. Best. *The English Housewife: Containing the Inward and Outward Virtues which Ought to be in a Complete Woman: As Her Skill in Physic, Cookery, Banqueting-Stuff, Distillation, Perfumes, Wool, Hemp, Flax, Dairies, Brewing, Baking, and all Other Things Belonging to a Household.* Kingston: McGill-Queen's University Press, 1986.

Mason, Laura. *Food Culture in Great Britain.* Westport, Conn.: Greenwood Press, 2004.

Meads, Chris. *Banquets Set Forth: Banqueting in English Renaissance Drama.* Manchester: Manchester University Press, 2001.

Mennell, Stephen. *All Manners of Food: Eating and Taste in England and France from the Middle Ages to the Present.* Oxford: B. Blackwell, 1985.

Orlin, Lena Cowen. *Elizabethan Households: An Anthology.* Washington, D.C.: Folger Shakespeare Library, 1995.

Pearson, Lu Emily Hess. *Elizabethans at Home.* Stanford: Stanford University Press, 1957 [1959].

Picard, Liza. *Elizabeth's London: Everyday Life in Elizabethan London.* London: Weidenfeld & Nicolson, 2003.

Pritchard, R.E. *Shakespeare's England: Life in Elizabethan and Jacobean Times.* Phoenix Mill, U.K.: Sutton Publishing, 2003.

Raleigh, Walter Alexander, Sidney Lee, and C. T. Onions. *Shakespeare's England; An Account of the Life & Manners of His Age.* Oxford: Clarendon Press, 1916. 2 vols.

Rogers, James E. Thorold. *A History of Agriculture and Prices in England.* Oxford: Clarendon Press, 1963.

Rosengarten, Frederic. *The Book of Spices.* Wynnewood, Pa.: Livingston Pub. Co., 1969.

Sass, Lorna. *To the King's Taste.* New York: The Metropolitan Museum of Art, 1975.

Sass, Lorna. *To the Queen's Taste.* New York: The Metropolitan Museum of Art, 1976.

Scholliers, Peter. *Food, Drink and Identity: Cooking, Eating and Drinking in Europe since the Middle Ages.* Oxford: Berg, 2001.

Segan, Francine. *Shakespeare's Kitchen: Renaissance Recipes for the Contemporary Cook.* New York: Random House, 2003.

Sim, Alison. *Food and Feast in Tudor England.* New York: St. Martin's Press. 1997.

Sim, Alison. *Tudor Housewife.* Montreal: McGill-Queen's University Press, 1996.

Singman, Jeffrey. *Daily Life in Elizabethan England.* Westport, Conn.: Greenwood Press, 1995.

Spencer, Colin. *British Food: An Extraordinary Thousand Years of History.* New York: Columbia University Press, 2002.

Spencer, Colin. *The Heretic's Feast: A History of Vegetarianism.* Hanover and London: University Press of New England, 1995.

St. Clare Byrne, M. *The Elizabethan Home: Discovered in Two Dialogues by Claudius Hollyband and Peter Erondell.* London: Methuen and Company, 1949.

Thorne, W.B. "A Seventeenth Century Cookery Book." *The Library,* New Series, vol. 4, no. 14, (1903): 180–88.

Wilson, C. Anne. *"Banquetting Stuffe": The Fare and Social Background of the Tudor and Stuart Banquet.* Edinburgh: Edinburgh University Press, 1991.

Wilson, C. Anne. *The Country House Kitchen Garden, 1600–1960: How Produce Was Grown and Used.* Vol. 10. London: Sutton Pub. in association with National Trust Enterprises, 1998.

Wilson, C. Anne. *Food & Drink in Britain from the Stone Age to Recent Times.* London: Constable, 1973.

Zyvatkauskas, Betty and Sonia Zyvatkauskas. *Eating Shakespeare: Recipes and More from the Bard's Kitchen.* Toronto: Prentice-Hall Canada, 2003.

## ONLINE RESOURCES

The Encyclopaedia Britannica's Guide to Shakespeare. http://search.eb.com/shakespeare/.

The Folger Shakespeare Library's exhibit on food in Shakespeare's England, based on the book *Fooles and Fricassees.* http://www.folger.edu/html/exhibitions/fooles_fricassees/.

Life in Elizabethan England: A Compendium of Knowledge. http://elizabethan.org/compendium/.

# INDEX

Page numbers in **bold** type indicate recipes.

## About the Authors

MARK MORTON is Senior Instructional Developer (Technology) in the Centre for Teaching Excellence at the University of Waterloo. Previously, he taught courses in Shakespeare, Modern Drama, and Creative Writing at the University of Winnipeg. His other books include *Cupboard Love: A Dictionary of Culinary Curiosities* (1996), *The End: Closing Words for a Millennium* (1999), and *The Lover's Tongue: A Merry Romp through the Language of Love and Sex* (2003). Mark also writes a quarterly column for *Gastronomica: A Journal of Food and Culture*, and has also written and broadcast more than a hundred columns about language for CBC Radio.

ANDREW COPPOLINO is a freelance writer, restaurant reviewer, and newspaper columnist with a special interest in food writing. He has published in *Restaurant Report*, *Culinary Trends*, *Whisky Magazine*, *CityFood Magazine*, *Gremolata*, and *Canadian Gaming Business*, as well as a number of food and lifestyle magazines.